LEARNING
SolidWorks®
2009

by

Thomas Short
Munro & Associates, Inc.
Troy, Michigan

Michael Pritchett
Design Engineer
Waterford, Michigan

Publisher
The Goodheart-Willcox Company, Inc.
Tinley Park, Illinois
www.g-w.com

Copyright © 2009

by

The Goodheart-Willcox Company, Inc.

All rights reserved. No part of this work may be reproduced, stored, or transmitted in any form or by any electronic or mechanical means including information storage and retrieval systems, without the prior written permission of The Goodheart-Willcox Company, Inc.

Manufactured in the United States of America.

Library of Congress Catalog Card Number 2009009476

ISBN: 978-1-60525-166-0

1 2 3 4 5 6 7 8 9 – 09 – 14 13 12 11 10 09

Cover image courtesy of Dassault Systèmes SolidWorks Corp.

The Goodheart-Willcox Company, Inc., Brand Disclaimer: Brand names, company names, and illustrations for products and services included in this text are provided for educational purposes only and do not represent or imply endorsement or recommendation by the author or the publisher.

The Goodheart-Willcox Company, Inc., Safety Notice: The reader is expressly advised to carefully read, understand, and apply all safety precautions and warnings described in this book or that might also be indicated in undertaking the activities and exercises described herein to minimize risk of personal injury or injury to others. Common sense and good judgment should also be exercised and applied to help avoid all potential hazards. The reader should always refer to the appropriate manufacturer's technical information, directions, and recommendations; then proceed with care to follow specific equipment operating instructions. The reader should understand these notices and cautions are not exhaustive.

The publisher makes no warranty or representation whatsoever, either expressed or implied, including but not limited to equipment, procedures, and applications described or referred to herein, their quality, performance, merchantability, or fitness for a particular purpose. The publisher assumes no responsibility for any changes, errors, or omissions in this book. The publisher specifically disclaims any liability whatsoever, including any direct, indirect, incidental, consequential, special, or exemplary damages resulting, in whole or in part, from the reader's use or reliance upon the information, instructions, procedures, warnings, cautions, applications, or other matter contained in this book. The publisher assumes no responsibility for the activities of the reader.

Library of Congress Cataloging-in-Publication Data
Short, Thomas.
   Learning SolidWorks 2009 / by Thomas Short, Michael Pritchett. -- 1st ed.
     p. cm.
   Includes index.
   ISBN 978-1-60525-166-0
  1. Computer graphics. 2. SolidWorks. 3. Computer-aided design. I. Pritchett, Michael.
II. Title.
T385.S4557 2009
620'.00420285536--dc22   2009009476

Introduction

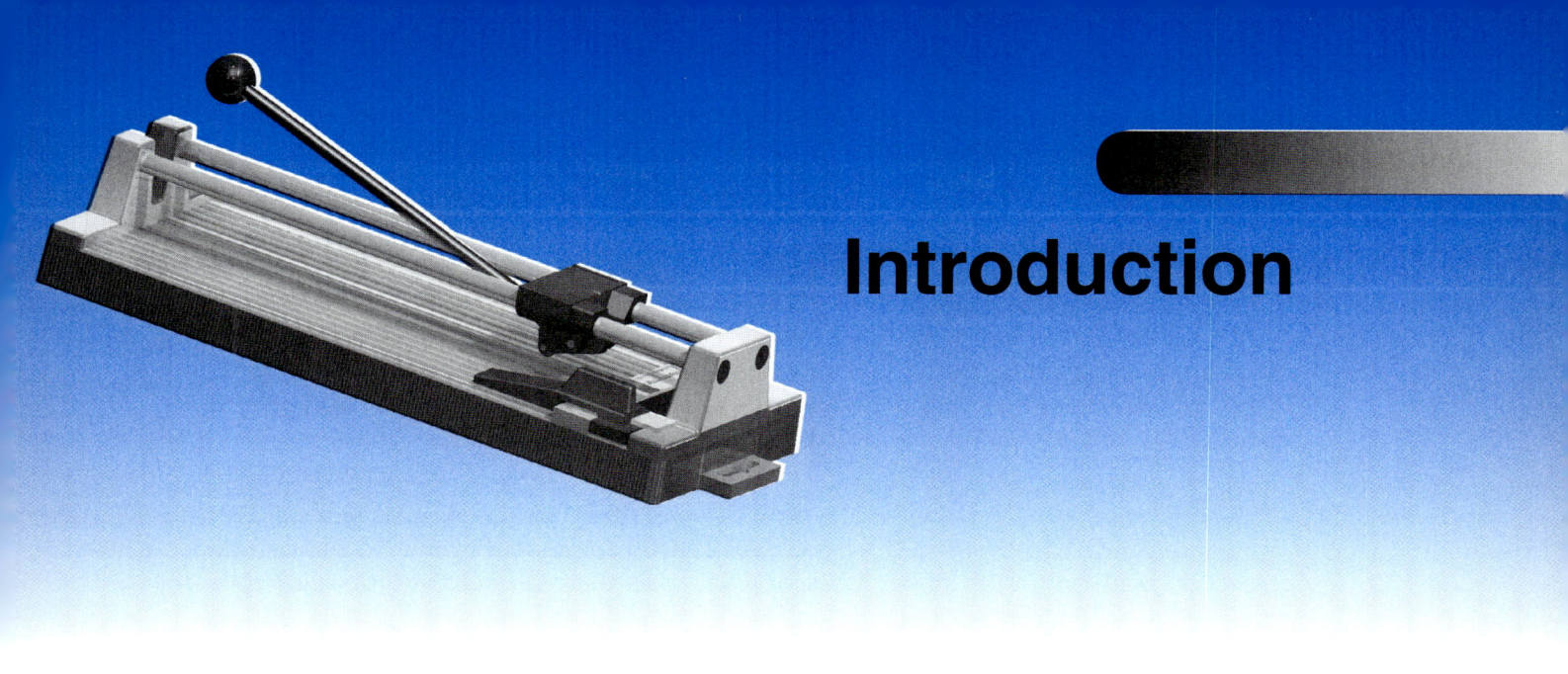

Learning SolidWorks 2009 is a text designed with the student as well as the engineering professional in mind. You will find it is presented in a manner designed to facilitate learning—practical examples and clear instructions. If you are looking for loads of theory, you will not find it in this text. The intention of this text is to recreate the actual workflow experienced by professionals as they use the software. After all, this text was written by those very same professionals. By the time you have finished this text, you will have a keen understanding of the methods used to produce a viable solid model part or assembly in SolidWorks.

Parametric design is very important in SolidWorks. You will encounter this a great deal. Throughout this text you will find example after example of parametric design principles. It cannot be stressed enough. The fact that your solid model should not be a static part, but a dynamic part able to withstand revision after revision, is of great importance. You will hear this principle echoed throughout the text. The software was designed for this capability, so take advantage of it.

The goal of *Learning SolidWorks 2009* is to present an approach to the SolidWorks tools, options, and techniques based on how they are used by an actual CAD operator. In addition, this text offers the following features.

- Step-by-step introductions to SolidWorks tools.
- Easily understandable explanations of how and why the tools function as they do.
- Numerous examples and illustrations to reinforce concepts.
- Professional tips explaining how to use SolidWorks effectively and efficiently.
- Practices involving tasks to reinforce chapter topics.
- Chapter tests for reviewing tools and key SolidWorks concepts.
- Chapter exercises to supplement each chapter.

Fonts Used in This Text

Different typefaces are used throughout the chapters to define terms and identify SolidWorks tools. Important terms always appear in ***bold-italic, serif*** type. SolidWorks menus, tools, dialog box names, and button names are printed in **bold-face, sans serif** type. File names, folder names, paths, and selections in drop-down lists appear in

Roman, sans serif type. Keyboard keys are shown inside of brackets [ ] and appear in Roman, sans serif type. For example, [Enter] means to press the enter (return) key.

Flexibility in Design

Flexibility is the key word when using *Learning SolidWorks 2009*. This text is an excellent training aid for individual as well as for classroom instruction. *Learning SolidWorks 2009* teaches you to apply SolidWorks to real-world problems. It is also a useful resource for professionals using SolidWorks in the work environment.

Notices

There are a variety of notices you will see throughout the text. These notices consist of technical information, hints, and cautions that will help you develop your SolidWorks skills. The notices that appear in the text are graphically identified as shown here.

PROFESSIONAL TIP

These are ideas and suggestions aimed at increasing your productivity and enhancing your use of SolidWorks tools and techniques.

NOTE

A note alerts you to important aspects of the tool or activity that is being discussed.

CAUTION

A caution alerts you to potential problems if instructions are not followed or tools are used incorrectly, or if an action could corrupt or alter files, folders, or disks. If you are in doubt after reading a caution, consult your instructor or supervisor.

Reinforcement and Evaluation

The chapter examples, practices, tests, and exercises are set up to allow you to select individual or group learning goals. Thus, the structure of *Learning SolidWorks 2009* lends itself to the development of a course devoted entirely to SolidWorks training. *Learning SolidWorks 2009* offers several ways for you to evaluate performance. Included are:

- **Examples.** The chapters include tutorial examples that offer step-by-step instructions for producing SolidWorks drawings, parts, and assemblies. The examples not only introduce topics, but also serve to help reinforce and illustrate principles, concepts, techniques, and tools.
- **Practices.** Chapters have short sections covering various aspects of SolidWorks. A practice composed of several instructions is found at the end of many sections. These practices help you become acquainted with the tools and techniques just introduced. They emphasize a specific point.
- **Chapter Tests.** Each chapter includes a written test. Questions may require you to provide the proper tool, option, or response to perform a certain task. You may also be asked to define industry terms and describe how they apply to SolidWorks.

- **Chapter Exercises.** A variety of drawing exercises follow each chapter. The exercises are designed to make you think and solve problems. They are used to reinforce the chapter concepts and develop your skills.

Student Website

Each chapter consists of examples, practices, and exercises. Most of these activities require a file that has been created and supplied to you on the student website (www.g-wlearning.com/CAD). At various points throughout this text, you will be instructed to open or access a file. The file will be used to develop, emphasize, and reinforce SolidWorks concepts and techniques. The required files are supplied on the student website in ZIP files. Before beginning work on a chapter, download the ZIP file for the chapter and unzip it using the "Use folder names" option.

In addition, the chapter practices and exercises are on the student website. Point your browser to www.g-wlearning.com/CAD and use the navigation menu to access the appropriate material. Once you have the instructions displayed on screen, use the [Alt][Tab] key combination to switch between the instructions and SolidWorks. The appendix is also included on the student website.

About the Authors

The authors are professionals with experience in design and training using SolidWorks. Their wide range of skills help make this book successful.

Thomas Short

Thomas Short is a nationally recognized expert in 3D solid/surface modeling. He is a registered mechanical engineer in Michigan and has his B.S. and M.S. in mechanical engineering. He was a faculty member in the Mechanical Engineering Department at Kettering University (formerly General Motors Institute). He is also a member of the Society of Manufacturing Engineers and the Society of Automotive Engineers.

Tom has been using, teaching, and consulting in CAD since 1975. In 1984, he founded CommandTrain, Inc., which was a CAD training center. He is now a consulting engineer for Munro & Associates in Troy, Michigan. He is a Certified Technical Instructor. He has written for, and taught, many courses in software. He has taught classes in the United States, Mexico, Brazil, Canada, and England.

As a CAD consultant and trainer, Tom has worked for many companies, including Ford Motor Company, General Motors, Visteon, 3M, and McDonnell Douglas. He has helped several tooling and manufacturing companies in the Detroit area implement successful strategies for solid modeling systems.

Michael Pritchett

Michael Pritchett is a Design Engineer, formerly with Munro & Associates in Troy, Michigan. He is currently pursuing a degree in Mechanical Engineering with a concentration in Mechanical Systems Design from Kettering University. Mike has been using SolidWorks for nearly 10 years and has completed training at Fischer Unitech in advanced modeling and COSMOS analysis. He is also currently pursuing certification as a Certified SolidWorks Professional.

Notice to the User

This text is designed as a complete entry-level SolidWorks teaching tool. The authors present a typical point of view. Users are encouraged to explore alternative techniques for using and mastering SolidWorks. The authors and publisher accept no responsibility for any loss or damage resulting from the contents of information presented in this text. This text contains the most complete and accurate information that could be obtained from various authoritative sources at the time of production. The publisher cannot assume responsibility for any changes, errors, or omissions.

Acknowledgments

The authors and publisher would like to thank the following individuals for their assistance and contributions.

Mike Berna
David Boomer
Fern Espino
Jim Irvine
Lawrence Maples
Jerry McNaughton
Doug Montgomery
Rick Oprisu
Eliza Perry
Del Radloff
Edward R. Rose

Brief Contents

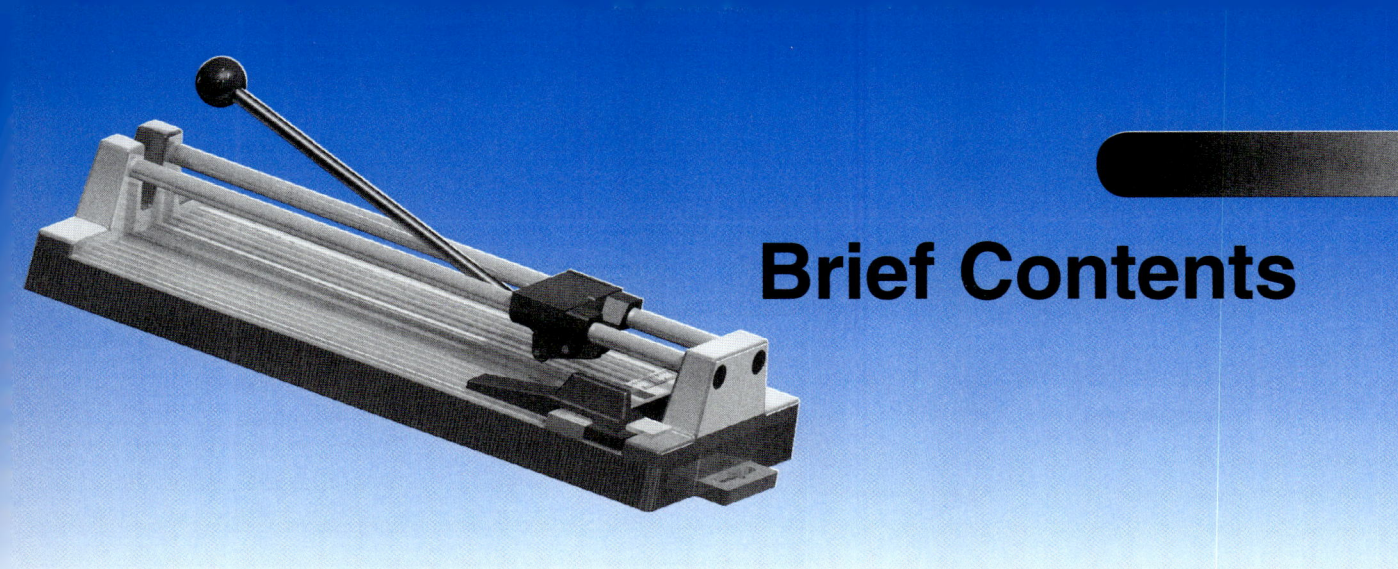

Chapter 1:	Introduction to SolidWorks	15
Chapter 2:	User Interface	25
Chapter 3:	Sketching, Relations, and the Base Feature	45
Chapter 4:	Complex Sketching, Equations, and Construction Geometry	71
Chapter 5:	Secondary Sketches and Reference Geometry	85
Chapter 6:	Adding Features	109
Chapter 7:	Adding More Features	135
Chapter 8:	Creating Part Drawings	153
Chapter 9:	Dimensioning and Annotating Drawings	173
Chapter 10:	Sweeps and Lofts	191
Chapter 11:	Building Assemblies with Mates	207
Chapter 12:	Working with Assemblies	227
Chapter 13:	Mechanical Assembly Mates	243
Chapter 14:	Configurations and Design Tables	251
Chapter 15:	Surfaces	259
Chapter 16:	Assembly Drawings	269
Chapter 17:	Exploded Views and Animations	283
Index		299

Learning SolidWorks 2009

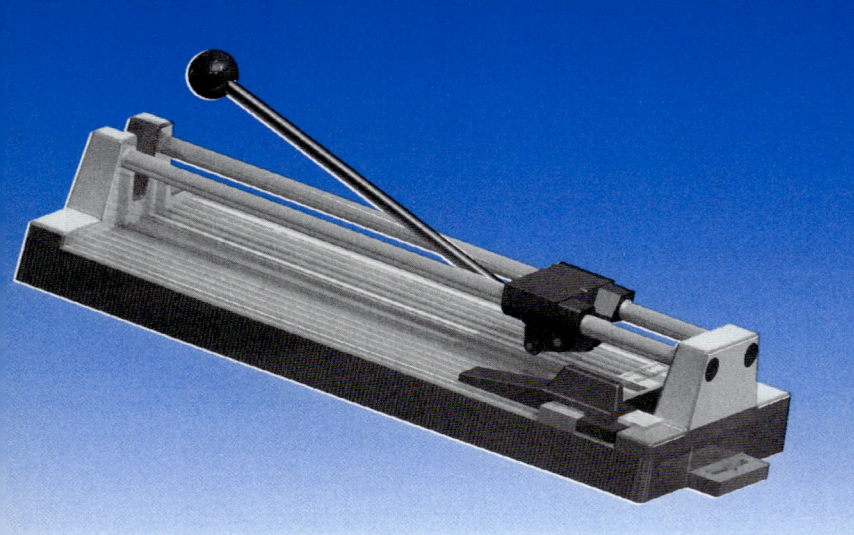

Expanded Contents

Chapter 1

Introduction to SolidWorks 15

Getting Started 15
Feature-Based Modeling 16
    Sketched Features 17
    Placed Features 18
    Reference Geometry 18
Parametric Modeling 18
Assembly Modeling 20
Modeling Motion 21
2D Drawings 21
Animations 22
eDrawing Files 22
SolidWorks Explorer 23
Pack and Go 23

Chapter 2

User Interface 25

User Interface Overview 25
Menu Bar 26
    New 26
    Open 27
    Save 28
    Undo and Redo 28
    Rebuild 28
View Navigation Tools 29
    Zoom to Fit 30
    Zoom to Area 30
    Previous View 31
    Viewpoint 31
    Display Style 31
    Pan 31

Command Manager 32
Feature Manager 32
      Changing Dimensions 34
      Renaming Features 35
      Shortcut Menu 36
      Working with Features 36
Pull-Down Menus 38
   File Pull-Down Menu 38
   Edit Pull-Down Menu 38
   View Pull-Down Menu 38
   Insert Pull-Down Menu 39
   Tools Pull-Down Menu 39
   Window Pull-Down Menu 40
   Help Pull-Down Menu 41
File Management 41

Chapter 3

Sketching, Relations, and the Base Feature 45

Process for Creating a Part 45
Sketching 47
      Relations 51
      Dimensions 52
      Relationship to the Origin 55
      Extruding the Part 56
      Editing the Feature and the Sketch 58
      Circles, Tangent and Horizontal Relations, and Trimming 59
      Arcs and More Relations 62
      Drawing an Arc from within the Line Tool 64
Things That Can Go Wrong with Sketches 65
Review of All Relations 66

Chapter 4

Complex Sketching, Equations, and Construction Geometry 71

Creating Complex (Ambiguous) Profiles 71
Using Equations in Sketch Dimensions 72
Construction Geometry 76
Sketch Mirror Entities Tool 79
Revolved Boss/Base Tool 80

Chapter 5

Secondary Sketches and Reference Geometry 85

Creating Secondary Sketches and Adding Features 85
End Condition Extrusion Options 88
Start Condition Extrusion Options 91
Converting Geometry and Projecting It to the Sketch Plane 93
Default Planes and Mid Plane Construction 95

Using the Combine Tool 99
Creating and Using Reference Geometry 101
    Creating Reference Planes 101

Chapter 6

Adding Features 109

Adding Nonsketch Features to the Part 109
Hole Tool 109
    Threaded Holes 112
    Pipe Thread Holes 113
    Clearance Holes 114
    Counterbored and Countersunk Holes 114
Cosmetic Thread Tool 115
Fillets and Rounds 117
    Applying Fillets and Rounds 117
    More Fillet Tool Options 119
    Variable-Radius Fillets and Setbacks 121
Adding Chamfers 123
Linear and Circular Patterns 126
    Linear Patterns 126
    Curve-Driven Linear Patterns 126
    Circular Patterns 127
    Pattern the Entire Part 128
Mirror Tool 130

Chapter 7

Adding More Features 135

Shell Tool 135
    Basic Shell Operation 135
    Multiple Shell Thicknesses 136
    Shelling Multiple Features and Combining Bodies 139
Rib Tool 139
Creating Text 143
Wrapping Features onto Non-Planar Faces 144
Drafts 145
    Neutral Plane 145
    Other Drafts 147
Split Tools 148
    Using the Split Tool 149
    Using the Split Line Tool 149

Chapter 8

Creating Part Drawings 153

Creating a 2D Part Drawing 153
Creating the Drawing Views 157
    Creating a Base View 157
    Projecting Views 159

Creating other Views 160
    Full Section View 160
    Half Section View 161
    Partial Section 161
    Aligned Section View 162
    Auxiliary Views 163
    Detail Views 164
    Broken-Out Section Views 164
    Broken Views 165
    Relative Views 167
Cropping Views 168
Creating Sketches in Drawing Files... 168
Editing Drawing Views 169
    Rotating Views 169
Changing the Model 170

Chapter 9

Dimensioning and Annotating Drawings 173

Preparing to Annotate a Drawing Layout 173
Drafting Standards 173
Adding Centerlines 175
Dimensioning in SolidWorks 176
    Adding Model and Reference Dimensions................................. 177
    Dimension Styles 178
    Layers 179
    Adding Hole or Thread Notes 179
    Adding Surface Texture Symbols... 180
    Adding Text 180
    Baseline Dimensions and Ordinate Dimensions 183
    Chamfer Dimensions 184
    Dimensioning Isometric Views 185
Editing the Title Block 185
Creating a Revision Table.. 188

Chapter 10

Sweeps and Lofts..191

Sweeps and Lofts... 191
Creating Sweep Features 191
    Creating a Sweep Path 192
    Creating a Cross-Sectional Profile 192
    Creating the Sweep 192
    Profile Not Perpendicular to the Path... 192
    Closed Paths 194
Practical Example of Sweeps 194
    Creating the Sweep Path.. 194
    Creating the Cross Section 195
    Completing the Part 196
3D Sweeps 197
Editing a 3D Sweep 199

    Lofts 199
        Basic Loft 200
        Loft with a Guide Curve 201
        Closed-Loop Loft 203
        Editing a Loft Feature 204

Chapter 11

Building Assemblies with Mates 207

Creating an Assembly 207
Building the Assembly 207
    Placing the First Part 208
    Rotating the Part 209
    Removing Degrees of Freedom Using Mates 210
    Applying Smart Mates 214
    Multiple-Mate Mode 215
    Placing the Bearing Block 216
    Placing the Bushing Using the Pre-Selection Method 216
    Determining the Cap Screw Specifications 218
    Placing Fasteners from the SolidWorks Toolbox Library 220
    Copying an Inserted Part 221
Constraining Edges of Parts 222
Tangent Mate 223

Chapter 12

Working with Assemblies 227

Creating Parts in the Assembly View 227
    Creating the New Part 227
    Constraining the New Part 228
Collision Detection 230
Angle Mate 231
Introduction to Animation 232
Constraining Reference Planes and Axes 233
Adaptive Parts 236
    Adaptive Location 236
    Adaptive Size 238

Chapter 13

Mechanical Assembly Mates 243

Mechanical Mates 243
Gear Mate 243
    Opposite Direction of Rotation 244
    Same Direction of Rotation 244
Rack and Pinion Mate 245
Rack and Pinion Mate—Second Solution 246
Cam Mate 247

Chapter 14
Configurations and Design Tables 251
Working with Configurations 251
Creating a New Configuration 251
Controlling Configurations with a Design Table 254
    Creating Configurations in a Design Table 254
    Editing a Design Table 256
    Creating a Design Table from Configurations 257

Chapter 15
Surfaces 259
Extruded Surfaces 260
Revolved Surfaces 260
Lofted Surfaces 262
Swept Surfaces 262
Thickening and Offsetting Surfaces 263
Surfaces as Construction Geometry 263
Knitted Surfaces 265

Chapter 16
Assembly Drawings 269
Creating Views 269
    Section Views 271
Creating Annotations 273
    Adding Dimensions 273
    Adding Leader Text 276
    Creating a Bill of Materials (BOM) 276
    Adding Balloons 280

Chapter 17
Exploded Views and Animations 283
Exploded Views 283
    Creating an Exploded View 284
    Animating Exploded Views 286
    Editing Exploded Views 287
    Adding Exploded Views to a Drawing 288
Creating Multiple Exploded Views 290
Using Exploded Views in Animations 292
    Creating the Exploded View 294
    Creating the Animation 294
    Editing the Animation 294

Index **299**

Student Website Content

www.g-wlearning.com/CAD

Chapter Practices
Chapter Exercises
Chapter Tests
Appendix
Related Websites

Chapter 1

Introduction to SolidWorks

Objectives

After completing this chapter, you will be able to:
- Describe a feature in SolidWorks.
- Explain the difference between sketched features and placed features.
- Explain how to edit a part.
- Describe an assembly in SolidWorks.
- Explain how to model motion in SolidWorks.
- Explain the purpose of SolidWorks eDrawings.

Getting Started

SolidWorks is a mature parametric solid modeling program that has been in use for about 15 years. It is built for mechanical design and is in wide use throughout the world. With this program, you can design 3D models of complex parts, determine their engineering properties, and create dimensioned detail drawings. Then, you can combine the parts into assemblies along with standard components, such as fasteners, from a built-in library. Assemblies can be animated to study their motion and to check for part interference. Assembly drawings with parts lists and balloons are easy to create and, like part drawings, are directly related to the model. In PhotoWorks and SolidWorks Motion, you can create realistic renderings and video files of animated assemblies.

This book uses a process-based approach. This approach offers a measured pace for the learner. A wealth of examples and exercises, along with the intuitive nature of SolidWorks, will allow you to become proficient and confident using SolidWorks with a moderate amount of study and practice.

Feature-Based Modeling

To explore the *feature-based* aspect of SolidWorks, refer to **Figure 1-1**. This figure shows a part tree in the **Feature Manager** for a completed part. The **Feature Manager** is an important part of the user interface. The *design tree* in the **Feature Manager** lists the components and processes that make up the part. SolidWorks refers to constructed components as *features*. If you think about any "single" part, it is really the end result of several features. The .sldprt file extension is used for SolidWorks part files.

The **Feature Manager** design tree shows several features that together form the actual solid geometry of the final part. Referring to **Figure 1-1**, these features are named and have a colored icon next to their name that represents the type of feature. In this example, features include tooth profile, tooth copies, boss rib, and cutout. These descriptive names were entered by the designer. By default, a feature is created with a generic name that represents the feature, such as Extrude1 for an extrusion or Revolve1 for a revolution.

All of the features are listed in the **Feature Manager** design tree in the order in which they were created, with the first feature at the top. Features may be reordered by simply picking and dragging them to a new position in the design tree. Reordering features may alter the part. In addition, features cannot be moved above other features on which they are based. For example, if a hole has a fillet applied to it, the fillet feature cannot be moved above the hole feature. The last feature to be listed in any SolidWorks design tree is directly above the *rollback bar*. The rollback bar is displayed as a horizontal blue bar. The rollback bar serves as an "end-of-file" marker for the part and allows you to "roll back" a part to an earlier state in the design tree. Using the rollback bar is covered in a later chapter.

Features can be edited on an individual basis to change their size, shape, and, in some cases, location on the part. Features can also be suppressed. This means that the features are still in the design tree, but their effects on the part are not applied. To

Figure 1-1.
The **Feature Manager** design tree is displayed on the left side of the user interface. The design tree contains all of the features that make up the part.

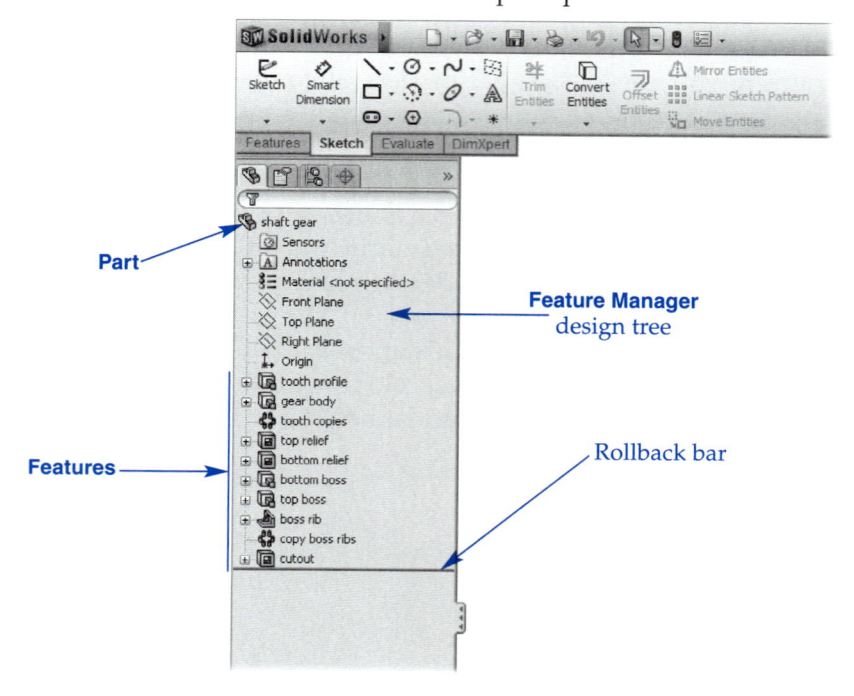

permanently remove a feature from the part, it is simply deleted. Features can even be exported for use in other parts.

The part that you are creating is never really edited; its *features* are edited. Since the part is made up of features, as the features are edited, the part is altered. SolidWorks is truly a feature-based solid modeling program and features form the heart of the system.

Features created in SolidWorks can be classified as sketched and placed features. As you work through this book, you will become very familiar with features and the tools used to create and edit them. Sketched and placed features are discussed in the next sections. You will also be introduced to the common types of reference geometry used when creating parts.

Sketched Features

A 2D *sketch* forms the basis for a *sketched feature*. This sketch can be drawn, or sketched, as any 2D geometry from lines, arcs, circles, and splines. The geometric relationship of the sketch geometry may then be constrained to a final shape by adding relations and applying dimensions. See **Figure 1-2**. A *fully defined sketch* completely describes the size, shape, and location of the sketched geometry so SolidWorks cannot inadvertently change the design in future operations. You will learn much more about sketches in later chapters.

Base feature

The *base feature* is typically the most fundamental feature making up a part. It is normally a sketched feature and is used as a "base" in constructing other features. For

Figure 1-2.
This is a fully defined sketch of a part with relations and dimensions applied. The part is designed to be created as a revolved feature.

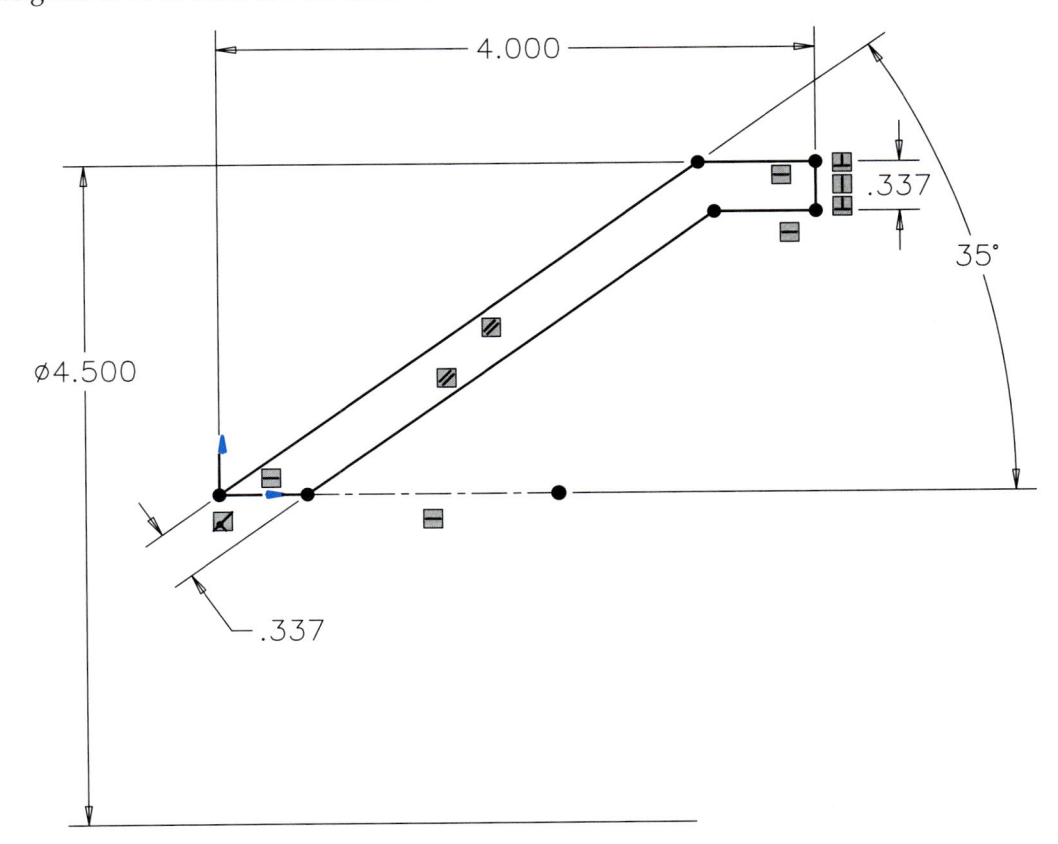

example, you may construct a motor shaft by sketching a circular profile and extruding it into a shaft to create the base feature. You may then add additional features to the base feature, such as a keyseat or beveled end.

Placed Features

A *placed feature* is not based on a sketch. Instead, the designer uses tools to "place" the feature onto an existing part. Placed features are similar to machining processes and can be thought of as operations performed on an existing part. Examples of placed features include fillets, chamfers, and holes.

Reference Geometry

Reference geometry is used for construction purposes. Reference geometry includes planes, axes, coordinate systems, and points. In a 3D environment, sometimes there is nothing on which to base a 2D sketch except a reference plane. A reference plane serves as the "drafting table" for the sketch's "paper." A reference axis can serve as a centerline of revolution. A reference point can serve as an anchor point for a 3D path.

The designer may elect to give reference geometry descriptive names, such as Plane for Extrusion. Reference geometry can be displayed in the graphics window or hidden when not needed. Reference geometry that is not visible in the graphics window is grayed out in the design tree.

Parametric Modeling

As you have seen, a SolidWorks part is made up of features. This is why Solid-Works is considered a *feature-based* solid modeling program. However, SolidWorks is also a *parametric* solid modeling program. A **parametric model** contains parameters, or dimensions, that define the model. In SolidWorks, the features that make up a part have dimensions that control the size, shape, and location of the features. By altering the dimensions (parameters), the features are altered.

For example, suppose you need to design a rectangular plate. The preliminary design indicates the plate is 8" × 4" × .25". To create the plate, you first sketch a rectangle that is roughly 8" × 4" on a sketch plane (the "paper"). Then, you apply a horizontal and a vertical dimension to the sketch and edit the values to 8" and 4". See **Figure 1-3**. The sketch completely describes the shape and size of the plate's top view. Next, you extrude the sketch .25" to fully describe the part in three dimensions. See **Figure 1-4**.

Figure 1-3.
A rectangle is sketched and dimensioned.

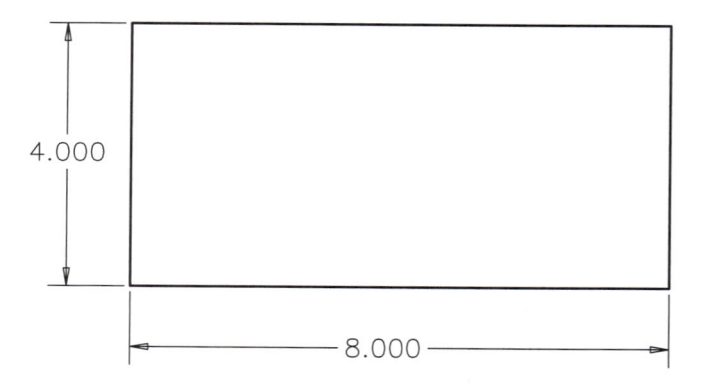

Figure 1-4.
The sketch from Figure 1-3 is extruded .25″ to create a solid part.

Since SolidWorks is a parametric modeler, you can now alter any or all of the three dimensions (parameters) to change the part.

Another powerful aspect of SolidWorks' parametric modeling is the ability to establish relationships between dimensions and features. For example, suppose the plate described above will always be half as wide as it is long, no matter what the length dimension is. An equation can be entered to specify a dimension to accomplish this. Every dimension, or parameter, in SolidWorks has a unique name. By default, the first dimension name is D1, the second is D2, and so on. Sketch dimensions and feature dimensions have a unique designator as part of the dimension name. For example, the dimension name D1@Sketch1 refers to the first dimension applied to a sketch, and the dimension name D1@Extrude1 refers to the extrusion depth dimension of the extruded feature named Extrude1. As you will learn, dimension names can be renamed to descriptive names as needed. Now, for the plate, since the vertical distance (D2@Sketch1) needs to be one-half of the horizontal distance (D1@Sketch1), instead of entering a number for the dimension, the simple equation "D2@Sketch1" = "D1@Sketch1"/2 is entered for the value of D2@Sketch1. See **Figure 1-5.** As D1@Sketch1 (the horizontal distance) is altered, D2@Sketch1 changes so the vertical distance is one-half of the horizontal distance. This is known as *specifying design intent*. It is the intention of the designer that this plate always maintains its aspect ratio of 2:1 length to width. The sketch is thus dimensioned to reflect this design intent.

PROFESSIONAL TIP

Equations may be created in SolidWorks using the **Equations** dialog box. This dialog box is accessed by selecting **Equations...** from the **Tools** pull-down menu. In the previous example, note that the dimension names used in the equation are enclosed in quotation marks. This is the standard format used when specifying dimension names in equations. Dimension names can be entered automatically in the **Add Equation** dialog box by selecting the displayed dimension in the drawing.

As mentioned, the default dimension names (D1, D2, etc.) can be renamed. Descriptive names, such as Length and Width, are meaningful to the drafter and designer. A year after the part is created, anybody can open the part file and instantly know what the dimension controls. Also, designers and drafters are almost always part of a team. Using descriptive names allows other team members to interpret your design intent. This is further enhanced by adopting a standard naming convention in your department or company.

Chapter 1   Introduction to SolidWorks

Figure 1-5.
Equations can be used to control relationships between dimensions. In the sketch shown, an equation that is based on the length dimension is entered for the width dimension. The value of the width dimension is displayed with an equation symbol (Σ) to indicate the dimension is controlled by an equation. Note the default names used for the sketch dimensions.

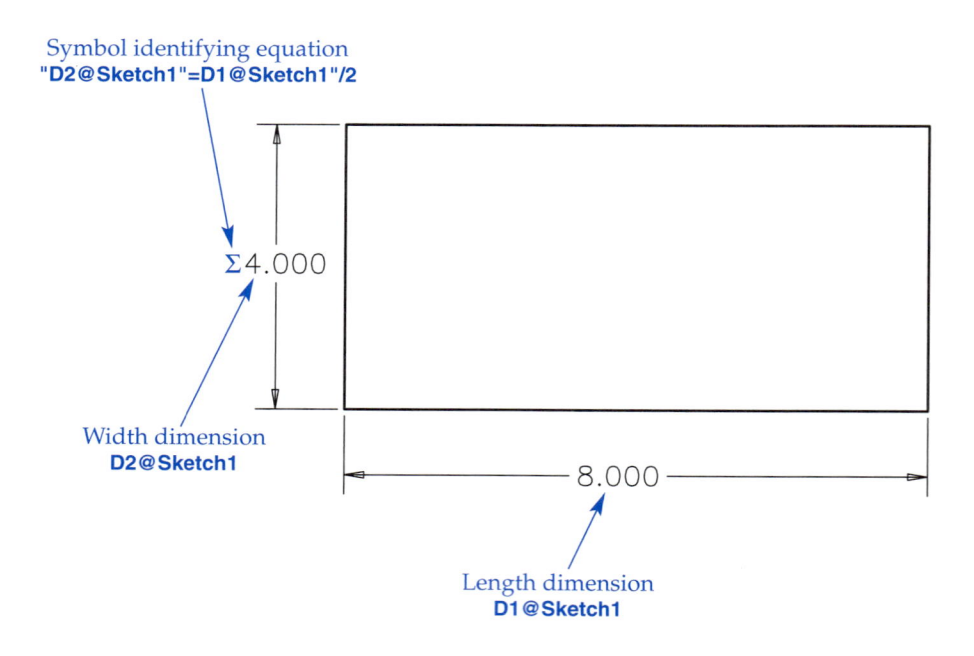

Symbol identifying equation
"D2@Sketch1"="D1@Sketch1"/2

Σ4.000

Width dimension
D2@Sketch1

8.000

Length dimension
D1@Sketch1

Another use of named dimensions is to "manufacture" different versions of a part based on data in a spreadsheet. See **Figure 1-6.** As the part is "manufactured," the designer is prompted to enter values for various parameters. The prompts are based on the dimension names. Therefore, Pipe Length is a meaningful name, where D1 is not.

Assembly Modeling

SolidWorks does a great job modeling parametric parts. However, the most powerful aspect of SolidWorks is the ability to create assemblies. As a part is a collection

Figure 1-6.
By using descriptive names, you can build a spreadsheet that is used to "manufacture" different versions of the part.

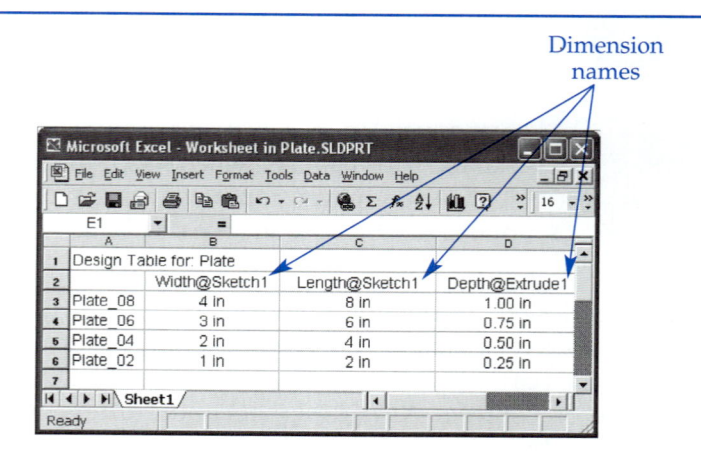

Dimension names

	Width@Sketch1	Length@Sketch1	Depth@Extrude1
Plate_08	4 in	8 in	1.00 in
Plate_06	3 in	6 in	0.75 in
Plate_04	2 in	4 in	0.50 in
Plate_02	1 in	2 in	0.25 in

Figure 1-7. This is a complex assembly. A number of individual parts were placed into the assembly and constrained to finish the assembly.

of features, an assembly is a collection of parts. See **Figure 1-7.** Each part is created and saved. Then, the parts are placed into an assembly file. An assembly file has a .sldasm file extension. Parts are only referenced in the assembly. The part files remain separate, but changes made to the part file are reflected in the assembly. Finally, the spatial relationships between parts are defined, or constrained, within the assembly file. In SolidWorks, assembly constraints are called *mates*.

A partially constrained part can be dynamically dragged to analyze its movement within the assembly. The extent of its movement is the part's *work envelope* in the assembly. You can also move parts in an assembly and then measure distances to determine design data for additional parts.

Modeling Motion

Assembly mates can be "driven," or animated. The numeric values used in the mate can be dynamically changed over a specified range to model a part's movement within the assembly. This allows you to animate the motion of an assembly. Several types of motion can be animated:
- Rotational (gears).
- Rotational-translational (rack and pinion).
- Translational (cam and cam follower).

2D Drawings

Prints of 2D drawings are always required for the machinists, assemblers, and other workers in the shop. Often, drawings must also be prepared for customers. These drawings must follow accepted drafting conventions for lineweight, linetype, and symbol use. SolidWorks provides tools for creating 2D drawings of parts and assemblies. SolidWorks drawings have an .slddrw file extension. Parts and assemblies are referenced into the drawing and displayed using orthographic projection rules. Changes made to the part are automatically reflected in the drawing.

Animations

If a picture is worth a thousand words, then how many words is a movie worth? As previously discussed, motion can be simulated by animating an assembly. Using the features available in SolidWorks, you can capture an animation to digital video. The animation can be saved as a video file or presented in an eDrawings file. SolidWorks eDrawings files are discussed in the next section.

Animations are commonly created to visually represent the process for building an assembly. Animations are also made from motion studies, exploded assembly views, and view changes to display different aspects of the design. See **Figure 1-8.**

eDrawings Files

An eDrawings file is meant to act as a communication tool between those collaborating on the design. SolidWorks eDrawings files have a compressed format and are typically sent to others electronically via e-mail. SolidWorks eDrawings files can be created from part, assembly, and drawing files. They can then be viewed in the SolidWorks eDrawings software. The SolidWorks eDrawings software provides markup and viewing tools for reviewing models, as well as basic animation tools and modification tools for moving assembly components.

A handy utility in the SolidWorks eDrawings software allows you to add notes to a part or feature that are not intended to be part of the final 2D drawing. See **Figure 1-9.**

Figure 1-8.
An animated exploded assembly presentation, such as this one, can be saved as an AVI file and played in Windows Media Player. (Image Courtesy of Garmin International, Inc.)

Figure 1-9.
A SolidWorks eDrawings file can be used to share comments that are not actual drawing annotations.

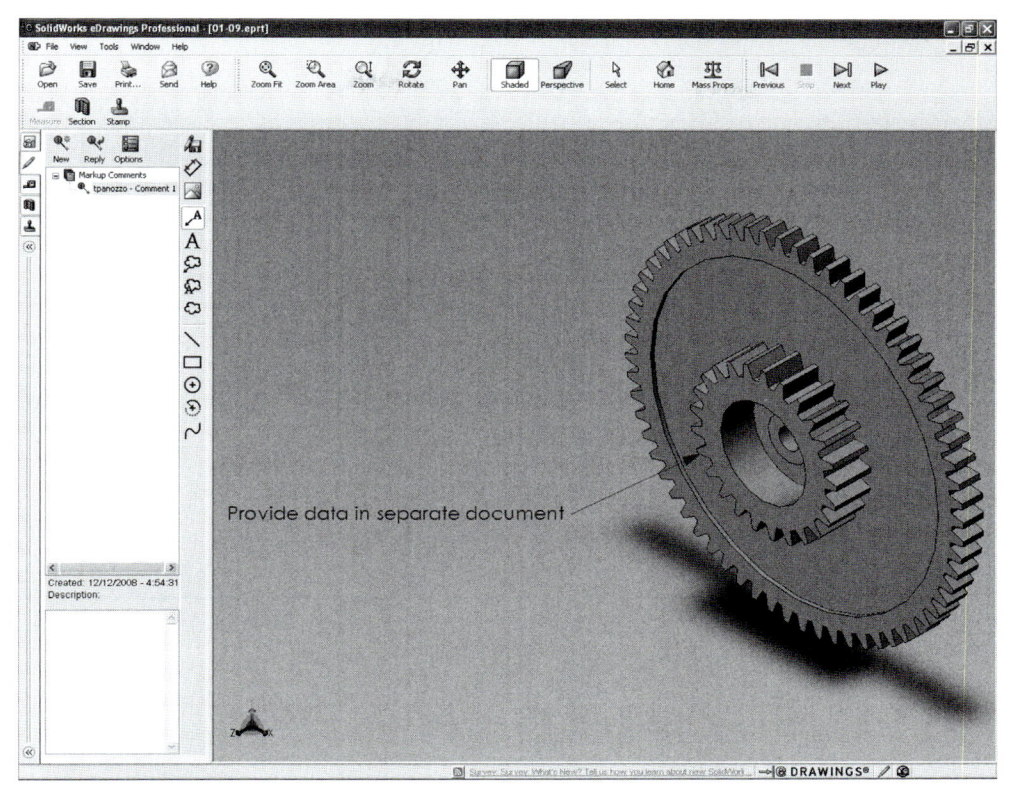

Notes can be inserted so that they appear in the graphics window at a specific location near the annotated part. Notes that are added appear in a design tree in the **Markup** tab in the **eDrawings** manager on the left side of the user interface. Notes are identified by user name in the design tree, and comments may be added to the notes without placing the text in the graphics window. This is a useful environment for communicating information between multiple users working on a design.

SolidWorks Explorer

In the process of creating parts, subassemblies, and an assembly, you may end up with hundreds of files. SolidWorks Explorer is a utility that acts as a file management system, **Figure 1-10.** It can track items such as revision number, design status, and configuration data. SolidWorks Explorer also provides common search functions and is a great utility for managing SolidWorks files.

Pack and Go

Another very useful utility, called **Pack and Go**, allows you to select an assembly and copy all of the parts, subassemblies, design views, etc., in the assembly to a destination folder. Then, you can zip all of the files and e-mail the zipped file. **Pack and Go** can be accessed within an open SolidWorks document or from SolidWorks Explorer.

Figure 1-10.
SolidWorks Explorer serves as a file management system.

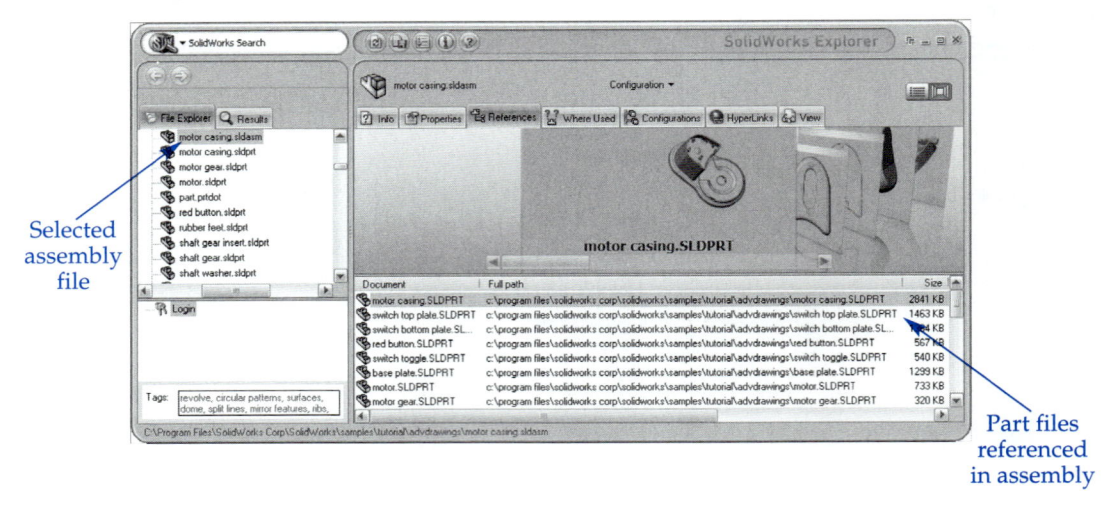

Chapter Test

Answer the following questions on a separate sheet of paper or complete the electronic chapter test on the student website.
www.g-wlearning.com/CAD

1. What are *features* in SolidWorks?
2. How is SolidWorks a feature-based modeling program?
3. How do sketched features and placed features differ?
4. What type of geometry is used for construction purposes?
5. What is the basic process for editing a part?
6. How is SolidWorks a parametric modeling program?
7. Give one example of where you would establish a relationship between a part's parameters.
8. What is an *assembly*?
9. How can motion be modeled in SolidWorks?
10. What is the purpose of an eDrawings file?

Chapter 2

User Interface

Objectives

After completing this chapter, you will be able to:
- Explain the various components of SolidWorks' user interface.
- Locate the various components of the user interface.
- Open an existing file.
- Create a new file.
- Set the unit of measure.
- Edit feature dimensions.
- Use the view navigation tools.

User Interface Overview

When SolidWorks is launched, most of the user interface is not displayed. To display the complete user interface, open a file or start a new file. Once a file is open, look at the user interface. See **Figure 2-1.** At the top of the screen are the **Menu Bar** and **Command Manager**. Along the left side of the screen is the **Management Panel**. At the top of the graphics window are the view navigation tools.

The **Command Manager** and **Management Panel** are *context sensitive*; that is, they change as you work in different modes. When a part file (SLDPRT) is open, the **Command Manager** contains the **Features**, **Sketch**, **Evaluate**, **DimXpert**, and **Office Products** tabs. Throughout this book, you will be using the tools found in the **Sketch** and **Features** tabs of the **Command Manager**.

Figure 2-1.
The default graphic interface for SolidWorks with a part file open.

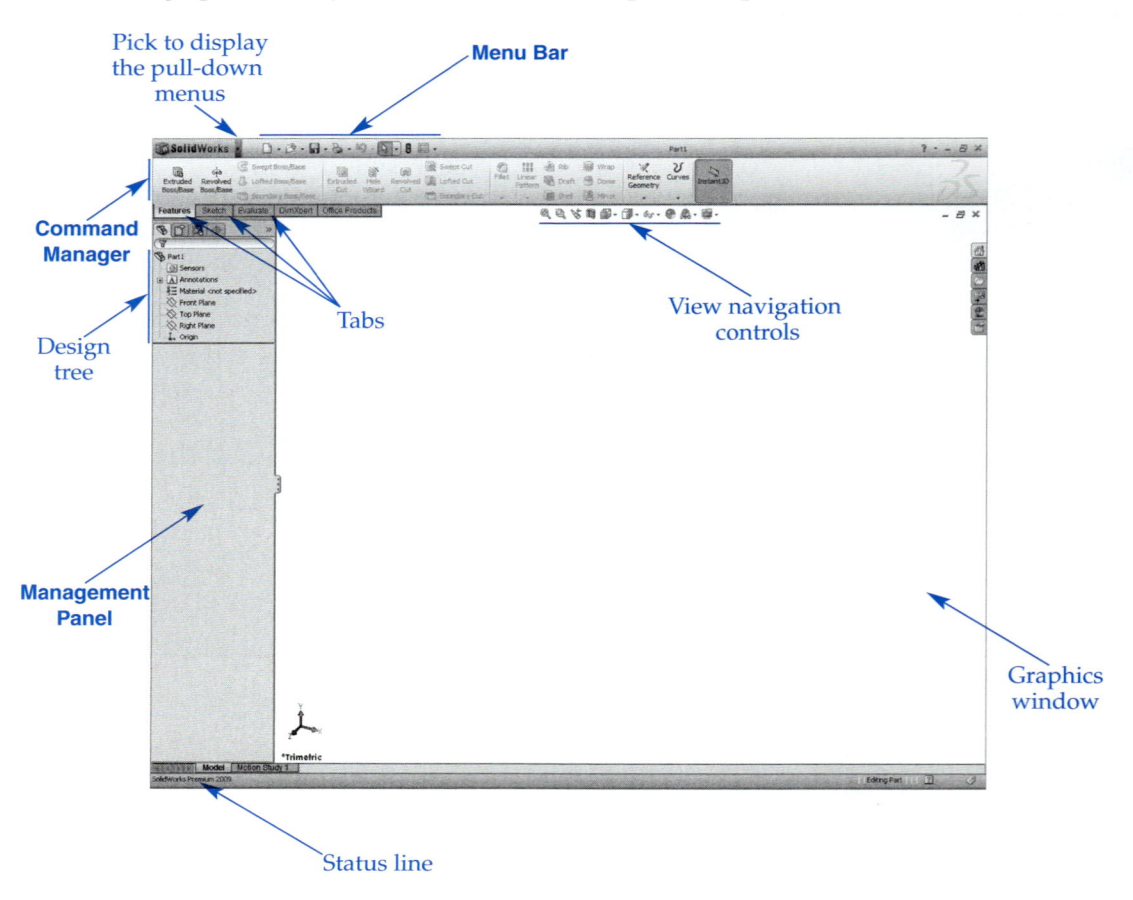

Labels: Pick to display the pull-down menus; Menu Bar; Command Manager; Design tree; Tabs; View navigation controls; Management Panel; Graphics window; Status line

Menu Bar

The buttons on the **Menu Bar** are primarily used for file-management tasks. See **Figure 2-2.** All of the common utility functions (**New**, **Open**, and **Save**) are located on this toolbar. It also contains the pull-down menus, which are hidden by default to minimize screen clutter. To show the pull-down menus, move the cursor over the arrow next to the SolidWorks logo. The pull-down menus then "flyout" on top of the **Menu Bar**. To keep the pull-down menus displayed, pick the pushpin button at the right-hand end of the pull-down menus. This also shifts the other tools in the **Menu Bar** to the right so they remain visible.

New

Picking the **New** button on the **Menu Bar** displays the **New SolidWorks Document** dialog box, **Figure 2-3.** In this dialog box, you can choose between a new part, assembly, or drawing file. To the right of the **New** button is a drop-down list. Pick the arrow to display the drop-down list. There are three options in this list that match the options in the **New SolidWorks Document** dialog box. These options allow you to start a new file directly without using the dialog box.

Part files are the basis of everything in SolidWorks. They are used to create assemblies as well as drawings. When a new part file is started, it is based on the default template for the default unit of measure. The default name is Part$x$, where x is a number. Part files are saved with a .sldprt file extension.

Figure 2-2.
A—The SolidWorks **Menu Bar**. B—Picking the arrow next to the SolidWorks logo displays the pull-down menus.

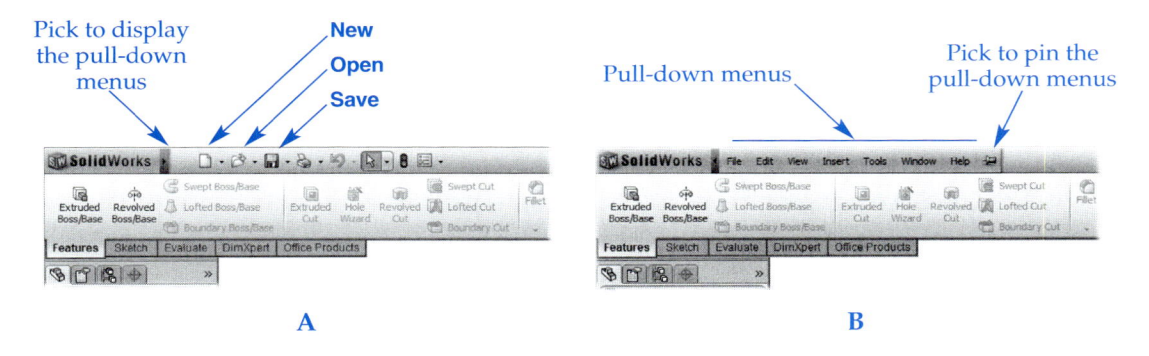

Figure 2-3.
Starting a new file in SolidWorks. Pick the button for the type of file and then pick the **OK** button to start the file.

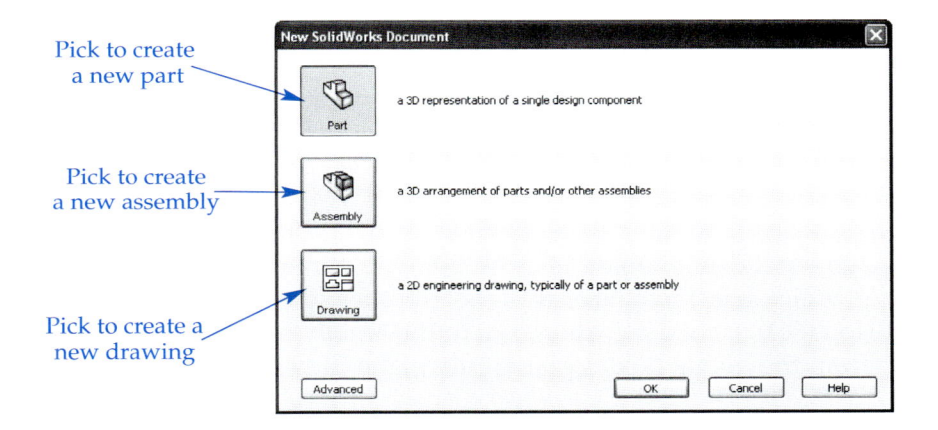

An *assembly file* is a collection of part files that are related to one another to create a completed product. A new assembly file is based on the template corresponding to the default unit of measure, which was specified when SolidWorks was installed. The unit of measure for any file can be changed in the options dialog box, as you will see later. The default name for an assembly file is Assem$x$, where x is a number. When the file is saved, you have the opportunity to give it a more meaningful name. Assembly files are saved with a .sldasm file extension.

Drawing files are used to create 2D orthographic and 3D pictorial views of parts and assemblies. The default name is Draw$x$, where x is a number. Drawing files are saved with a .slddrw file extension.

Open

Picking the **Open** button displays the **Open** dialog box. This is a standard Windows "open" dialog box. It is used to locate and open an existing SolidWorks file.

Near the bottom of the **Open** dialog box is the **Files of type:** drop-down list. This list includes all of the file types that can be opened in SolidWorks. SolidWorks uses three file types: SLDASM, SLDDRW, and SLDPRT. The DWG file type is the native AutoCAD format. The DXF, IGES, SAT, and STEP file types are used to exchange 3D information with other CAD systems.

Save

When working on a new file that has yet to be saved and the **Save** button is picked, the **Save As** dialog box is displayed. See **Figure 2-4**. This dialog box is not displayed when saving a file that has previously been saved. The **Save As** dialog box is a standard Windows "save" dialog box.

Use the **Save in:** drop-down list to navigate to the folder where the file is to be saved. When specifying a filename, you do not need to type the extension. SolidWorks assumes the file type, which will be the type displayed in the **Save as type:** drop-down list. The **Save as type:** drop-down list contains many other file types and is used to export SolidWorks files as other types.

Undo and Redo

Selecting the **Undo** button reverses the last action, except view-related operations such as **Zoom** or **Pan**. The **Redo** tool reverses the effect of the **Undo** button. A redo basically undoes the undo. The **Redo** tool is located in the **Edit** pull-down menu. As with undo, view-related operations are not affected by a redo. Both the **Undo** and **Redo** tools can be used multiple times to step backward or forward through undo and redo operations.

Rebuild

As described in Chapter 1, SolidWorks is a parametric modeler. Parts and assemblies designed in SolidWorks can be changed time and time again. The **Rebuild** tool is used to update a part or assembly after a modification has been made so the file reflects the changes. See **Figure 2-5**.

Open Example_02_01.sldprt. Right-click on Extrude1 in the design tree and pick the **Edit Sketch** button from the shortcut toolbar, **Figure 2-6**. The dimensions for the extrusion and the sketch on which it is based appear in the graphics screen. Double-click on the diameter dimension (66), change its value to 70 in the **Modify** dialog box, and pick the check mark button in the dialog box or press [Enter]. The dimension of the feature

Figure 2-4.
When a file is first saved, the **Save As** dialog box appears. This dialog box is also displayed when **Save As...** is selected from the **File** pull-down menu.

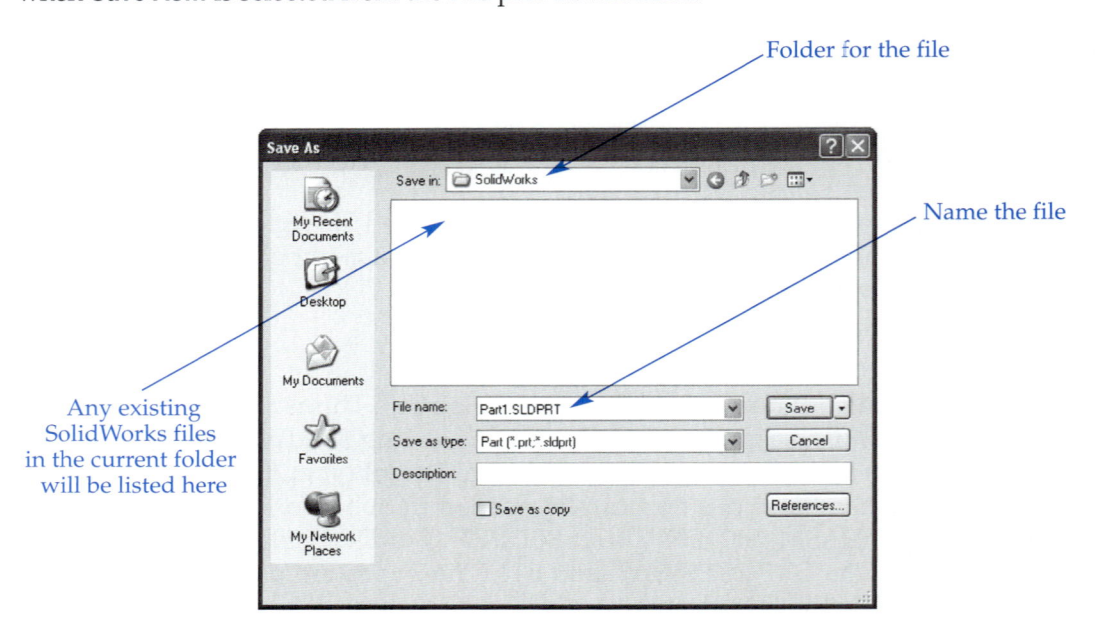

Figure 2-5.
Sometimes, you will need to rebuild the part or assembly after a modification has been made.

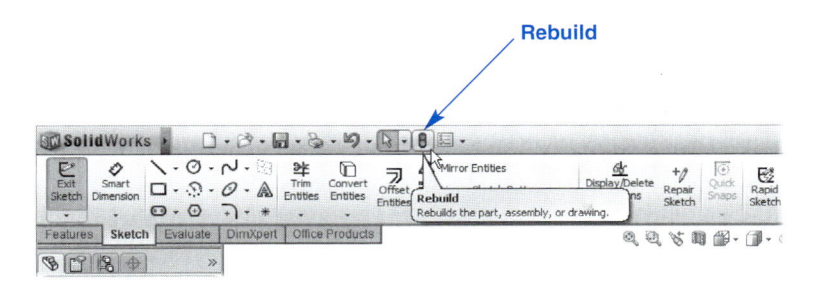

Figure 2-6.
When you right-click on a feature in the design tree, a shortcut menu is displayed. Often, a shortcut toolbar is also displayed.

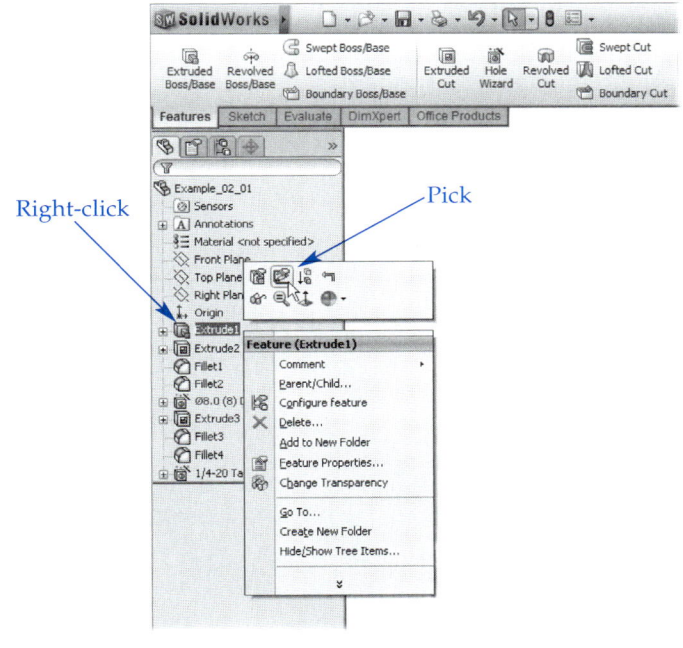

has been changed; however, the part is not yet rebuilt to reflect the change. Pick the **Rebuild** button on the **Menu Bar** to update the part. After examining the change, pick the **Undo** button until the change is reversed.

PROFESSIONAL TIP

One of the main uses for the **Rebuild** tool is for updating parts in assembly mode when you are working on a large assembly with subassemblies.

View Navigation Tools

At the top of the graphics window are several view navigation tools. See **Figure 2-7.** Other view navigation tools are available in the shortcut menu displayed by right-clicking in the graphics window. See **Figure 2-8.**

Chapter 2 User Interface

Figure 2-7.
Many navigation tools are displayed at the top of the graphics window.

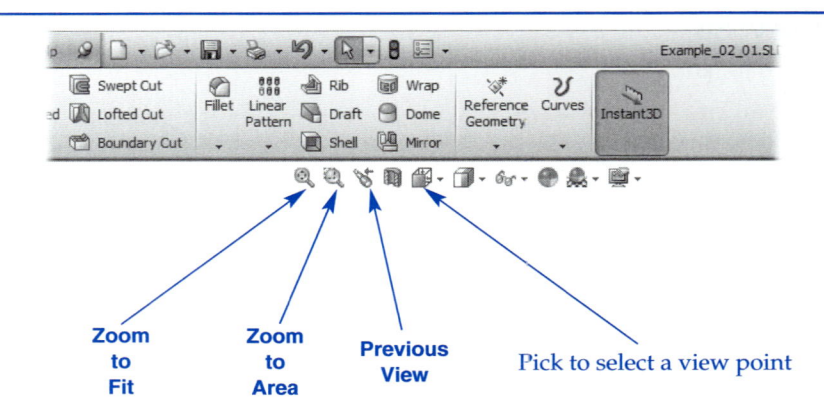

Zoom to Fit   Zoom to Area   Previous View   Pick to select a view point

Figure 2-8.
When you right-click in the graphics window, a shortcut is displayed that contains navigation tools. The shortcut menu shown here is displayed when nothing is selected.

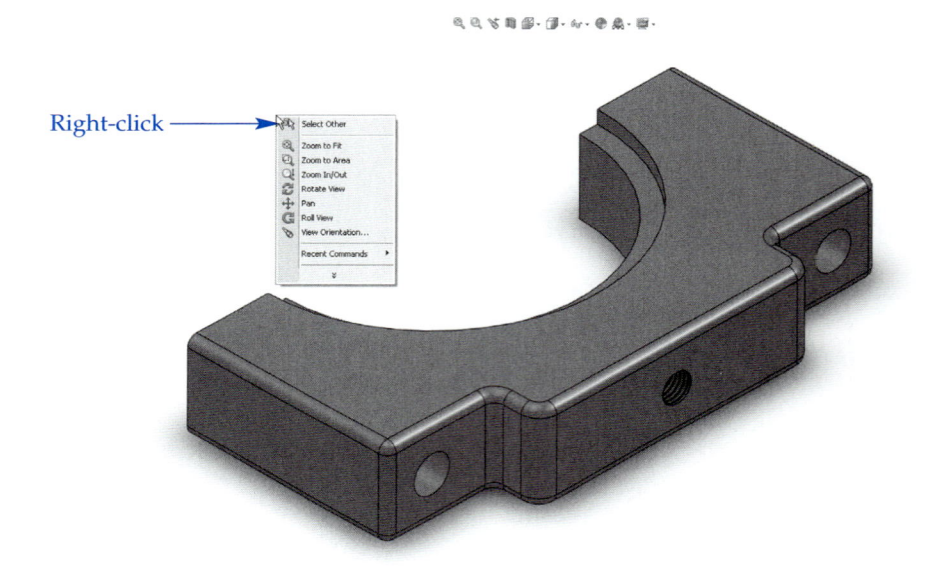

Right-click

Zoom to Fit

The **Zoom to Fit** button is used to fill the graphics window with all of the part or assembly. The display will zoom out or in as needed.

Zoom to Area

The **Zoom to Area** button is used to fill the graphics window with a selected rectangular area of the display. After picking the button, select two points to define the window. The two points are defined using a pick-and-drag method. SolidWorks zooms to fill the graphics window with that area. Remember, **Undo** does not undo view-related operations.

PROFESSIONAL TIP

A great trick is to simply use the mouse's roller wheel to zoom—roll the wheel toward you to magnify or away from you to reduce the image.

30 Learning SolidWorks 2009

Previous View

The **Previous View** button restores the previous display. In effect, this is an undo button for view changes. You can pick the button multiple times to step back through the previous views.

Viewpoint

The *viewpoint* is the location from which the model is viewed. Often, you will be working in an isometric view. This is a 3D viewpoint of the model. To select a viewpoint, pick the appropriate button in the **View Orientation** flyout. You can select an orthographic view, such as top or left. You can also select a pictorial view, such as isometric, trimetric, or dimetric.

The **Normal To** button is also located in the **View Orientation** flyout. When you pick this button, you are prompted to select a planar face or surface. Once you make the selection, a view is displayed that is parallel to the selected face. In other words, the viewpoint is normal, or perpendicular, to the face. This tool can be very useful to display a plan view when creating a sketch.

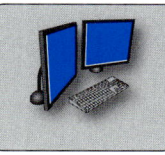

> **PROFESSIONAL TIP**
>
> To orbit the view in 3D, press the mouse wheel button and move the mouse. This allows you to rotate the view of the part or assembly to see other sides.

Display Style

The buttons in the **Display Style** flyout are used to change the shading of the part. The **Shaded with Edges** button displays the part as a colored object with solid line on the edges of the faces. The **Shaded** button produces a similar display, but without the edges. The **Hidden Lines Removed** button displays the part as a white object with those lines that would normally be hidden not shown. The **Hidden Lines Visible** button produces a similar display, but with the hidden lines shown. The **Wireframe** button displays no shading and all lines are shown. In other words, the part is shown as a wireframe. See **Figure 2-9.**

Pan

The **Pan** tool is used to shift the display within the graphics window. The tool is located in the shortcut menu. To display this menu, right-click in the graphics window. After selecting the **Pan** tool, the panning cursor appears in the graphics window. To pan around the graphics window, press and hold the left mouse button and drag to obtain the desired display. When done, press [Esc]. Panning can be done at any time, even within a tool.

A quick way to select the **Pan** tool is to press the [Ctrl] key and the mouse wheel button at the same time. Then, you can pan the view as described above.

> **NOTE**
>
> If something is selected when you right-click to display the shortcut menu, you must first select **Zoom/Pan/Rotate** to display a cascading menu that contains the view navigation tools. Also, there are additional navigation tools located in the shortcut menu, such as **Roll View** and **Rotate View**.

Chapter 2   User Interface

Figure 2-9.
There are several different ways in which the model can be displayed. A—Shaded with edges. B—Hidden lines removed. C—Hidden lines visible. D—Wireframe.

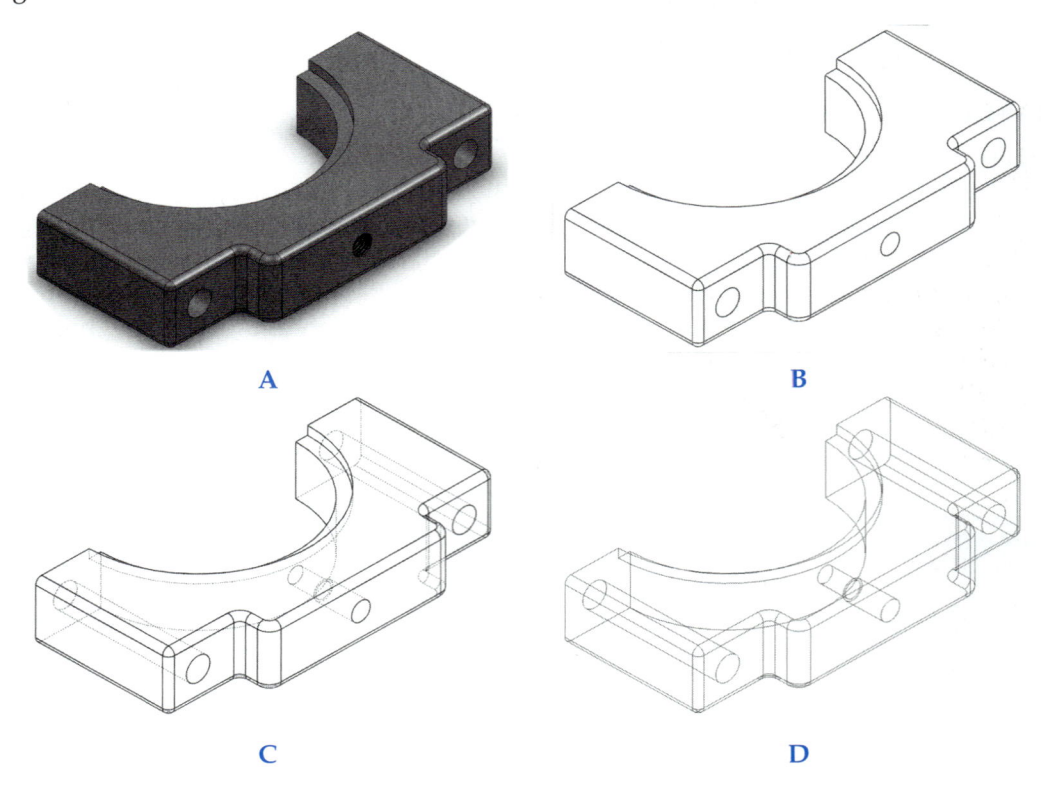

A

B

C

D

Command Manager

The **Command Manager** is the main interface for SolidWorks tools. It contains tabs that in turn contain buttons for tools. Which tabs are displayed and which tools are available depend on the type of file being edited and in which mode you are working (sketch, part, assembly, etc.). The **Command Manager** tabs automatically change to match the current file and mode.

Some of the buttons in the **Command Manager** have associated drop-down lists. These are denoted by a small black arrow below or next to the button name. If you pick on the arrow, a drop-down list is displayed that contains additional tools.

SolidWorks has an "expert mode" for the buttons in the **Command Manager**. In expert mode, the explanatory text for each button is hidden; only the icon is displayed. **Figure 2-10** shows the **Sketch** tab in the **Command Manager** in expert mode. Notice the text is gone and only the icon is shown on the button. To enter expert mode, right-click on the background of the **Command Manager** and uncheck **Use Large Buttons with Text** in the shortcut menu. To exit expert mode, select **Use Large Buttons with Text** from the shortcut menu so it is checked.

Feature Manager

The design tree in the **Feature Manager** is the heart of SolidWorks. You will spend a great deal of time using it to manage features and navigate assemblies. SolidWorks creates parametric parts that are based on parametric features. The features are, in turn, based on sketches. All of the items used to build a part or assembly are listed in

Figure 2-10.
When the **Command Manager** is in expert mode, only the icons are displayed on the buttons. There is no descriptive text.

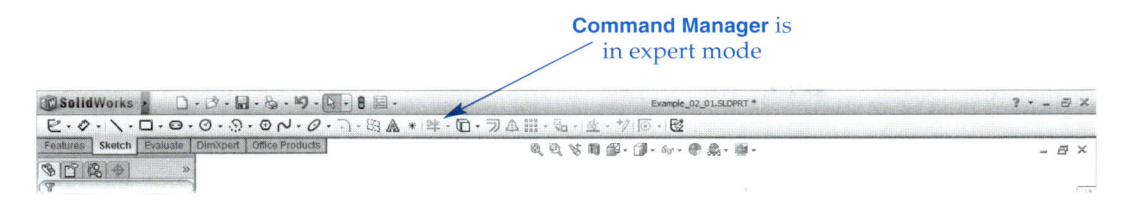

the *design tree* as they are created. The design tree is also used to access the parameters of a feature.

Figure 2-11 shows the design tree for Example_02_01.sldprt. If you move your cursor over the name of a feature, a shaded box appears around the feature name. Also, the feature is highlighted by an orange wireframe in the graphics window as long as the cursor is over the feature name. If you pick a feature in the design tree, such as Extrude1, it is highlighted in blue in the graphics window and the dimensions used to create feature are shown.

More than one feature can be selected in the design tree. To select consecutively listed features, pick the first one in the tree, hold down the [Shift] key, and pick the last one. To select individual features, hold down the [Ctrl] key and pick the features in the tree.

In most CAD systems, geometry is selected in the graphics window only. In SolidWorks, geometry can be selected in the graphics window or the design tree. This is extremely useful because in some situations you can *only* select items from the design tree.

Often, the flyout **Feature Manager** design tree is displayed in the upper-left corner of the graphics window. This occurs when a **Property Manager** is displayed in the

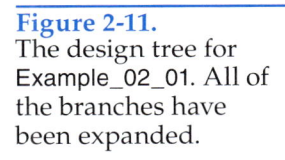

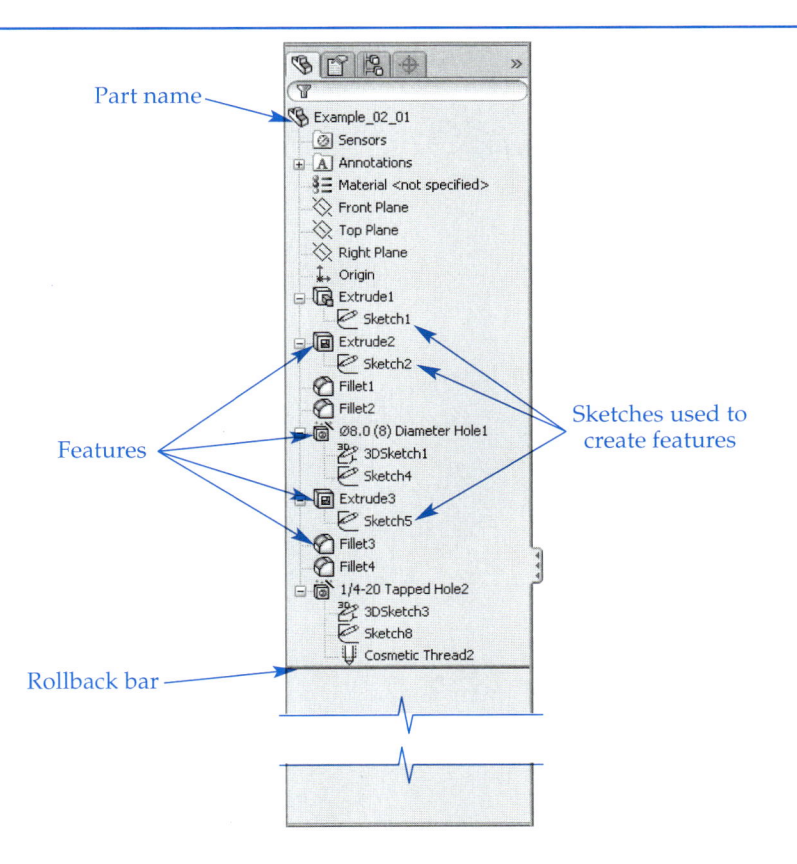

Figure 2-11.
The design tree for Example_02_01. All of the branches have been expanded.

Chapter 2   User Interface

Management Panel. The flyout design tree is the same as the design tree in the **Feature Manager**. You can expand the tree and select features in it during an operation.

With the file Example_02_01.sldprt open, pick the plus sign next to Extrude1 in the design tree. This expands the Extrude1 branch in the design tree to show the sketch on which the feature is based. Features defined by a sketch, such as this extrusion, are called *sketched features.* Some of the features in the design tree, such as the fillets, do not have a plus sign next to them. These are called *placed features* and are not defined by a sketch. Rather, they are "placed" on other features.

Double-click on Sketch1 under Extrude1. You can also right-click on the sketch or feature name and pick the **Edit Sketch** button from the shortcut toolbar that appears. Your screen should look like **Figure 2-12**. Sketch mode has been entered and the graphics window displays the 2D sketch that is the basis of Extrude1. Notice that the **Sketch** tab in the **Command Manager** has been made active. Also, notice that all of the features and sketches in the design tree, other than Sketch1, are grayed out. These items are currently unavailable.

At this point the sketch can be edited—perhaps the dimensioning scheme needs to be changed or some geometry added or removed. Exit the sketch by picking the **Exit Sketch** button on the **Sketch** tab. You can also pick the return button that appears in the top-right corner of the graphics window.

Changing Dimensions

As shown above, you can edit a sketch to change dimensions. However, you can change dimensions in part mode, too. To change the dimensions controlling a feature while in part mode, select the feature in the design tree. For example, with Example_02_01.sldprt

Figure 2-12.
Editing the sketch on which the feature Extrude1 is based.

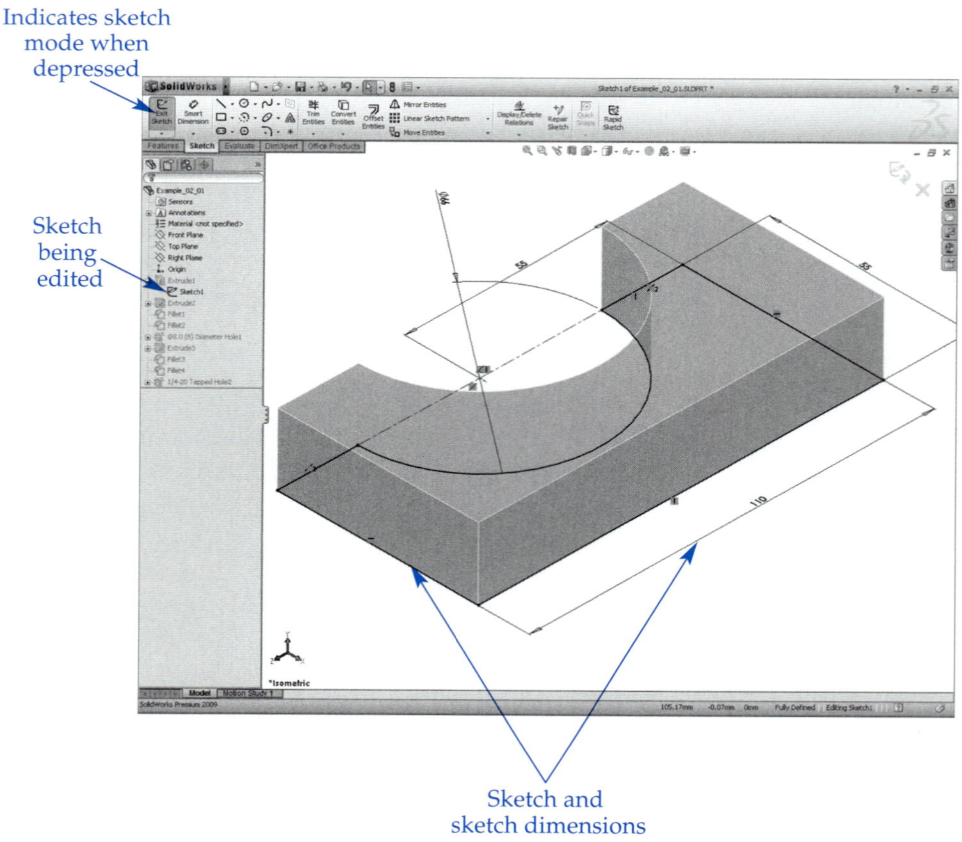

open, pick Extrude1 in the design tree. The associated dimensions are shown in the graphics window. Locate the ⌀66 mm dimension and single-click on it. A text box appears in place of the dimension with the current dimension value displayed. See **Figure 2-13.**

Change the value to 30 mm and press the [Enter] key. The dimension changes and the part is updated. This example illustrates the parametric capabilities of SolidWorks. The diameter dimension is a parameter of the feature and, in turn, the part. By changing this parameter, the feature and part are altered. In software that is not parametric, once the feature is created, you do not have access to the parameters on which the feature is based.

Renaming Features

As features are created, SolidWorks automatically names them. The default feature names, such as Extrude1, are often not very descriptive. The **Feature Manager** can be used to rename features. With Example_02_01.sldprt open, left-click two single times on Extrude1 in the design tree; do not double-click. See **Figure 2-14.** The name is replaced by a text box and the current name is highlighted. Now, type a new name, such as Base Feature, and press [Enter].

Feature names are very important. For example, the hole features in Example_02_01.sldprt are provided names by SolidWorks that are descriptive—the names indicate the size of the hole and if it is tapped. However, the extrude and fillet operations all have generic names. You do not want to have a finished part containing 50 features with names Extrude1 through Extrude50. The little extra time required to rename features can save hours of headaches later trying to figure out which feature is which. In this example, Extrude2 may be renamed to Notch and Extrude3 may be renamed to Flange Seat. Likewise, the fillets may be renamed to indicate which edge they are applied to and their radius. Sketches and reference geometry can be renamed, too.

Figure 2-13.
Changing the diameter dimension in the sketch on which Extrude1 is based.

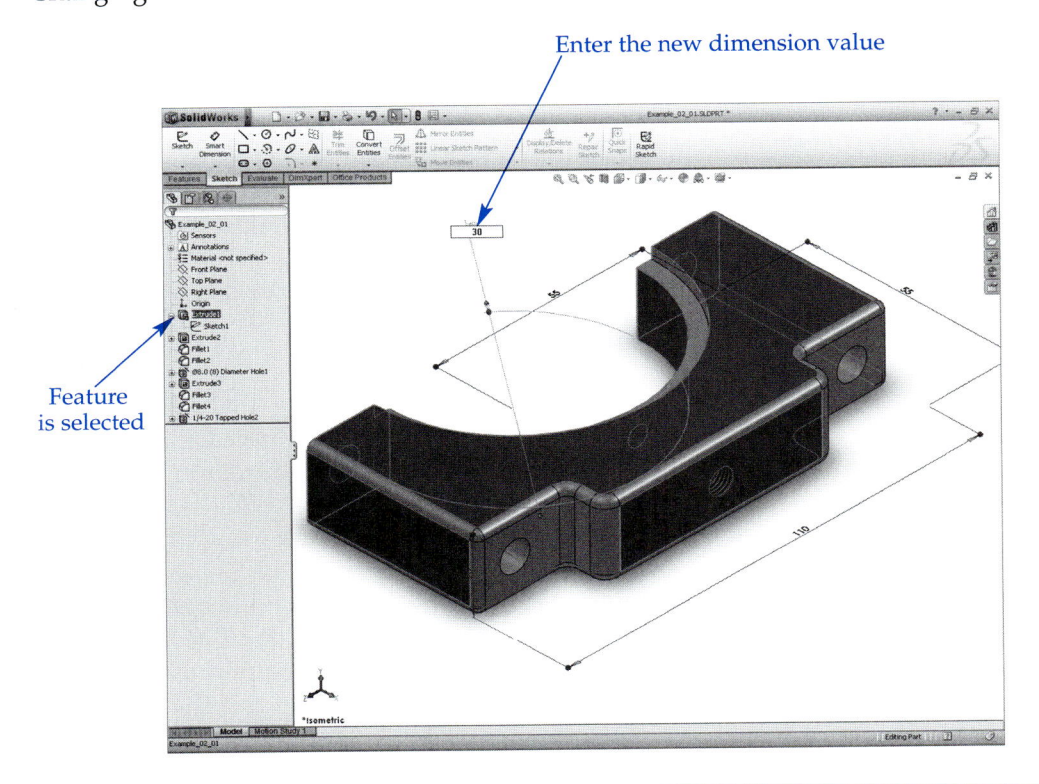

Chapter 2   User Interface

Figure 2-14. Renaming a feature. A—Single-click two times on the name to display the text box. B—Type a new name and press the [Enter] key.

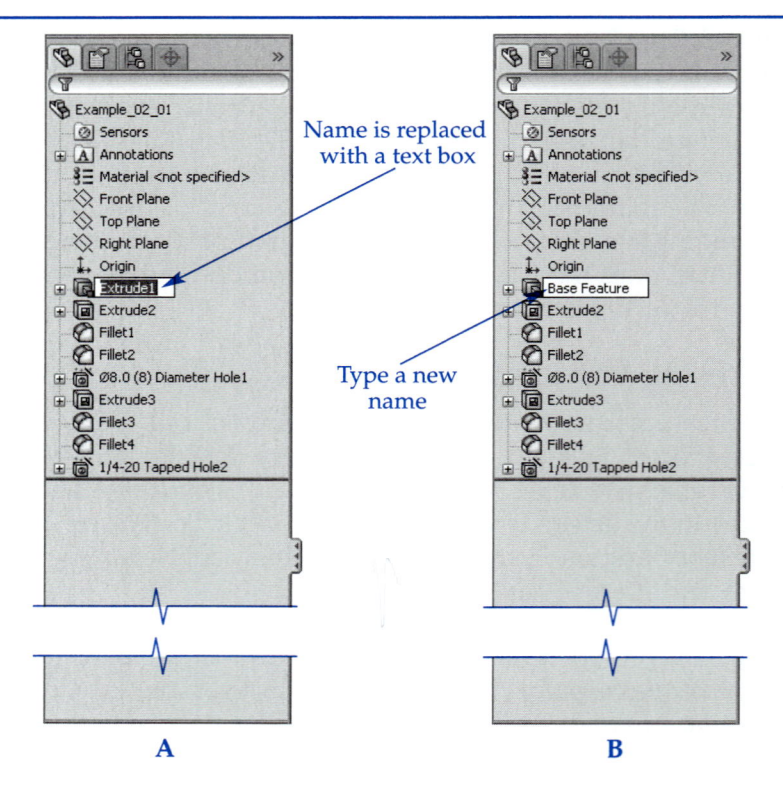

Shortcut Menu

Right-clicking on a sketched feature displays a shortcut menu and, in some cases, a shortcut toolbar. See **Figure 2-15.** The options in this menu are context specific and differ based on the current situation. Typical options are discussed below. These options may be available as an entry in the shortcut menu or a button on the shortcut toolbar.

- **Edit Feature.** Allows you to edit how the feature was created, but not the sketch on which it is based. Use of this option is covered in later chapters.
- **Edit Sketch.** Displays in sketch mode the sketch on which the feature is based. This is an alternative to double-clicking on the feature's sketch in the design tree.
- **Suppress.** Simplifies the part or temporarily removes a feature from the part.
- **Rollback.** Suppresses the feature and any dependent features from the part.
- **Hide.** Hides the feature or the body that was modified by the feature.
- **Zoom to Selection.** Zooms the image to the geometry affected by the feature.
- **Normal To.** Displays a view that is parallel to the sketch plane used to create the feature.
- **Appearances.** Allows you to assign various colors and textures to a body, feature, or face.

Working with Features

The top branch of the design tree is the name of the currently open document. The icon next to the name also identifies the type of file. There is a different icon for each type of SolidWorks file: part, assembly, and drawing.

Immediately below the document name are branches containing information about the part. Depending on the situation, these branches may be Sensors, Annotations, Solid Bodies, and Surface Bodies. Below these branches are the Materials branch and branches for the three standard planes and the origin. See **Figure 2-16.** The origin is the coordinate system's origin (0,0,0). The standard planes correspond to the planes formed by the coordinate system's X, Y, and Z axes. These planes and the origin are

Figure 2-15.
The shortcut menu and shortcut toolbar displayed by right-clicking on a feature.

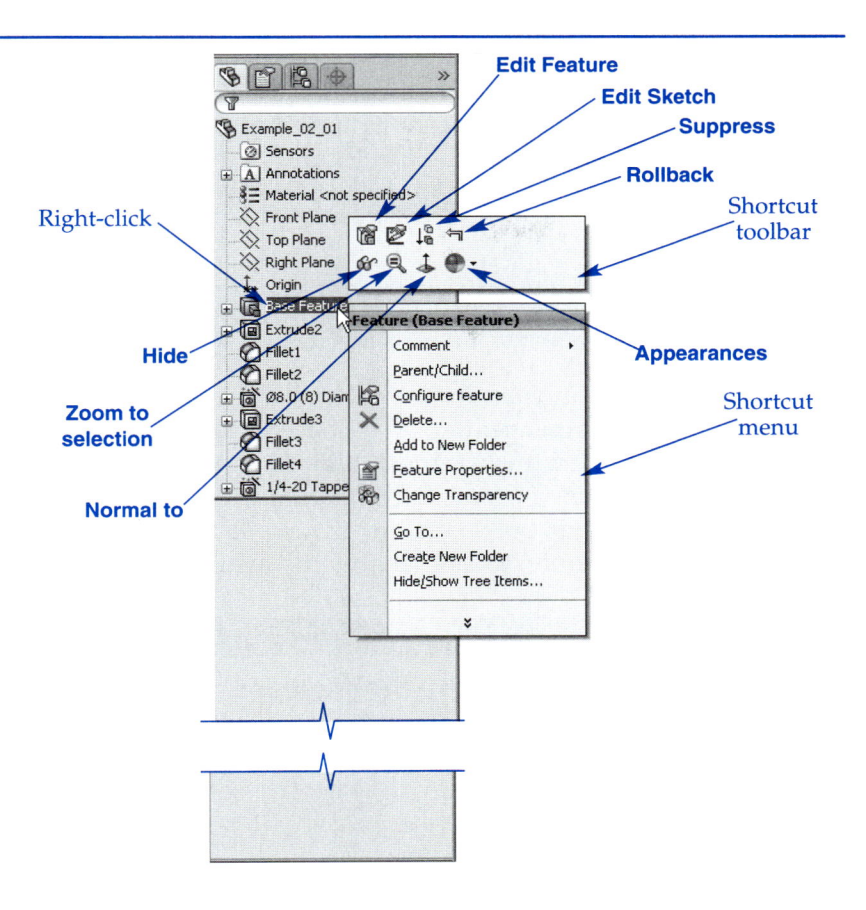

Figure 2-16.
Every SolidWorks part and assembly file contains the three standard planes and the origin in the design tree.

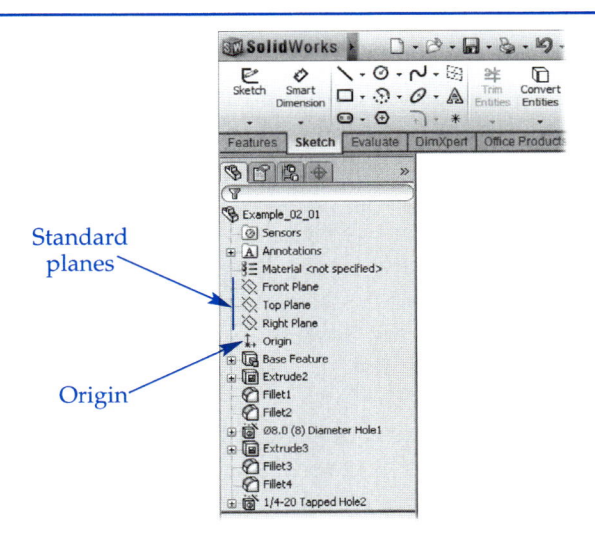

important in part modeling, as well as constraining assemblies. Throughout this book there are references to these planes and the origin.

The last element of the design tree is a special feature called the rollback bar. The *rollback bar* denotes the end of the feature listing, but it also has specific uses. For example, with Example_02_01.sldprt open, pick on the rollback bar, drag it up the tree, and drop it below the Origin branch. Notice that all features are grayed out in the design tree and are no longer displayed in the graphics window. The rollback bar represents the end of the features list—the end of the database. After the move, it is higher in the tree than any of the features, so the features are basically no longer in the part.

Chapter 2   User Interface

Now, drag-and-drop the rollback bar below the first part feature, Extrude1 (or Base Feature, if you renamed it earlier). The basic shape that was used to start this part is displayed in the graphics window and is no longer grayed out in the design tree. Continue to drag-and-drop the rollback bar down one feature at a time. This reveals the method(s) used to construct this part. This is a great way to see how the part was built.

Pull-Down Menus

The pull-down menus are located on the **Menu Bar**. To display the pull-down menus, pick the arrow next to the SolidWorks logo. There are seven pull-down menus—**File**, **Edit**, **View**, **Insert**, **Tools**, **Window**, and **Help**. They contain important tools with which you need to become familiar. Many of the tools are also available on tabs in the **Command Manager**, but some are only available in the pull-down menus. The next sections discuss common tools that are only available in the pull-down menus.

> **NOTE**
>
> Depending on which add-ins you have active, other pull-down menus may be displayed. Only the standard pull-down menus are discussed here.

File Pull-Down Menu

Selecting the **Make Drawing from Part** option in the **File** pull-down menu starts a new SolidWorks drawing file. When the drawing file is started, you must first select a drawing sheet size. After the sheet size is selected, you must place a view of the drawing. Drawings are discussed in detail in Chapters 8, 9, and 16.

The **Make Assembly from Part** option starts a new assembly file with the current part ready to be placed. An assembly is a file containing parts related to each other through the use of mates. Assemblies are discussed in detail in Chapters 11 through 14.

The **Save As** dialog box is displayed when the **Save As...** option is used. This option saves the current file under a new name. In essence, the software simply renames the current file. However, this option is also used to save the file as a different file type, such as JPEG, DWF, or STL. In the **Save As** dialog box, select the appropriate file type in the **Save as type:** drop-down list.

The **Save All** option saves the active file and all other currently open files. This option does not, however, save any dependent files. For example, suppose you have an assembly file open that consists of several parts. Each of these part files is a dependent of the assembly file. Picking **Save All** will save the assembly file because it is open, but it will *not* save the dependent part files unless they are also open.

Edit Pull-Down Menu

The **Edit** pull-down menu contains standard options such as **Cut** and **Paste**. It also contains options for rebuilding the part or assembly, suppressing configurations, and changing the appearance of a face or feature.

View Pull-Down Menu

The **View** pull-down menu contains options for displaying or hiding various items, such as reference planes and axes and sketch relations. It also contains options for changing the view in the graphics window and the appearance of the display.

The **View** pull-down menu is used to display various toolbars. Some users may prefer to select tools in a toolbar rather than the **Command Manager** or a pull-down menu. To display a toolbar, select **Toolbar** in the **View** pull-down menu to display a cascading menu. The cascading menu contains a list of all available toolbars. Pick the name of the toolbar to display. The icon next to the name is depressed for any toolbar that is currently displayed.

There are many other options in the **View** pull-down menu. These are covered throughout the text as needed.

Insert Pull-Down Menu

The **Insert** pull-down menu offers every tool available in SolidWorks. As mentioned earlier, the **Command Manager** contains many tools, but not all tools. All tools can be accessed by choosing the appropriate subcategory in the **Insert** pull-down menu.

Tools Pull-Down Menu

The options in the **Tools** pull-down menu have many uses. Later chapters cover many of the options in the pull-down menu. The focus in this section is on the **Options...** selection. Picking this entry displays the options dialog box. There are two tabs in this dialog box: **System Options** and **Document Properties**. The name of the dialog box reflects which tab is active.

System Options

Settings pertinent to the SolidWorks environment are set in the **System Options** tab of the options dialog box. See **Figure 2-17**. These settings are saved in the SolidWorks registry and apply to all documents that are opened in SolidWorks.

On the left side of the tab is a tree containing branches for several system categories. Once you select a category in the tree, the options and settings in that category are displayed on the right-hand side of the tab. For example, to change the screen colors,

Figure 2-17.
Settings that apply to all documents in SolidWorks are made in the **System Options** tab of the options dialog box.

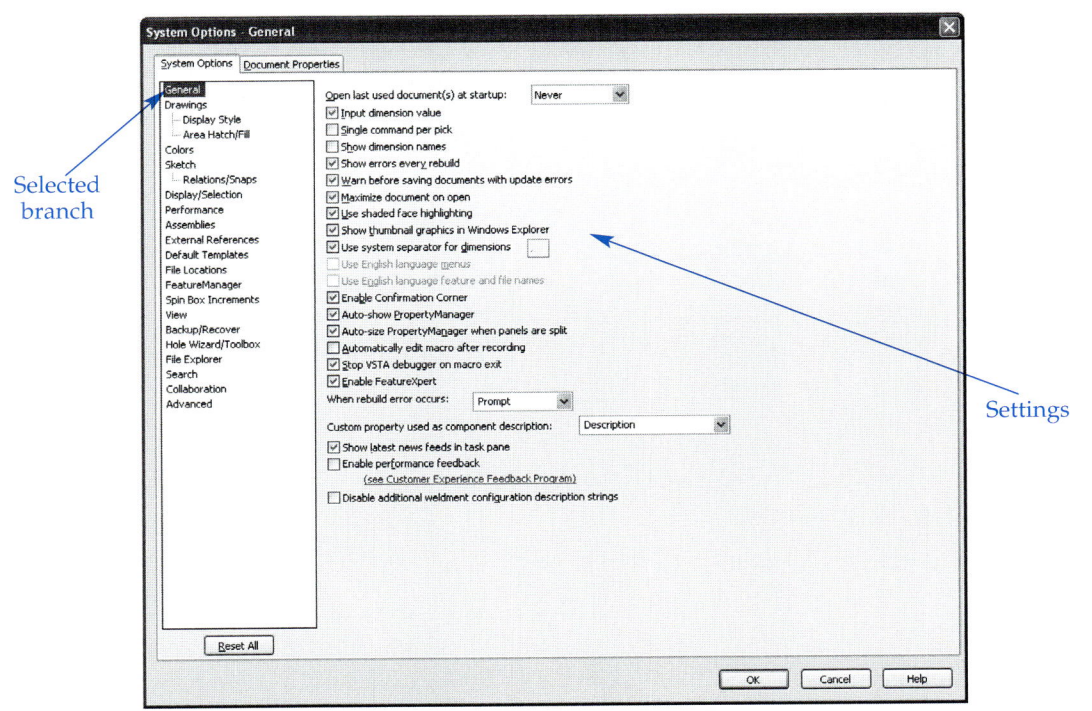

Chapter 2 User Interface

select the Colors branch. Then, on the right-hand side of the tab, change the color for interface elements as needed. Once you pick the **OK** button to close the dialog box, the new settings are applied.

Document Properties

The settings in the **Document Properties** tab are saved in the current document. Other documents are not affected by changes to settings in this tab. On the left side of the tab is a tree containing branches for several document categories. Once you select a category in the tree, the options and settings in that category are displayed on the right-hand side of the tab.

One document setting you may need to change is the unit of measure. To do this, select the Units branch. The unit settings are then displayed on the right-hand side of the tab, **Figure 2-18.** There are several units of measure from which to select. Pick the radio button corresponding to the unit of measure you wish to use. Then, pick the **OK** button to close the options dialog box and apply the setting.

Another setting you may wish to make to the document properties is related to threads. By default, threads are not shown as a shaded representation. If your graphics card can handle the extra calculations needed to show shaded threads, you may wish to enable this feature. Shaded threads look more realistic in part and assembly files. To enable shaded threads, pick the Detailing branch in the **Document Properties** tab. Then, check the **Shaded cosmetic threads** check box on the right-hand side of the tab. See **Figure 2-19.** Then, pick the **OK** button to apply the setting.

Window Pull-Down Menu

Several files can be open at the same time in SolidWorks. The display of these files is managed via the **Window** pull-down menu. Switching between the open files

Figure 2-18.
Settings that apply to only the current document in SolidWorks are made in the **Document Properties** tab of the options dialog box. Here, the unit of measure is being set.

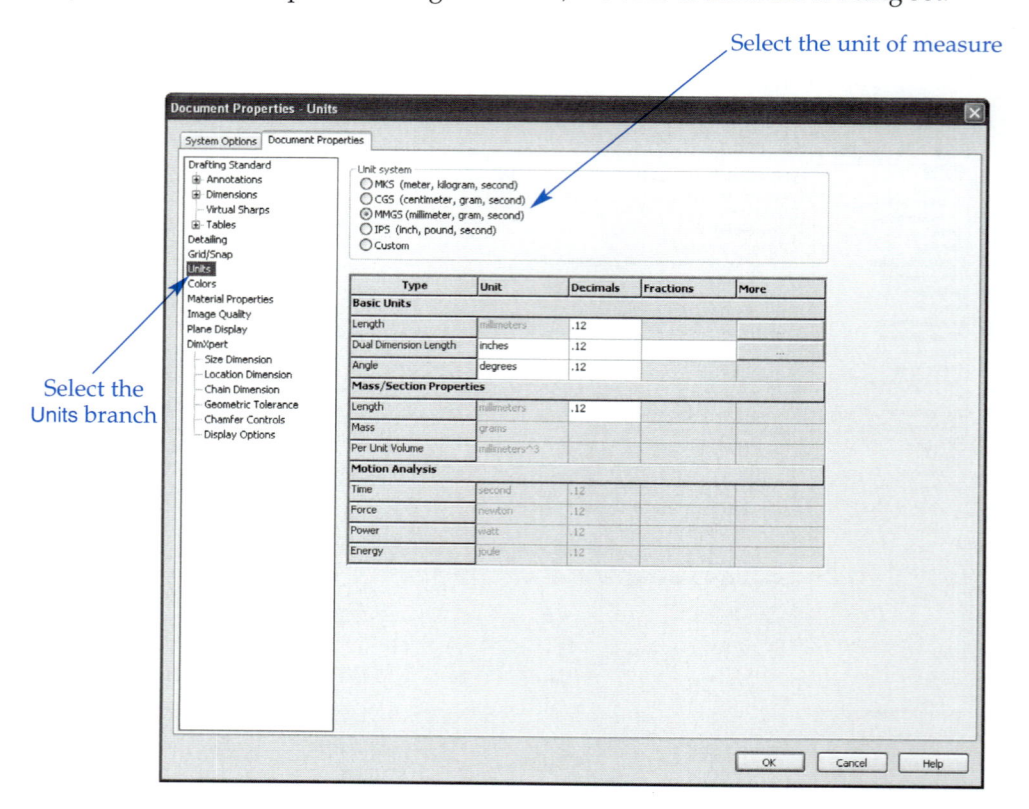

Figure 2-19.
Changing the display of cosmetic threads to shaded. Shaded threads appear more realistic in the document.

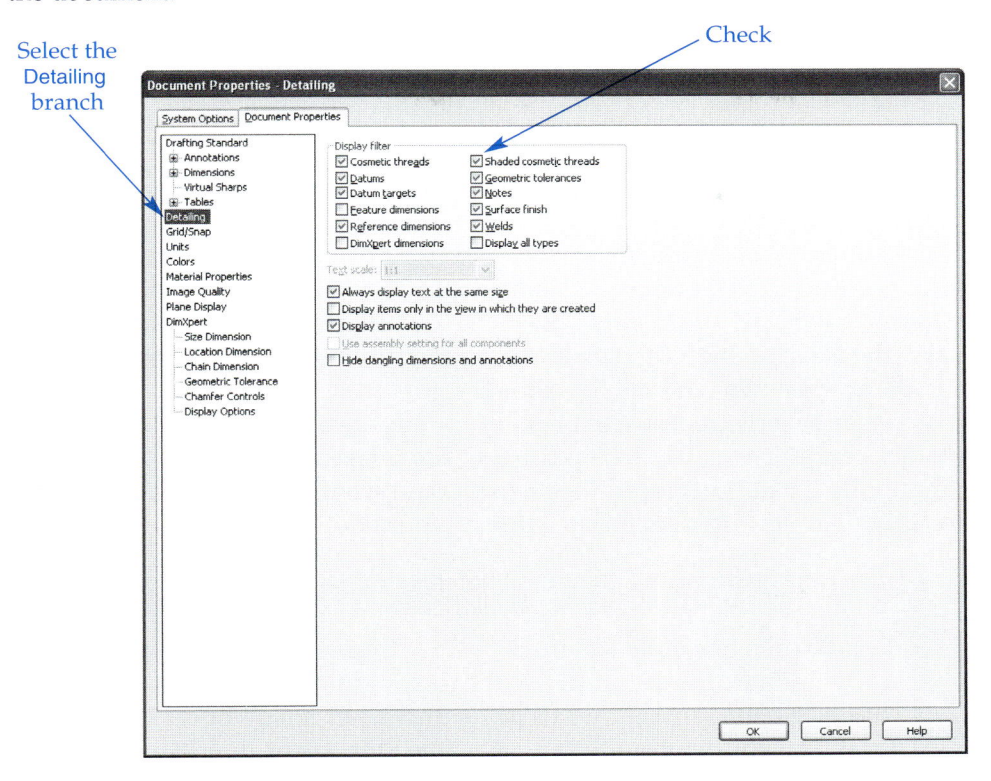

is as simple as selecting the file name in the pull-down menu. One of the advantages of having multiple files open is that geometry can be copied from one document into another. Also, when creating an assembly, the open part files are automatically available for insertion. This saves time because you do not need to browse for files.

Help Pull-Down Menu

The **Help** pull-down menu provides access to a comprehensive help system. It gives a user a complete guide to the software. Tutorials are also offered in the pull-down menu. Using the **Help** pull-down menu, you can check for software updates and manage your software license.

File Management

Many of the SolidWorks file types depend on other files. For example, an assembly file (SLDASM) is composed of part files (SLDPRT) or subassemblies. When the assembly is opened for editing, SolidWorks must be able to locate those part files. As another example, when a drawing file (SLDDRW) is opened, the part or assembly that it depicts must be located. If the part or assembly cannot be located, then you have a serious problem. You may end up with nothing shown on the screen.

If you move files from their original folders or rename them and try to open a file that depends on those files, you will encounter a warning. See **Figure 2-20**. This warning is telling you that SolidWorks cannot locate the file. You have the opportunity to manually locate the needed file. Pick the **Yes** button to display a standard Windows "open" dialog box. Then, browse to the file, select it, and pick the **Open** button.

Figure 2-20.
If SolidWorks cannot locate a dependent file, this warning is displayed. You are offered the chance to manually locate the missing file.

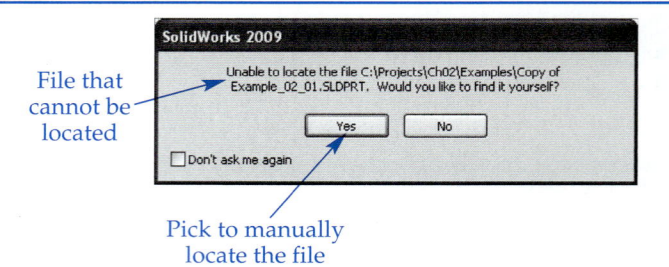

For example, open Example_02_02.sldasm. You will receive the warning because SolidWorks cannot find the file Copy of Example_02_01.sldprt. Pick the **Yes** button to display the **Open** dialog box. In this case, Example_02_01.sldprt and Copy of Example_02_01.sldprt are identical, so select Example_02_01.sldprt. Then, pick the **Open** button. The assembly file now knows where to look for the part file.

This process can become tedious, especially for a large assembly. For example, if you move a folder containing a hundred parts that are referenced by an assembly, you will have to manually locate a hundred files when you open the assembly. Therefore, it is best to carefully plan your folders before starting to model anything.

PROFESSIONAL TIP

SolidWorks has a file-renaming utility that can be used to automatically update references. To use the tool, right-click on the name of the file to rename in Windows Explorer and select **SolidWorks>Rename...** from the shortcut menu. The **Rename Document** dialog box that is displayed shows the file and all files of which it is a dependent. When you rename the file, the parent files are also updated to reflect the new name.

Chapter Test

Answer the following questions on a separate sheet of paper or complete the electronic chapter test on the student website.
www.g-wlearning.com/CAD

1. What does it mean that the **Command Manager** and **Management Panel** are *context sensitive*?
2. Where are the pull-down menus located and how are they displayed?
3. List the three types of SolidWorks files.
4. What is the purpose of the **Rebuild** tool?
5. What is the *viewpoint*?
6. The _____ is the main interface for SolidWorks tools.
7. What purpose does the *design tree* serve?
8. Define *sketched feature* and *placed feature*.
9. How can features be renamed in the design tree and why should you do this?
10. Settings made in the _____ tab of the options dialog box are applied to the current file, while settings made in the _____ tab are applied to SolidWorks itself and affect all files.

Chapter Exercises

Complete the chapter exercises on the student website.
www.g-wlearning.com/CAD

Exercise 2-1 Ring Gear.
Complete the exercise on the student website.

Exercise 2-2 Swivel Yoke.
Complete the exercise on the student website.

Exercise 2-3 Piston.
Complete the exercise on the student website.

The SolidWorks help system provides a comprehensive resource for user help. Included are search functions for help topics, examples illustrating SolidWorks tools, and user tutorials. Help system features are accessed from the **Help** pull-down menu on the **Menu Bar**.

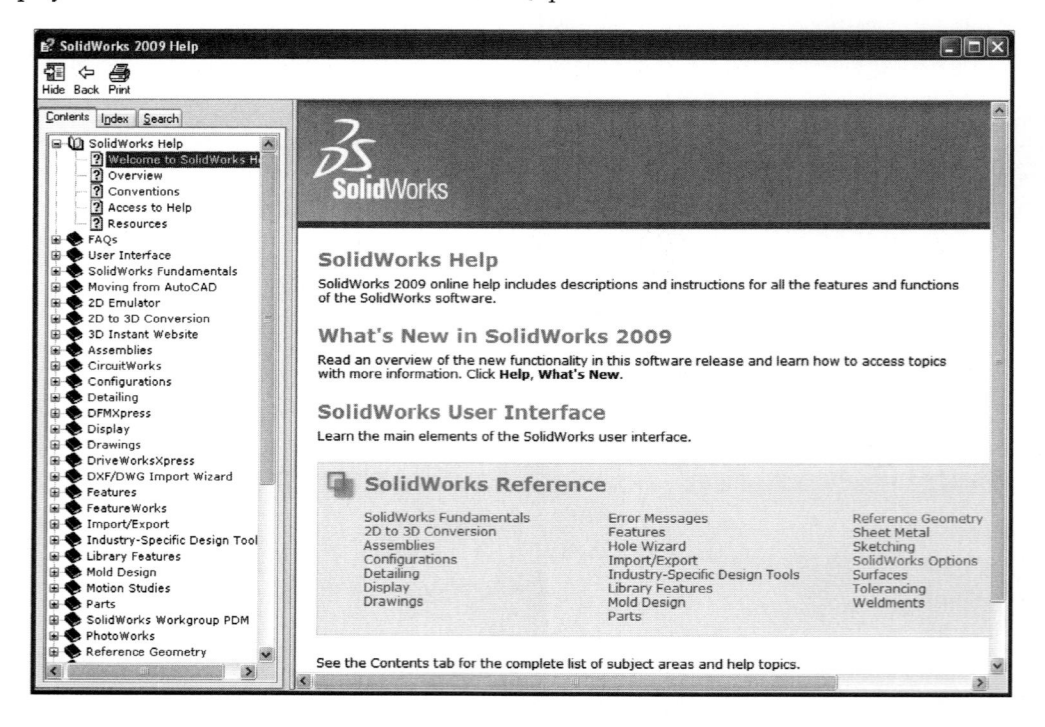

Chapter 3

Sketching, Relations, and the Base Feature

Objectives
After completing this chapter, you will be able to:
- Describe the procedure for creating a base sketch.
- Sketch curves, including lines and arcs.
- Explain the geometric relations that SolidWorks can apply.
- Apply geometric relations.
- Add dimensions to define a sketch.
- Extrude solid parts from a sketch.

Process for Creating a Part

All parts in SolidWorks start with a base 2D profile that is extruded, revolved, or swept into a solid. The profile is called a *sketch*. A sketch is constructed from geometric shapes: lines, arcs, circles, and splines. The sketch cannot cross over itself, but it can have interior islands or separated closed shapes. Valid and invalid shapes for solid profiles are shown in **Figure 3-1**. In this chapter, you will learn how to create single, closed shapes. These are called *unambiguous profiles*. You will also learn how to extrude these profiles into solid parts.

Figure 3-1.
The shapes on the left are valid 2D profiles for extruding. The shapes on the right are invalid.

Valid　　　　　　　　Invalid

Two lines that cross

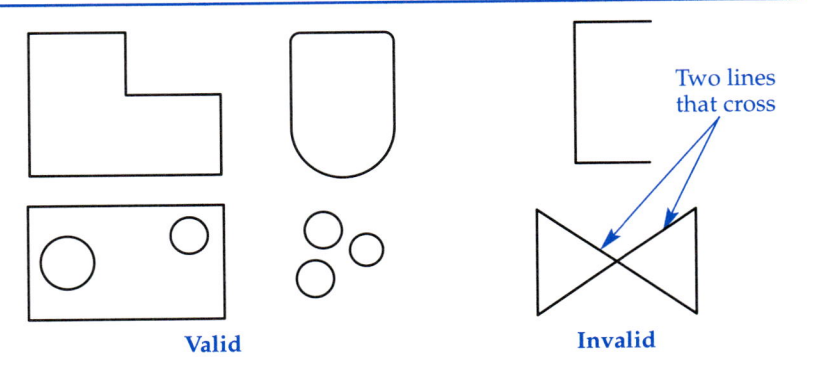

45

A SolidWorks sketch made up of six lines is shown in **Figure 3-2**. All lines, arcs, and circles in SolidWorks are considered curves. The curves (lines) in Figure 3-2 are called *intelligent objects* because they each contain, or "know," unique information about themselves and each other. For example, line AB was constructed in a horizontal fashion and SolidWorks remembers this by automatically attaching a horizontal relation to the line. Line BC knows that it is vertical and the vertical relation symbol is displayed. Lines AB and AF also know they are connected to origin and the coincident symbol is displayed at that intersection.

Relations define and maintain the relationships between the geometry in the sketch. By default, SolidWorks applies horizontal and vertical relations whenever possible in place of parallel and perpendicular relations. Horizontal, perpendicular, coincident, and parallel are all geometric relations. You can also apply dimensional relations. Adding and deleting relations are discussed later in this chapter.

The sketch in **Figure 3-2** was drawn in metric units. When line AB was constructed, it was not drawn to the exact length of 170 mm. After the sketch is drawn, dimensions (dimensional relations) can be added. Adjusting a dimension value changes the associated geometry. The fully dimensioned sketch is shown in **Figure 3-3**.

Figure 3-2.
This is a sketch created in SolidWorks. All lines, arcs, and circles in SolidWorks are called curves.

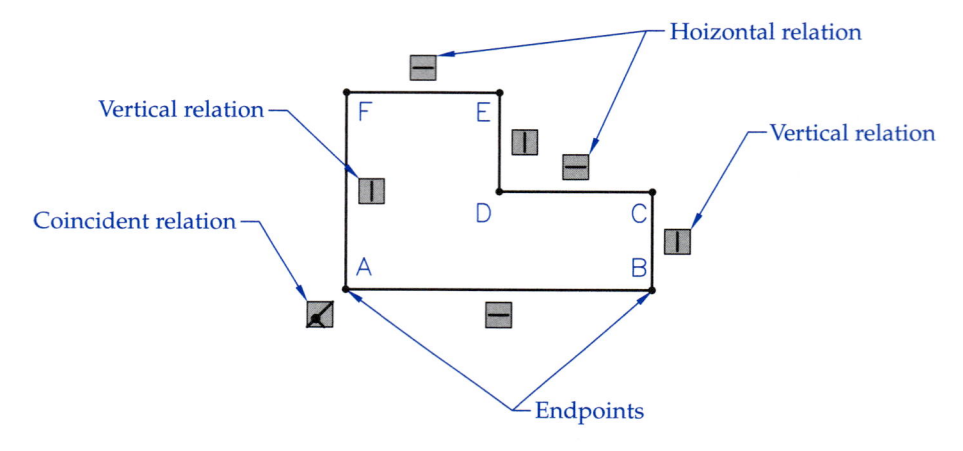

Figure 3-3.
This is the sketch from Figure 3-2 fully dimensioned and constrained.

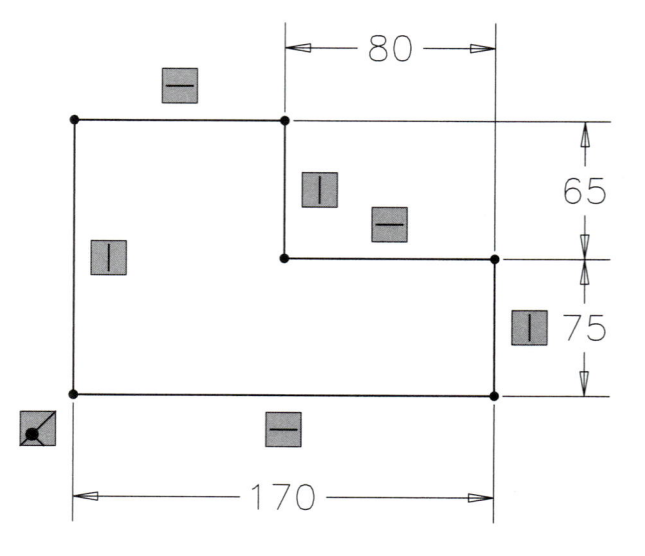

Even though you do not need to initially construct your sketch precisely, you do want to be reasonably close. Large changes in part size made by editing dimensions may distort the sketch beyond repair. You may be forced to undo the changes and start again. Based on these ideas, here are some sketching guidelines:
- Sketch the size reasonably close.
- Sketch so the relations are exact.
- Precisely dimension the sketch.

In addition, make the base sketch representative of the fundamental feature of the part, yet as simple as possible. This will give you control of all of the added features for making quick changes. For example, a bracket and its base sketch are shown in **Figure 3-4**. The fillets, cutouts, and holes were all added as features.

In some cases, you may not add the dimensions. For example, this may be a preliminary design study and the dimensions may not be known. Of course, the dimensions can be added later. In another example, you may want to control the size of the part (its dimensions) by the position of other parts in the assembly. Parts of this nature are said to have *externally referenced geometry* and are discussed in Chapter 12.

Sketching

Now you will learn how to create a base feature from a sketch. First, you will sketch the 2D profile shown in **Figures 3-2** and **3-3**. Then, you will extrude this sketch to create a solid. Begin by starting a new part file and setting the units to metric:
1. Select **New...** from the **File** pull-down menu, pick the **New** button on the **Menu Bar**, or press [Ctrl][N].
2. In the **New SolidWorks Document** dialog box that appears, select the **Part** button and then pick the **OK** button. A new, blank part file is started. See **Figure 3-5**.

Figure 3-4.
A—This is the completed part.
B—The base sketch used to create the part (shown in an isometric view).

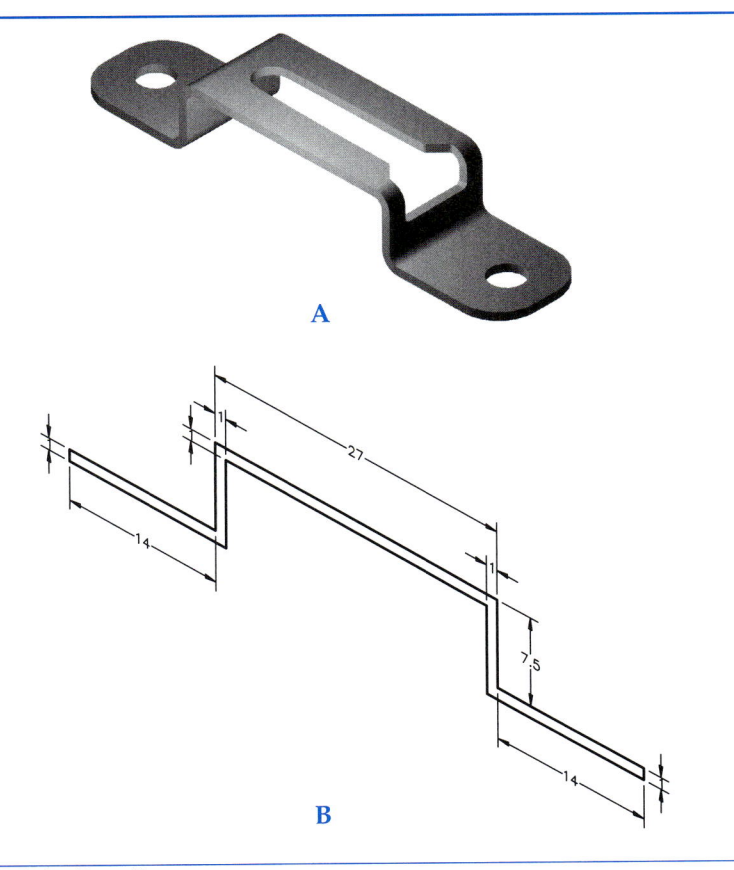

Chapter 3 Sketching, Relations, and the Base Feature

Figure 3-5.
The SolidWorks screen after starting a new part.

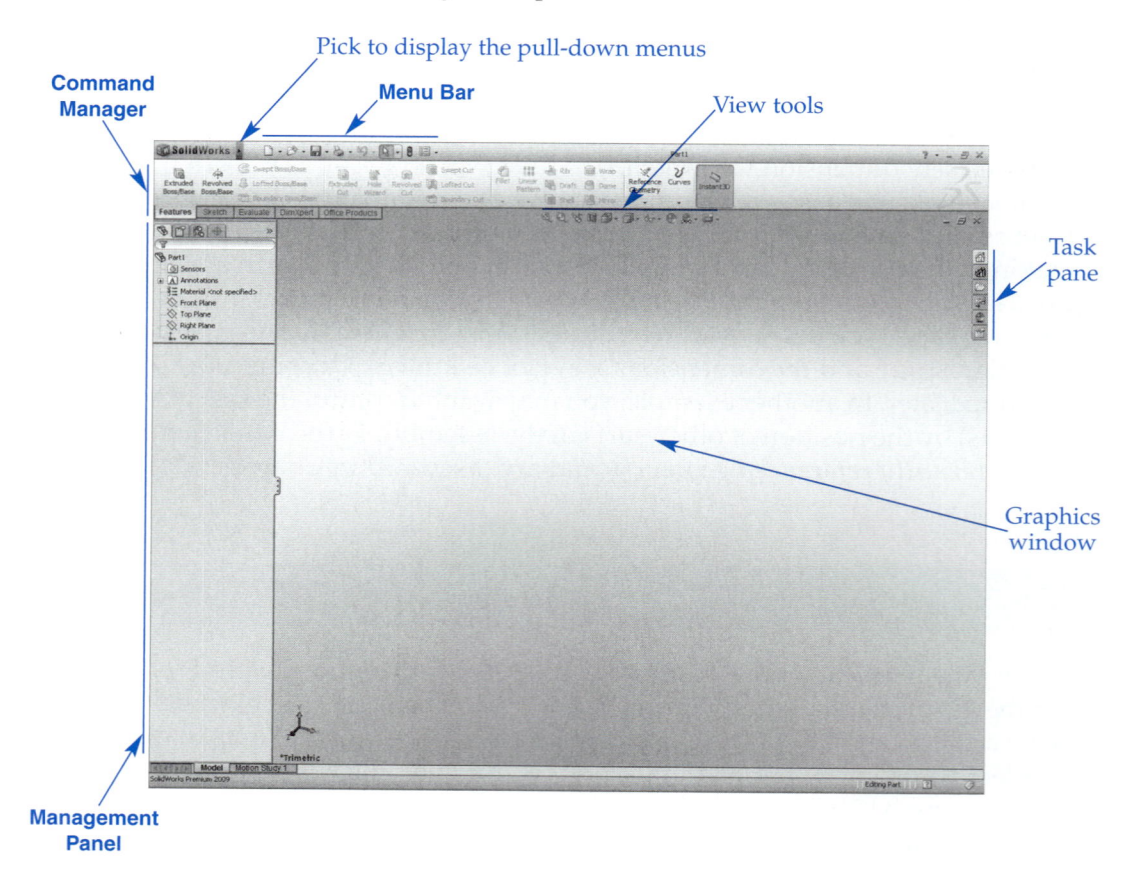

Callouts: Command Manager; Menu Bar (Pick to display the pull-down menus); View tools; Task pane; Graphics window; Management Panel

3. Set the units to MMGS (millimeter, gram, second) in the options/properties dialog box. Select **Tools>Options...** in the pull-down menu, then pick the **Document Properties** tab in the options/properties dialog box. In the tree on the left-hand side of the tab, select **Units**. Then, pick the **MMGS** radio button in the **Unit System** area on the right-hand side of the tab.
4. Pick the **OK** button to close the options/properties dialog box.

In the **Feature Manager**, notice the new part file contains front (XY), top (XZ), and right (ZY) planes and an origin. See **Figure 3-6**. You will use one of these planes to create a base sketch. These planes can also be used to create other reference geometry, including axes and other planes. This is discussed in a later chapter. The default name of the file is Part1 (or Part2, Part3, etc.). Later, when the file is saved, it can be given a more appropriate name.

Activate the **Sketch** tab in the **Command Manager**. Then, pick the **Sketch** button. The three planes are displayed in the graphics window. A message is displayed in the **Property Manager** in the **Management Panel** asking you to choose a plane on which to begin a 2D sketch. See **Figure 3-7**. For this example, the sketch is created on the front (or XY) plane. Either select the front plane in the flyout **Feature Manager** design tree or simply select the plane in the graphics window. After the plane is selected, a view normal to the sketch plane is displayed in the graphics window. Notice that the **Exit Sketch** button on the **Sketch** tab in the **Command Manager** is depressed. This indicates you are in sketch mode.

You can zoom out to display more of the work area. Right-click in the graphics window to display the shortcut menu. Then, pick the **Zoom/Pan/Rotate** to display a cascading menu. Pick **Zoom In/Out**. Then, pick anywhere in the graphics window and drag the cursor down to zoom out or up to zoom in. Now, right-click with the tool

48   Learning SolidWorks 2009

Figure 3-6.
SolidWorks contains three default planes and an origin point. When starting a sketch, you can select one of these planes on which to sketch.

Figure 3-7.
Selecting the front plane as the sketch plane.

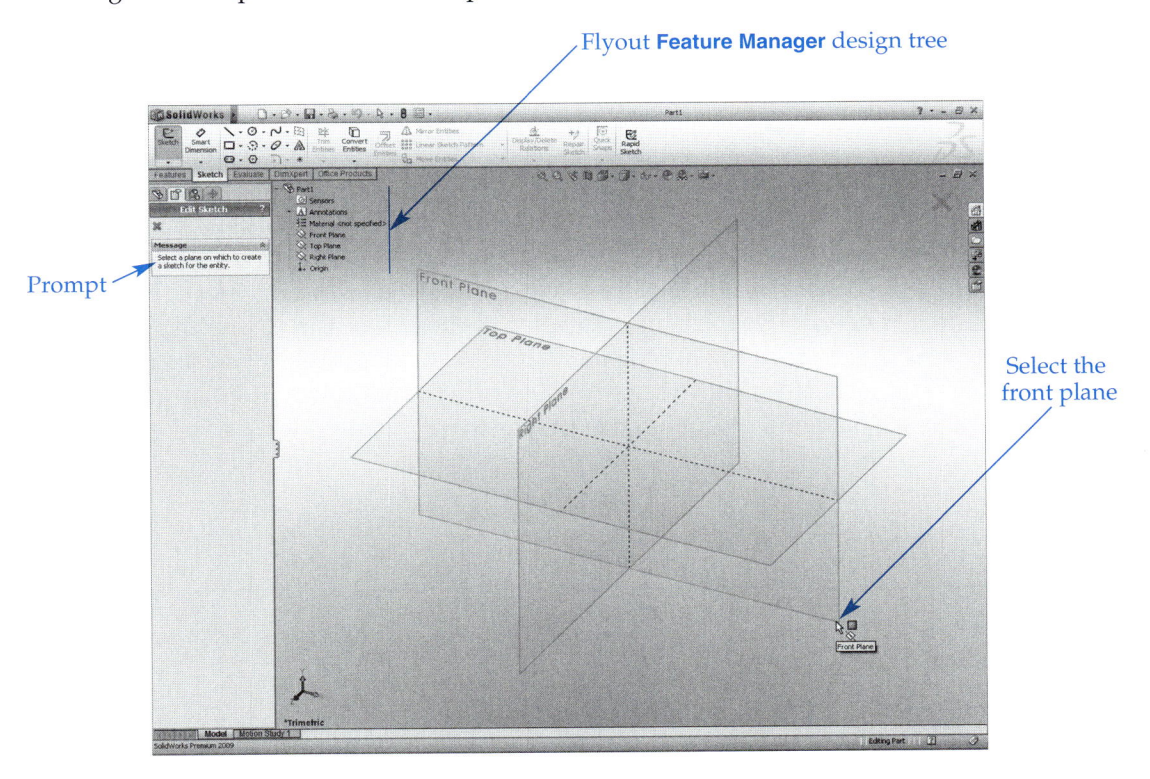

still active and select **Pan**. Pan the view so the origin is in the lower-left corner of the screen. Press [Esc] to exit the **Pan** tool.

If you have a roller-wheel mouse, you can roll the wheel to zoom. If the wheel also acts as a button, press the [Ctrl] key and hold the wheel down to pan. These methods may be quicker than using the shortcut menu or pull-down menu to access the **Zoom** and **Pan** tools.

The intersection of the three planes is called the *origin* and has the coordinates 0,0,0. In this example, you are sketching on the front (XY) plane, so the origin has the coordinates X= 0, Y= 0. This is where you will start sketching. Starting at the origin is

Chapter 3 Sketching, Relations, and the Base Feature 49

not necessary, but you will find it very useful when using reference planes, which is introduced in Chapter 5.

The sketching tools are available in the **Sketch** tab of the **Command Manager**. If you hover the cursor over a button, a tooltip is displayed. Note that several of the buttons have an arrow for displaying a drop-down list. For example, picking the arrow next to the **Corner Rectangle** button displays a drop-down list that contains five tools for creating a rectangle. The button you pick from a drop-down list remains "on top" as the default button after you are done using the tool.

Now, it is time to draw the first line, line AB. Refer to **Figures 3-2** and **3-3**. First, activate the **Line** tool by picking the **Line** button in the **Sketch** tab of the **Command Manager**. The **Line** button is shaded (depressed) to indicate the tool is active.

Move the cursor to the origin. As you move the cursor, the coordinates are shown on the status bar below the graphics window. When the cursor is over the origin, the coincident relation symbol appears next to the cursor. This indicates that if you pick, the endpoint will be constrained coincident to the origin. With this symbol displayed, pick to set the first endpoint of the line on the origin.

Now, move the cursor to the right. A line appears attached to the cursor and the first endpoint. If you move the cursor horizontally, the horizontal relation symbol is displayed next to the cursor. This symbol indicates that a horizontal relation will be applied. If you move the cursor vertically, the vertical relation symbol is displayed.

Notice the coordinates displayed on the status line below the graphics window. See **Figure 3-8**. These represent the X, Y, and Z coordinates of the cursor position. Since you are sketching on the XY plane, the Z value is zero. Also, as you move the cursor, the length of the line is displayed near the cursor. If the line matches the set snap angle, that angle is also displayed. For example, the default snap angle is 45°. When the line is at 45°, 90°, 135°, etc., that angle is displayed.

Move the cursor to the right so the line is horizontal and about 170 mm in length; *about* means between 160 and 180. Pick to set the second endpoint of the first line, line AB.

Now, draw the other five lines in the sketch using the following steps. Remember, the lengths do not need to be exact at this point, rather *about* the correct length.

1. Move the cursor straight up. Notice that a vertical symbol appears next to the cursor. This indicates that the automatic vertical relation will be applied. When the line is vertical and about 60 mm in length, pick to set the second endpoint of line BC.

Figure 3-8.
As you draw, various information is displayed. Also, notice the relation symbol that is displayed next to the cursor.

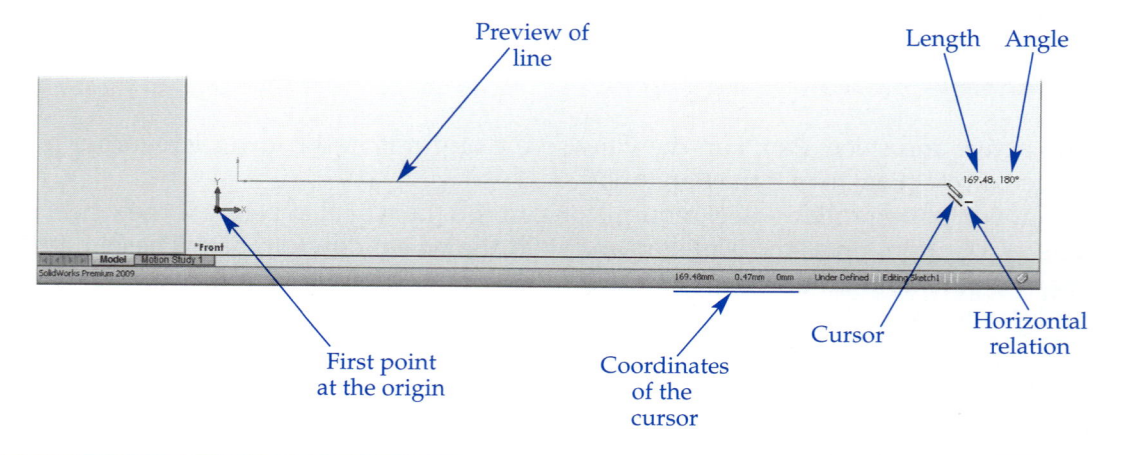

2. Draw line CD by moving the cursor to the left. Notice that a horizontal symbol appears next to the cursor. This indicates that the automatic horizontal relation will be applied. When the line is horizontal and about 80 mm in length, pick to set the second endpoint of line CD.
3. Move the cursor straight up. Notice that the automatic vertical relation will be applied. When the line is vertical and about 65 mm in length, pick to set the second endpoint of line DE.
4. Move the cursor to the left. Notice that the automatic horizontal relation will be applied. When you move the cursor above the first endpoint of line AB, a dotted vertical line appears indicating what SolidWorks thinks is a logical endpoint for the next line. This helps you locate the second endpoint of line EF. When the dotted line appears and line EF is horizontal, pick to set the second endpoint of line EF. Note: you may need to pan if this point is behind the flyout **Feature Manager** design tree. Use [Ctrl] and hold the mouse wheel.
5. Now, move the cursor to the first endpoint of line AB, which is the origin in this case. The dotted line appears as you move the cursor straight down. Also, the automatic vertical relation will be applied. When the cursor is directly on top of the first endpoint of line AB, an orange dot appears. Also, the concentric relation symbol appears next to the cursor that indicates the two endpoints will be connected. Pick on the first endpoint of line AB to draw line FA and close the sketch.
6. Exit the **Line** tool by pressing the [Esc] key.

If you make a mistake while drawing the profile, pick the **Undo** button on the **Menu Bar**, press the [Ctrl][Z] key combination, or select **Undo** from the **Edit** pull-down menu. This deletes the last line segment and cancels the **Line** tool. To continue drawing the profile, pick the **Line** button, move the cursor to the endpoint of the last line, and pick when the orange dot appears. Then, finish sketching the profile.

Relations

Relations, often referred to as *constraints*, define and maintain the relationships between the geometry in the sketch. The two types of constraints are geometric (such as parallel or perpendicular) and dimensional (defining a distance, angle, or length). Dimensional relations are discussed in the next section.

As you saw in the previous example, you can automatically place geometric relations on the sketch as you draw. If for some reason you want to prevent the automatic relations from being applied, hold down the [Ctrl] key as you draw.

SolidWorks shows the relationships between curves in a sketch by displaying small symbols, or glyphs, where appropriate in the graphics window. To select a curve, pick the **Select** button on the **Menu Bar**, then pick the curve in the graphics window. Selecting a curve displays the **Property Manager** with the properties of the curve displayed. You are given information about existing relations on the curve, adding relations, and line parameters. In the **Existing Relations** rollout, you can view and manage all of the relations that have been applied to the curve. See **Figure 3-9**. For example, to make line AB diagonal, you first must delete the horizontal relation. Select the horizontal relation in the **Existing Relations** rollout and press the [Delete] key. However, in this example, leave the horizontal relation on line AB.

The **Add Relations** rollout in the **Property Manager** displays buttons for all of the relations that SolidWorks is able to apply to the selected curve. Picking the button for one of the displayed relations applies that relation to the selected curve. The new relation then appears in the **Existing Relations** rollout in the **Property Manager**.

To add a relation between two or more curves, select the curves by holding the [Ctrl] key and picking each individual curve. Selected curves are displayed in light blue (by default). SolidWorks displays buttons in the **Add Relations** rollout of the **Property Manager**

Chapter 3   Sketching, Relations, and the Base Feature

Figure 3-9.
The properties for a line are displayed in the **Line Properties** Property Manager.

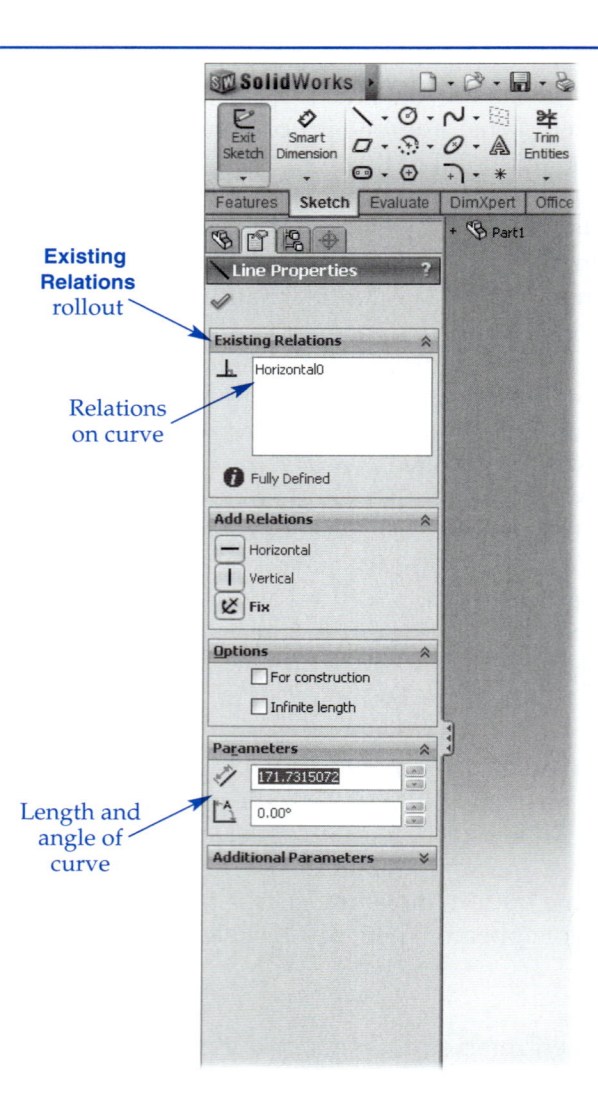

for all relations it can solve on the selected curves. After choosing the desired relation, the curves may adjust themselves to fit their new constraints. If you make a mistake, simply undo the operation.

> **NOTE**
>
> As you add more relations, you will notice SolidWorks begins numbering them in pairs, as indicated near the relation icons in the graphics window. This is a way to help you identify which relations correspond to each other.

Dimensions

Since there are currently no dimensions on the sketch, you can dynamically change the geometry in the sketch. Select a line or an intersection of two lines, hold down the mouse button, and then drag the geometry to the new location. Try this by selecting any corner in your sketch and moving it to a new location. However, notice that as you move the corner, the two lines attached to it remain constrained by the geometric relations that were automatically placed as you drew the profile. This is a useful technique for preliminary design work.

You have two choices for applying the dimensions needed to accurately size the part. You can apply automatic dimensions, in which case SolidWorks decides where the dimensions should be placed. Alternately, you can manually apply and place each dimension.

Automatic dimensions

For this example, first apply automatic dimensioning. Right-click in the graphics window to display the shortcut menu. Then, select **Fully Define Sketch...** in the **Relations** area of the shortcut menu. The **Fully Define Sketch Property Manager** is displayed, **Figure 3-10**. Expand the rollouts to see all of the options. In the **Entities to Fully Define** rollout, pick the **All entities in sketch** radio button. Notice that when you expanded the **Relations** and **Dimensions** rollouts that a check mark appears in each rollout title bar. This means the feature, geometric relations or dimensions, will be applied. In each rollout, you can choose which specific relations will be applied.

Finally, pick the **Calculate** button in the **Entities to Fully Define** rollout. SolidWorks fully defines the sketch with geometric and dimensional relations. This is reported on the right-hand side of the status bar at the bottom of the screen. Also, all of the curves are displayed in black in the graphics window. Curves that are not fully defined are displayed in blue. Pick the green check mark button at the top of the **Fully Define Sketch** panel to accept the dimensions and close the panel.

PROFESSIONAL TIP

Notice that SolidWorks has applied different dimensions than those shown in **Figure 3-3**. However, in both cases, the dimensions are correct to fully define the sketch. This shows that there is more than one way to achieve the same design intent.

Figure 3-10.
Using the "fully define" feature.

Pick to apply the relations

Select which geometric relations to apply

Check to apply the relation

Select the scheme for dimensional relations

Chapter 3 Sketching, Relations, and the Base Feature

Manual dimensions

In many cases, it is best to manually apply dimensions. This allows you to control which dimensions are applied to better maintain the design intent. To remove the automatic dimensions placed in the last section, pick the **Undo** button on the **Menu Bar** or press [Ctrl][Z] until the dimensions have been removed.

To manually apply a dimension, pick the **Smart Dimension** button in the **Sketch** tab of the **Command Manager**. Then, pick the geometry to which you want the dimension applied. The dimension appears attached to the cursor. Drag the dimension to the desired location and pick. The **Modify** dialog box is displayed by the dimension, **Figure 3-11**. Enter the exact dimension and pick the green check mark button.

You do not need to enter the "mm" for millimeters, as this is a metric part and the units are set to MMGS (millimeter, gram, second). If other units are desired, you need to include the unit abbreviation, such as 6.6929 in, 0.558 ft, or 17 cm. Any of these entries will change the dimension to 170 mm. Regardless of the units entered, the dimension on the sketch will always display the millimeter value since the units are set to MMGS.

Manually apply the dimensions shown in **Figure 3-3**. To end the **Smart Dimension** tool, press the [Esc] key or pick the green check mark button in the **Dimension Property Manager**.

Editing placed dimensions

Once a dimension is placed, you can reposition it. Simply pick on the number when the "move" cursor is displayed. Then, drag the dimension to a new location. All sketch tools must be inactive to do this.

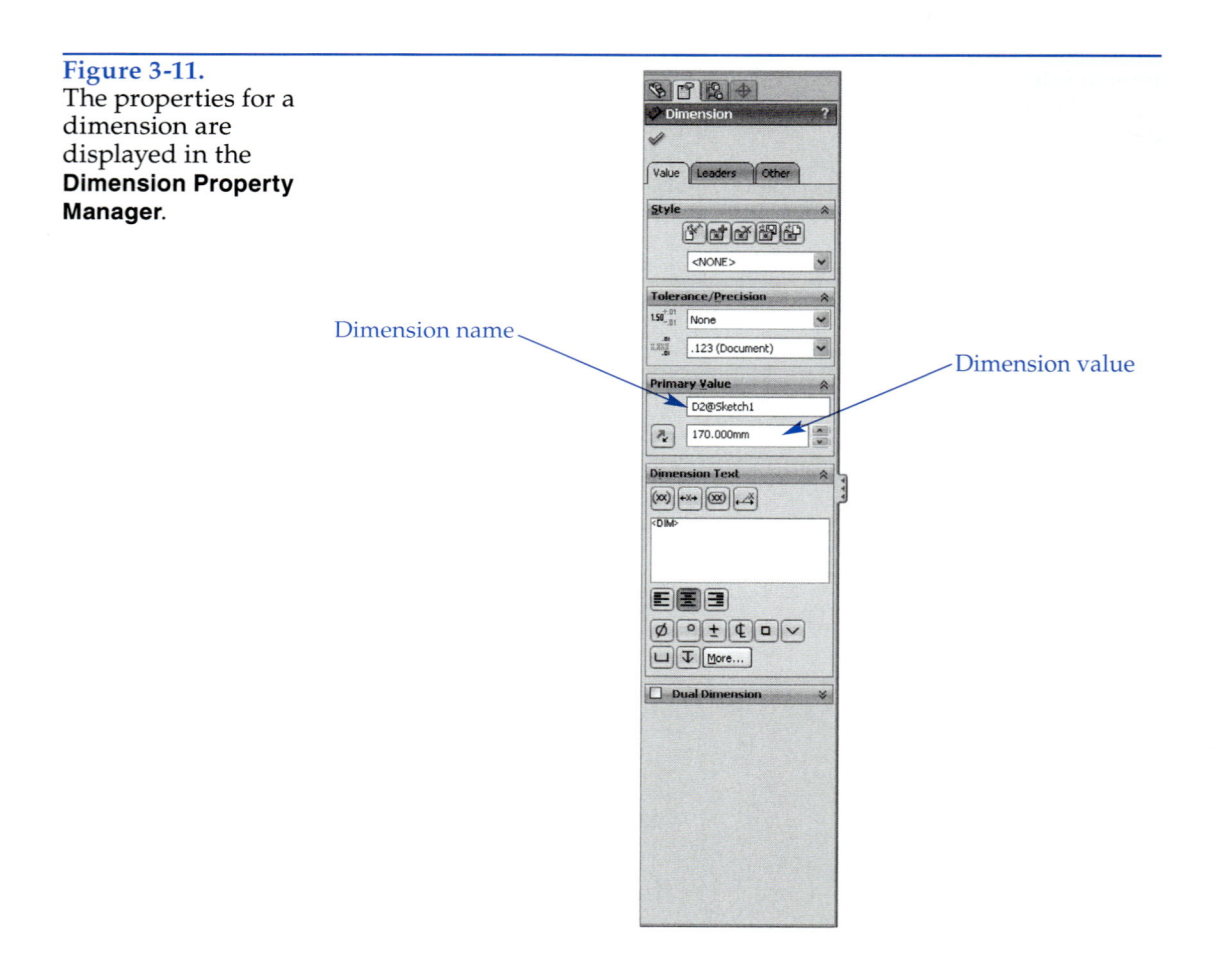

Figure 3-11. The properties for a dimension are displayed in the **Dimension Property Manager**.

Dimensions are what allow you to draw the sketch at its approximate size. Once a dimension is placed, it can be edited to an exact value. When a dimension is manually placed, the **Modify** dialog box is automatically displayed for editing the dimension value. Since the associated geometry is constrained by the dimension, it is updated to match the exact value. For example, double-click on the 170 mm dimension across the bottom. The **Modify** dialog box is displayed. Type 200 in the text box and pick the check mark button to set the dimension and close the dialog box. Notice how the length of the line changes, while all lines remain constrained by the applied relations. Edit the dimension again and change the value back to 170. The sketch again changes to match the applied relations.

When you double-click on a dimension, the **Dimension Property Manager** is displayed. It is also displayed when a dimension is selected with a single pick. This panel displays the properties for the selected dimension. See **Figure 3-11**. You can change the value of the dimension using the lower text box in the **Primary Value** rollout. Also, each dimension has a name that is, initially, assigned by SolidWorks. In this case, the name is D2@Sketch1. This appears in the top text box in the **Primary Value** rollout. Depending on how you drew your sketch, this name may be different, but it will start with the letter D. In the next chapter, you will learn how to rename dimensions and relate dimensions to each other. To close the **Dimension Property Manager**, pick the green check mark button at the top of the panel.

Relationship to the Origin

The sketch is now dimensionally and geometrically constrained. Also, since you started drawing line AB at the origin, the sketch is locked, or *fixed*, to the coordinate system. This means that the geometry cannot be moved around in the XY plane of the coordinate system. Fixing the sketch to the coordinate system allows you to take advantage of the existing work planes.

However, depending on how you created the sketch, it may not be automatically fixed to the origin. You can manually fix the geometry in the sketch. To see how to do this, first delete the relation automatically added to the sketch at the origin by Solid-Works. Pick the **Select** button on the **Menu Bar**. Then, select the common endpoint of line AB and line AF. The **Point Property Manager** is displayed, **Figure 3-12**. The **Existing Relations** rollout displays all relations on the selected entity. In this case, there is a coincident relation between the endpoint and the origin and a dimensional relation. Select the coincident relation in the list and press the [Delete] key. This removes the relation. Notice that the message at the bottom of the rollout now states the entity is under defined. Pick the green check mark button to close the panel.

Since the sketch is no longer constrained to the origin, it is now free to move. Also notice that all lines are displayed in blue, indicating they are under defined. Select the endpoint at the origin and drag. The sketch can now be freely moved around the plane with respect to the origin. Move the sketch so the origin is visible.

Now, with the **Select** button on, hold down the [Ctrl] key and pick the origin and line AB. The **Properties Property Manager** is displayed. The two entities are listed in the **Selected Entities** rollout. Also, notice no relations are listed in the **Existing Relations** rollout, which also reports the geometry is under defined. In the **Add Relation** rollout, pick the **Coincident** button to apply a coincident relation. Line CD and line EF change color from blue to black to indicate they are fully defined. This is because they have dimensional relations to line AB, which is now constrained to the Y axis. The **Existing Relations** rollout also now reports the selected entities are fully defined.

Deselect the line and the origin by pressing the [Esc] key or by picking the green check mark button at the top of the **Properties Property Manager**. You can now move the sketch left and right. However, it cannot be moved up and down. This is because the Y values of line AB are constrained, or locked, to the coordinate system. Lines CD and EF are locked to line AB by dimensional relations.

Chapter 3 Sketching, Relations, and the Base Feature

Figure 3-12.
Displaying the relations on a selected point.

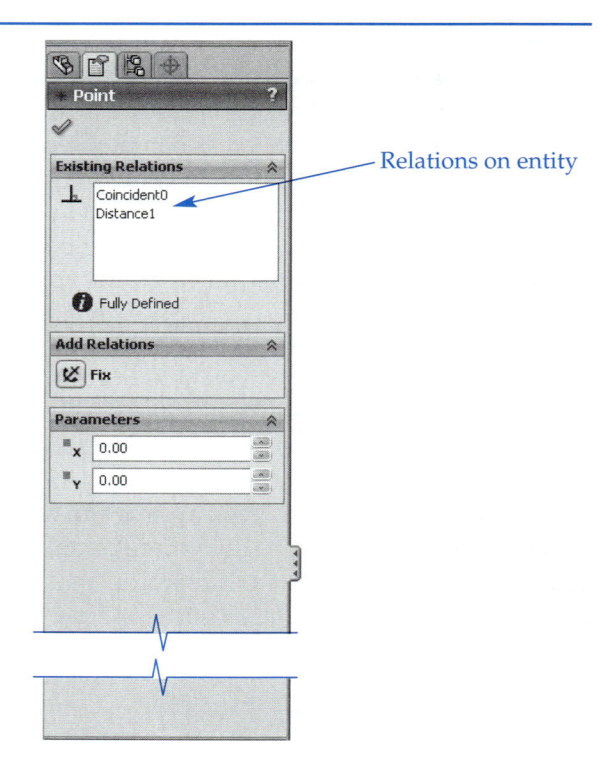

Now, select the origin and line AF. Using the **Property Manger**, apply a coincident relation. Press the [Esc] key to deselect the origin and Line AF. Now, all of the lines in the sketch have changed to black, indicating that the sketch is fully defined. If you attempt to drag the lines, none of them can be moved.

> **PROFESSIONAL TIP**
>
> To delete a relation, you can simply select the icon in the graphics window and press the [Delete] key. This may be much quicker than using the **Property Manager**, however you may select the wrong icon.

Extruding the Part

Now that the sketch is fully defined, it can be extruded into a solid. First, you must exit sketch mode. Pick the **Exit Sketch** button on the **Sketch** tab of the **Command Manager**. The button is replaced with the **Sketch** button, indicating you are now in part modeling mode. This is a good place to save your work. Pick the **Save** button on the menu bar or press [Ctrl][S]. In the **Save As** dialog box that appears, save the file as Example_03_01.sldprt in your working folder.

Once you have exited sketch mode, select the **Features** tab in the **Command Manager**. This tab contains many of the available tools for creating solid geometry. Some of the tools are available in the drop-down list, similar to some of the tools in the **Sketch** tab. To display a 3D view of the developing part, pick the **Isometric** button in the **View Orientation** flyout in the view tools. These tools are located at the top of the graphics window.

Next, pick the **Extruded Boss/Base** button in the **Features** tab. The **Extrude Property Manager** is displayed with a message indicating what to do. Select the sketch you just created, either in the graphics window or from the flyout **Feature Manager** design tree located in the upper-left corner of the graphics window. This tool does several things:

- If a curve in the sketch is selected and the sketch is an unambiguous profile, the tool selects the profile.

- The tool displays the properties of the extrusion in the **Extrude Properties Manager**, **Figure 3-13**.
- A shaded wireframe preview of the profile extruded with the default settings is displayed.

The **Depth** text box in the **Direction 1** rollout is where the height of the extrusion above the sketch plane is set. For this example, change the value to 60 mm. The preview changes to reflect the value when you pick in a different text box or press the [Enter] key. Now, in the graphics window, pick the end of the gray arrow displayed in the preview and drag it up and down (or back and forth). The distance value in the **Direction 1** rollout changes to reflect the change in the preview. When done, reset the value to 60 mm. The **Direction 2** rollout is used to set the height of the extrusion below the sketch plane. For this example, make sure the value is zero.

The direction of the extrusion can be changed by picking the **Reverse Direction** button at the top of the **Direction 1** rollout. This reverses "direction 1" and "direction 2." To equally apply the height on each side of the sketch plane, select Mid Plane in the **End Condition** drop-down list. When this is selected, one-half of the extrusion distance is applied to each side of the sketch, as shown in the preview. For this example, select Blind in the **End Condition** drop-down list and make sure "direction 1" is applied on the positive Z axis. You can determine axis direction by looking at the axes triad in the lower-left corner of the graphics window.

Normally, you will create a solid part from the complete area defined by the sketch. However, you can also extrude a thin-walled part based on the sketched profile. For example, from a sketch of a single circle, you can create a straight section of pipe. To create a thin-walled feature, expand the **Thin Feature** rollout and check the box in its

Figure 3-13.
Extruding a sketch into a solid.

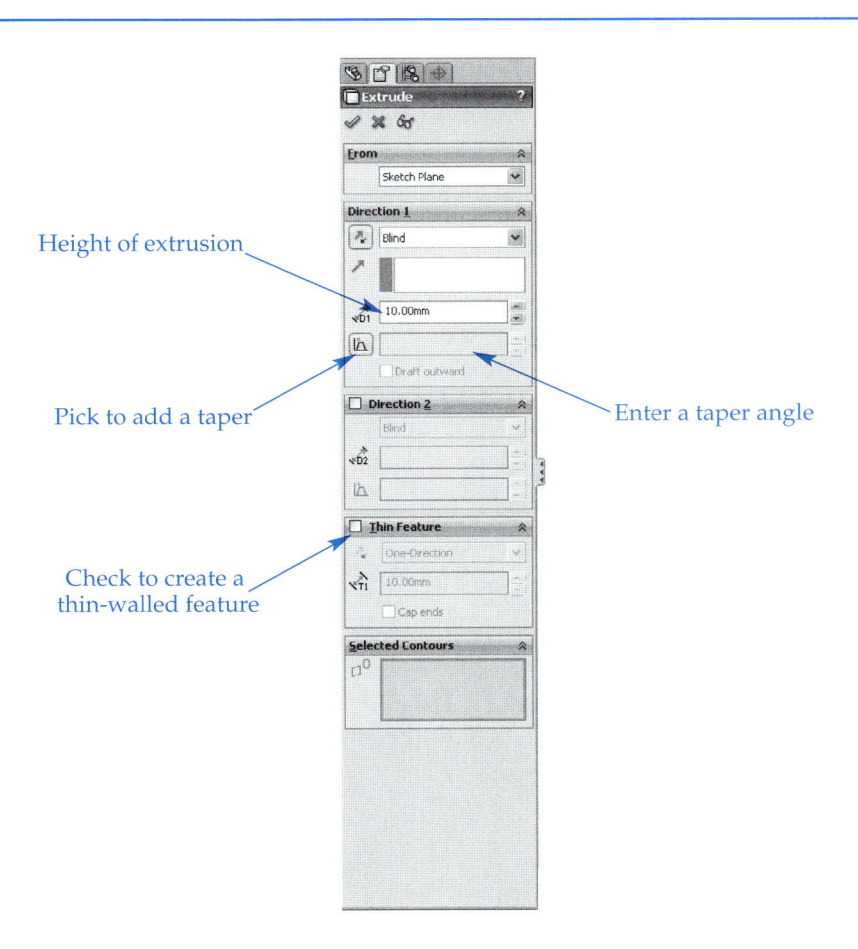

Chapter 3   Sketching, Relations, and the Base Feature   57

title bar. This enables the options in the rollout. Then, set the wall thickness and how it is applied. Extruding profiles into a surface, which has zero thickness, requires the use of a different toolset. This is covered in a later chapter. For this example, you are not creating a thin-wall section, so make sure the check box in the **Thin Feature** rollout is unchecked.

By default, the sides of the extrusion are perpendicular to the sketch plane. However, you can add a taper to the sides. This is often done to represent a draft that allows a part to be removed from a mold. To add a taper, pick the **Draft On/Off** button in the **Direction 1** rollout. There is also a **Draft On/Off** button in the **Direction 2** rollout to apply a taper to "direction 2." Once the button is picked, enter the taper angle in the text box. For this example, enter 20 and press [Enter] once to update the preview. Notice that the part tapers to the inside. If you check the **Draft outward** check box, the part tapers to the outside. For this example, uncheck the **Draft outward** check box so the part tapers to the inside.

To finalize the extrusion, pick the green check mark button at the top of the **Extrude Property Manager**. The part is extruded with a taper angle on all faces, as shown in **Figure 3-14**.

Editing the Feature and the Sketch

The **Feature Manager** design tree for Part1, or Example_03_01 if you saved the file, now includes Extrude1 at the bottom of the tree. If you expand this branch, Sketch1 appears below Extrude1. Right-click on Extrude1 to display a shortcut menu and toolbar with many options, **Figure 3-15**. There are two options in the shortcut toolbar above the shortcut menu that allow you to change the size and shape of the part: **Edit Feature** and **Edit Sketch**.

Pick the **Edit Sketch** button to view the sketch used to create the Extrude1 feature. You can now change, add, or delete the dimensions or geometric relations in the sketch. For example, double-click on the 170 mm dimension and change it to 150 mm. Then, pick the green check mark button to close the **Dimension Property Manager**. Pick the

Figure 3-14.
The completed part. Notice the taper angle.

Figure 3-15.
This shortcut menu is displayed when you right-click on the extrusion name in the design tree.

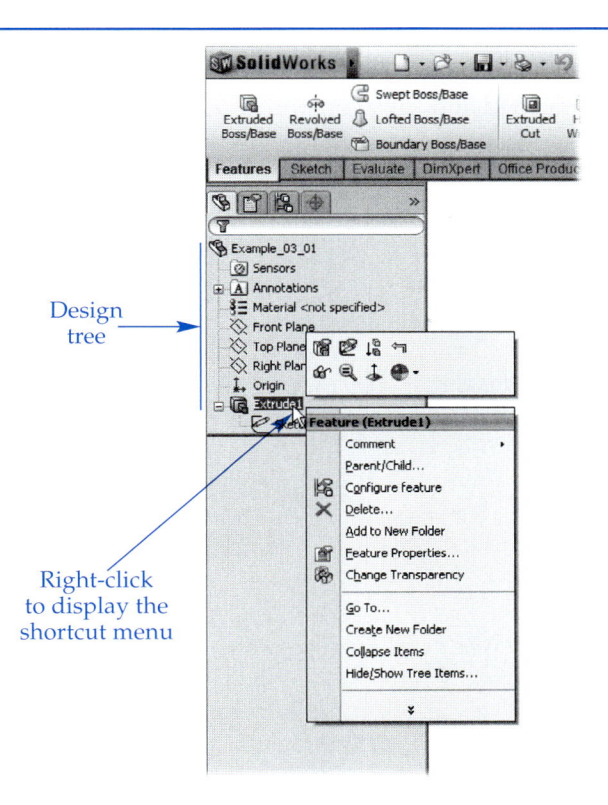

Design tree

Right-click to display the shortcut menu

Exit Sketch button on the **Sketch** tab in the **Command Manager** to exit sketch mode. You can also pick the **Rebuild** button on the **Menu Bar**. The part is then updated.

To exit sketch mode without applying the change, pick the red X at the top-right corner of the graphics window. Any changes made to the sketch are discarded and sketch mode is exited. The part is displayed in its state prior to when the **Edit Sketch** button was picked. For this example, accept the change.

The second option that allows you to modify the part is **Edit Feature**. When the **Edit Feature** button is picked in the shortcut toolbar, the **Extrude1** (the name of the feature) **Property Manager** is displayed. In this panel, changes can be made to the extruded distance, direction, end condition, and draft angle. For example, in the **Direction 1** rollout, deselect the **Draft On/Off** button. Notice the preview has changed and the taper is no longer applied to the feature. To accept the change, pick the green check mark button to close the panel and update the part. To reject the change, pick the red X button at the top of the panel. The panel is closed and the change is discarded. For this example, discard the change. Then, save and close the file.

PROFESSIONAL TIP

When editing the sketch, it may be easier to work with a "flat" view of the sketch. Pick the **Normal To** button in the **View Orientation** flyout in the view tools at the top of the graphics window. The view is changed so the plane on which the sketch was created is parallel to the screen.

Circles, Tangent and Horizontal Relations, and Trimming

In this section, you will use the **Circle** and **Line** tools to construct the part shown in **Figure 3-16A**. You will also apply tangent and horizontal relations to the sketch before extruding the profile. Start a new part file and set the units to MMGS. Then, start a new sketch on the front (XY) plane.

Chapter 3 Sketching, Relations, and the Base Feature **59**

Figure 3-16.
A—The completed part. B—Start the sketch used to create the part by drawing two circles. C—The sketch is completed and fully constrained.

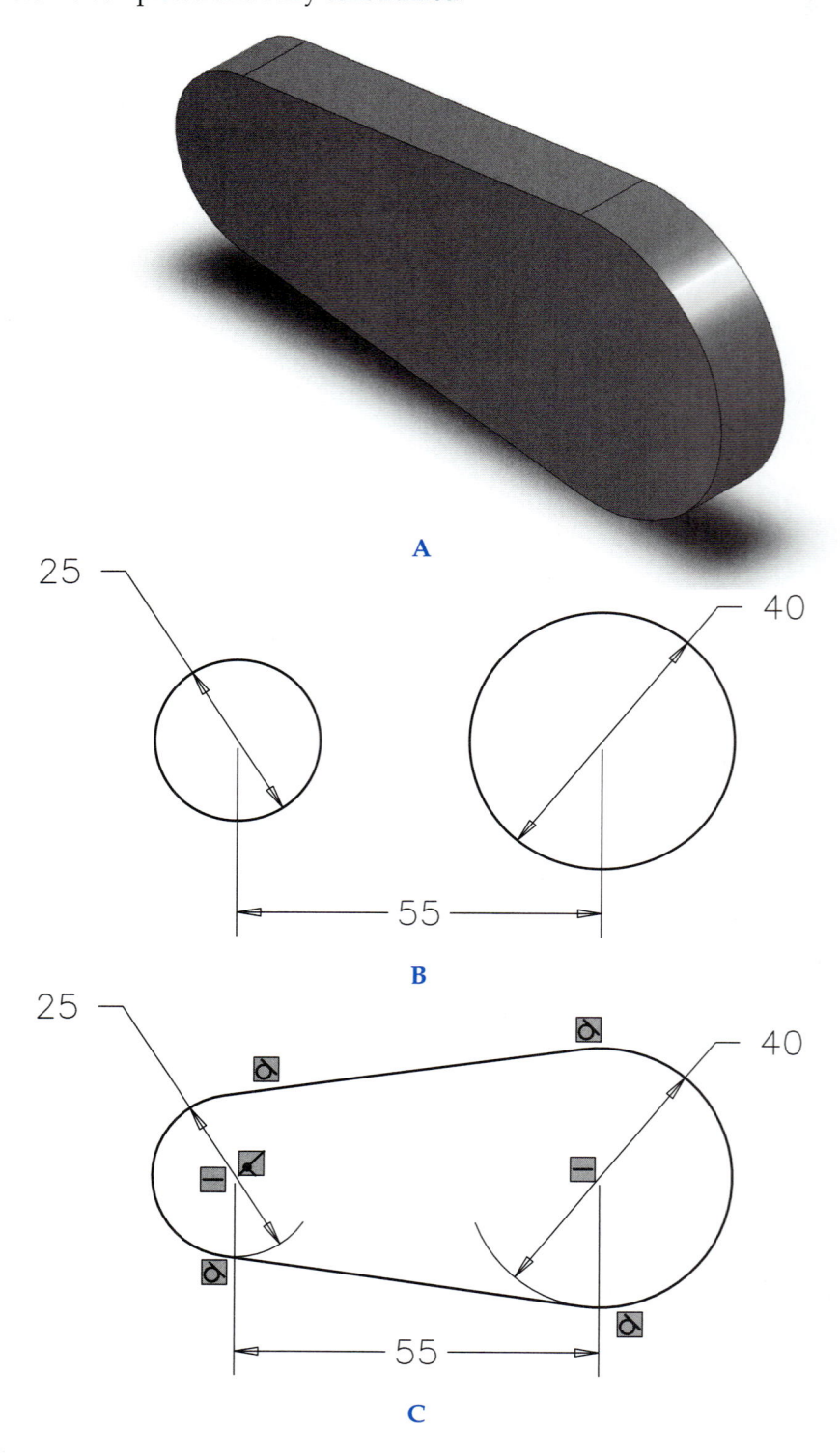

Pick the **Circle** button in the **Sketch** tab of the **Command Manager**. Construct two circles as shown in **Figure 3-16B**. Pick once to place the center of the circle. Pick the origin as the center of the small circle. Then, move the cursor and pick to set the diameter. The radius of the circle (not the diameter) is displayed beside the cursor as you drag. Remember, you can draw the circles to an approximate size and later edit the dimensions to exact values.

Learning SolidWorks 2009

The **Circle** tool remains active, so draw the larger circle. You can align the center points by moving the cursor until it is inline with the center point of the small circle, then moving the cursor to the right. As you move the cursor, a dashed line appears as long as the cursor is in an exact line from the center. Pick to set the center of the larger circle, then drag and pick to set the diameter. However, this does *not* apply a relation between the two circles. Once the second circle is drawn, pick the green check mark button at the top of the **Circle Property Manager** to close the panel and end the tool.

Next, apply dimensions and edit them to the exact values. To put a diameter dimension on a circle, pick the **Smart Dimension** button in the **Sketch** tab of the **Command Manager**. Then, pick anywhere on the circumference of the circle and drag the dimension to the desired location. You can pick on either the circumferences or the center points of the circles to place the 55 mm linear dimension. Pick the green check mark button at the top of the **Dimension Property Manager** to set the dimensions and end the tool.

Notice that the small circle is black and the large circle is blue. The small circle is constrained to the origin, but there is no geometric relation on the large circle. Now, place a horizontal relation between the center points of the two circles to vertically align them. Right-click anywhere in the graphics window to display the shortcut menu. Then, select **Add Relation...** in the **Relations** section of the menu. Next, pick the center point of the small circle. Finally, pick the center point of the large circle.

The **Add Relations Property Manager** is displayed. A list of relations that can be applied is displayed in the **Add Relations** rollout. See **Figure 3-17**. Pick the **Horizontal** button. If the circles were drawn so their centers are not horizontal (different Y values), the large circle moves to reflect the relation. Think of this relation acting as if a horizontal line is drawn between the two circle centers.

To complete the sketch, you need to draw two lines and trim the circles. Pick the **Line** button in the **Sketch** tab of the **Command Manager**. Then, pick the first endpoint of the line anywhere on the top of the smaller circle except the quadrant point. The cursor displays the coincident relation symbol when hovered over the circle. Next, hover the cursor on the larger circle and move it around until you see both the coincident and

Figure 3-17.
Applying a horizontal relation to the center points.

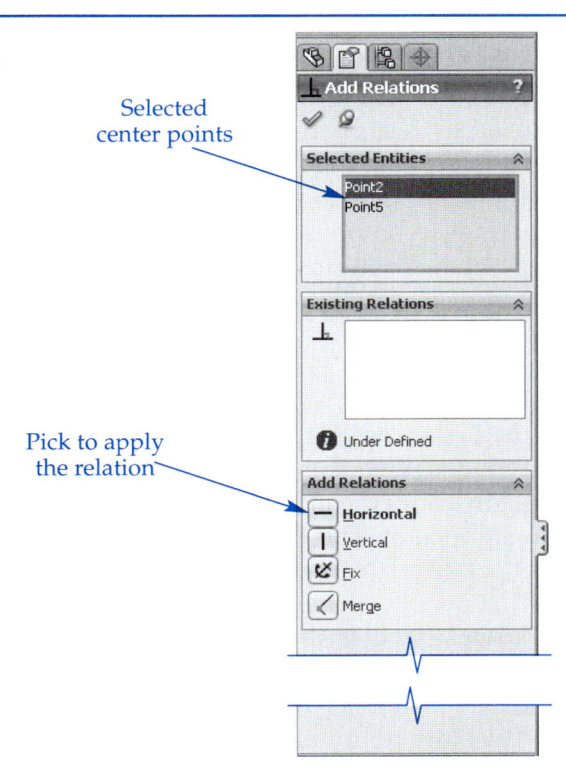

tangent relation symbols. Pick this point to finish the line. Press the [Esc] key to end the **Line** tool.

The existing relation icons are displayed. Notice that the line is both coincident and tangent to the large circle. In addition, SolidWorks may have automatically applied a tangent relation between the line and the small circle. If not right-click in the graphics window and select **Add Relation...** from the shortcut menu. Then, pick the line and the small circle. Finally, add a tangent relation using the **Add Relations Property Manager**. The first endpoint of the line moves to a location so that the line is tangent to the small circle. The second endpoint of the line also moves slightly so the line remains tangent to the large circle.

Use a similar process to draw a line across the bottoms of the circles. Both lines have two coincident and two tangent relation symbols displayed near them in the graphics window. This is because each endpoint is on (coincidental to) a circle and each line is tangent to each circle.

Currently, the sketch is an ambiguous profile, which simply means there is more than one possible profile. Ambiguous profiles are discussed in the next chapter. To make the sketch unambiguous, which allows it to be automatically selected for extrusion, the inner portions of the circles need to be removed. The **Trim Entities** tool is used to do this. Pick the **Trim Entities** button in the **Sketch** tab in the **Command Manager**. Then, pick near the inside edge of the small circle and drag the cursor across the inside edge. The portion of the circle between the two lines is removed by the tool. In the same manner, trim the inside edge of the large circle, **Figure 3-16C**. Then, pick the green check mark button at the top of the **Trim** panel.

After using the **Trim** tool, you may still see a portion of an arc. This arc is actually the dimension line for the diameter dimension. Since the dimension is not part of the geometry, this does *not* create an ambiguous sketch.

The sketch is complete, fully defined, and unambiguous. You can now extrude it into a solid part. Finish the sketch by selecting the **Exit Sketch** button in the **Sketch** tab. Display a 3D view of the model. Finally, extrude the profile 10 mm using the **Extruded Boss/Base** tool in the **Features** tab in the **Command Manager**. Save the file as Example_03_02.

Arcs and More Relations

Five lines and an arc are required to construct the part shown in **Figure 3-18A**. Three relations will be used to locate the arc: equal, collinear, and coincident. Start a new part file and set the units to IPS (inch, pounds, seconds). Then, start a new sketch on the front (XY) plane. Using the **Line** tool, draw the five lines shown in **Figure 3-18B**. Make sure to leave the gap between lines AB and CD. Apply a fix relation to lines AB and AF, which will keep them from moving as other lines are dynamically moved. Now, dimension the sketch as shown in **Figure 3-18B**.

Notice that the only relationship between lines AB and CD is that they are both horizontal. In fact, if you pick on line CD, you can drag it independent of line AB and line DE. By adding a collinear relation to lines AB and CD, the lines are constrained to the same Y values. If the lines were vertical, they would be constrained to the same X values. Select lines AB and CD. In this case, the order is not important. However, the second line picked is constrained collinear to the first line picked, so in the case of angled lines, the order is important. The **Properties Property Manager** is displayed. In the **Add Relations** rollout, pick the **Collinear** button. Then, pick the green check mark button to close the panel.

Now, the arc needs to be added to the sketch. Pick the **Three Point Arc** button in the **Sketch** tab of the **Command Manager**. This button is located in the drop-down list displayed by picking the arrow next to the **Center Point Arc** button. Three-point arcs are drawn by selecting the start point, endpoint, and then middle point (not center

Figure 3-18.
A—The completed part. B—Start the sketch used to create the part by drawing the line segments shown here. Be sure to leave the gap between points B and C.

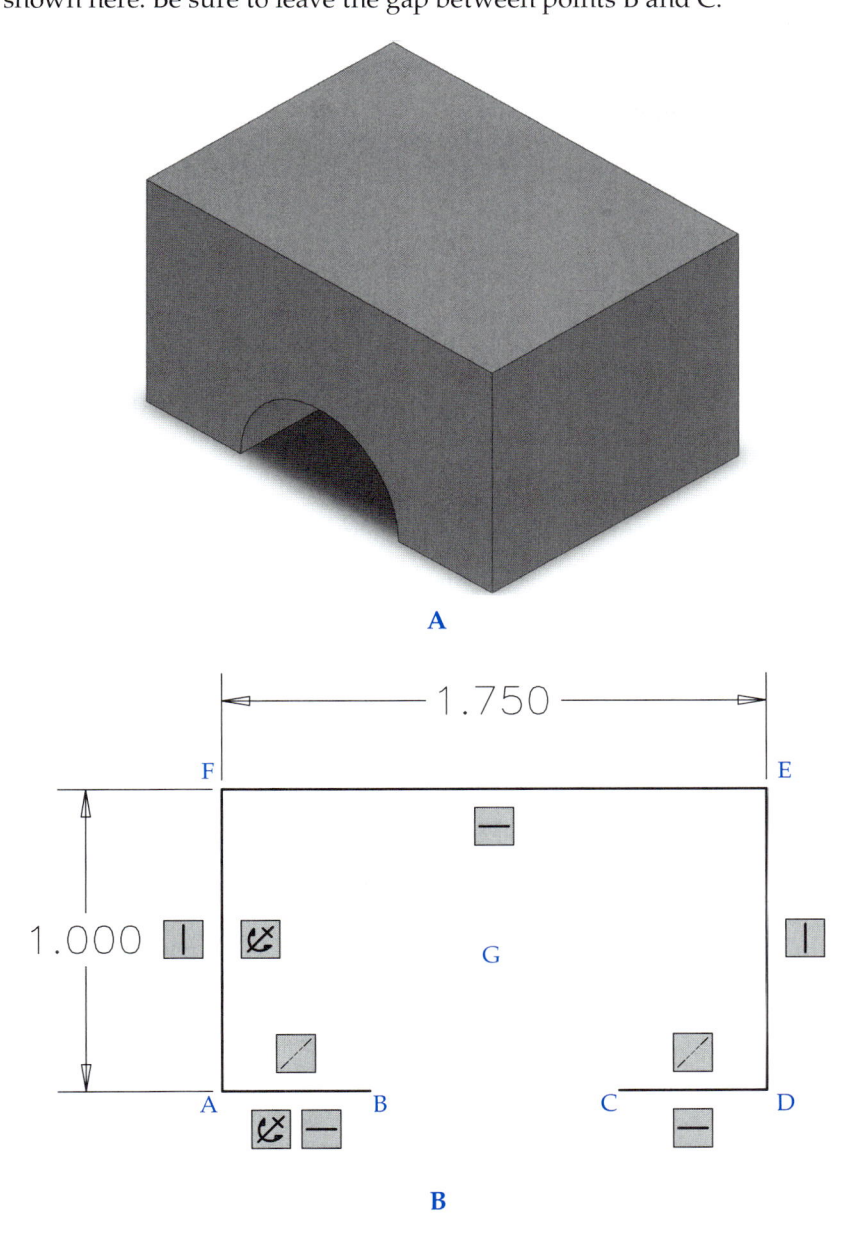

point). Pick the right-hand endpoint of line AB; an orange dot appears on the endpoint. Then, pick the left-hand endpoint of line CD. Finally, pick at approximately point G (shown in **Figure 3-18**). The Y coordinate of the center of the arc is approximately the same as the Y coordinate for lines AB and CD. Pick the green check mark button in the **Arc Property Manager** to end the tool.

An equal relation applied to lines AB and CD will horizontally center the arc between the lines. This is because the endpoints of the arc are constrained to the endpoints of the lines. Select lines AB and CD. Then, in the **Add Relations** rollout in the **Properties Property Manager**, pick the **Equal** button. Finally, pick the green check mark button to close the panel.

The arc now needs to be vertically constrained. This can be done by applying a coincident relation to the center of the arc and line CD (or line AB). Holding the [Ctrl] key, pick the center of the arc (the dot) and line CD. In the **Add Relation** rollout in the

Chapter 3 Sketching, Relations, and the Base Feature

Properties Property Manager, pick the **Coincident** button. Then, pick the green check mark button to close the panel.

The last relation that needs to be added to the sketch is a dimension for the size of the arc. This will constrain not only the size of the arc, but the length of lines AB and CD. Pick the **Smart Dimension** button in the **Sketch** tab in the **Command Manager**. Then, pick the arc and drag the dimension to the desired location. Finally, enter .40 for the radius value and close the **Dimension Property Manager**.

Add a dimension to line AB. You will receive a message indicating that applying the dimension will over define the sketch. See **Figure 3-19A**. You must correct an over-defined sketch before it can be used to create a part. The length of line AB is already defined by the radius of the arc and the equal relation between lines AB and CD. For this example, pick the **Leave this dimension driving** radio button and pick the **OK** button. A message is now displayed in a balloon on the status bar, **Figure 3-19B**. Pick the **Undo** button to remove the dimension.

The sketch is complete, fully defined, and unambiguous. Exit the sketch and display a 3D view. Complete the part by extruding the sketch 1.25". You may need to select the profile. Also, save the file as Example_03_03.

> **PROFESSIONAL TIP**
>
> Several sketching tools can be accessed through the shortcut menu when in sketch mode. Press the [Esc] key to cancel any tools you may have selected. Right-click on an empty area of the graphics window to display the pop-up menu. Then, select the sketching tool you wish to use.

PRACTICE 3-1

Complete the practice problem on the student website.
www.g-wlearning.com/CAD

Drawing an Arc from within the Line Tool

Tangent and perpendicular arcs can also be constructed from *within* the **Line** tool. For example, the sketch shown in **Figure 3-20** can be constructed, not including dimensions, using only one session of the **Line** tool. This is a little tricky, but, once mastered, you will find it very useful.

Start a new part file and set the units to MMGS. Start a new sketch on the front plane. Draw a line from point A to point B about 170 mm long. Now, move the cursor over point B and let it "hover." The endpoint of the line will turn orange; do not pick.

Figure 3-19.
If you attempt to apply a dimension that will over define the sketch, a warning appears. A—You can choose to apply the dimension as a driven or driving dimension. B—If the dimension is applied as driving, a warning is displayed.

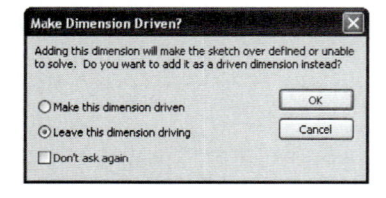

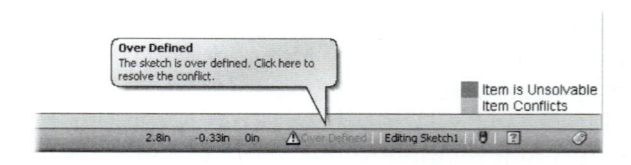

A

B

Figure 3-20.
All curves in this sketch can be drawn in a single session of the **Line** tool.

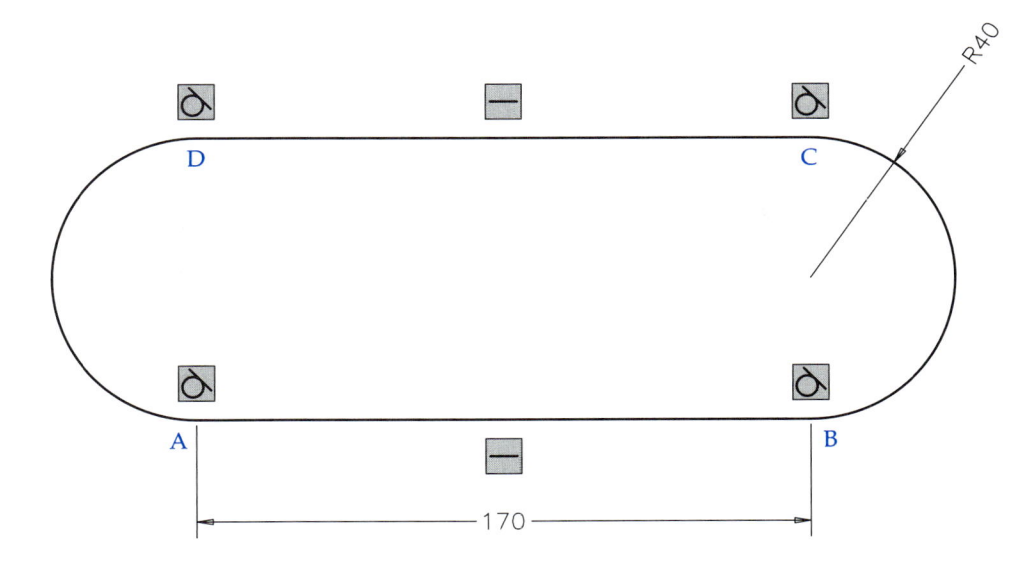

Swing the cursor to the right and up, as if you were sketching an arc. A dashed preview of the arc is displayed. Pick when the radius is about 40, as shown beside the cursor. The arc segment is constructed. Then, draw line CD normally. Finally, use the same "swing" method to draw the second arc from point D to point A.

Make sure both arcs are tangent to both lines. If not, add the necessary tangent relations. Now, if you were going to finish the part, you can add dimensions and adjust their values. Then, finish the sketch and extrude the part.

PRACTICE 3-2
Complete the practice problem on the student website.
www.g-wlearning.com/CAD

Things That Can Go Wrong with Sketches

There are several mistakes you can make in the construction of sketches that will generate errors when you attempt to use the **Extruded Boss/Base** tool. The two most common errors are having gaps at corners and having overlapping lines. For example, open the Example_03_04.sldprt file. There is a very small gap between the two lines in the upper-right corner, as shown in **Figure 3-21**.

Pick the **Extruded Boss/Base** button in the **Features** tab of the **Command Manager** and select the profile. In the **Extrude Property Manager**, notice that the check mark in the title bar of the **Thin Feature** rollout is checked. Because of the gap, SolidWorks assumes this sketch is to be extruded into a thin-walled feature. In the **Thickness** text box in the **Thin Feature** rollout, enter .001. A preview of the thin-walled feature should be displayed in the graphics window. However, you want this to be a solid, so try to uncheck the check box in the title bar of the **Thin Feature** rollout. You cannot uncheck it. This is the first clue that something is wrong with the sketch. SolidWorks will only allow a thin-walled feature to be created from this open sketch. To fix the problem, you will have to investigate the geometry and find any gaps that may exist. This will

Chapter 3   Sketching, Relations, and the Base Feature

Figure 3-21.
At a "normal" zoom level, the sketch on the left appears to be closed. However, if you zoom in on the upper-right corner of the sketch, there is a small gap, as shown in the detail.

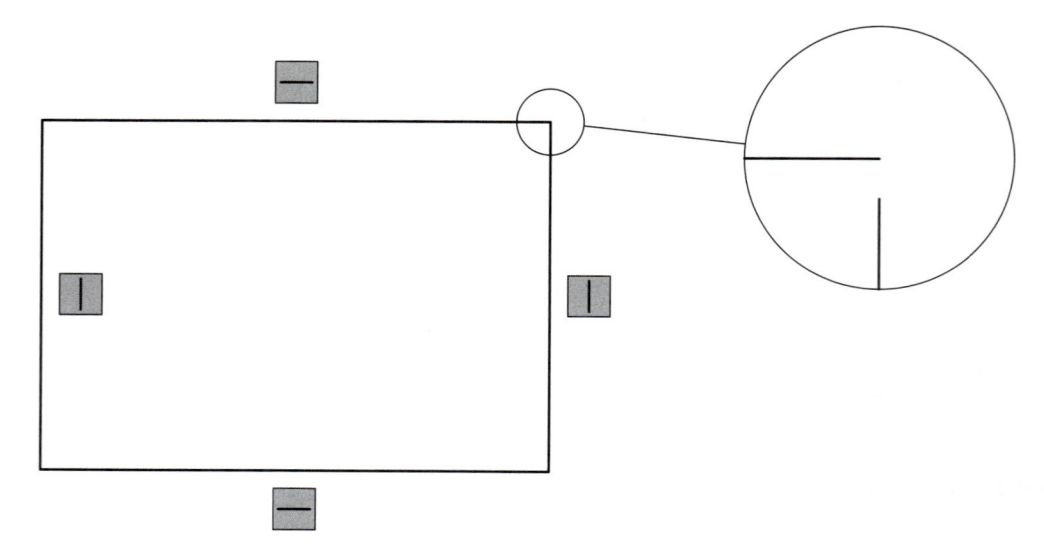

sometimes require you to zoom in very close and check each corner in the sketch. Once gaps are found, lines can be redrawn to fix the problem.

For another example of a sketch with a problem, open the Example_03_05.sldprt file. The bottom line in this sketch is actually two lines that overlap. Pick the **Extruded Boss/Base** button in the **Features** tab of the **Command Manager**. Notice that the **Extrude Property Manager** displays a message asking you to select a sketch. Select the sketch and notice SolidWorks does not offer a shaded preview. This means SolidWorks cannot locate a closed profile. This is again a hint that something is wrong. You must locate the problem in the sketch. Cancel the **Extruded Boss/Base** tool. Right-click on the sketch name in the design tree and pick the **Edit Sketch** button in the shortcut toolbar. Notice that the lower line has two points between its endpoints. This means there are either three segments or two overlapping segments. In this case, there are two overlapping segments. Select one segment and delete it by pressing the [Delete] key. Then, drag the endpoint of the remaining segment to the endpoint of the vertical line next to it to close the gap. Now, you can exit the sketch and extrude the feature.

Review of All Relations

Various geometric relations available in the **Add Relations** rollout in the curve **Property Manager**. The symbol that appears in the **Property Manager** is the same symbol that appears as an icon in the graphics window. The chart in **Figure 3-22** reviews the choices for common geometric relations. In order to become more familiar with the available relations, copy this chart by hand to a blank sheet of paper. Be neat so you can use the sheet as a reference as you work in SolidWorks. Other relations will be introduced as you work through this text.

Figure 3-22.
Review of common geometric relations. Commit the icons to memory.

Symbol	Relation Name	Entities
	Coincident	Point and a line, arc, or ellipse
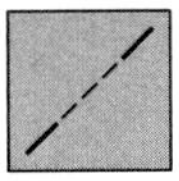	Collinear	Two or more lines
	Concentric	Two or more arcs or a point and an arc
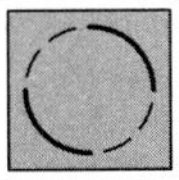	Coradial	Two or more arcs
	Equal	Two or more lines or two or more arcs
	Fix	Any entity
	Horizontal	One or more lines; two or more points
	Intersection	Two lines and a point
	Merge Points	Two points
	Midpoint	Two lines or a point and a line
	Parallel	Two or more lines
	Perpendicular	Two lines
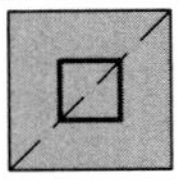	Symmetric	Centerline and two points, lines, arcs, or ellipses
	Tangent	Arc, ellipse, or spline and a line or arc
	Vertical	One or more lines; two or more points

Chapter Test

Answer the following questions on a separate sheet of paper or complete the electronic chapter test on the student website.
www.g-wlearning.com/CAD

1. Define *sketch* in SolidWorks.
2. All lines, arcs, and circles in SolidWorks are considered _____ objects.
3. What is a *relation* in SolidWorks?
4. What steps are required to start a sketch in SolidWorks after a new part file is started?
5. How can you use the mouse wheel button to pan the graphics window?
6. When using the **Line** tool, what information is provided near the cursor?
7. What are the two basic types of relations?
8. How can you prevent automatic relations from being applied as you draw?
9. When relations are displayed for geometry, how are they represented on-screen?
10. If you have drawn a line that is 150 mm in length, but it should be 148 mm in length, how can you correct this problem in SolidWorks?
11. Which tool allows you to manually apply a dimension?
12. What function does the fix relation serve?
13. Briefly describe how to extrude a fully defined, unambiguous sketch into a solid part.
14. Once you have extruded a sketch into a solid part, how can you edit the original sketch, in sketch mode, to change the part?
15. Briefly describe how to draw an arc from within the **Line** tool. Assume you have drawn one straight line segment.

Chapter Exercises

Complete the chapter exercises on the student website.
www.g-wlearning.com/CAD

Exercise 3-1 Test Sample. *Complete the exercise on the student website.*

Exercise 3-2 Clamp Block. *Complete the exercise on the student website.*

Exercise 3-3 Plate.
Complete the exercise on the student website.

Exercise 3-4 Pipe Bracket.
Complete the exercise on the student website.

Exercise 3-5 Shear Blade.
Complete the exercise on the student website.

Exercise 3-6 Taper Wedge.
Complete the exercise on the student website.

Exercise 3-7 U-Bracket.
Complete the exercise on the student website.

Exercise 3-8 Cover Plate.
Complete the exercise on the student website.

Chapter 3   Sketching, Relations, and the Base Feature

Revolved parts are created from a profile and an axis. In this example, a centerline is used as the axis of revolution and diametric dimensions establish the overall dimensions of the part.

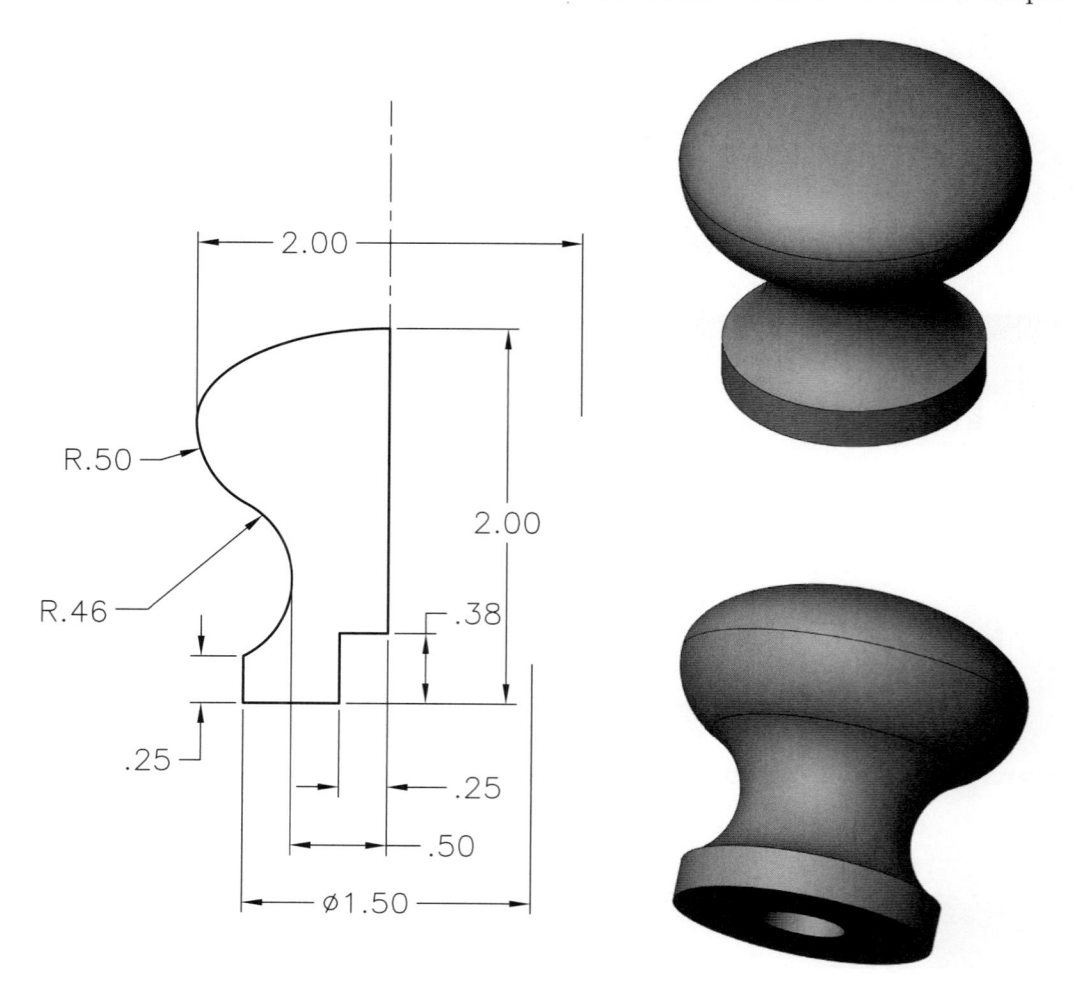

Chapter 4

Complex Sketching, Equations, and Construction Geometry

Objectives

After completing this chapter, you will be able to:
- Explain how to create and select ambiguous profiles.
- Use dimension names to create dimensions with equations.
- Create and use construction geometry and centerlines to locate sketch objects.
- Use the **Mirror Entities** tool in a sketch.
- Use the **Revolve Base/Boss** tool and explain its features.

Creating Complex (Ambiguous) Profiles

The sketches you created in Chapter 3 had no interior geometry, or "islands." There was only one choice for the profile; therefore, they were *unambiguous.* When you initiated the **Extruded Boss/Base** tool, there was only one profile that could be selected. If the sketch was selected prior to initiating the **Extruded Boss/Base** tool, SolidWorks automatically selected the only possible profile for you. In this chapter, you will work with sketches that have several possible profiles. These are called *ambiguous profiles.* You must select the specific profile to extrude. The islands in the sketch will extrude as *cutouts.* They are not called holes because there is a **Hole Wizard** tool, which is discussed in Chapter 6.

A SolidWorks sketch made up of four lines and two circles is shown in **Figure 4-1.** This geometry presents eight possible profiles that can be extruded, which are shown in the figure. To select the profile, pick the **Extruded Boss/Base** button in the **Features** tab of the **Command Manager** while still in sketch mode. Sketch mode is exited and the **Extrude Feature Manager** is displayed. The **Selected Contours** box in the **Selected Contours** rollout is selected (highlighted blue). Since this box is selected, SolidWorks cannot find an unambiguous profile and you are being asked to select the profile to extrude.

In the graphics window, pick within the area(s) you want to extrude. As you select each area, a shaded preview appears and a name, such as Sketch1-Region<1>, appears within the **Selected Contours** box. This represents the profile that will be extruded. You can remove an area from the selection by picking in that area again or right-clicking

Figure 4-1.
There are eight possible profiles from the sketch shown on the left. The possible profiles are shown on the right. The area that will be extruded is represented by the hatch lines.

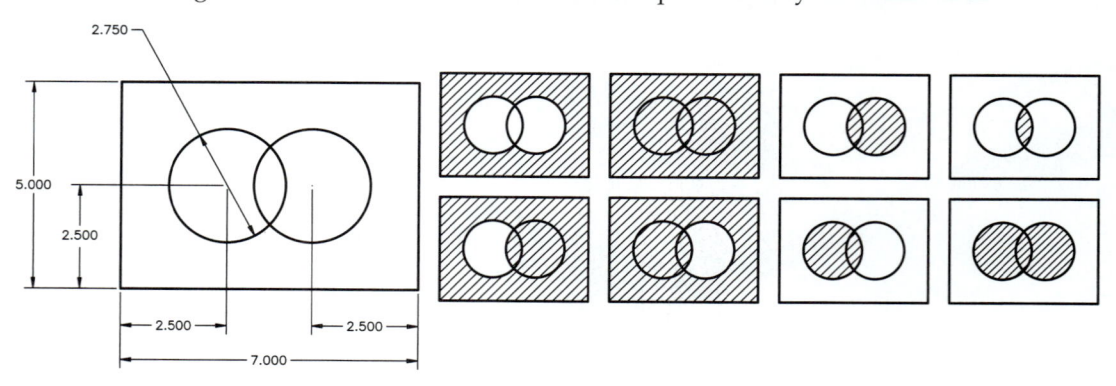

on the name in the **Selected Contours** box and picking **Delete** from the shortcut menu. Only the profile that will be extruded is shaded.

Open the file Example_04_01.sldprt. Ensure that you are in sketch mode. Then, pick the **Extruded Boss/Base** button in the **Features** tab of the **Command Manager**. In the **Extrude Property Manager**, notice that the **Selected Contours** box in the **Selected Contours** rollout is selected (highlighted blue). However, no shaded preview appears; the sketch is ambiguous. With the **Selected Contours** box selected, move the cursor over the sketch and pick the appropriate areas to create the 1" thick part shown in **Figure 4-2A**. Create the part. Then, right-click on Extrude1 in the **Feature Manager** and pick the **Edit Feature** button in the shortcut toolbar. Pick the **Selected Contours** box in the **Feature Manager** so it is highlighted blue. Then, select or deselect the areas to create the extruded part shown in **Figure 4-2B**. Pick the green check mark button in the **Feature Manager** to update the part.

When a sketch contains multiple profiles, more than one extrude feature can be created from the sketch. In the design tree in the **Feature Manager**, expand the Extrude1 branch and select Sketch1. This is the original sketch. Next, pick the **Extruded Boss/Base** button in the **Features** tab of the **Command Manager**. The **Extrude Feature Manager** is displayed. The **Selected Contours** box is automatically selected because SolidWorks cannot find an unambiguous profile. Select the football-shaped region in the middle of the part and extrude it 1.5". See **Figure 4-3**. Save and close the file.

> **NOTE**
>
> If you first exit sketch mode and then pick the **Extruded Boss/Base** button, you are asked to select a profile. However, you cannot directly select a region (contour). You will need to select the entire sketch using the flyout **Feature Manager** design tree. Then, you can continue as described above.

Using Equations in Sketch Dimensions

In Chapter 3, you learned how to add dimensions to constrain a sketch. Now, you will learn how to relate dimensions to each other. In this section, you will draw a circle in the center of a rectangle. Using dimensions, you can constrain the circle so it is always in the horizontal center of the rectangle.

Figure 4-2.
A—One possible part produced by extruding the sketch shown in Figure 4-1. B—Another possible part.

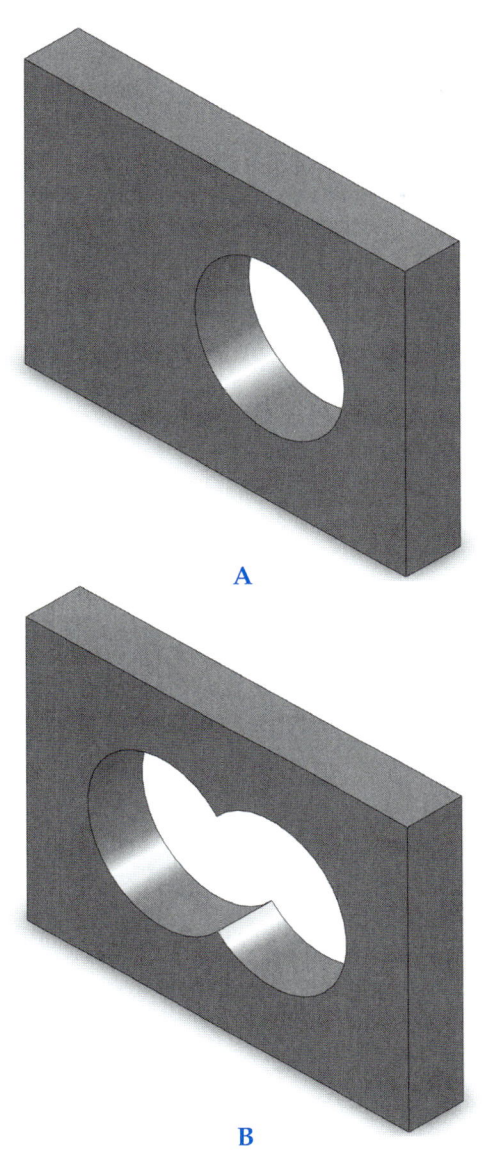

A

B

Start a new part file and set the units to IPS. Start a new sketch on the front plane. Next, pick the **Corner Rectangle** button in the **Sketch** tab of the **Command Manager**. Pick the first corner of the rectangle coincident to the origin. Move the cursor up and to the right until the rectangle is approximately 5" by 4" (X,Y) and pick to draw the rectangle. Next draw a circle about ⌀2" in the approximate center of the rectangle. Using the **Smart Dimension** tool, add size dimensions to the sketch. Next, place a dimension from the center of the circle to the left-hand edge of the part. Accept the default dimension value and then press the [Esc] key to end the **Smart Dimension** tool.

Every dimension has a unique name starting with an uppercase "D" and a number; the first dimension in the first sketch will be D1@Sketch1, the second D2@Sketch1, and so on. These names will be used to locate the center of the circle at the horizontal midpoint of the rectangle, regardless of the rectangle's width.

Double-click on the dimension that locates the center of the circle to open the **Modify** dialog box. Pick the arrow next to the dimension value to display the drop-down list and select Add Equation. The **Add Equation** and **Equations** dialog boxes are

Chapter 4 Complex Sketching, Equations, and Construction

Figure 4-3.
When a sketch contains multiple profiles, you can create multiple extrusions from the same sketch.

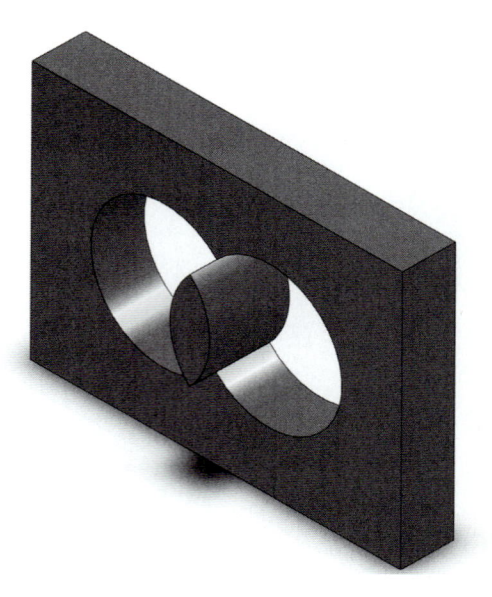

Figure 4-4.
A—The **Add Equation** dialog box is used to add an equation to the dimension in place of a numeric value. B—This equation results in the dimension D4@Sketch1 always being 1/2 of the value of the dimension D1@Sketch1.

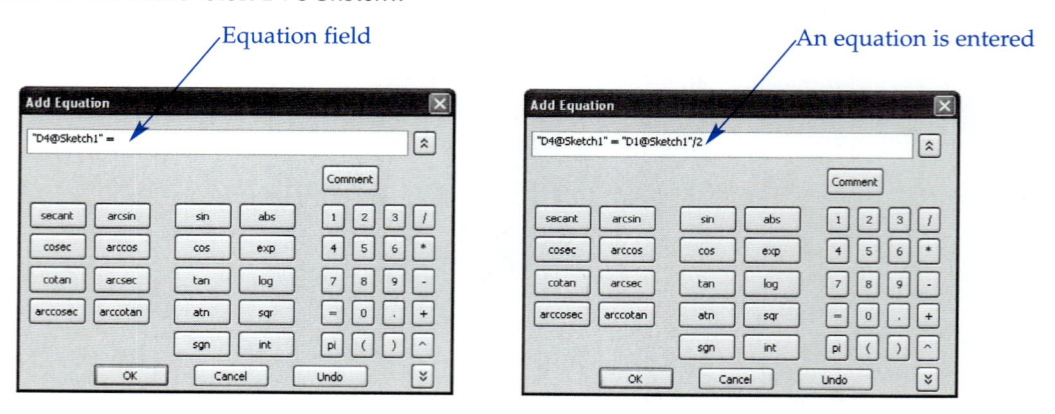

Equation field

An equation is entered

displayed in the graphics window. Initially, one dialog box may be on top of the other. In the **Add Equation** dialog box, "D4@Sketch1" = appears in the equation field. See **Figure 4-4A**. In this case, the name of the dimension is D4@Sketch1. The equation field indicates the equation for the dimension. With the **Add Equation** dialog box open, pick the 5″ dimension in the graphics window. The name of that dimension appears as the next value in the equation. Next, type /2 so the equation reads "D4@Sketch1" = "D1@Sketch1"/2, **Figure 4-4B**. This equation means that the value of D4@Sketch1 (the dimension from the center to the left edge) is the value of D1@Sketch1 divided by 2. In other words, the value of dimension D4@Sketch1 will always be one-half of the value of dimension D1@Sketch1. Press [Enter] or pick the **OK** button to update the dimension.

Once the dimension is updated, the **Equations** dialog displays the equation, **Figure 4-5**. If the sketch contained other equations, they would also be listed in the **Equations** dialog box. This dialog box can be used to manage all of the equations in the SolidWorks file. For now, close the dialog box.

Figure 4-5.
All equations in the part file are shown in the **Equations** dialog box, which is used to manage equations.

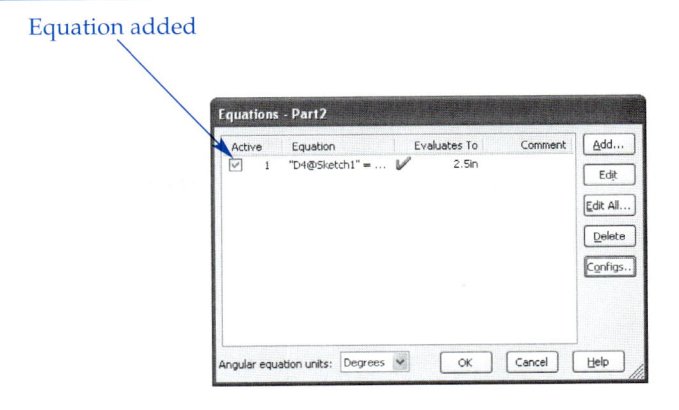

The value for D4@Sketch1 (the dimension locating the circle) is now shown as Σ 2.500. The symbol Σ (sigma) indicates that the dimension is a function of (related to) another dimension or is driven by an equation. Since the driving dimension is currently 5″, one-half of that value is 2.5″.

Now, change dimension D1@Sketch1 (the 5″ dimension) to a value of 10. The circle remains horizontally centered because dimension D4@Sketch1, which horizontally constrains the center of the circle, is defined as one-half of D1@Sketch1. Edit dimension D1@Sketch1 to a value of 5 and the circle returns to its original position.

Using a similar method, vertically constrain the center of the circle. Place a dimension from the center of the circle to the bottom edge of the part. Instead of accepting the default dimension value, select Add Equation from the drop-down list. With the **Add Equation** dialog box open, select the 4″ dimension. Type /2 after the name for the 4″ dimension and press [Enter]. Notice the **Equations** dialog box now shows two equations. Pick the **OK** button to close the **Equations** dialog box. The circle's vertical dimension is now constrained to one-half of the overall vertical dimension.

Now, you will constrain the size of the circle based on the overall size of the part. First, edit the diameter dimension on the circle. Then, add the equation "D3@Sketch1" = "D2@Sketch1"*.5, where D2@Sketch1 is the name of the overall vertical dimension and D3@Sketch1 is the diameter of the circle. This equation is the same as "D2@Sketch1"/2. Now, any time the overall vertical dimension is changed, the circle remains vertically centered *and* the diameter of the circle is one-half of the vertical distance.

If you select a dimension, the **Dimension Property Manager** is displayed. See **Figure 4-6.** Here, you can set the number of decimal places and the way the dimension is displayed. Using the **Primary Value** rollout, you can assign a descriptive name to each dimension. This comes in handy when sketches become complex. For example, you can change the name of the 5″ dimension from D1 to Long. Notice that the location designator (@Sketch1) remains. If Sketch1 is renamed, this suffix will also change.

Now, select **Tools>Equations...** from the pull-down menu to display the **Equations** dialog box, **Figure 4-7.** Each equation is shown in the Equation column and the solution is shown in the Evaluates To column. Notice that D1@Sketch1 has been replaced with Long@Sketch1 in the equation for D4@Sketch1 (which should be the first equation). You can select the **Edit** or **Edit All...** buttons to make changes to the existing equations. Close the **Equations** dialog box and exit sketch mode. Extrude the part .5″. Then, save the part as Example_04_02.

With the dimensions related to each other through the use of equations, the part can easily be updated in the future. You could even take it one step further and constrain the overall vertical dimension to 80% of the overall horizontal dimension, if needed. The value entered in the **Add Equation** dialog box can vary from arithmetic, trigonometric, or algebraic equations with the dimension names used as variables.

Chapter 4 Complex Sketching, Equations, and Construction

Figure 4-6.
The **Primary Value** rollout is used to rename the dimension.

Dimension name is changed

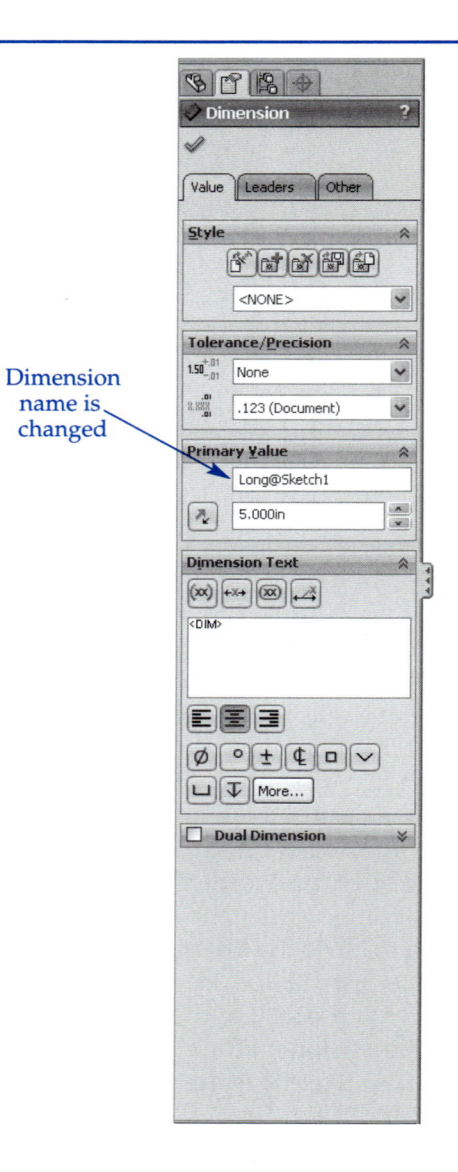

Figure 4-7.
Once a dimension is renamed, all equations referencing it are automatically updated.

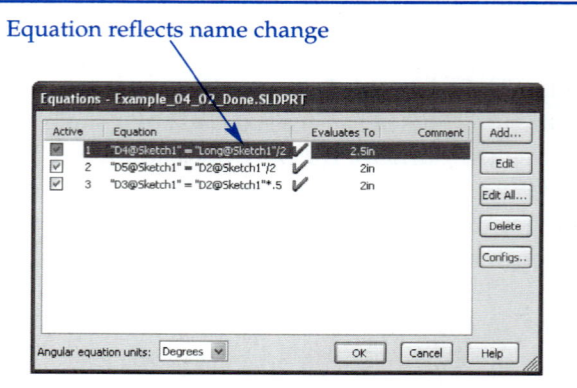

Equation reflects name change

Construction Geometry

Lines can be sketched in different styles. So far, you have only sketched in the normal style. This style creates solid (continuous) curves that are evaluated as part of the profile when the sketch is "finished." Two other available styles are construction and centerline, which appear the same. Geometry created in the construction style can be used with relations to locate geometry created in the normal style without the use of dimensions. Construction geometry is not part of the profile and has no effect on the model when the profile is extruded. In this section, you will locate a circle at the center of a rectangle using a line drawn in the construction style.

Start a new part file and set the units to MMGS. Start a sketch on the plane of your choice. Construct a 100 mm × 70 mm rectangle with one corner at the origin. Dimension the bottom and the left side. Next, pick the **Line** button in the **Sketch** tab in the **Command Manager**. In the **Options** rollout of the **Insert Line Property Manager**, check the **For construction** check box. This sets the line style to construction.

Draw a line from the lower-left corner of the rectangle to the upper-right corner. Notice that the line is thinner than the other lines drawn in the normal style and appears as a series of long and short dashes. This indicates the line is in the construction style. Press [Esc] to exit the **Line** tool.

Pick the **Circle** button in the **Sketch** tab on the **Command Manager**. Notice that there is not an option to draw the circle in the construction style. Locate the center point of the circle at the midpoint of the construction line by first drawing the circle in its approximate location and size. Then, apply a midpoint relation between the center of the circle and the diagonal construction line. You could also draw the circle at the midpoint by sliding the cursor along the construction line until the midpoint icon is displayed near the cursor, then picking. The midpoint grip is also displayed on the line when the cursor is over the midpoint. Since the construction line bisects the rectangle, the midpoint is also the geometric center of the rectangle. Finally, dimension the circle's diameter and change the value to 40 mm.

Change the length of the part from 100 mm to 150 mm. Notice that the circle stays in the center of the rectangle. Change the dimension back to 100 mm; the circle moves to stay in the center of the rectangle. The reason the circle stays at the center of the rectangle is that there is a midpoint relation applied between the center of the circle and the construction line. The endpoints of the construction line are constrained to the corners of the rectangle by automatically applied coincident relations. Therefore, as the corner of the rectangle is moved, the endpoint of the construction line moves. In turn, the center of the circle follows the midpoint of the construction line.

To complete this example, you will use the circle to construct a five-sided (pentagon) shape. Since the circle will not be part of the profile, it should be changed to the construction style. First, select the circle. Selected curves are displayed in light blue. With the circle selected, check the **For construction** check box in the **Options** rollout in the **Circle Property Manager**. The circle is changed to a construction circle.

Now, you can construct the pentagon. The easiest method to draw a pentagon is with the **Polygon** tool. However, here you will use the **Line** tool to gain practice applying relations. Each segment of the pentagon will be constrained tangent to the circle and equal to the other segments. See **Figure 4-8A**.

With the **Line** tool, draw the left side of the pentagon vertical. Remember, the starting point and length can be "about" correct. SolidWorks will automatically apply a vertical relation to the line. Then, holding down the [Ctrl] key to prevent automatic relations, sketch the other four sides at approximate sizes and locations. Make sure the last endpoint of the last segment is connected to the first endpoint of the first segment (release the [Ctrl] key so the automatic coincident relation is applied).

Now, apply a tangent relation between each of the five line segments and the circle. Holding the [Ctrl] key, select a line and the circle, then apply a tangent relation. Pick the green check mark button or pick anywhere in the graphics window to deselect the line and circle. Do this for each of the five lines. Then, apply an equal relation to the lines so they are equal to each other. Holding the [Ctrl] key, select all five lines at once and then apply the equal relation. Finally, exit sketch mode, display a 3D view, and extrude the profile 10 mm. Since the construction objects are not analyzed by SolidWorks, the correct

Chapter 4   Complex Sketching, Equations, and Construction

Figure 4-8.
A—Using construction objects and relations to construct a circumscribed pentagon. B—The sketch is extruded into a part.

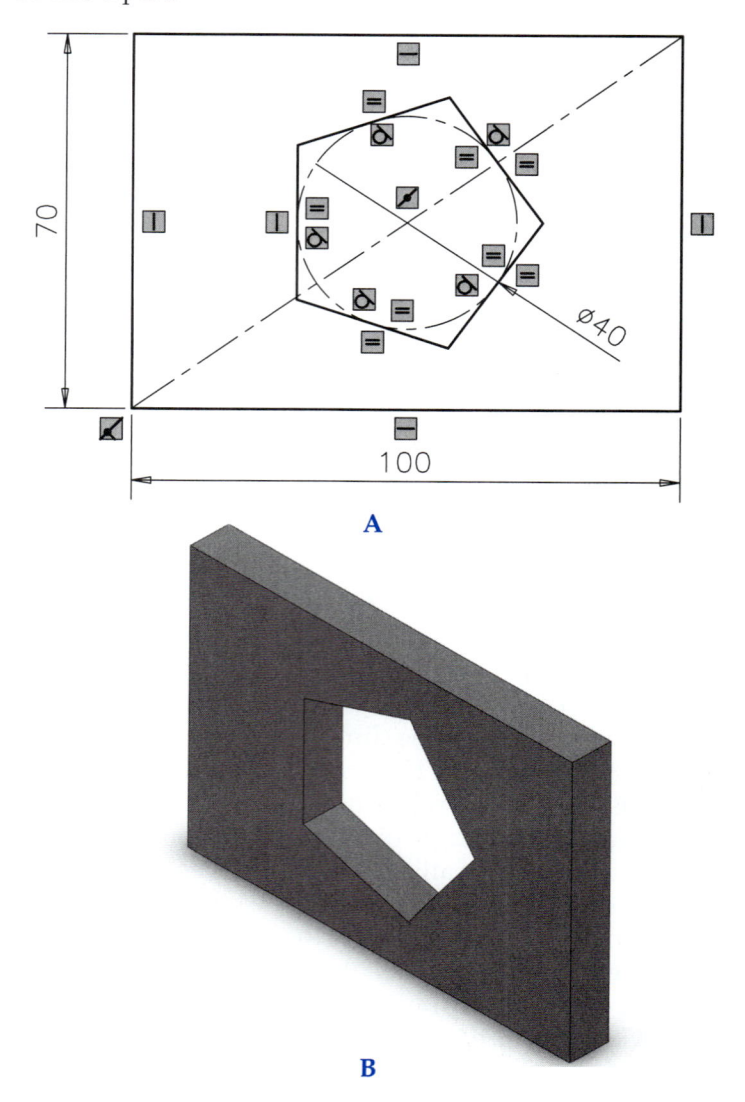

A

B

profile is selected. Notice that SolidWorks automatically removes the island to create a cutout (hole). See **Figure 4-8B.** Save the file as Example_04_03 in your working folder.

PROFESSIONAL TIP

As you saw with the circle, you can quickly change the style of an existing curve by selecting it and then checking the **For construction** check box in the **Options** rollout. Holding the [Ctrl] key allows multiple curves to be selected and then changed using this method.

PRACTICE 4-1

Complete the practice problem on the student website.
www.g-wlearning.com/CAD

78 Learning SolidWorks 2009

Sketch Mirror Entities Tool

The **Mirror** tool is used to create a mirror of geometry or objects by reflecting about a centerline. There are actually two mirror tools in SolidWorks. One is found in the **Features** tab of the **Command Manager** and the other is found in the **Sketch** tab of the **Command Manager**. In this section, you will look at the **Mirror Entities** tool in the **Sketch** tab. It is used to mirror sketched curves about any line in the sketch.

Open the file Example_04_04.sldprt, **Figure 4-9**. In this example, the arc and two short lines will be mirrored about a line from the midpoint of line AD to the midpoint of line BC. First, using the **Line** tool, draw a line from the midpoint of line AD to the midpoint of line BC. The line can be in any style, but in this case, pick the **Centerline** button in the **Line** drop-down list on the **Sketch** tab to create a centerline. A centerline acts the same as any straight line in the construction style. Draw the centerline between midpoints of lines AD and BC. Press the [Esc] key to end the **Line** tool. You can manually add the midpoint relations after the line is drawn, if you desire.

Now, use the **Mirror Entities** tool. Pick the **Mirror Entities** button in the **Sketch** tab of the **Command Manager**. The **Mirror Property Manager** is displayed. See **Figure 4-10**. If any entities were selected when the tool was initiated, they will be listed in the **Entities to mirror:** box in the **Options** rollout. To select entities to mirror, pick this box so it is active (highlighted in blue). Then, select the two short lines and the arc on the sketch. When selected, the lines are displayed in light blue and listed in the **Entities to mirror:** box. If needed, you can remove entities from the list by picking it in the graphics window.

Next, pick the **Mirror about:** box in the **Options** rollout so it is active (highlighted in blue). Select the centerline you just constructed on the sketch. A preview of the mirrored entities appears in yellow. Finally, pick the green check mark button at the

Figure 4-9.
The "tab" feature on this sketch will be mirrored to create a second tab.

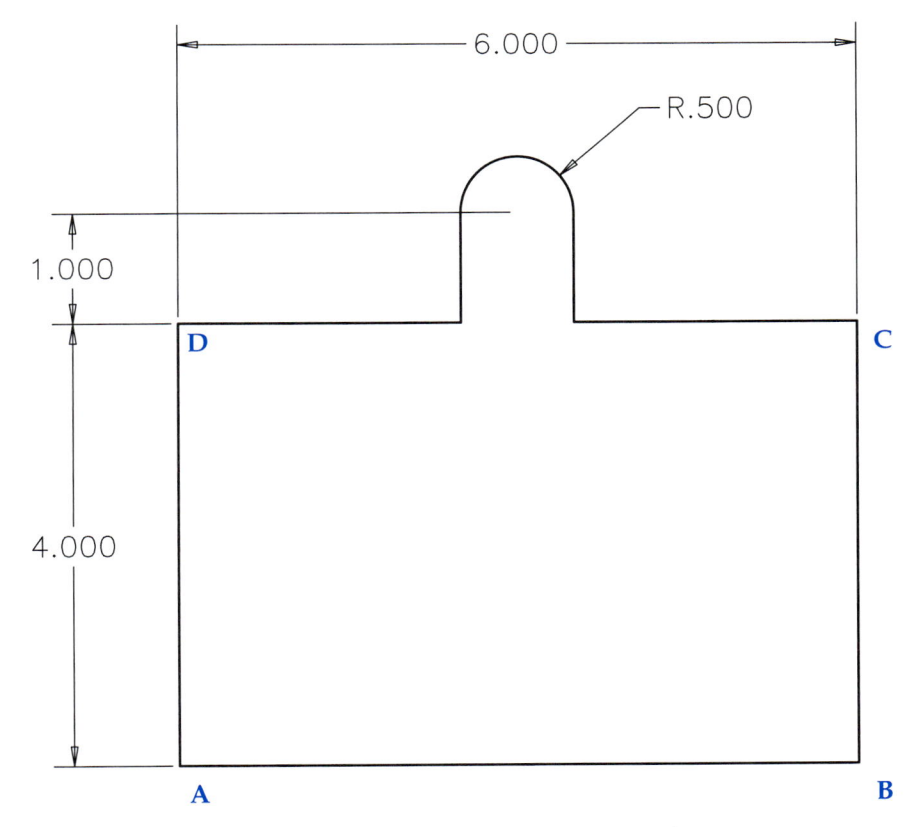

Figure 4-10.
Selecting the curves and mirror axis to mirror entities.

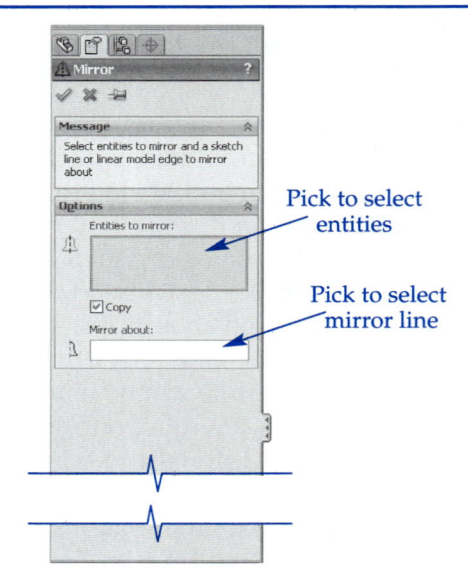

top of the **Mirror Property Manager** to complete the operation. The **Mirror** tool applies the symmetric relation to the arc and the endpoints of the lines that are mirrored.

To complete the part, use the **Trim Entities** tool in the **Sketch** tab of the **Command Manager** to trim the center portion of line AB. Then, exit sketch mode, display a 3D view, and extrude the profile .25″. Save the file.

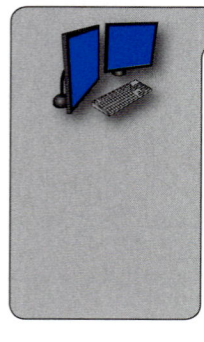

> **PROFESSIONAL TIP**
>
> When using tools such as the **Mirror Entities** tool, you may save time by selecting the entities you wish to mirror and the mirror axis before activating the tool. Holding down the [Ctrl] key, select the lines and arc you wish to mirror and the centerline axis. The order in which you select these elements is not important. With the entities selected, activate the **Mirror Entities** tool. SolidWorks automatically selects the centerline as the mirror axis and assumes the other selected entities will be mirrored. The operation is automatically completed.

Revolved Boss/Base Tool

The **Revolved Boss/Base** tool creates cylindrical parts by revolving a profile about an axis. The axis must be a straight line that, if extended indefinitely, would never cross the profile. However, the axis can touch the profile, such as an axis line that is tangent to a circle. This method produces a cylindrical model without a hole.

The axis can be in any line style. However, the advantage of using a centerline is that when you place dimensions in a sketch, they are placed as diametric dimensions, even though the complete diameter is not shown. *Diametric dimensions* measure the diameter of circular geometry. Place these dimensions by picking the geometry and the centerline and placing the dimension on the opposite side of the center as the geometry. Be aware that if you pick the endpoint of the centerline, the dimension will be radial, not diametric.

Open the file Example_04_05.sldprt. See **Figure 4-11.** Line BD is a construction line. Point B is the origin of the coordinate system. The top of the sketch is made of two

Figure 4-11.
This sketch will be used to create a symmetrical, circular part. Notice the centerline and the diametric dimension.

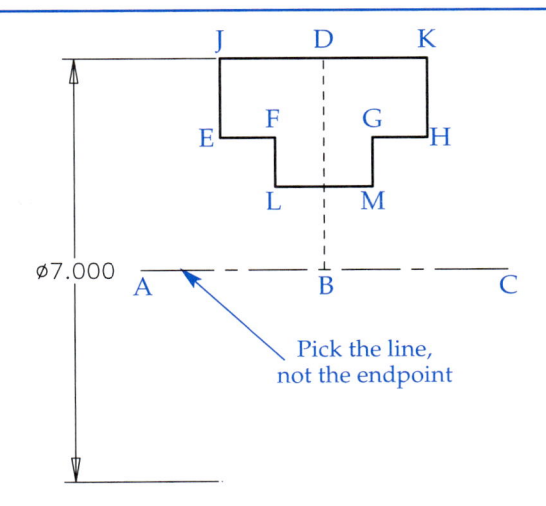

separate lines, lines JD and DK. First, select line BD and apply a vertical relation. Next, apply an equal relation to lines JD and DK, and to lines EF and GH. This horizontally centers the sketch.

Now, place a dimension between line EF and the centerline (line AC) and change the value to 4.5″. Be sure to pick on the side of line AC that is opposite of line EF. Notice how the dimension is placed as a diametric dimension. Also, the dimension does not measure from the centerline to line EF. Rather, it measures from a point on the opposite side of the centerline to line EF. Also, place a diametric dimension between line LM and the centerline. Enter this dimension value as 2.5″. The fully dimensioned sketch is shown in **Figure 4-12.** Display a 3D view and exit sketch mode.

Now, you can revolve the profile about the centerline to complete the part. Pick the **Revolved Boss/Base** button in the **Features** tab of the **Command Manager**. The **Revolve Property Manager** is displayed, **Figure 4-13.** Select the centerline in the sketch. SolidWorks assumes the centerline will be the axis of revolution and the closed profile will be revolved about it. A shaded preview of the revolution is displayed.

If you have multiple profiles in a sketch, expand the **Selected Contours** rollout in the **Revolve Property Manager** and pick the list box so it is active (highlighted blue). Then, select the profiles in the graphics window. Like the **Extrude Boss/Base** tool, you can select multiple profiles. If there is more than one possible axis of revolution, or if the axis is not drawn in the centerline style, pick the **Axis of Revolution** box in the **Revolve Parameters** rollout so it is active (highlighted blue). Then, pick the axis in the graphics window.

Figure 4-12.
The fully dimensioned sketch that will be revolved.

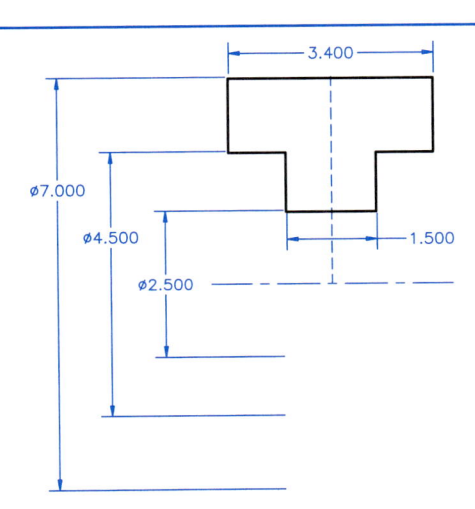

Chapter 4 Complex Sketching, Equations, and Construction

Once the profile and axis are selected, pick the green check mark button at the top of the **Revolve Property Manager**. A solid model is created by revolving the profile through 360° (which is set in the **Revolve Parameters** rollout). See **Figure 4-14.** Save the file. There are other options with the **Revolved Boss/Base** tool that are discussed later in the book.

Figure 4-13.
When selecting the sketch for the revolve operation, pick the centerline. In this way, SolidWorks will automatically set it as the axis of revolution and select the closed profile as the entities to revolve.

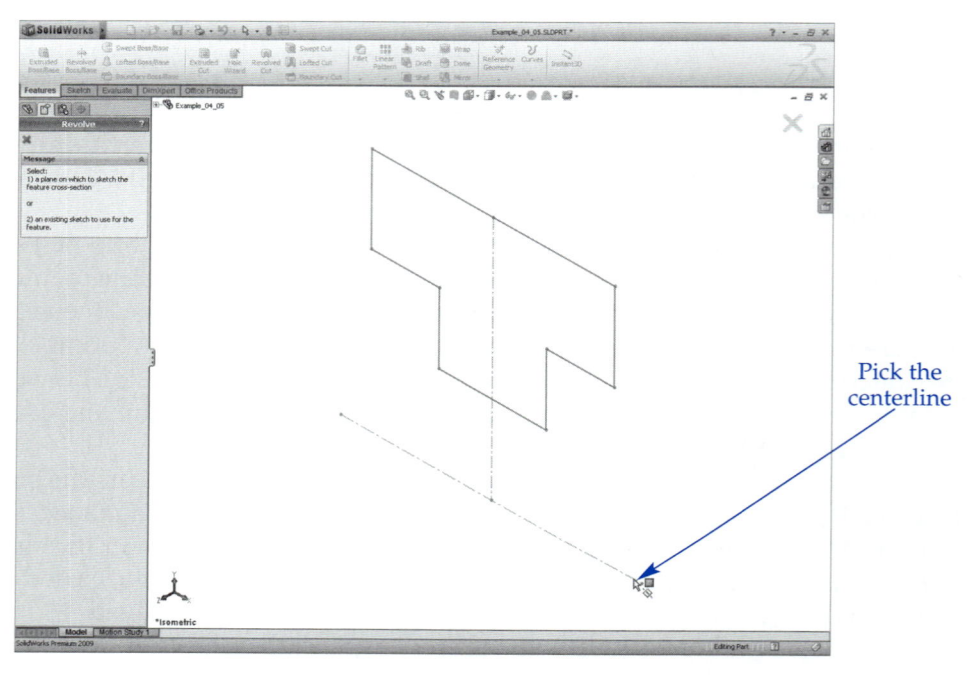

Figure 4-14.
The sketch shown in Figure 4-12 is revolved to create this part.

Chapter Test

Answer the following questions on a separate sheet of paper or complete the electronic chapter test on the student website.
www.g-wlearning.com/CAD

1. A sketch containing islands is considered a(n) _____ profile.
2. An island is also called a(n) _____ once the sketch is extruded.
3. Briefly describe how to create more than one extruded feature from a single sketch containing multiple profiles. Assume you have already extruded one feature.
4. How can you set the dimension D4@Sketch1 so it is always equal to D3@Sketch1 divided by D2@Sketch1?
5. Briefly describe how to rename a dimension.
6. What is the advantage of using the construction style to draw construction lines?
7. Once a line is drawn, how can you change its line style?
8. What is the function of the sketch **Mirror Entities** tool?
9. What relationship must the axis of revolution have to the profile when using the **Revolve Boss/Base** tool?
10. When using the **Revolved Boss/Base** tool, what is the advantage of drawing the axis of revolution in the centerline style?

Chapter Exercises

Complete the chapter exercises on the student website.
www.g-wlearning.com/CAD

Exercise 4-1 Link. *Complete the exercise on the student website.*

Exercise 4-2 Valve. *Complete the exercise on the student website.*

Exercise 4-3 Stamping. *Complete the exercise on the student website.*

Exercise 4-4 Mirror Part. *Complete the exercise on the student website.*

Exercise 4-5 Cap.
Complete the exercise on the student website.

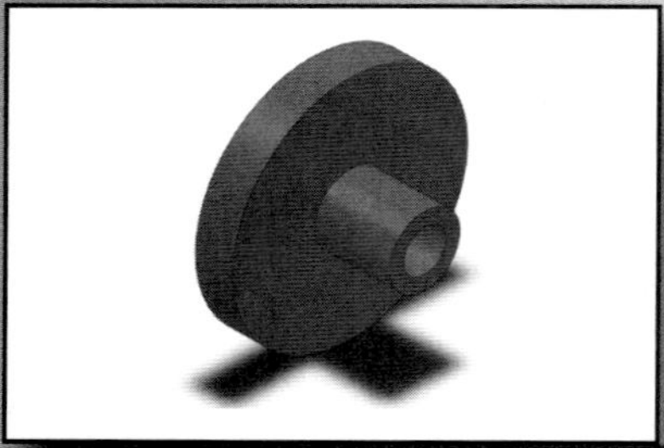

Exercise 4-6 Wheel.
Complete the exercise on the student website.

Exercise 4-7 Blanked Cam Plate.
Complete the exercise on the student website.

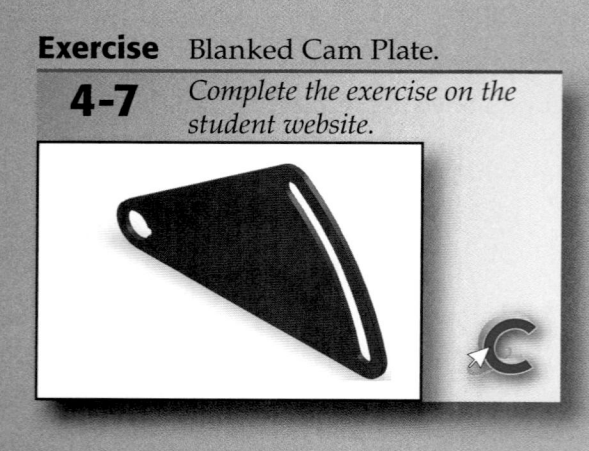

Exercise 4-8 Locking Cam.
Complete the exercise on the student website.

Chapter 5

Secondary Sketches and Reference Geometry

Objectives

After completing this chapter, you will be able to:

- Explain how to create secondary sketches.
- Explain and use the start condition and end condition options for extruded features.
- Project geometry onto a sketch plane using the **Convert Entities** tool.
- Use the **Add**, **Subtract**, and **Common** options of the **Combine** tool.
- Display, adjust, and use the three default planes to create a sketch.
- Create and use reference geometry.

Creating Secondary Sketches and Adding Features

The parts you created in Chapters 3 and 4 were all based on a primary sketch created on one of the three default planes. In this chapter, you will look at how to create additional, secondary sketches on the faces of the part and on reference planes. Open the file Example_05_01.sldprt. This part has five planar (flat) faces that can be used as sketch planes. It also has one curved face that *cannot* be used as a sketch plane. See **Figure 5-1.**

In this section, you will create a boss on the top face. The procedure is to select the planar face on which to sketch, create the sketch, and extrude the profile. This basic procedure can be used to create a new feature on any planar face.

85

Figure 5-1.
This part has five planar faces that can be used as sketch planes. The curved face cannot be used as a sketch plane.

Curved face cannot be used as a sketch plane

PROFESSIONAL TIP

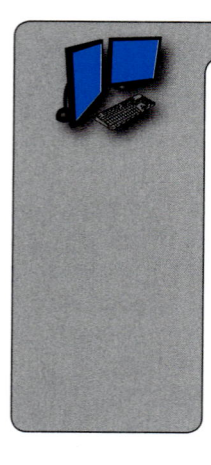

SolidWorks provides tools for changing the display color and other visual characteristics of part faces. Changing the color setting of a face may provide a visual reference when working with different sketch planes. To access the color setting for a face, right-click on the face and pick on the **Appearances** drop-down list located on the shortcut toolbar. Select the color box next to the **Face** option. This displays the **Appearances Property Manager**. In the **Color** rollout, select a color using the swatch window, crosshairs cursor, or slider bars. Then, pick the green check mark button. The face is now displayed in the selected color. You can change the color of any face, feature, or body using this procedure.

1. Pick the **Sketch** button in the **Sketch** tab of the **Command Manager** to initiate a sketch. A geometry icon appears next to the cursor in the graphics window indicating that you need to select a sketch plane. You must select a plane on which to sketch before a sketch can be created.
2. Move the cursor over any face on the part. The edges of the face are highlighted.
3. Move the cursor over the top face and pick to select it.

Notice that a new local origin is on the selected face. This indicates that the current coordinate system coincides with the selected face. You may align your view normal to the sketch plane to make things easier by selecting the **Normal To** button in the **View Orientation** flyout in the view tools at the top of the graphics window.

Now, draw the sketch and extrude it into the boss:

1. Using the **Circle** tool, sketch a circle anywhere on the sketch plane. Use the default **Circle** tool option. This draws a center-based circle. For this example, do not pick the center of the circle coincident to the center of the arc on the part.
2. Apply a concentric relation between the circle and the arc. Select the curved edge of the part and the circle to apply the relation.
3. Dimension the circle's diameter. Then, edit the dimension to a value of 25 mm.
4. Exit the sketch to return to part mode.

5. Pick the **Extruded Boss/Base** button in the **Features** tab of the **Command Manager**. If the sketch is not automatically selected, you must select the sketch. After selecting the sketch, the interior area of the circle is highlighted and a shaded preview of the extrusion is displayed.
6. In the **Extrude Property Manager**, make sure the **Merge result** check box is checked. Then, set the depth to 22 mm. See **Figure 5-2A.** Also, make sure the Blind option is selected in the **End Condition** drop-down list. This creates an extrusion at a specified depth. The **End Condition** options are discussed in the next section.
7. Pick the green check mark button at the top of the **Extrude Property Manager** to extrude the feature, **Figure 5-2B.** Notice that the extrusion is given a different name in the **Feature Manager** design tree, such as Extrude2, rather than being added to the previous extrusion.

You can rename the components of the part in the **Feature Manager** design tree. For example, Extrude2 is really not very descriptive. Instead, Boss would be a meaningful description. To rename the boss extrusion:

1. Right-click on the extrusion name in the design tree and select Feature Properties... from the shortcut menu. The **Feature Properties** dialog box is displayed. See **Figure 5-3**.
2. In the **Name** text box, type Boss. After selecting **OK**, the name of the extrusion is changed to Boss in the design tree.

PROFESSIONAL TIP

A quick way to rename features and other items in the design tree is to select the name of the item and then pick on the name again. This displays an edit box, which you can use to type a new name. After typing the new name, press the [Enter] key.

Figure 5-2.
A—The settings for extruding the sketch. B—The extrusion is added to the part.

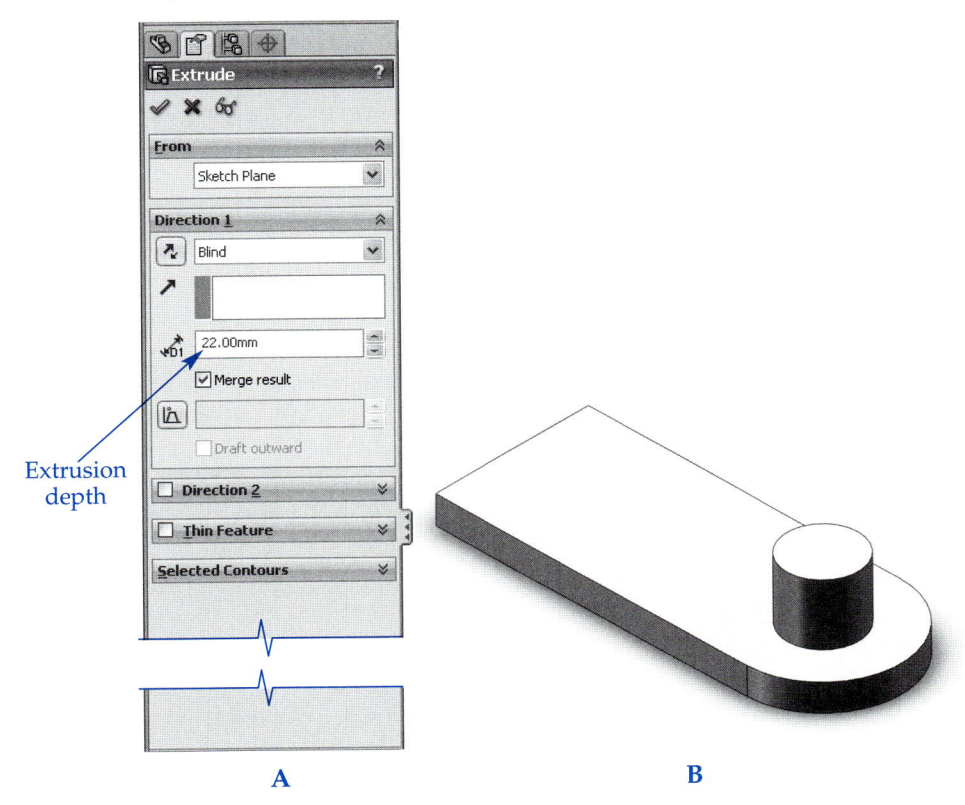

Chapter 5 Secondary Sketches and Reference Geometry

Figure 5-3.
Changing the name of a feature using the **Feature Properties** dialog box.

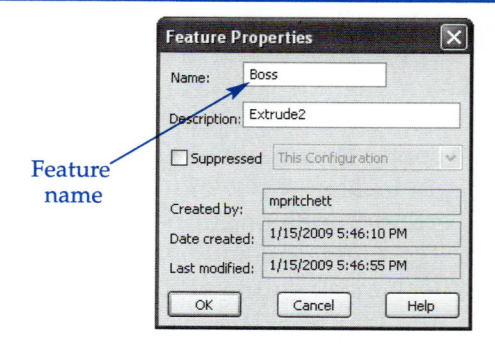

Feature name

End Condition Extrusion Options

The **End Condition** options available with the **Extruded Boss/Base** tool are used to specify how the extrusion is generated and how "far" it extends. The same options are available when using the **Extruded Cut** tool. The **End Condition** options are selected from the **End Condition** drop-down list in the active **Property Manager**. The **Start Condition** options available in the **Start Condition** drop-down list are used to define the starting plane for the extrusion. To this point in the book, you have used the default Sketch Plane start condition option. The other start condition options are discussed in the next section.

The Blind end condition option is active by default. The Blind option specifies an exact length for the extrusion, which is what you have used so far. The Through All option specifies that the extrusion will extend through all geometry in the part. The Up To Next option specifies that the extrusion will terminate at the next surface it intersects when extended. The Up To Vertex option specifies that the extrusion will extend to a plane that lies parallel to the sketch plane and passes through the selected vertex. The Up To Surface option is used to select a face to which the extrusion will extend. The Offset From Surface option is similar to the Up To Surface option, but it allows you to specify an offset from the termination surface. The Up To Body option is used to select a body to which the extrusion will extend. The Mid Plane option specifies an exact length for the extrusion and divides that length equally on either side of the sketch plane.

In this next operation, you will use the Through All option and the **Extruded Cut** tool. If you have not created the boss as described in the previous section, do so now. Then, continue as follows.

1. Pick the **Sketch** button in the **Sketch** tab of the **Command Manager**. Then, select the face on the top of the boss as the sketch plane.
2. Pick the **Normal To** button in the **View Orientation** flyout in the view tools at the top of the graphics window. This establishes a top view. This step is not necessary, but it may make locating the new sketch easier.
3. Sketch a circle with its center at the center of the boss. This constrains it concentric to the boss. Place a diameter dimension on the circle and edit the dimension to a value of 10 mm.
4. Exit the sketch to return to part mode. Then, pick the **Extruded Cut** button in the **Features** tab of the **Command Manager**. Select the small circle as the sketch to extrude.
5. In the **Extrude Property Manager**, select Through All from the **End Condition** drop-down list. See **Figure 5-4**.
6. In the **Direction 1** rollout, pick the **Draft On/Off** button to create the feature with a draft angle. Enter an angle of 10° and select the **Draft Outward** option. The **Draft Outward** option increases the size of the feature as it is extruded.

88   Learning SolidWorks 2009

Figure 5-4.
The settings for extruding the sketch.

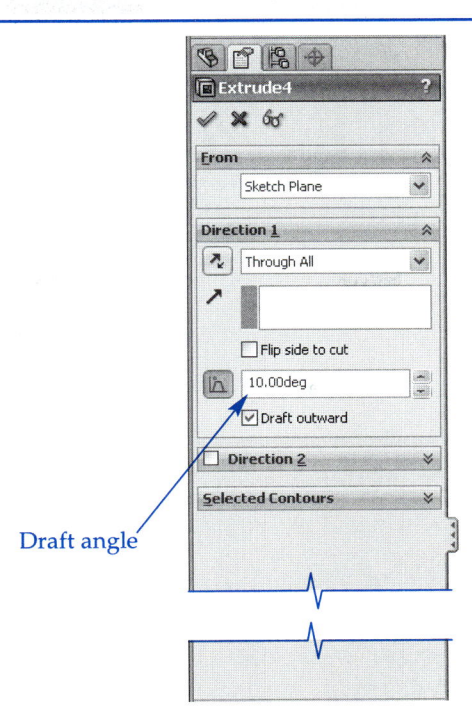

Draft angle

7. Pick the green check mark button to extrude the sketch. The finished part is shown in **Figure 5-5** with half of the part removed to show the interior extrusion.

Now, open the file Example_05_02.sldprt. This is a U-shaped part, **Figure 5-6.** You will add a cutout (hole) to one leg of the part, but not the other. The Up To Surface extruded cut option allows you to do this by limiting the extent of the extrusion to the next face that the extrusion encounters. The "up to surface" face can be either flat or curved. To create the cutout:

1. Pick the **Sketch** button in the **Sketch** tab of the **Command Manager** and select the top face of the part as the sketch plane.

Figure 5-5.
The part after making the extruded cut. The sketch was on the top face of the boss, which is why a positive draft angle results in the bottom of the cutout being larger than the top. Note: The part is shown sliced through the middle for illustration.

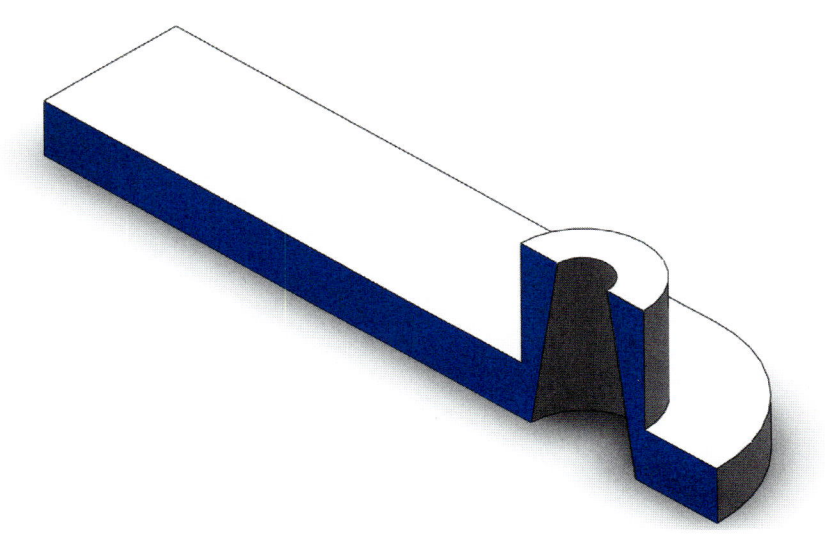

Chapter 5   Secondary Sketches and Reference Geometry

Figure 5-6.
A cutout (hole) will be added to one leg of this U-shaped part.

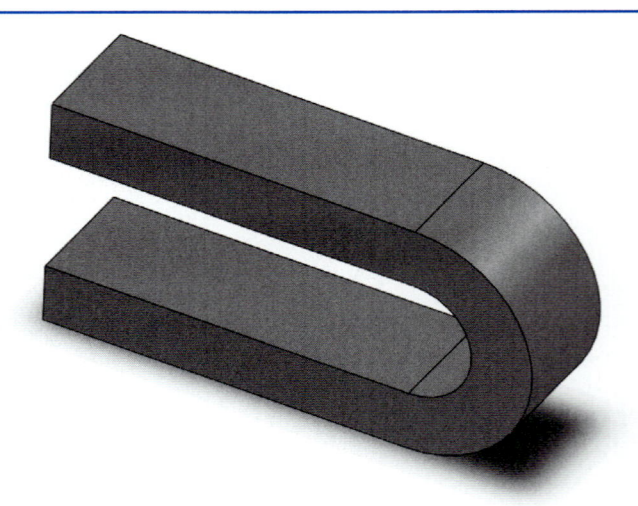

2. Draw a construction line from the midpoint of the short, left-hand edge. If the relation does not already exist, add a perpendicular relation to make the construction line perpendicular to the edge. Dimension the line as shown in **Figure 5-7.**
3. Draw a circle with its center at the endpoint of the construction line. This centers the circle in the local Y direction and constrains it coincident with the end of the line. Dimension the circle as shown in **Figure 5-7.**
4. Exit the sketch to return to part mode. Then, pick the **Extruded Cut** button in the **Features** tab of the **Command Manager**. Select the circle as the sketch to extrude.
5. In the **Extruded Cut Property Manager**, select Up To Next from the **End Condition** drop-down list. See **Figure 5-8.**
6. Pick the green check mark button to create the extrusion. The updated part is shown in **Figure 5-9.** Notice how the cutout (hole) does not pass through both legs of the part. You may want to use the **Rotate** tool to rotate the view and better see the feature.

Figure 5-7.
Sketching the circle that will be extruded to create the cutout.

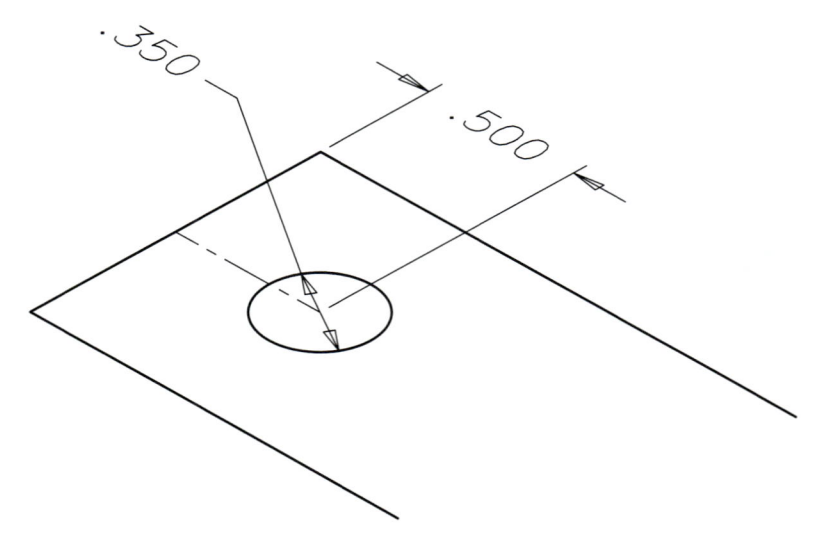

Learning SolidWorks 2009

Figure 5-8.
The Up To Next option is used for extruding the sketch to create a cutout (hole) in one leg only.

Figure 5-9.
The extrusion is "cut out" from one leg only.

Start Condition Extrusion Options

The **Start Condition** options available in the **From** rollout in the **Extrude Property Manager** allow you to start the extrusion from a plane other than the sketch plane. In the next example, you will use the start and end condition extrusion options to create an extruded feature in an existing part.

Open Example_05_03.sldprt. This part is similar to the U-shaped part with which you have been working. However, one leg has a small lip projecting to the interior of the part. See **Figure 5-10.** In this example, you will add a pin to the leg that extends only as far as the lip. The Up To Surface extrude option allows you to do this. The circle

Chapter 5 Secondary Sketches and Reference Geometry

Figure 5-10.
An extrusion that extends to the same plane as the lip will be added to this part.

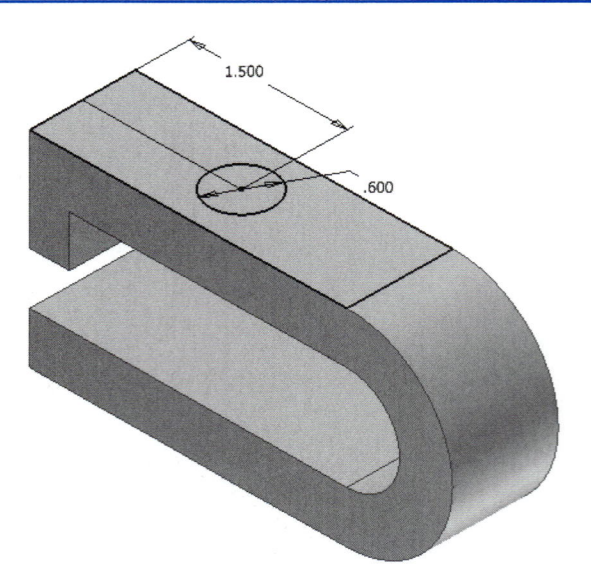

sketch that you will extrude is already drawn and is located on the top surface of the part. You will select a different plane from which to extrude the sketch by using the Surface/Face/Plane option in the **Start Condition** drop-down list in the **Extrude Property Manager**. The options in this drop-down list allow you to start the extrusion from a specified plane. You can specify the start condition as a face, reference plane, vertex, or as an offset distance from the sketch plane. The start surface can be either planar or curved. These options provide a number of ways to define the location where the extrusion starts. Proceed as follows.

1. Pick the **Extruded Boss/Base** button in the **Features** tab of the **Command Manager** and select the circle as the sketch to extrude.
2. In the **Extrude Property Manager**, select Up To Surface as the end condition. Pick the **Reverse Direction** button to change the direction of the extrusion, if needed.
3. With the **Face/Plane** box active, pick the bottom of the lip feature. The color of this face has been changed to blue in the file to help you select the correct face. Rotate the view as needed to better see the face.
4. Once you pick the face, it is highlighted in purple and its name is displayed in the **Face/Plane** box. The face is treated as an infinite plane and does not have to intersect the path of the extrusion.
5. In the **Start Condition** drop-down list, select Surface/Face/Plane as the start condition.
6. With the **Select A Surface/Face/Plane** box active, pick the interior surface underneath the top surface. The color of this face has been changed to red in the file to help you select the correct face. Rotate the view as needed. Once you pick the face, it is highlighted in green and its name is displayed in the **Select A Surface/Face/Plane** box.
7. Pick the green check mark button in the **Extrude Property Manager** to create the new feature. See **Figure 5-11**.

PRACTICE 5-1

Complete the practice problem on the student website.
www.g-wlearning.com/CAD

Figure 5-11.
The extrusion is added to the part. Notice how it extends to the same plane as the lip.

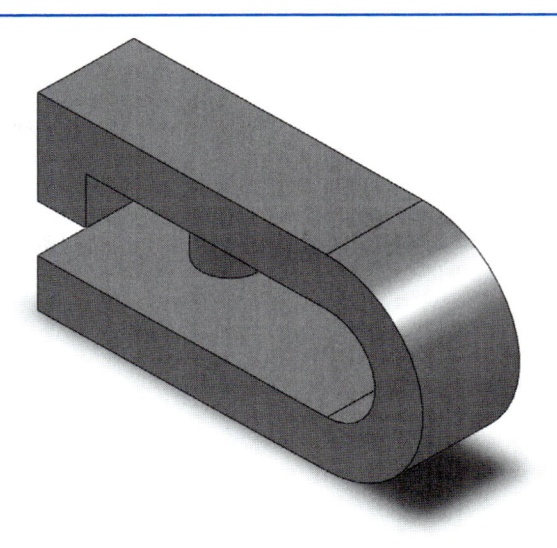

Converting Geometry and Projecting It to the Sketch Plane

Open the file **Example_05_04.sldprt**. **Figure 5-12A** shows the part as a solid in the isometric view. The curved surface of the part has been changed to blue. **Figure 5-12B** shows the same part in the front view as a wireframe. The line on the right side of the wireframe represents the extent of the curved surface. This type of line (curve) is called a *silhouette curve,* but, in reality, there is no edge there. The line is displayed

Figure 5-12.
A—An isometric view of the part. Face A indicated here is used as the sketch plane. B—The front view of the part. The silhouette curve representing the curved face will be projected onto the sketch plane.

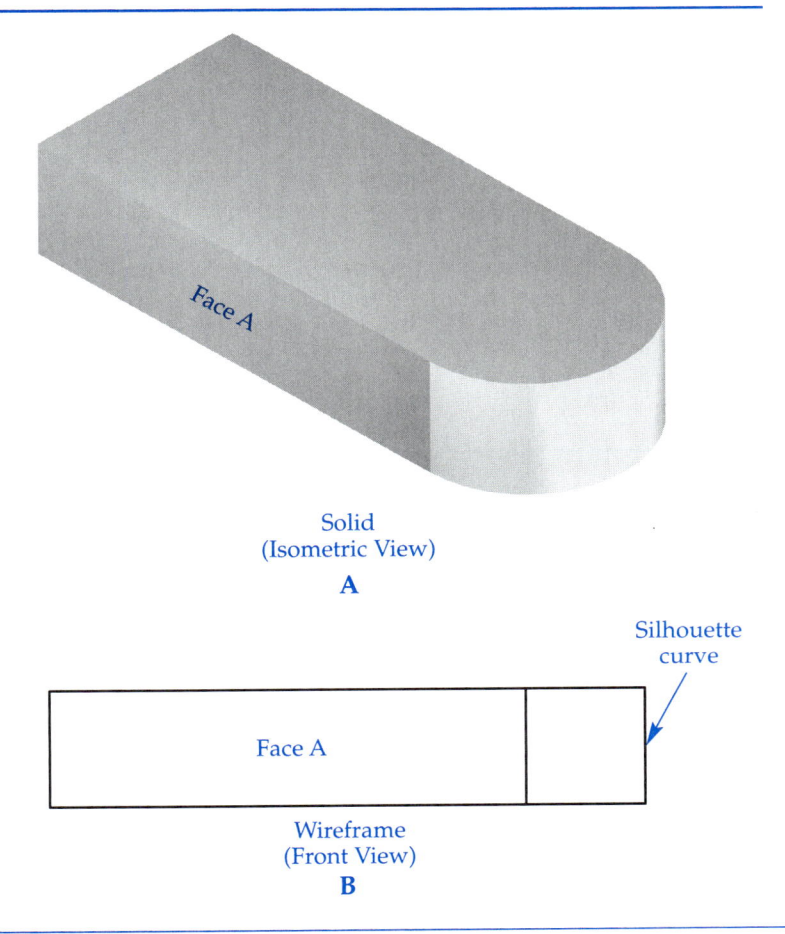

Solid
(Isometric View)
A

Silhouette curve

Wireframe
(Front View)
B

Chapter 5 Secondary Sketches and Reference Geometry

to make the part "look right." The edges of the part can be used to define a sketch, but a special technique is necessary to use a silhouette curve. A silhouette curve must be projected onto the sketch plane. The **Convert Entities** tool is used to do this.

Now, you will construct a slot through the curved end of this part.

1. Pick the **Sketch** button in the **Sketch** tab of the **Command Manager**. Then, select face A as the sketch plane. Face A is indicated in **Figure 5-12**.
2. Select the vertical line that represents the end of the curved face. See **Figure 5-13**. Be sure not to select the entire curved face.
3. Pick the **Convert Entities** button in the **Sketch** tab of the **Command Manager** to project the selected silhouette curve onto the sketch plane.
4. Sketch two construction circles, as shown in **Figure 5-14**. Apply tangent relations to constrain the large circle tangent to the top and bottom edges of the part. Apply a concentric relation between the small circle and the large circle. Dimension the small circle's diameter to a value of .2".
5. Sketch the three lines forming the profile of the slot. Apply a perpendicular relation between each long line and the projected line. Apply a tangent relation between each long line and the small circle. Use a dimension to constrain the location of the short line relative to the left edge of the part, as shown in **Figure 5-14**.
6. Exit the sketch to return to part mode.
7. Pick the **Extruded Cut** button in the **Features** tab of the **Command Manager**. Using the **Selected Contours** box in the **Selected Contours** rollout, select one of the edges defining the rectangular area formed by the projected line and the three lines you just constructed. As an alternative, you can select the two internal areas within the rectangular boundary to create the intended slot.

Figure 5-13.
Projecting the silhouette curve onto the sketch plane.

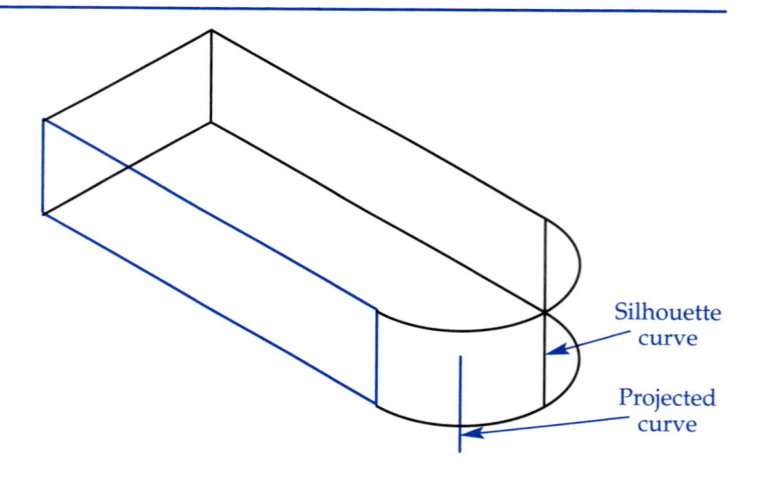

Figure 5-14.
Drawing the sketch that will be extruded into the cutout. Notice how two construction circles are used to center the cutout.

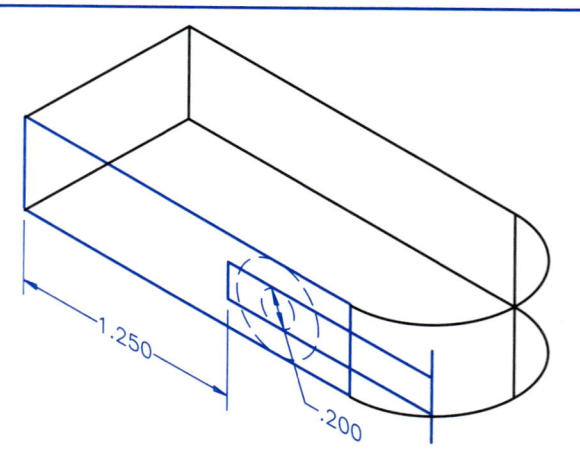

Figure 5-15.
The extrusion is subtracted from the part to create the cutout (slot).

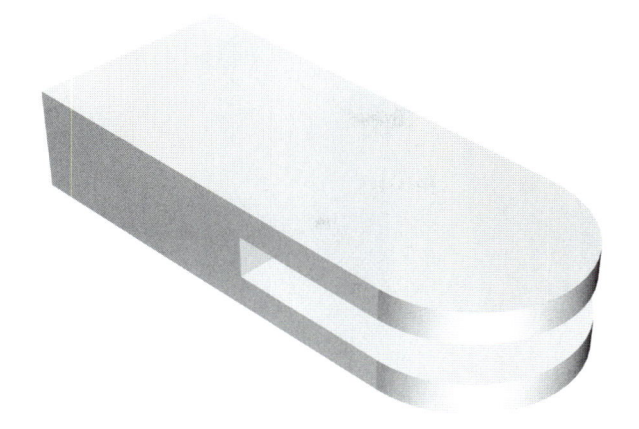

8. Select Through All as the end condition in the **Extrude Property Manager**. Then, pick the green check mark button to extrude the sketch and remove its volume from the part. See **Figure 5-15.**

Default Planes and Mid Plane Construction

As you saw in the previous section, the planar faces of the part can be used to define sketch planes. In addition, you can use the default planes to define the sketch plane. The *default planes* are construction planes that can be used to help in creating sketches and features. There are three default planes in every SolidWorks part file—front, top, and right. These planes correspond to the three principal drawing views. By default, the visibility of the default planes is turned off, but the planes are listed in the **Feature Manager** design tree.

In this section, you will use one of the default planes to construct the part shown in **Figure 5-16.** Only one plane will be used. Start a new part file and set the units to IPS (inches, pounds, seconds). Display the isometric view. Right-click on Front Plane in the design tree to display the shortcut toolbar and select the **Show** option. The front plane is now visible in the graphics window and the icon next to the plane in the design tree has been shaded.

When the front plane's name is selected in the design tree, the plane is highlighted in the graphics window. What you have selected is an object representing an infinite plane; the highlighted edges are not true "edges."

You can move the plane around in the graphics window. The plane can even be resized. To move the plane, select an edge of the plane; the move cursor is displayed. Pick and drag the plane to a new position. You can resize the plane by moving the cursor to any of the spheres at the corners and sides of the plane. This may help if the plane is displayed inside of a shaded part and, therefore, is not visible. You can also resize a plane using the **Autosize** option. This automatically adjusts the size of the plane based on any existing part geometry. To use this option, right-click on the plane in the graphics window or its name in the design tree. Then, select the **Autosize** option in the shortcut menu. Remember, since the plane is infinite, changing the size or location has no effect on the use of the plane, just its display.

CAUTION
When moving a plane in an isometric view, it may appear as if you are changing the elevation (local Z value) of the plane. However, you are not.

Chapter 5   Secondary Sketches and Reference Geometry

Figure 5-16.
This part is created using a single plane (the default front plane).

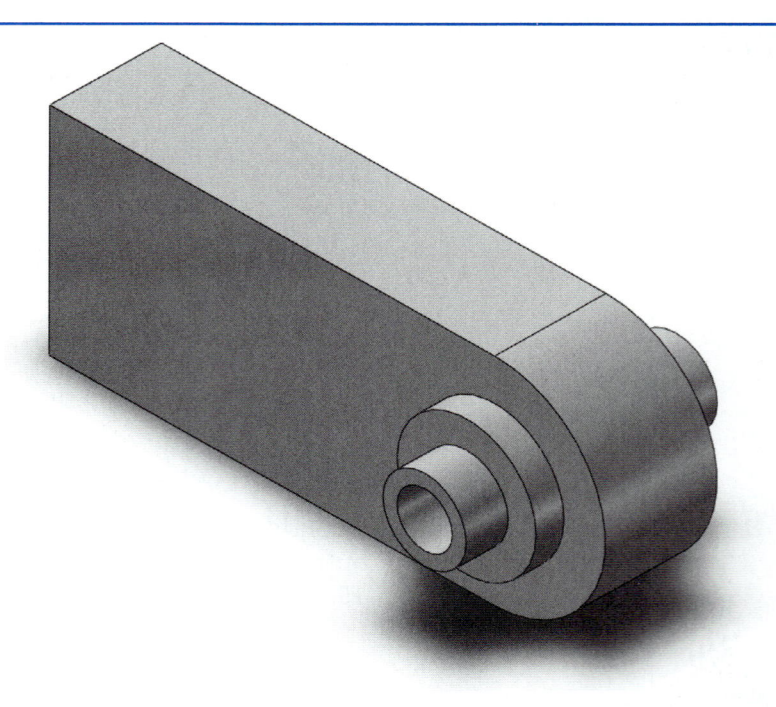

Turning on the visibility of the origin can also be useful. The origin represents the origin of the coordinate system, which is the intersection of the front, top, and right planes. The origin is fixed; it does not move when different sketch planes are active. When its visibility is turned on, the origin is represented by a red icon (in a sketch) or a blue icon (in a part). The icon is made up of a set of XY axes. The intersection of the axes represents the origin point. To turn the visibility of the origin on or off, right-click on Origin in the design tree. Then, select **Shows origin** or **Hides origin** in the shortcut toolbar.

To draw the part shown in **Figure 5-16,** continue as follows.
1. Begin a sketch on the front plane.
2. Sketch a circle centered on the origin. This ensures the center of the circle is at the coordinate system origin for future sketches.
3. Dimension the circle diameter to 2″.
4. Construct the three straight lines and place the two dimensions shown in **Figure 5-17** (only one of the two dimensions is required; determine which one and apply it). Apply the appropriate relations. You can trim the inside portion of the circle, as shown in the figure, but this is not necessary.
5. Exit the sketch to return to part mode. Display the isometric view, if it is not already displayed.

Figure 5-17.
Creating the first sketch to be extruded.

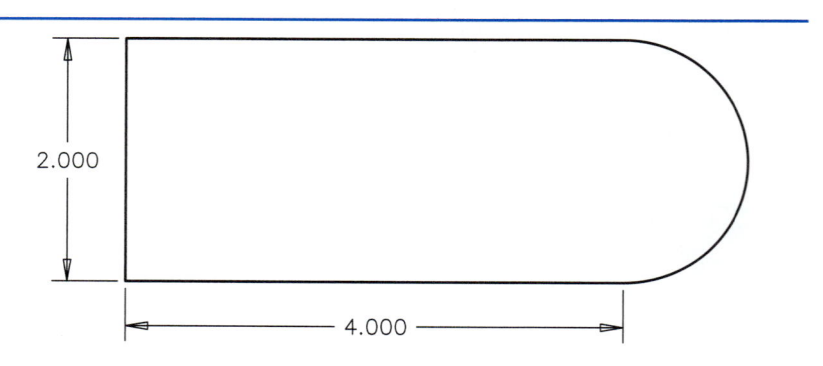

2.000

4.000

96 Learning SolidWorks 2009

6. Pick the **Extruded Boss/Base** button in the **Features** tab of the **Command Manager**. If you did not trim the circle in the sketch, select the appropriate contours to extrude in the sketch. In the **Extrude Property Manager**, select Mid Plane from the **End Condition** drop-down list and set the distance to 1". Notice that the preview in the graphics window shows the extrusion equally divided about the front plane. Pick the green check mark button to create the extrusion.
7. Pick the **Sketch** button in the **Sketch** tab of the **Command Manager**. Select the front plane as the sketch plane; pick an edge. This is why you turned on the visibility of the front plane. Otherwise, you could right-click on the name of the plane in the design tree and select **Sketch** from the shortcut toolbar. You can also pick the **Sketch** button in the **Sketch** tab of the **Command Manager** and then select the plane in the flyout **Feature Manager** design tree.

The sketch plane passes through the part. By using the front plane and the Mid Plane extrusion option, you can easily create the entire part. Continue creating the part as follows.

8. Using the **Circle** tool, draw a center-based circle with the center at the origin.
9. Dimension the diameter and edit the value to 1.25".
10. Exit the sketch to return to part mode. Pick the **Extruded Boss/Base** button in the **Features** tab of the **Command Manager**.
11. In the **Extrude Property Manager**, check the **Merge result** check box. Also, select Mid Plane from the **End Condition** drop-down list and set the distance to 1.50". Pick the green check mark button to create the extrusion.
12. Using the same procedure, sketch a .75" diameter circle and extrude it 2.25". Make sure the Mid Plane end condition is selected.
13. Sketch a .50" diameter circle and use the **Extruded Cut** tool and Mid Plane end condition to make a cutout all the way through the part.

The part is complete and should look like **Figure 5-16**. To turn off the visibility of the front plane, right-click on it in the graphics window or on its name in the design tree. Then, select **Hide** in the shortcut toolbar.

Open the file Example_05_05.sldprt. This is a revolved part to which you will add a cutout (hole) through one side of the outer shell, as shown in **Figure 5-18**. You will create a sketch on one of the default planes and use the Surface/Face/Plane and Up To Surface extrusion options to construct the new cutout feature.

Right-click on Front Plane in the design tree and select **Show** in the shortcut toolbar. Pick the **Sketch** button in the **Sketch** tab of the **Command Manager**. Then, pick the front plane as the sketch plane and continue as follows.

Figure 5-18.
The cutout (hole) shown here will be added to the outer shell of this part.

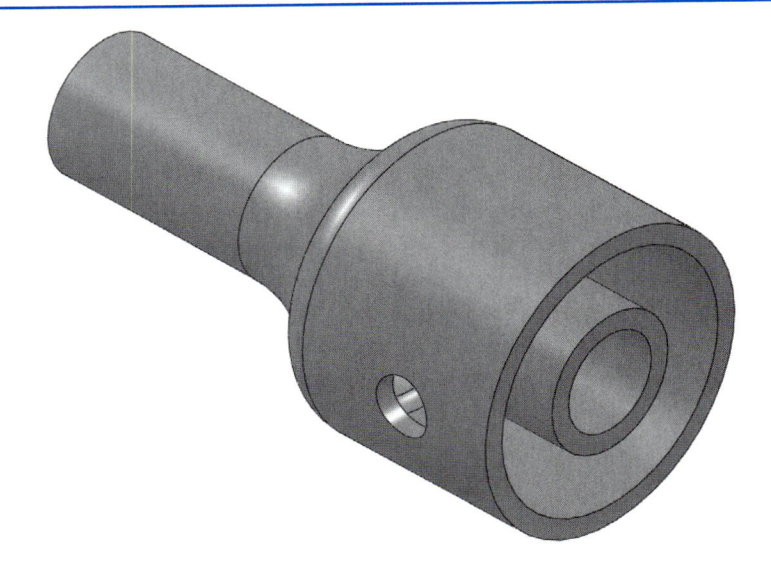

1. Select the edge of the large cylinder and then pick the **Convert Entities** button in the **Sketch** tab of the **Command Manager**. This will project the edge of the cylinder as a line onto the sketch plane. Select this new line and check the **For construction** check box in the **Line Properties Property Manager**.
2. Pick the **Centerline** button in the **Line** drop-down list on the **Sketch** tab of the **Command Manager**. Then, pick on the origin in the graphics window and draw a line along the X axis.
3. Now, draw a circle. Dimension it as shown in **Figure 5-19**.
4. Apply a coincident relation between the center of the circle and the X axis centerline, if it does not already exist. Exit the sketch to return to part mode.
5. Pick the **Extruded Cut** button in the **Features** tab of the **Command Manager**.
6. Select the sketch of the circle as the sketch to extrude.
7. In the **Extrude Property Manager**, select Surface/Face/Plane from the **Start Condition** drop-down list.

The Surface/Face/Plane option is used to pick a plane or face to define the start of the extrusion. The extruded feature does not have to touch the plane on which you created the sketch. Once you select this option, you will need to select the start plane or face. See **Figure 5-20**. Continue as follows.

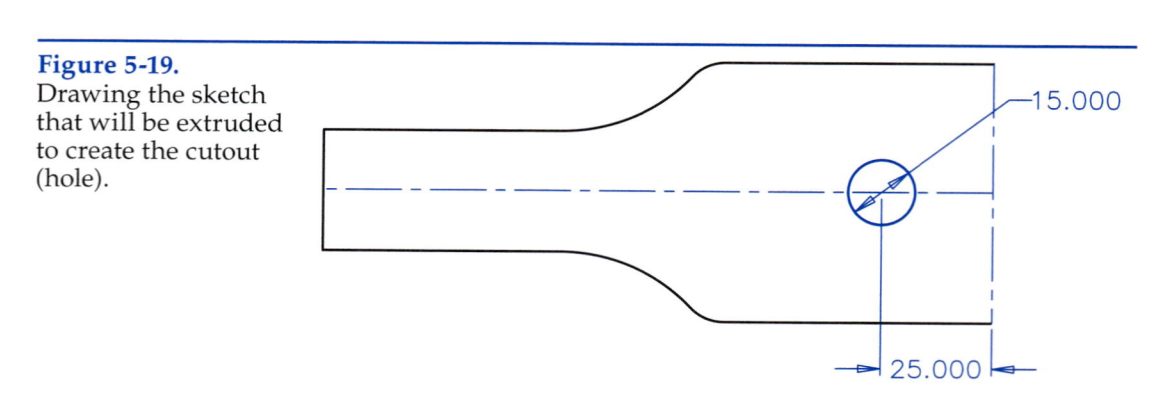

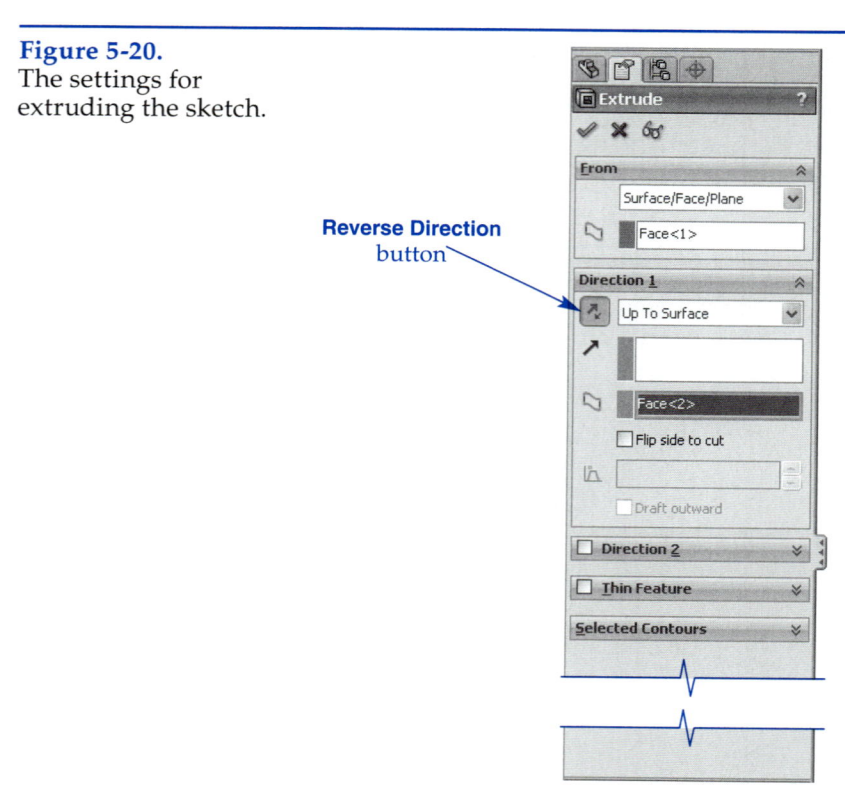

Figure 5-19.
Drawing the sketch that will be extruded to create the cutout (hole).

15.000

25.000

Figure 5-20.
The settings for extruding the sketch.

Reverse Direction button

98

Learning SolidWorks 2009

8. Pick the inside surface of the outer shell of the part.
9. In the **End Condition** drop-down list, pick Up To Surface. Select the outside surface of the outer shell of the part. If needed, pick the **Reverse Direction** button next to the **End Condition** drop-down list to change the direction of the extrusion.
10. Pick the green check mark button to extrude the sketch.

The part is completed and should look like **Figure 5-18.**

PRACTICE 5-2
Complete the practice problem on the student website.
www.g-wlearning.com/CAD

Using the Combine Tool

The **Combine** tool creates a solid of the volume that is an intersection of two or more solid bodies. The effects of the three options of this tool—**Add**, **Subtract**, and **Common**—are shown in **Figure 5-21.**

In this section, you will use the **Common** option of the **Combine** tool to create a part that would be difficult to create any other way. Open Example_05_06.sldprt. See **Figure 5-22.** The default front and right planes are visible. On each plane is a sketch. Continue as follows.

1. Using the **Extruded Boss/Base** tool, extrude the left-hand sketch 300" to the right. The distance can also be entered as 25′.
2. Using the **Extruded Boss/Base** tool, extrude the right-hand sketch. Set the distance to 25′.
3. Uncheck the **Merge result** button in the **Extrude Property Manager**. If needed, pick the **Reverse Direction** button so the preview shows the extrusion going into the existing part.
4. Pick the green check mark button to create the extrusion.

You now have two separate solid bodies that partially occupy the same space. SolidWorks has automatically added a new Solid Bodies folder to the design tree. Expand this folder to see each solid body. SolidWorks uses the name of the last feature that affected a body as its default name. If you select a body from the Solid

Figure 5-21.
A—A wireframe representation of two separate solid bodies. Using the **Combine** tool can result in one of three parts, depending on the option selected. B—**Add**. C—**Subtract**. D—**Common**.

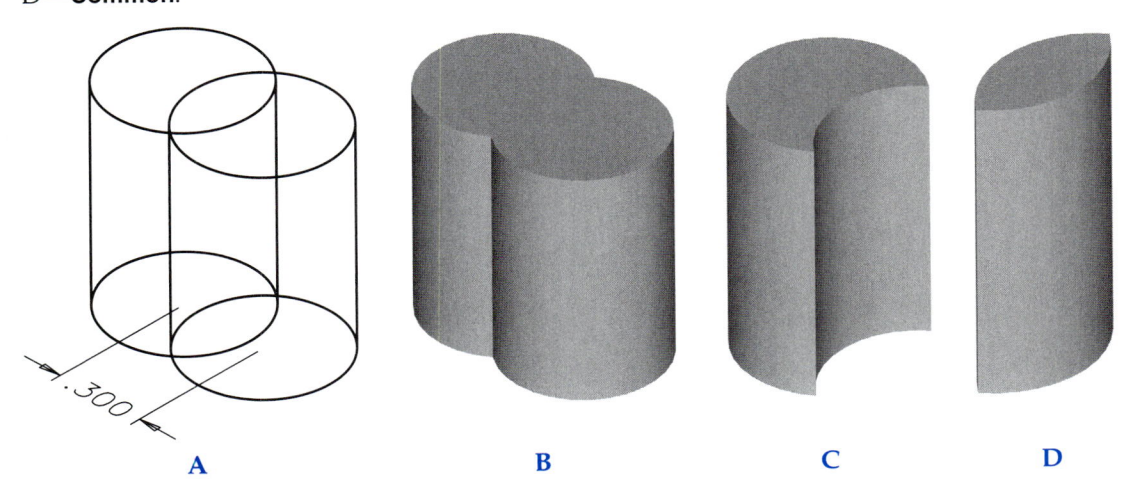

A   B   C   D

Chapter 5 Secondary Sketches and Reference Geometry

Figure 5-22.
These are two separate sketches that will be extruded into two separate bodies and then combined into a single body using the **Combine** tool.

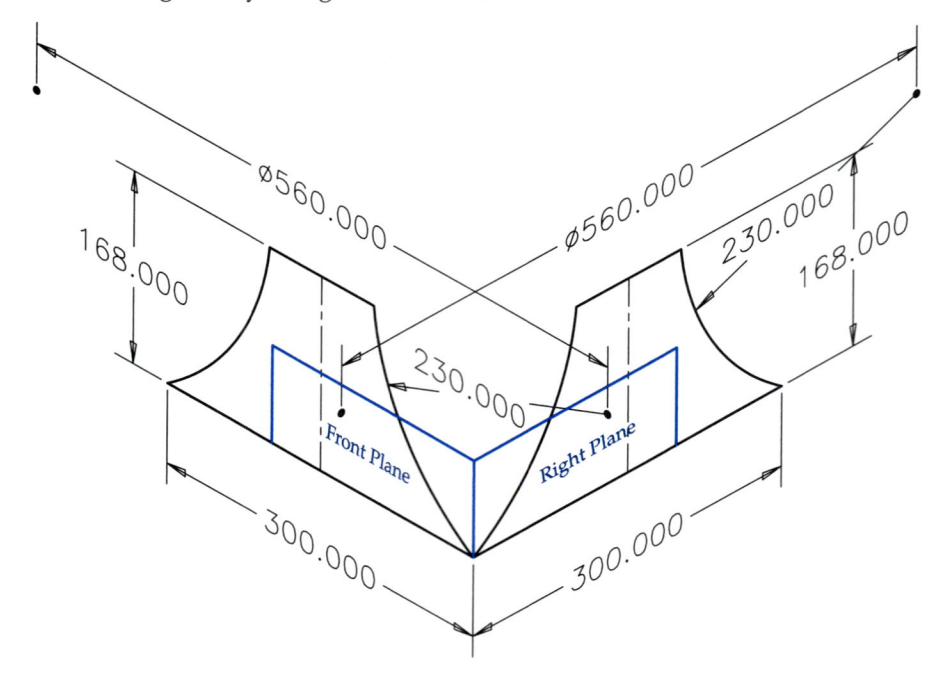

Bodies folder in the design tree, the body is highlighted in the graphics window.
   5. Using the [Ctrl] key, select both solid bodies from the design tree.
   6. Right-click and select **Combine** from the shortcut menu.
   7. In the **Combine Property Manager**, make sure both bodies are selected, and then choose **Common.**
   8. Pick the green check mark button to exit the **Combine Property Manager** and view the results.
   9. The result is the pagoda roof shown in **Figure 5-23**.

Figure 5-23.
This part is the result of extruding the sketches shown in Figure 5-22 and using the **Combine** tool to create a single body from the shared volume of the two extrusions.

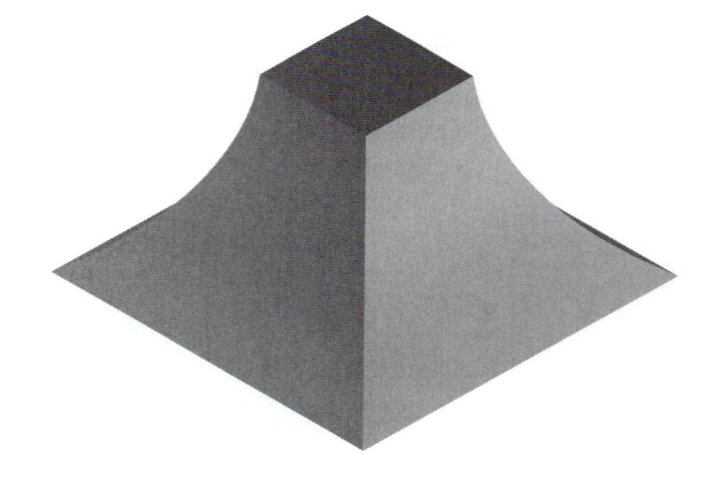

Creating and Using Reference Geometry

Reference geometry is used for construction purposes. The types of reference geometry that can be created in SolidWorks include planes, axes, points, and coordinate systems. This chapter discusses reference planes, axes, and points.

A *reference plane* is used when it is necessary to establish a working plane other than one of the default planes or an existing part surface. Reference planes are used to create sketches and features and can be used for other design purposes.

A *reference axis* is a fixed construction line. You cannot sketch on a reference axis as you can a plane. However, reference axes can be used in creating features or reference planes, and in applying mates.

A *reference point* is a fixed point. Reference points are used in the creation of features as well as other types of reference geometry.

You will encounter many uses for reference geometry throughout this book. This chapter focuses on the use of reference planes and presents related applications for reference axes and points.

Creating Reference Planes

Reference planes can be created from part faces, edges, axes, points, and the default planes. Reference planes are used to terminate extrusions, to provide angled and offset sketch planes, and to serve as references for dimensions and relations. The latter application is very useful for the assembly mates that you will use for assemblies in Chapter 11.

The **Plane** tool is used to create a reference plane. The basic procedure is to first activate the tool by selecting Plane from the **Reference Geometry** drop-down list, which is located in the **Features** tab of the **Command Manager**, and then pick some combination of reference entities. The position and orientation of the new plane depend on which reference entities you pick and how you pick them. Reference entities that can be selected include faces, edges, endpoints (vertices), existing planes, reference points, and reference axes. The next sections present several different options for creating reference planes.

Offset from an existing face or plane

A reference plane can be created that is offset a specific distance from a face or existing plane. This technique is often used when creating a feature attached to a cylinder. Typically, the required reference plane for creating the sketch can be created from a default plane or an existing part surface. Since it is impossible to move an existing plane, a new one is created a set distance away from the old plane. Now, sketching the required shape is possible.

For example, the part in **Figure 5-24A** is the existing part. The finished part is shown in **Figure 5-24B**. To create the new feature, you will offset the default right plane. Open Example_05_07.sldprt. Right-click on Right Plane in the design tree and select **Show** from the shortcut toolbar to display the plane. Then, continue as follows.

1. Pick Plane from the **Reference Geometry** drop-down list in the **Features** tab of the **Command Manager**. Then, pick the right plane in the graphics window. A preview of an offset plane should appear.
2. In the **Plane Property Manager**, enter a value of 100 mm in the **Offset Distance** text box. Then, press [Enter] or pick the green check mark button at the top of the **Plane Property Manager**.

Figure 5-24.
A—The original part.
B—A feature is added to the part.

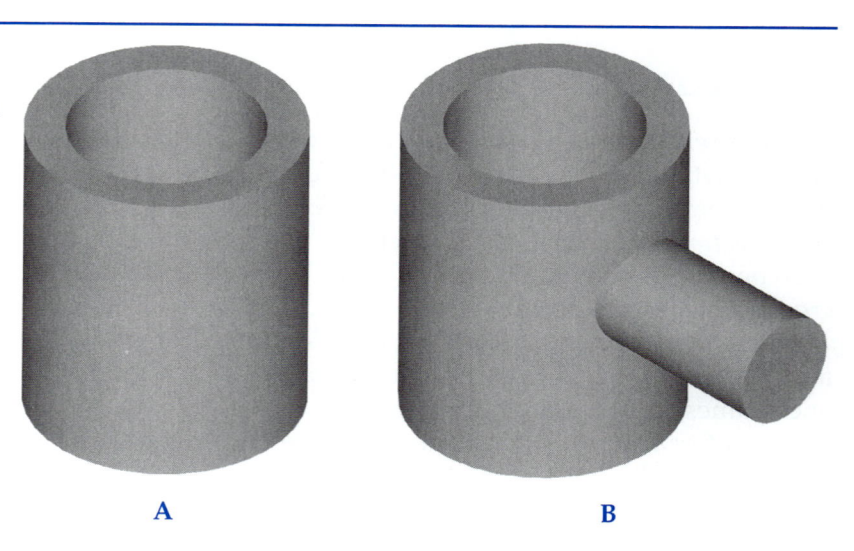

A   B

3. Pick the **Sketch** button in the **Sketch** tab of the **Command Manager**. Pick the new reference plane as the sketch plane.
4. Using the **Convert Entities** tool, project the top and bottom of the part onto the sketch plane. Change the two converted lines to construction geometry.
5. Draw a construction line between the midpoints of the two projected lines.
6. Draw a circle. Dimension the diameter and edit the value to 35 mm.
7. Apply a coincident relation between the center of the circle and the construction line you drew in step 5.
8. Add a dimension between the projected top edge and the center of the circle. Edit the dimension to a value of 40 mm. See **Figure 5-25**.
9. Exit the sketch and pick the **Extruded Boss/Base** button in the **Features** tab of the **Command Manager**.
10. Select the circle as the sketch to extrude.
11. In the **Extrude Property Manager**, check the **Merge result** check box and select Up To Surface as the end condition. Then, pick the outside surface of the cylinder.
12. Pick the green check mark button to create the extrusion. The new feature is added to the part.

Figure 5-25.
Creating the sketch that will be extruded into the feature shown in Figure 5-24B.

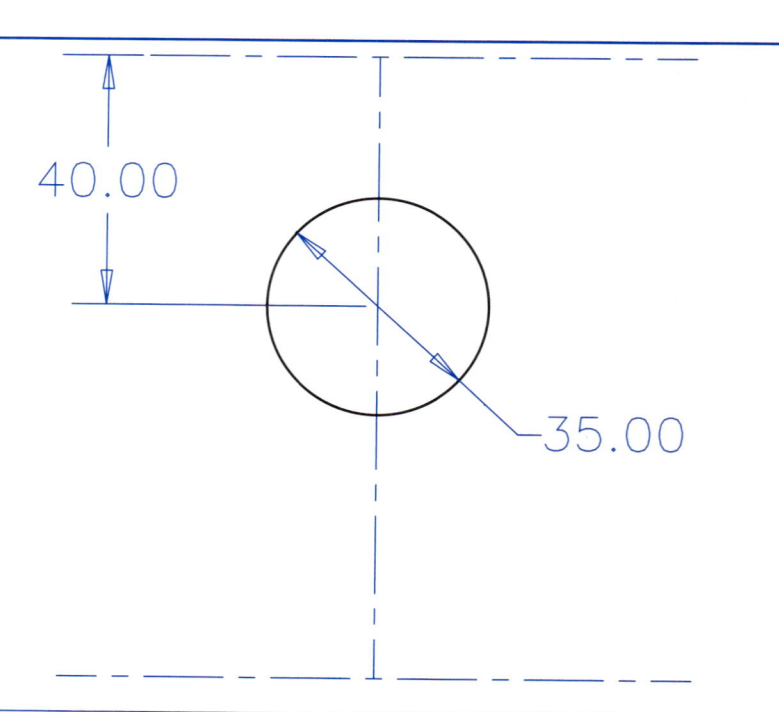

40.00

35.00

102   Learning SolidWorks 2009

Angled from a face or existing plane

A reference plane can be created at an angle to a face or existing plane. The new plane will pass through an edge on the part, an axis, or a sketched line, depending on the reference entity selected. For example, look at the existing and finished parts in **Figure 5-26**. Notice how the added feature, the pin, is not extruded perpendicular to the face. In order to do this, a reference plane must be created at an angle to the face. Open Example_05_08.sldprt. Then, continue as follows.

1. Pick Plane from the **Reference Geometry** drop-down list in the **Features** tab of the **Command Manager**.
2. Pick face A as indicated in **Figure 5-26**.
3. Pick edge B as indicated in **Figure 5-26**. Do not pick an endpoint or the midpoint.
4. In the **Plane Property Manager**, enter an angle of 30° in the **At Angle** text box. The feature you are adding is angled 30° from perpendicular to the face. Then, press [Enter] or pick the green check mark button to create the new reference plane.
5. Pick the **Sketch** button in the **Sketch** tab of the **Command Manager**. Pick the new reference plane as the sketch plane.
6. Using the **Convert Entities** tool, project the four edges of face A onto the sketch plane. This can be done in one step by moving the cursor over the face until all four edges are highlighted, picking the face, and then picking the **Convert Entities** button in the **Sketch** tab of the **Command Manager**. Change the four converted lines to construction geometry.
7. Draw a construction line from the midpoint of the top projected line to the midpoint of the bottom projected line.
8. Draw a circle with its center at the midpoint of the construction line, as shown in **Figure 5-27**. Dimension the circle's diameter to 30 mm.
9. Exit the sketch and pick the **Extruded Boss/Base** button in the **Features** tab of the **Command Manager**.
10. Select the circle as the sketch to extrude. Also, check the **Merge result** check box in the **Extrude Property Manager**. Then, select Up To Surface as the end condition and select face A.
11. Pick the green check mark button to create the extrusion. The new feature is added to the part.

Figure 5-26.
A—The existing part. B—A feature is added to the part.

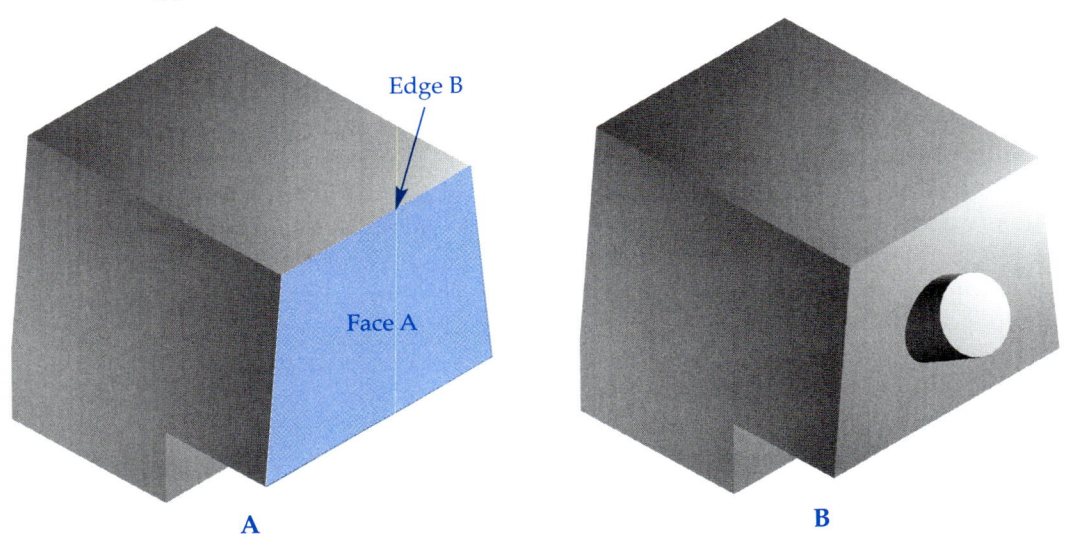

Figure 5-27.
Creating the sketch that will be extruded into the feature shown in Figure 5-26B.

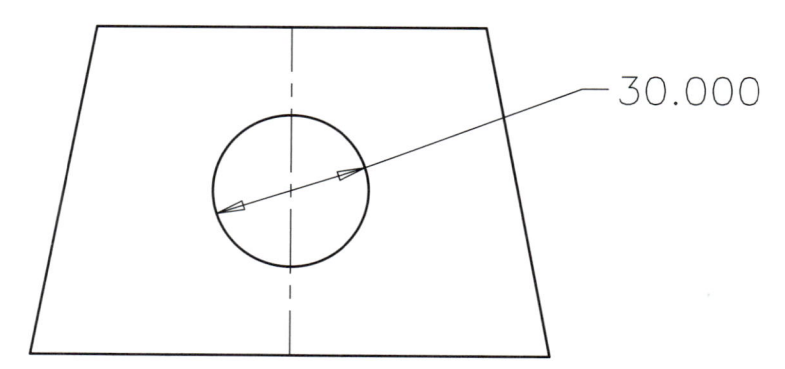

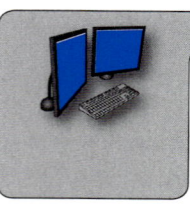

PROFESSIONAL TIP

If there is no edge on the part at the position where you want the reference plane to pass through, you can sketch a construction line on an existing plane or face. Then, select the construction line as the "edge" through which the new reference plane will pass.

PRACTICE 5-3

Complete the practice problem on the student website.
www.g-wlearning.com/CAD

Through lines/points

The Through Lines/Points option in the **Plane Property Manager** is used to create a reference plane using a sketch line, axis, or edge, and a point. You can also select three points as reference entities to create a reference plane using this option. For example, you may have two cylinders and need to create a new reference plane that passes through the center of each cylinder. To create the plane, we will use a reference axis through the center of one cylinder and a reference point at the center of the other cylinder's end face as the reference entities.

First, to create a reference axis, select Axis from the **Reference Geometry** drop-down list in the **Features** tab of the **Command Manager**. Then, pick one of the two cylinders. Do not pick the end face. Then, pick the green check mark button at the top of the **Axis Property Manager**. This creates the reference axis. A reference axis is displayed as a line consisting of a series of long and thin dashes similar to a construction line.

Next, select Point from the **Reference Geometry** drop-down list in the **Features** tab of the **Command Manager**. Place a point at the center of either end face on the other cylinder.

Now, using the **Plane** tool, select the axis and the point in any order. A reference plane is created that passes through the center of each cylinder. See **Figure 5-28**.

A reference plane can also be defined by three points that do not lie on the same line. By definition, any two points define a line. Therefore, a plane can also be defined by an edge (line) and a point that is not on that edge.

Another way to create a work plane is to select two edges whose endpoints lie in the same plane. Using the **Plane** tool, select an edge and a point, or two edges. The order of selection is not important. Note that selecting an edge and a point is the same as selecting a reference axis and a point, as discussed in the previous example.

Figure 5-28.
Creating a reference plane through the centers of two cylinders.

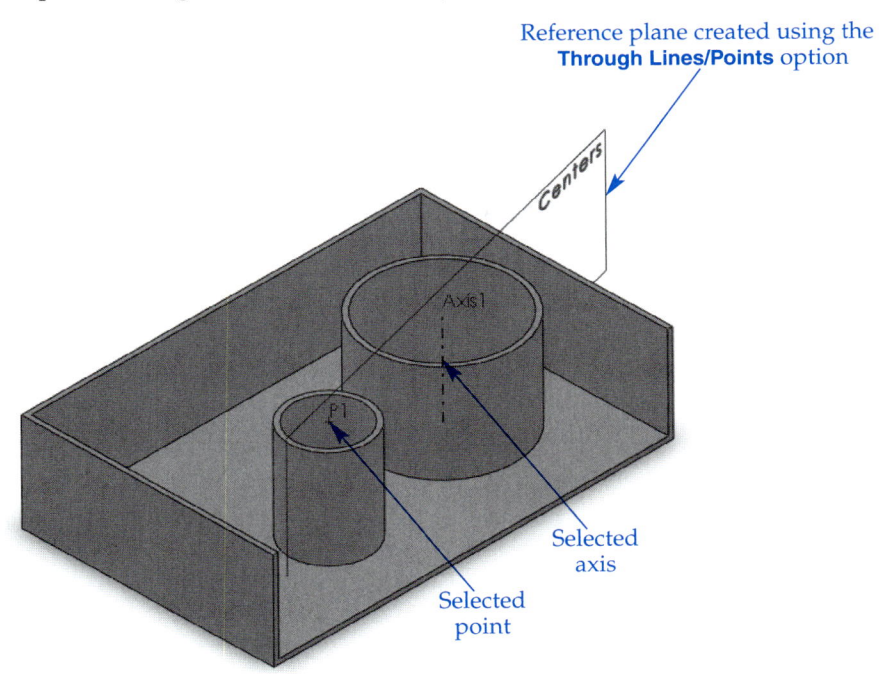

Parallel at a point

You can create a reference plane parallel to a planar face or existing plane at a specified point using the Parallel Plane at Point option. To use this option, access the **Plane** tool. Pick the **Parallel Plane at Point** button in the **Plane Property Manager** and select the face or plane. Then, select a point, such as an endpoint or midpoint of an edge. The new reference plane is created parallel to the selected face or plane and through the selected point.

Normal to a curve

To create a reference plane at a point on, and normal to, a curve, use the Normal to Curve option. After selecting this option in the **Plane Property Manager**, select the curve and pick a point along that curve at which you want the reference plane.

You can use this method to create a plane at a specific point along a spline or a radius. First, create a reference point on the curve at the desired location. Then, use the **Plane** tool to create a plane normal to the curve at the point.

On surface

You can create a reference plane on a curved or angular surface using the On Surface option. After selecting this option in the **Plane Property Manager**, select the required reference entities. For example, you can create a reference plane that is tangent to the curved surface of a cylinder by selecting the surface and a point on the surface. First, sketch a point that locates the endpoint of a line from the center of the cylinder to the circumference (at the intended point of tangency). See **Figure 5-29.** Then, using the **Plane** tool, select the curved surface and the sketch point.

Chapter 5   Secondary Sketches and Reference Geometry

Figure 5-29.
Creating a reference plane tangent to a cylinder at a specific point.

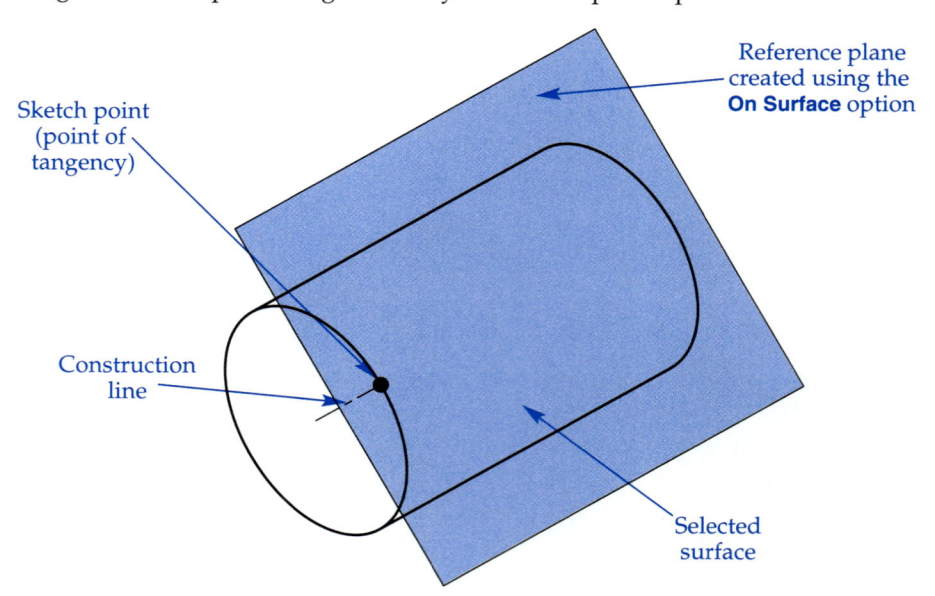

Chapter Test

Answer the following questions on a separate sheet of paper or complete the electronic chapter test on the student website.
www.g-wlearning.com/CAD

1. Which faces of a part can be used as sketch planes?
2. How can you change the color of a face?
3. Suppose you have created an extrusion that has the default name Extrusion1. How can you change the name to Pin, Locking?
4. Explain the Blind end condition option of the **Extruded Boss/Base** tool.
5. Explain the Through All end condition option of the **Extruded Boss/Base** tool.
6. Explain the Up To Next end condition option of the **Extruded Boss/Base** tool.
7. Explain the Up To Surface end condition option of the **Extruded Boss/Base** tool.
8. Explain the Mid Plane end condition option of the **Extruded Boss/Base** tool.
9. Explain the Surface/Face/Plane start condition option for extruded features.
10. Define *silhouette curve*.
11. How do you project a silhouette curve onto the current sketch plane?
12. How many default planes are there? Name them.
13. Explain how to turn on the visibility of a default plane.
14. Explain the difference between the **Add**, **Subtract**, and **Common** options of the **Combine** tool.
15. Define *reference plane*.
16. Which tool is used to create a reference plane?
17. Name four types of reference entities that can be used, in part, to define a new reference plane.
18. Give three applications where reference planes may be used.
19. Define *reference axis*.
20. Suppose you have drawn two cylinders. How can you create a sketch on a plane that passes through the center of each cylinder?

Chapter Exercises

Complete the chapter exercises on the student website.
www.g-wlearning.com/CAD

Exercise Boss.
5-1 Complete the exercise on the student website.

Exercise Bracket.
5-2 Complete the exercise on the student website.

Exercise Cutouts.
5-3 Complete the exercise on the student website.

Exercise Tapered Part.
5-4 Complete the exercise on the student website.

Exercise Mirror Part.
5-5 Complete the exercise on the student website.

Exercise Yoke.
5-6 Complete the exercise on the student website.

Exercise Brace.
5-7 Complete the exercise on the student website.

Chapter 5 Secondary Sketches and Reference Geometry

The **Hole Wizard** tool is used to create standard size holes. Holes created with this tool are placed features. This part includes two counterbored holes and two tapped holes.

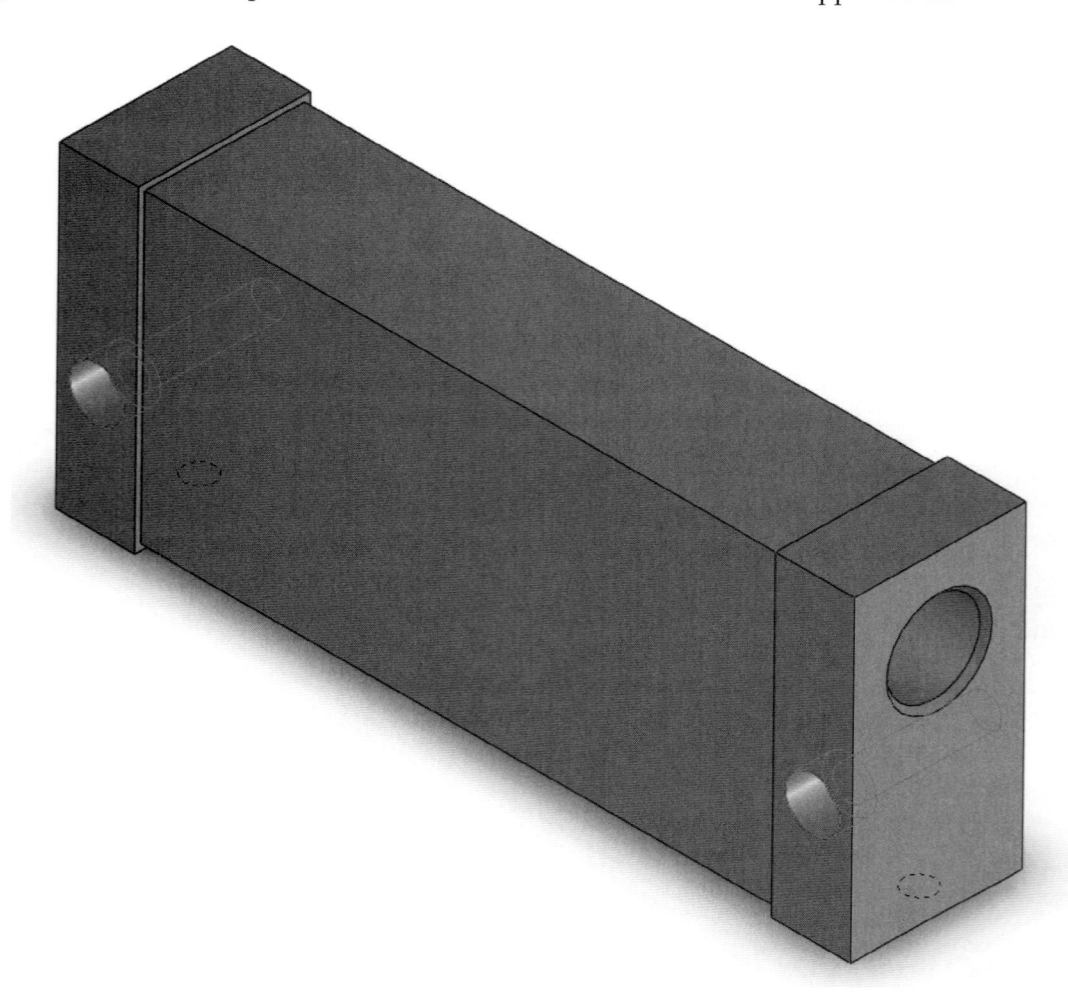

Chapter 6
Adding Features

Objectives

After completing this chapter, you will be able to:

- Add holes to a part.
- Add threads to a part.
- Fillet edges on a part.
- Chamfer edges on a part.
- Create rectangular and circular patterns.
- Mirror features.

Adding Nonsketch Features to the Part

There are several features that can be added to a part without drawing a sketch profile. The tools for creating most of these features are found in the **Features** tab of the **Command Manager**. For some, you will need to use a sketch plane. For the **Mirror** tool, selection of a reference plane or planar surface is required. However, for other tools, like the **Fillet** tool, you need only select the edge(s) to be modified. In this chapter, seven of these feature tools are discussed—**Hole Wizard**, **Thread**, **Fillet**, **Chamfer**, **Mirror**, **Linear Pattern**, and **Circular Pattern**. Other feature tools are discussed in the next chapter.

Hole Wizard Tool

So far, you have created holes as *cutouts* by extrude-cutting circles. However, the **Hole Wizard** tool has several advantages over extruded circles. Refer to **Figure 6-1** and the list below.

- The holes can be drilled, counterbored, or countersunk in a single operation.
- Counterbores and countersinks can be automatically sized for standard fasteners.
- Thread sizes and specifications can be easily applied.
- Cosmetic threads can be displayed in the shaded image.

Figure 6-1.
These holes were created using the **Hole Wizard** tool. When done in this manner, threads appear correctly in the part drawing and tables can be created.

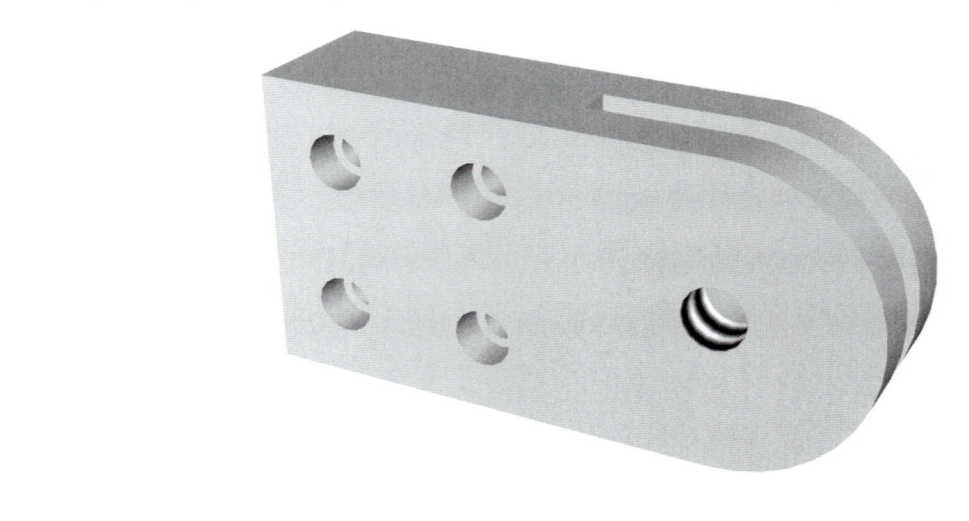

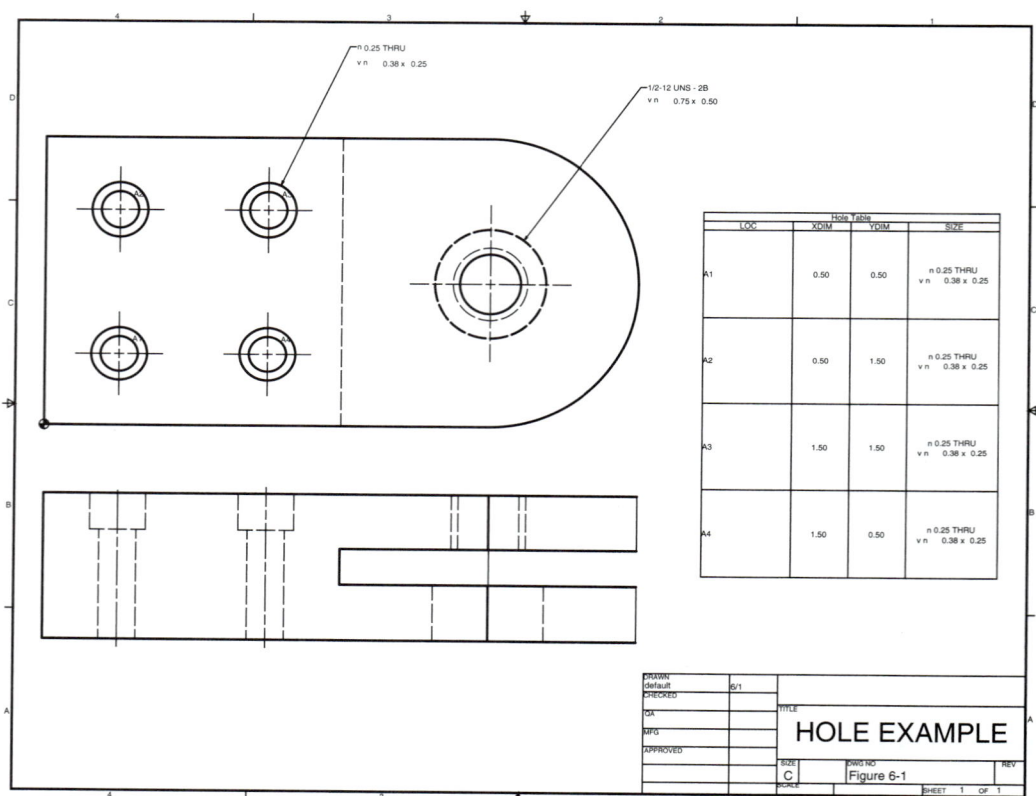

- Threaded holes will correctly display in the part drawings.
- Hole notes can be automatically applied to the part drawings.
- Hole tables can be created in the part drawings.

Open Example_06_01.sldprt. In the **Features** tab of the **Command Manager**, pick the **Hole Wizard** button. First, you must select a face on which to place the holes. Select the large front face. Next, display the **Positions** tab in the **Property Manager**. This tab is used to locate the hole centers. Pick two points on the selected face, then press the [Esc] key. Notice the shaded preview of the holes. With the **Positions** tab still displayed, right-click in the graphics window and select **Add relations...** from the shortcut menu.

Select both points and apply an "along Y" relation to them. This will keep them in a line parallel to the Y axis.

Next, dimension the hole centers as shown in **Figure 6-2** using the **Smart Dimension** tool in the **Sketch** tab of the **Command Manager**. When done dimensioning, pick the green check mark button in the **Dimension Property Manager** to close the panel. The **Positions** tab is again displayed in the **Property Manager**.

Pick the **Type** tab in the **Property Manager**. This is where you specify the type and size of the holes created in this session of the hole wizard. Refer to **Figure 6-3.** All of the holes created in one hole wizard session have the same size and characteristics.

Expand the **Hole Type** rollout and select the **Hole** button at the top of the rollout. This will create a simple hole. In the **Standard:** drop-down list, select ANSI Inch. In the **Type:** drop-down list, select Fractional Drill Sizes. Specify the diameter of the hole in the **Hole Specifications** rollout. Select 1/2 from the **Size:** drop-down list in the rollout. By selecting these options, you have specified the hole as a simple hole with a diameter of 1/2". This type of hole will be placed at each point you selected using the **Positions** tab. The two shaded previews reflect the settings.

By checking the **Show Custom Sizing** check box in the **Hole Specifications** rollout, you can set the angle of a pointed drill bit. This is set in the **Angle at Bottom** text box. For this example, use the default angle value.

Next, the end condition of the hole needs to be defined. The end condition specifies how the bottom of the hole will be created. There are six options in the **End Condition** drop-down list in the **Hole Specification** rollout—Blind, Through All, Up To Next, Up To Vertex, Up To Surface, and Offset From Surface. The Blind option is used to set a specific hole depth. The value is set by changing the dimension in the **Blind Hole Depth** text box in the rollout. For this example, select the Blind option and set the depth as .5".

Holes have a direction. The direction can be reversed or "flipped" by picking the **Reverse Direction** button next to the **End Condition** drop-down list. If the preview of the hole is "outside" of the part, SolidWorks will not be able to properly create the hole. Holes must be to the interior of a part.

Figure 6-2.
Locating the centers of two holes.

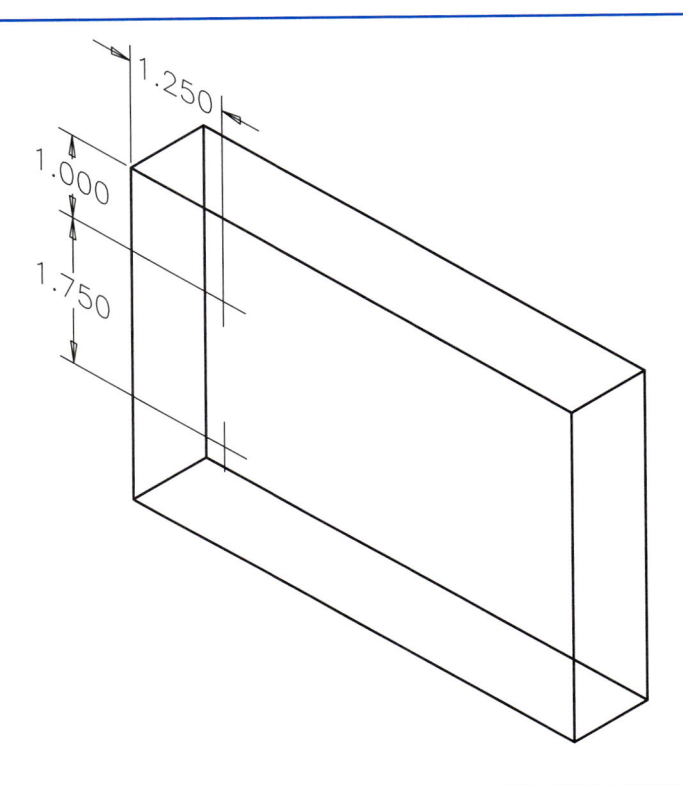

Figure 6-3.
The **Hole Specification Property Manager** is used to create holes.

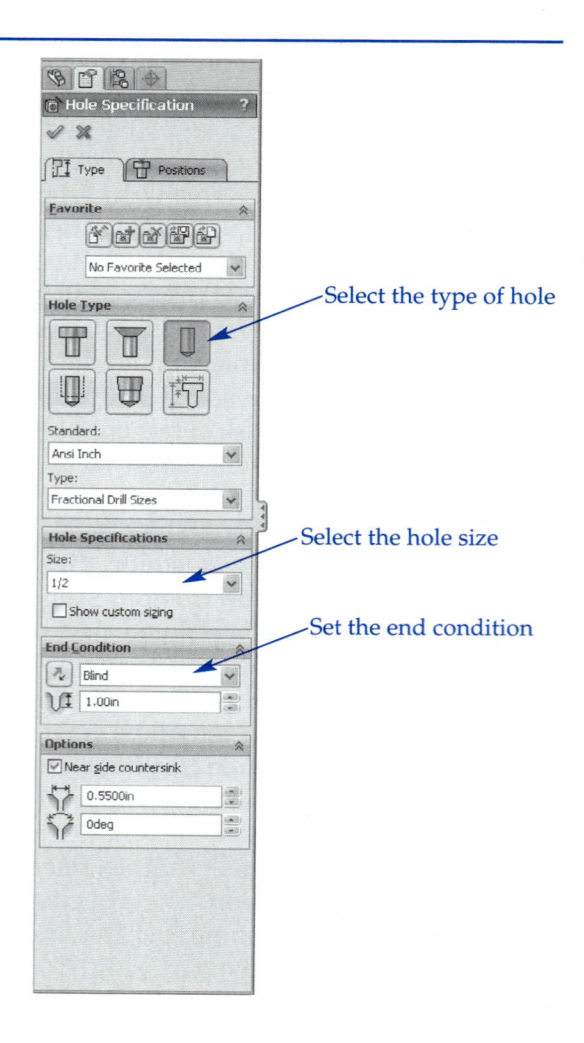

Now, pick the green check mark button in the **Property Manager** to create the two holes. Using the **Rotate** tool (**View>Modify>Rotate**), rotate the view to see the holes. Notice how they do not pass through the part. Change to a wireframe display with hidden lines visible. Then, rotate the view so you can see the side of the holes. Notice how the bottom is tapered according to the angle set in the **Hole Specifications** rollout.

Threaded Holes

Adding threads to the holes can be done when the holes are created or later by editing the feature. Display the isometric view of Example_06_01.sldprt and shade the view. Now, right-click on the hole feature in the design tree in the **Feature Manager**. Pick the **Edit Feature** button in the shortcut toolbar. The **Hole Specification Property Manager** is displayed.

In the **Hole Type** rollout, pick the **Tap** button to change the hole type to a threaded hole. Notice that a **Thread:** drop-down list and text box have appeared in the **End Condition** rollout. These are used to specify threads for the hole. Also in the **Hole Type** rollout, select ANSI Inch in the **Standard:** drop-down list and Tapped hole in the **Type:** drop-down list.

In the **Termination** drop-down list at the top of the **End Condition** rollout, select Through All. This changes the holes so they completely pass through the part. Next, select Through All from the **Thread:** drop-down list, if not already selected. This specifies that the hole is threaded all of the way through the part. When the Blind option is selected in the **Thread:** drop-down list, the text box displayed below the drop-down list is used to specify the depth of thread. This is done if the hole will not be threaded over its entire depth.

In the **Hole Specifications** rollout, select 1/2-20 from the **Size:** drop-down list. This will create a ⌀.5″ hole with fine threads.

In the **Options** rollout, you can choose to create the hole by using the tap drill diameter, showing a cosmetic thread, or by removing the thread. For this example, select the **Cosmetic thread** button. Also, check the **Thread class** check box and then select 1B from the drop-down list that appears next to the check box.

Finally, pick the green check mark button at the top of the **Hole Specification Property Manager** to update the feature. See **Figure 6-4.** Save the file.

PROFESSIONAL TIP

Cosmetic threads can be displayed as an image representing the thread. To do so, open the options/properties dialog box (**Tools**>**Options...**) and display the **Document Properties** tab. Then, select Detailing in the tree. In the **Display filter** area on the right-hand side of the tab, check the **Shaded cosmetic threads** check box. Then, close the dialog box. The cosmetic threads now appear as shown in **Figure 6-4.**

Pipe Thread Holes

The previous type of hole had standard threads. You can also create pipe threads. Edit the hole feature you created in Example_06_01.sldprt. To create pipe threads, pick the **Pipetap** button in the **Hole Type** rollout. Now, the only option in the **Type:** drop-down list is Tapered Pipe Tap.

Next, select the size of fastener from the **Size:** drop-down list in the **Hole Specifications** rollout. Select 1/2″ for the diameter. Also, in the **Options** rollout, check the **Cosmetic thread** check box. Finally, pick the green check mark button at the top of the **Property Manager** to create the pipe threads. Save the file.

Figure 6-4.
Threads are added to the existing holes.

Chapter 6   Adding Features

Clearance Holes

A clearance hole is large enough to allow a specified fastener to pass through. The size of this hole is determined by the fastener that will be located in the hole. To create a clearance hole, pick Screw Clearance from the **Type:** drop-down list in the **Hole Type** rollout.

Edit the hole feature you created in Example_06_01.sldprt. In the **Hole Type** rollout in the **Hole Specification Property Manager**, pick the **Hole** button to create a simple hole. Then, select Screw Clearance from the **Type:** drop-down list. This specifies the hole will be a clearance hole.

Next, select the size of fastener from the **Size:** drop-down list in the **Hole Specifications** rollout. Below the **Size:** drop-down list is the **Fit:** drop-down list. You can specify a fit for the fastener using this drop-down list. For this example, select Normal. Based on these two selections, the hole diameter is automatically changed to .531". This is the proper hole size to accommodate the selected fastener at a normal fit.

Most clearance holes are made to allow a fastener to pass through the part and thread into an adjacent part. Therefore, in the **End Condition** rollout, select Through All from the drop-down list. To update the feature, pick the green check mark button at the top of the **Property Manager**.

Counterbored and Countersunk Holes

You have seen drilled holes that are simple, threaded, or clearance. Holes can also be created with a counterbore, spotface, or countersink. Counterbored and countersunk holes provide a clearance for the head of a fastener. Spotfaced holes provide a smooth seating surface for the fastener head.

Edit the hole feature you created in Example_06_01.sldprt. At the top of the **Hole Type** rollout, pick the **Counterbore** button. Notice the shaded preview now includes the counterbore, which makes room for the fastener head. The dimensions of the counterbore are automatically calculated based on fastener information. Change the fastener type to a hex head bolt by selecting Hex Bolt from the **Type:** drop-down list in the **Hole Type** rollout. In the **Hole Specifications** rollout, set the size to 1/2". Then, pick the green check mark button at the top of the **Property Manager** to update the part. See **Figure 6-5**.

Figure 6-5.
A counterbored clearance hole allows the head of the fastener to sit below the part surface.

Figure 6-6.
SolidWorks assumes that a flat head or oval head fastener will be used if you are creating a countersunk hole.

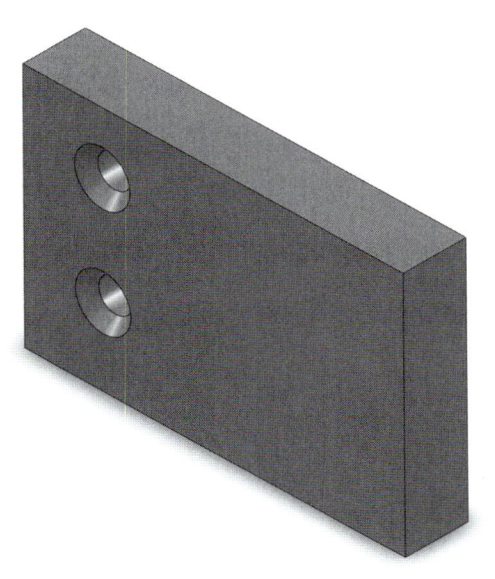

Edit the hole feature again. In the **Hole Type** rollout, pick the **Countersink** button. In the **Standard:** drop-down list, select ANSI Inch. Then, display the **Type:** drop-down list. Notice that the list contains flat and oval head styles. These are the fasteners used with a countersunk hole. For this example, select Flat Head Screw (82). In the **Hole Specifications** rollout, set the size to 1/2". You can specify additional head clearance for both counterbore and countersink holes by checking the **Head clearance** box in the **Options** rollout. This allows the head to be recessed below the surface of the part. For this example, do not add a clearance, so uncheck the **Head clearance** check box. Then, pick the green check mark button at the top of the **Property Manager** to update the part. See **Figure 6-6.** Save the file.

> **NOTE**
>
> The head type (fastener type) can only be selected for clearance holes.

Cosmetic Thread Tool

Threads can be applied to cylindrical features, not just to holes. The features can be external, such as a cylinder. The features can also be internal, such as cutouts created by extruding circles or revolving rectangular shapes. The **Cosmetic Thread** tool is used to do this.

Open Example_06_02.sldprt, which is a small metric part. You will add M12×1.75-6H thread to an external cylindrical face of the part. Select **Insert>Annotations>Cosmetic Thread** to activate the tool. The **Cosmetic Thread Property Manager** is displayed. With the **Circular Edges** selection box active (highlighted blue) in the **Thread Settings** rollout, move the cursor over the end of the outside diameter at point A shown in **Figure 6-7** and pick. A dashed line representing the thread appears on the end of the boss. In the **End Condition** drop-down list in the rollout, choose Blind. Then type 5 in the **Depth** text box in the rollout. In the **Minor Diameter** text box in the rollout, enter 10.106 mm. This is the minimum minor diameter allowed for a 12 mm×1.75-6H threaded boss. Type M12×1.75-6H in the text box

Figure 6-7.
Threads are added to the shaft on this object.

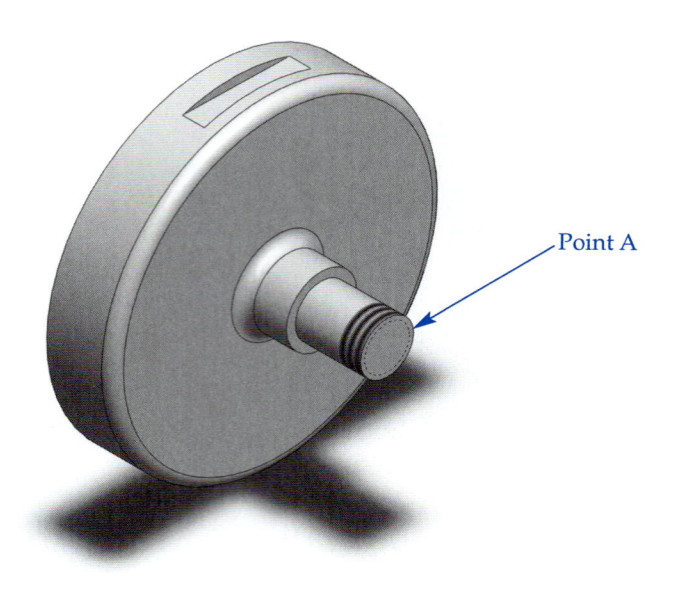

Figure 6-8.
Threads are represented in SolidWorks as a bitmap, however, the part drawing conforms to standards for representing threads.

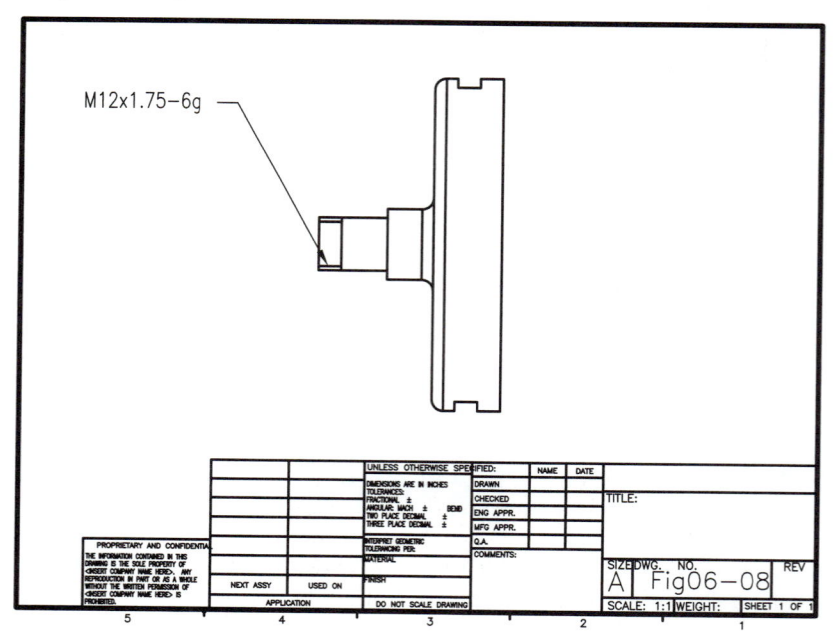

in the **Thread Callout** rollout. Entering the thread specification will aid in annotating 2D drawings, as you will see in later chapters. Pick the green check mark button at the top of the **Property Manager** to apply the thread.

By expanding the branch for the revolved feature in the **Feature Manager** design tree, you can see the branch for the cosmetic thread feature. To make changes to the threads, right-click on the branch and pick the **Edit Feature** button in the shortcut toolbar.

The visual representation of the threads does not show coarseness or direction of the thread. However, the threads will be properly displayed in the part drawing in the correct ANSI standard. See **Figure 6-8.** Creating part drawings is discussed in Chapter 8.

> **NOTE**
>
> Creating true thread features (modeled geometry) in SolidWorks requires many steps and the extra surfaces generated are demanding of system resources. It is usually of little value to add true thread features to a part.

Fillets and Rounds

The **Fillet** tool puts a radius on any or all edges of a part, including intersections of part features. A radius on an inside edge adds material to the part and is called a *fillet*. A radius on an outside corner removes material and is called a *round*. See **Figure 6-9.** The terminology may be a little confusing when working in SolidWorks as the **Fillet** tool creates both fillets and rounds.

Applying Fillets and Rounds

Open Example_06_03.sldprt. Pick the **Fillet** button in the **Features** tab in the **Command Manager**. The **Fillet Property Manager** is displayed, **Figure 6-10.** Pick the **Manual** button at the top of the **Property Manager**. There are four types of fillets that can be applied: constant radius, variable radius, face, and full round. The type of fillet is selected in the **Fillet Type** rollout. For this example, pick the **Constant radius** radio button to create a fillet with the same radius along its length.

The radius of the fillet is set in the **Radius** text box at the top of the **Items to Fillet** rollout. The **Fillet** tool allows you to set several radii in one session of the tool by checking the **Multiple Radius Fillet** check box. For this example, check the check box and enter .25" in the **Radius** text box. Then, pick the four top edges of the part. See **Figure 6-11A.** When the cursor is over an edge, the edge is displayed as a thick orange line. As you select edges, they are displayed in light blue to indicate where the round will be applied. Next, enter .5" in the **Radius** text box and select the four side edges of the part.

Notice that a leader is attached to each fillet with the radius displayed. Each individual radius can be edited by picking on the radius value in the leader balloon and typing a new value. Using this method, you can apply a variety of fillets and rounds

Figure 6-9.
Fillets and rounds.

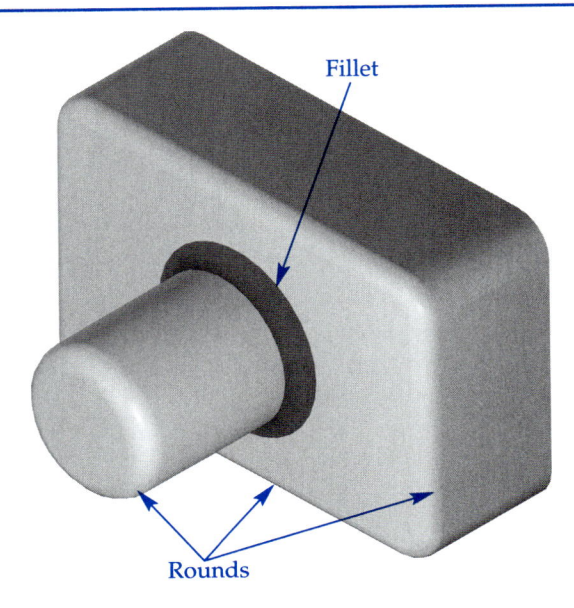

Figure 6-10.
Making settings for fillets and rounds.

Pick the type of fillet

Set the radius

Pick to select the features

Define a setback if needed

Figure 6-11.
A—Apply fillets and rounds as indicated here. B—The completed part.

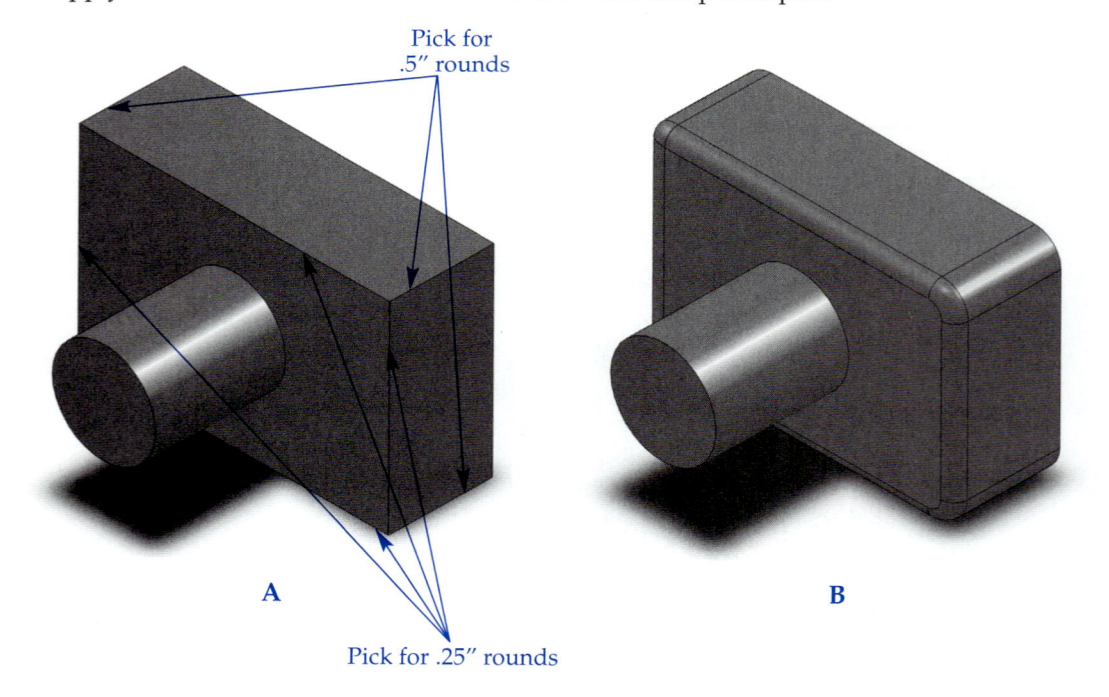

Pick for .5" rounds

A

B

Pick for .25" rounds

118 Learning SolidWorks 2009

with the same session of the **Fillet** tool. When all radii are set, pick the green check mark button at the top of the **Fillet Property Manager** to create the fillets and rounds. See **Figure 6-11B**.

Instead of individually selecting the four top edges, you can select them all with one pick. This is because they are considered a loop. Undo the previous operation. Then, activate the **Fillet** tool and enter .25" for the radius. Next, right-click on one of the top edges and choose **Select Loop** from the shortcut menu. The entire loop (all four edges) is selected and a yellow arrow is displayed near the edge on which you right-clicked. Since the one edge is a member of two loops, you can pick the yellow arrow to flip the loop selection. If needed, pick the arrow so the loop contains the four top edges. Then, pick the green check mark button to create the rounds.

Notice how the rounds are applied at the sharp corners. Edit the fillet feature. Then, check the **Multiple radius fillet** check box and enter .5" for the radius. Then, select the four side edges of the part as you did before. Pick the green check mark button to update the part. Notice how the rounds on the top edges are applied now that the corners are rounded. Save the file.

PROFESSIONAL TIP

The **Tangent Propagation** check box in the **Items to Fillet** rollout is normally checked. This results in all tangential edges in a loop being selected by picking one edge. When unchecked, you must pick individual edges in the loop or use the **Select Loop** option in the shortcut menu.

More Fillet Tool Options

The **Fillet Options** rollouts in the **Fillet Property Manager** provide additional options for creating fillets and rounds. When the **Keep Surface** radio button is on in the **Fillet Options** rollout, a constant fillet radius is applied along the edge, even if this means extending adjacent faces. See **Figure 6-12**. For example, open Example_06_04.sldprt. Put a .75" fillet on the intersection where the cylinder meets the base. Notice how face C is extended to keep the

Figure 6-12.
A—Face C is extended when the **Keep Surface** radio button is on. B—The end view of the part clearly shows how the face is extended.

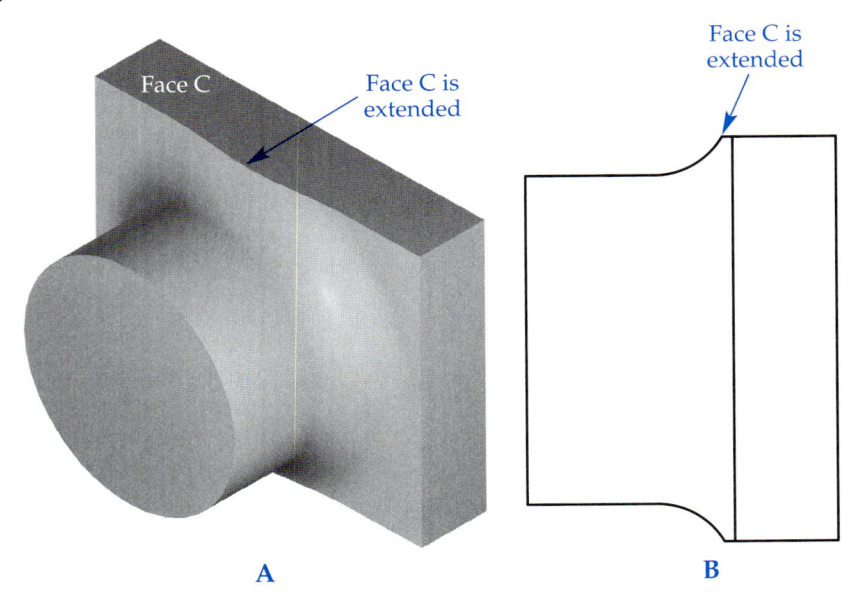

Chapter 6 Adding Features

constant radius. This is obvious in the end view. Now, edit the fillet feature and pick the **Default** radio button. After you update the part, notice how the fillet radius is now varied to keep the edge along face C a straight line. See **Figure 6-13**. This is done by varying the radius of the fillet.

The **Round Corners** check box in the **Fillet Options** rollout controls the intersection of edges. Open Example_06_05.sldprt. Place a .25" radius fillet on the four inside edges on the top of the cavity. Check the **Round Corners** check box and apply the fillet. The result of the operation is shown in **Figure 6-14A**. Notice how the corners are rounded, not sharp. Now, edit the fillet feature and uncheck the **Round Corners** check box. The result of the operation is shown in **Figure 6-14B**. Notice the sharp corners.

Figure 6-13.
A—Face C is not extended when the **Default** radio button is on. B—The end view of the part clearly shows how the face is not extended.

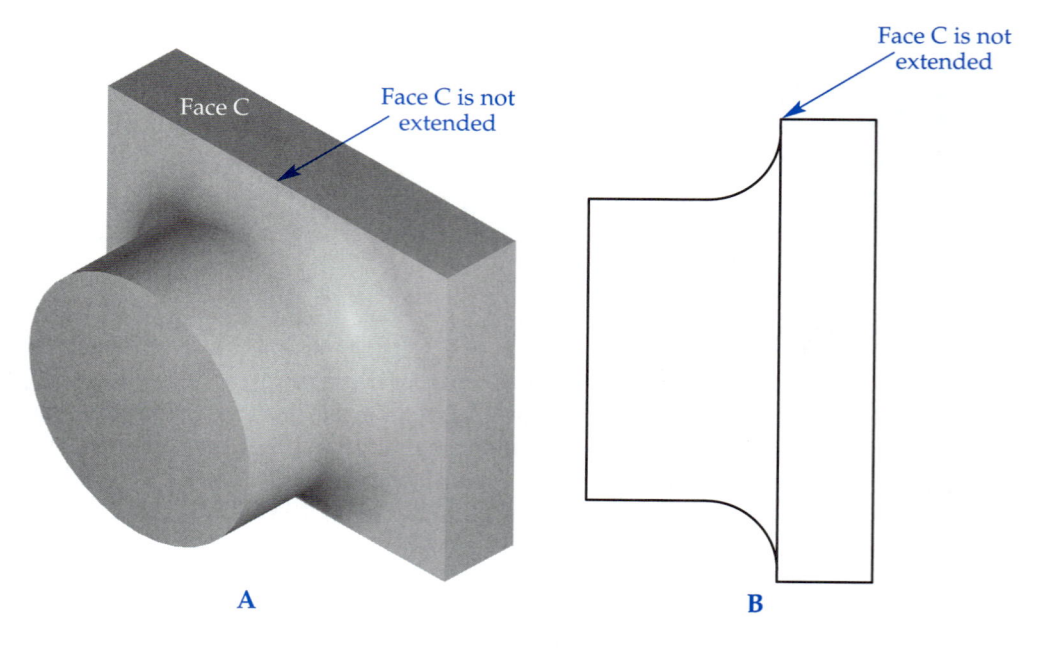

Figure 6-14.
A—The corners are rounded when the **Round Corners** check box is checked. B—Unchecking the check box results in sharp corners.

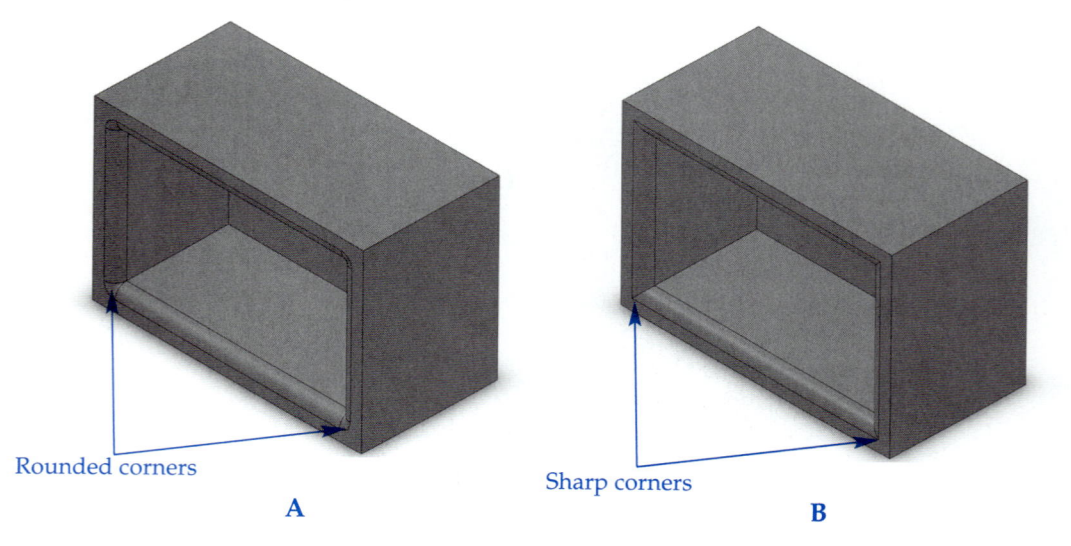

When the **Keep Features** check box in the **Fillet Options** rollout is checked, some features, such as holes, are retained when they intersect the fillet. Open Example_06_06.sldprt. Place a 1″ radius round (fillet) on the short edge of the top by the hole and the post. In the **Fillet Options** rollout, uncheck the **Keep Features** check box. When the round is applied, the hole and post disappear. See **Figure 6-15A.** In some cases, you will get an error message. Now, edit the fillet feature and check the **Keep Features** check box. When you pick **OK** to update the feature, the hole and post both reappear. See **Figure 6-15B.**

Variable-Radius Fillets and Setbacks

In some applications, the desired radius of a fillet must vary over the length of the edge. This is called a *variable-radius fillet.* Open Example_06_07.sldprt. Activate the **Fillet** tool and pick the **Variable radius** radio button in the **Fillet Type** rollout in the **Fillet Property Manager**. Then, pick the long, front edge of the top face. The edge appears in light blue, the two endpoints appear in gray and have radius leaders, and three points appear in orange on the edge between the endpoints.

The **Variable Radius Parameters** rollout is used to define the fillet or round. The **Radius** text box at the top of the rollout is used to set a fillet radius. The list box below the **Radius** text box lists the points that are selected to define the fillet or round. Currently, only the two endpoints are selected and appear in the list box. To assign a radius to a point, select it in the list box, enter the radius in the **Radius** text box, and pick the **Set Unassigned** button. You can also use the leader bubble to set the radius. Once assigned, the radius of the fillet at the point is given in the list box next to the point name. Set the radius of the first endpoint to .1″ and the second endpoint to 1.0″. Pick the green check mark button to apply the round. This setting creates a smooth, variable-radius round (fillet) between the two endpoints. See **Figure 6-16A.**

However, you can have multiple points along the length of the fillet, each with a different radius. By default, there are three points between the endpoints. The number of points is set in the **Number of Instances** text box at the bottom of the **Variable Radius Parameters** rollout. Undo the previous fillet operation. Then, activate the **Fillet** tool and select the long, front edge on the top. For this example, use four points along the edge, counting the endpoints, so enter 2 in the **Number of Instances** text box. Then, using the cursor, pick the two orange points between the two endpoints. As you pick the points, they turn light blue and are added to the list box in the **Variable Radius Parameters**

Figure 6-15.
A—When the **Keep Features** check box is unchecked, a fillet or round may remove some features. B—When the check box is checked, some features are retained. However, some features may still be removed by the fillet or round.

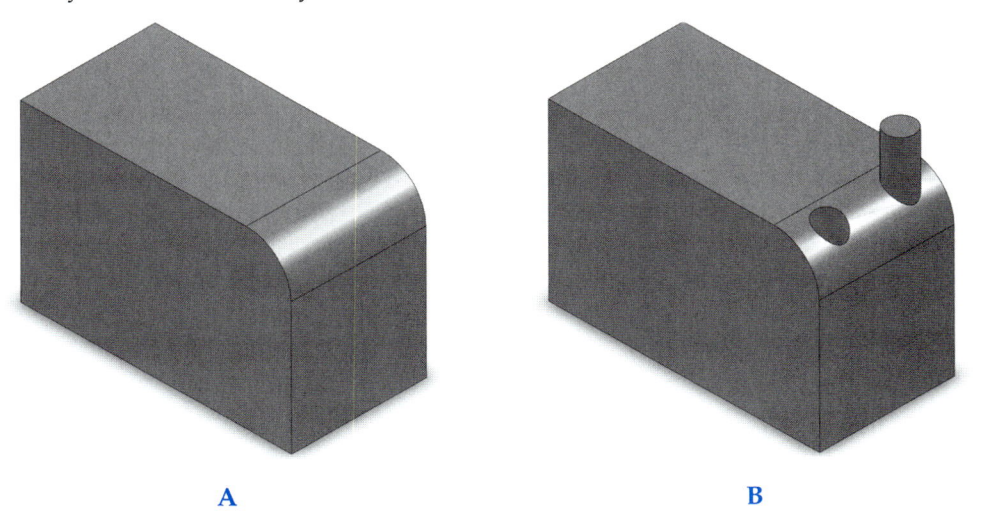

A   B

Chapter 6 Adding Features

Figure 6-16.
A—This is a variable-radius round (fillet). B—This variable-radius round has multiple transitions.

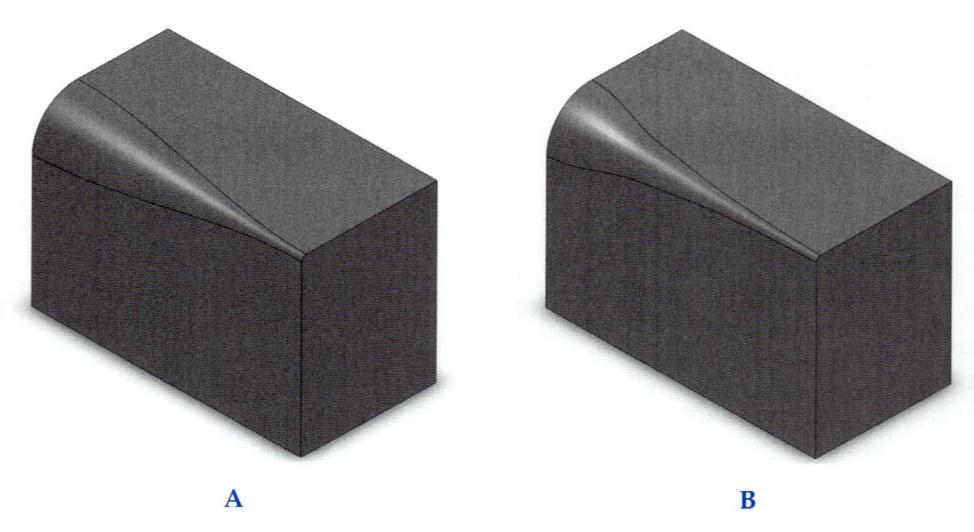

A   B

rollout. Also, a radius leader appears in the graphics window for each selected point. Change the radius values of the points so the fillet goes from .1, to .2, to .5, and to 1. If needed, you can change the location of the points by picking the percentage in the balloon and entering a new percentage. For this example, accept the default positions. Then, pick the green check mark button to apply the round. See **Figure 6-16B**.

A *setback* is the distance from the corner where three fillets or rounds meet. It is measured from the point where the edges would meet to form a square corner. See **Figure 6-17**. By increasing the setback, the fillets are blended together to smooth the corner. Open Example_06_08.sldprt. The block has a .5" fillet with no setback on three intersecting edges. See **Figure 6-18A**. Edit the fillet feature and expand the **Setback Parameters** rollout in the **Fillet Property Manager**. Pick the **Setback Vertices** box (the middle box) to activate it (highlighted blue). As you move the cursor over the part, an orange dot appears on valid vertices. Pick the corner where the three fillets intersect. In the **Setback Parameters** rollout, three edges are listed in the **Setback Distances** text box. Pick in the **Distance** box and change the value to 2", then select the **Set All** button. See **Figure 6-19**. You could also set a different setback for each edge by selecting the

Figure 6-17.
The setback is the distance from the theoretical sharp corner to the radius. A—No setback. B—Setback of 1.00.

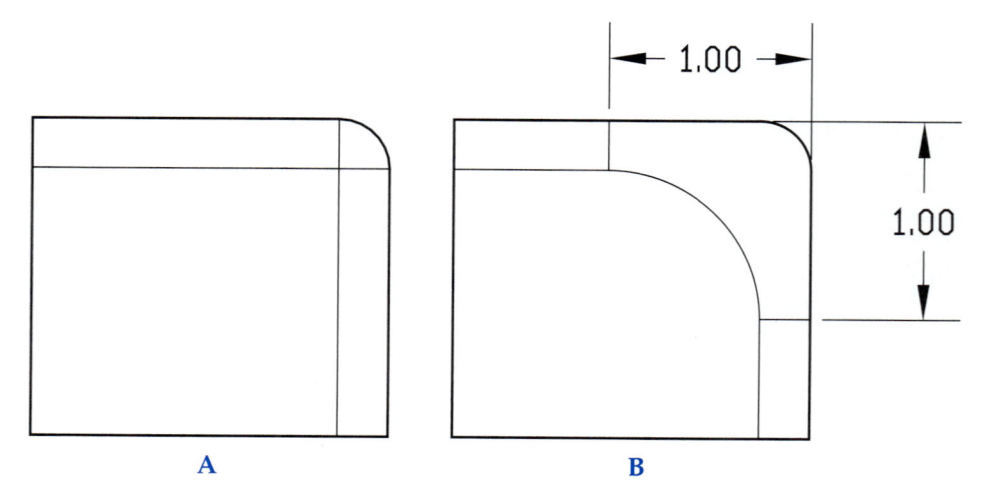

A   B

122   Learning SolidWorks 2009

Figure 6-18.
A—The intersection of these three rounds is created without setbacks. B—Setbacks allow you to smooth the corner.

A

B

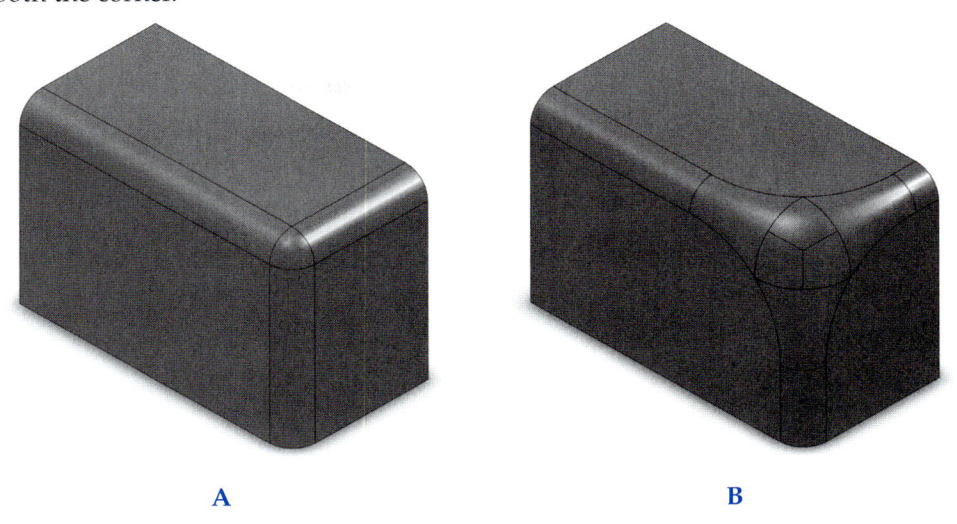

Figure 6-19.
Adding setbacks to the intersection of three fillets or rounds.

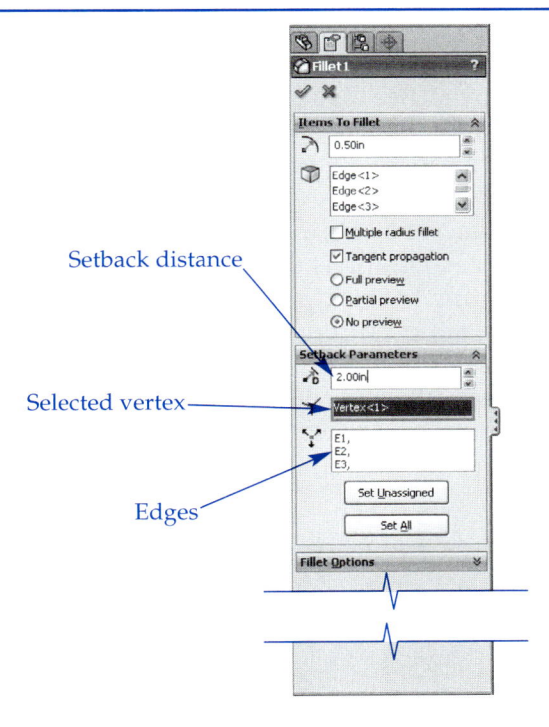

Setback distance

Selected vertex

Edges

edge in the text box, entering a setback distance, and picking the **Set Unassigned** button. When the setbacks are assigned, pick the green check mark button to update the rounds (fillets). The corner is smoothed, as shown in **Figure 6-18B**.

Adding Chamfers

A *chamfer* is a bevel—a flat sloping face—on the edge between two intersecting faces of the part. The faces can be flat or curved. Like fillets and rounds, chamfers add material to inside edges and remove material from outside edges. **Figure 6-20** shows chamfers applied to three types of edges.

Chapter 6   Adding Features

Figure 6-20.
A—The unchamfered part. B—Three different chamfers are applied to the part.

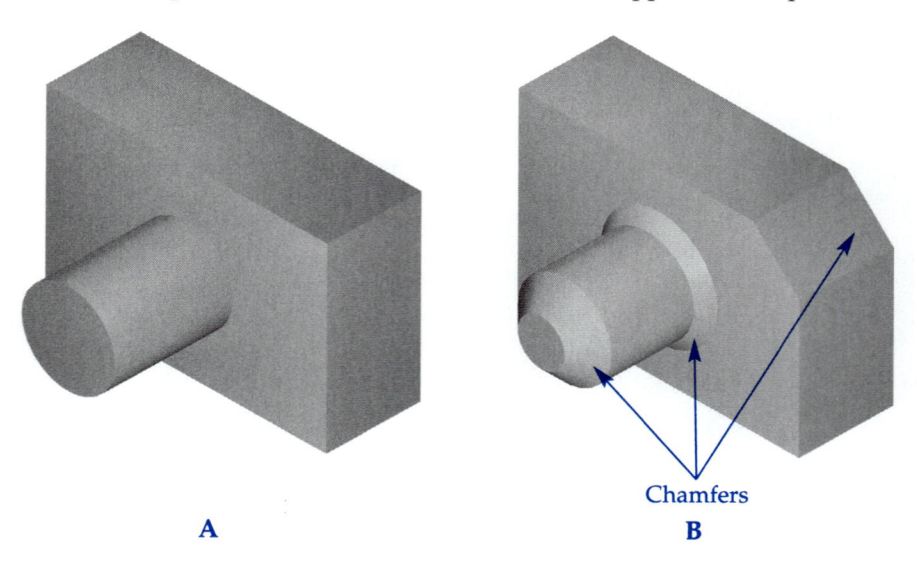

Chamfers

A   B

To create a chamfer, pick the **Chamfer** button in the **Features** tab of the **Command Manager**. The button is located in the flyout below the **Fillet** button. The **Chamfer Property Manager** is displayed. See **Figure 6-21.** There are three methods for defining the chamfer—angle and distance, two distances, and selecting a vertex. The three buttons in the **Chamfer Parameters** rollout allow you to choose between these methods.

- **Angle Distance radio button.** A chamfer is created a specified distance from the edge on one face and at a specified angle to the second face. With this option, specify the distance and angle, then pick the edge to chamfer. The distance is applied to the face in the direction of the preview arrow.
- **Distance Distance radio button.** Allows a different distance from the edge on each face. With this option, specify the two distances and pick the edge. SolidWorks automatically chooses the faces to which the distances are applied, but you can flip the order by reversing the text box entries.

Figure 6-21.
Applying a chamfer.

Pick to select a feature

Select a method

Enter the angle and distance as needed

124   Learning SolidWorks 2009

- **Vertex radio button.** Allows you to add a chamfer to the edges at a selected vertex. With this option, select the **Vertex** radio button in the **Chamfer Property Manager**, then choose a vertex to fillet. Finally, specify a distance for each edge that intersects the vertex. This option, in effect, "shaves" the corner.

Open Example_06_09.sldprt. Pick the **Chamfer** button in the **Features** tab of the **Command Manager**. Then, continue as follows.

1. In the **Chamfer Parameters** rollout, pick the **Angle distance** radio button.
2. In the **Distance** text box, change the distance to .5". In the **Angle** text box, specify a 45° angle.
3. Pick the edge at the end of the large cylinder (not the intersection with the base). A preview of the chamfer appears on the part in yellow wireframe.
4. In the **Chamfer Property Manager**, pick the green check mark button to place the chamfer.
5. Pick the **Chamfer** button in the **Features** tab of the **Command Manager**. Note: You can apply multiple chamfers of the same type in one session of the **Chamfer** tool, but you cannot apply multiple chamfers of different types.
6. In the **Chamfer Parameters** rollout, pick the **Angle distance** radio button.
7. Set the distance to .3" and the angle to 30°.
8. Pick the edge between the base and the large cylinder. A preview of the chamfer appears on the part in yellow wireframe.
9. In the **Chamfer Property Manager**, pick the green check mark button to place the chamfer.

When using the **Chamfer** tool, you can select a chain, or loop, of edges. However, the loop cannot contain sharp corners. Also, the corner radii must be tangent to the straight edges. The **Tangent Propagation** check box in the **Chamfer Parameters** rollout determines if a chain of edges or a single edge is selected. When checked, a chain is selected when a single edge is picked.

Open Example_06_10.sldprt. Face A has fillets on each corner; in other words, the face has no sharp corners. See **Figure 6-22A.** Face B, on the other hand, has three sharp corners and one smooth corner. Activate the **Chamfer** tool. Make sure the **Tangent propagation** check box is checked in the **Chamfer Parameters** rollout. Then, pick the

Figure 6-22.
A—The edge of face A does not have any sharp corners, while the edge of face B does. B—The chain or loop for a chamfer stops at sharp corners, which results in the chamfer on face B.

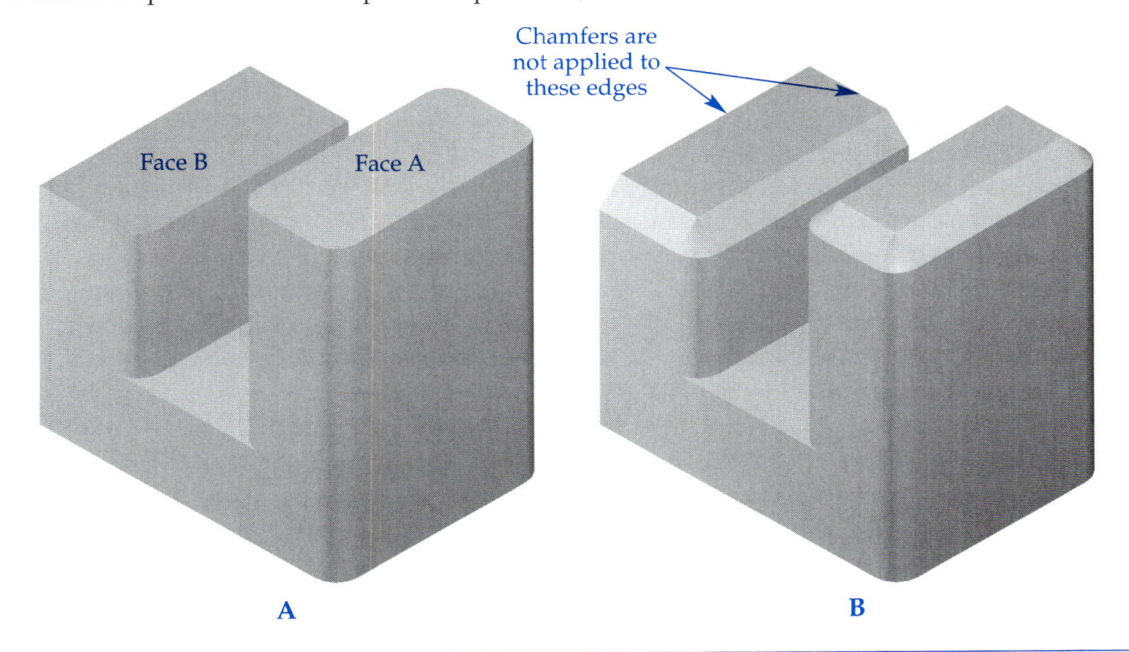

Chapter 6 Adding Features 125

Distance distance radio button and enter 5 mm in the **Distance 1** and **Distance 2** text boxes. Also, pick the **Full preview** radio button at the bottom of the **Chamfer Parameters** rollout. Next, pick a single edge on face A and a single edge on face B. Notice how the yellow preview of the chamfer appears on all edges of face A. However, on face B, the preview only appears on some of the edges. This is because the loop is broken by the sharp corners. If the **Tangent propagation** check box is unchecked, only the single edge you selected on each face is used for the chamfer operation. To place the chamfers, be sure the **Tangent propagation** check box is checked and then pick the green check mark button in the **Chamfer Property Manager**. See **Figure 6-22B**.

Linear and Circular Patterns

Patterns, or arrays, of features or sketches can be created in SolidWorks. The process is very similar for both features and sketches. There are two basic types of patterns—linear and circular. A *linear pattern* is an arrangement in rows and columns. A *circular pattern* is an arrangement about a center point or axis. Feature patterns are discussed here. Once you understand linear and circular patterns for features, you will be able to create curve-driven and sketch patterns with ease.

Linear Patterns

Open Example_06_11.sldprt. This is a metric part with a circular sketch that has been extruded through the part to create a cutout (hole). The color of the cutout feature has been changed to red. In the **Features** tab in the **Command Manager**, pick the **Linear Pattern** button. The **Linear Pattern Property Manager** is displayed. See **Figure 6-23**.

With the **Features to Pattern** selection box active (highlighted blue), pick the red extrusion as the feature. You can select it in the flyout **Feature Manager** design tree or on the part. Once the feature is selected, you need to define the pattern by setting directions and values for the columns and rows.

In the **Direction 1** rollout, pick the **Pattern Direction** selection box so it is activated (highlighted blue). Then, pick a long edge on the top face. An arrow appears on the part indicating the direction of the pattern. Next, enter 4 in the **Number of Instances** text box in the **Direction 1** rollout. This is the number of columns. Also, enter 40 mm in the **Spacing** text box in the rollout. This defines the distance between features. Depending on how the edge was selected, the preview may be shown opposite from the direction needed. If necessary, pick the arrow on the preview to flip the direction.

In the **Direction 2** rollout, pick the **Pattern Direction** selection box so it is activated (highlighted blue). Then, pick a short edge on the top face. The arrow on the part that indicates the direction of the pattern should point into the part, along the edge, and away from the hole. If not, pick the **Reverse Direction** button next to the **Pattern Direction** selection box in the **Direction 2** rollout. This is the same as picking the arrow on the preview. Next, enter 3 in the **Number of Instances** text box and 30 mm in the **Spacing** text box.

As you make changes in the **Linear Pattern Property Manager**, a preview of the pattern is shown in wireframe on the part. Once the pattern is defined, pick the green check mark button in the **Linear Pattern Property Manager**. The selected feature is arrayed in the defined pattern.

Curve-Driven Linear Patterns

In a curve-driven pattern, sketch entities can be selected as paths for the directions. The sketch entities can be lines, arcs, or splines. Open Example_06_12.sldprt. This part is similar to the one in the previous example. However, it contains an unconsumed sketch. The curve is a spline that is part of the unconsumed sketch.

Figure 6-23.
Defining a linear pattern.

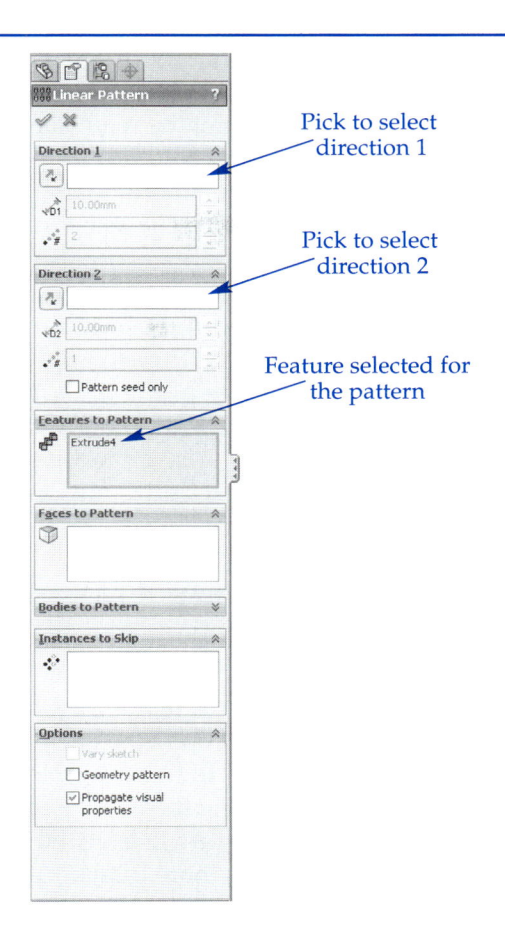

Pick to select direction 1

Pick to select direction 2

Feature selected for the pattern

Pick the **Curve Driven Pattern** button from the flyout below the **Linear Pattern** button in the **Feature** tab of the **Command Manager**. In the **Features to Pattern** rollout, pick the selection box so it is active (highlighted blue) and then select the hole feature. In the **Direction 1** rollout, pick the **Pattern Direction** selection box so it is activated (highlighted blue). Select the spline. Then, enter 5 for the number of instances and 15 mm for the spacing. Pick the green check mark button to create the pattern. Notice how the five holes follow the curve of the spline. See **Figure 6-24.**

Circular Patterns

To create a circular pattern, you must select an axis of rotation about which the feature is arrayed. This axis can be a reference axis or a circular feature. Open Example_06_13.sldprt.

Figure 6-24.
Using a curved line as a path applies the pattern along the curve.

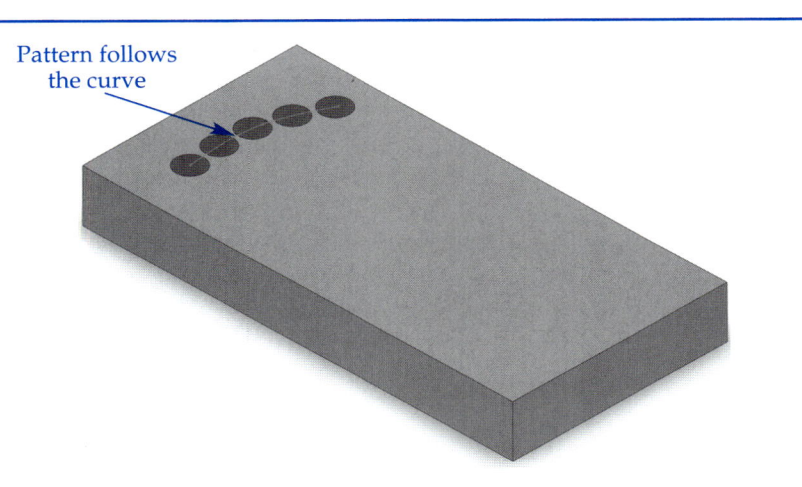

Pattern follows the curve

Chapter 6   Adding Features   *127*

This part has a single ear that needs to be arrayed about the centerline of the part. The ear contains an extrusion, hole (cutout), and two fillets. All features that compose the ear will be arrayed about the center of the main shaft.

Pick the **Circular Pattern** button from the flyout below the **Linear Pattern** button in the **Features** tab in the **Command Manager**. The **Circular Pattern Property Manager** is displayed, **Figure 6-25.** With the selection box in the **Features to Pattern** rollout active (highlighted blue), select all four features that compose the ear. You can select the features in the graphics window or flyout **Feature Manager** design tree.

Next, pick the **Pattern Axis** selection box in the **Parameters** rollout so it is active (highlighted blue). Since the three components of the main shaft share the same centerline, you can select any one of these features to define the axis. A preview of the array appears on the part. In the **Parameters** rollout, enter 3 in the **Number of Instances** text box to create three items. Also, enter 360 in the **Angle** text box to indicate the pattern will be rotated around the entire circumference. Finally, pick the green check mark button to create the pattern. See **Figure 6-26** for the result.

Pattern the Entire Part

It is possible to pattern the entire part. Open the part Example_06_14.sldprt. This part contains a reference axis that will be used to create the circular pattern. Pick the **Circular Pattern** button in the **Features** tab of the **Command Manager**. Expand the **Bodies to Pattern** rollout and activate the selection box. Then, select the body. A *body* is a collection of features all connected to each other. In this example, there is only one body. It can be selected in the graphics window or by using the flyout **Feature Manager** design tree. In the design tree, the bodies contained in the file are listed under the Solid Bodies branch. However, this branch only appears when there is more than one body in the part.

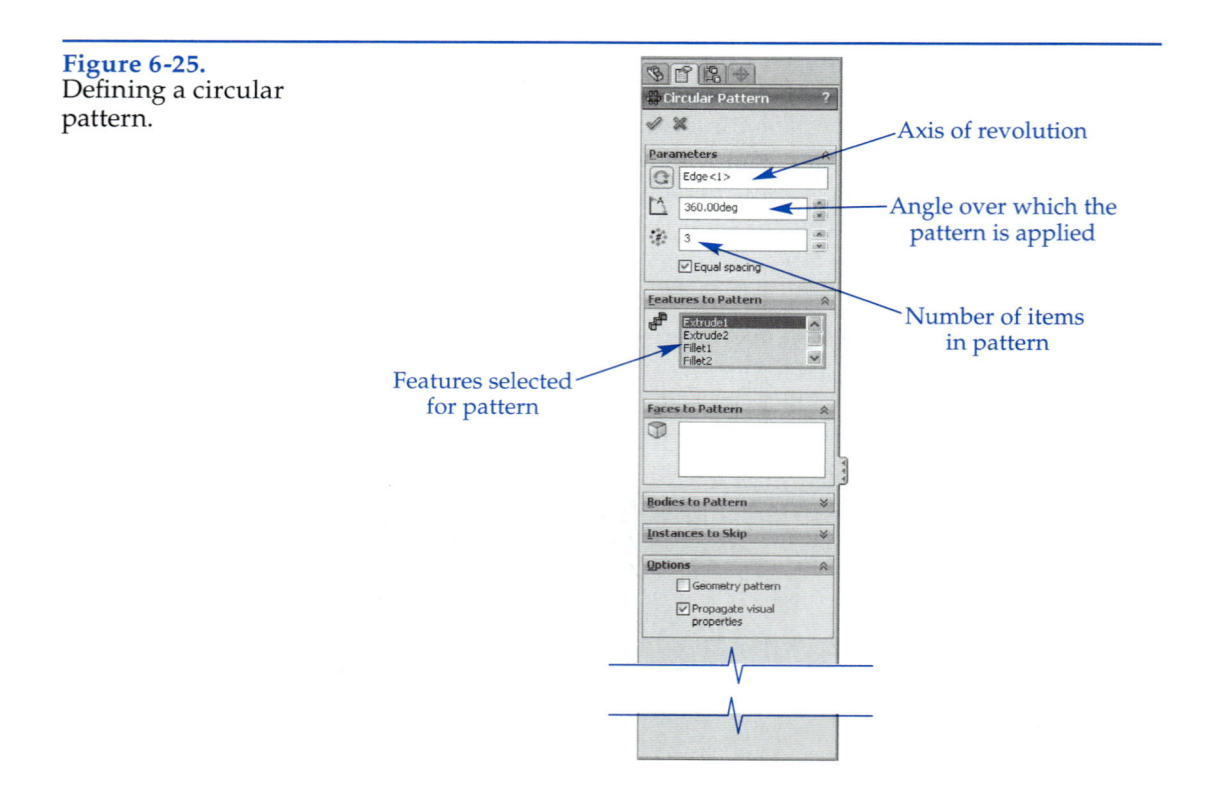

Figure 6-25.
Defining a circular pattern.

After selecting the body, pick the **Pattern Axis** selection box in the **Parameters** rollout so it is active (highlighted blue). Pick the reference axis as the axis of revolution. Now, set the number of instances to 4 and the angle to 360 degrees. Pick the green check mark button to complete the pattern. See **Figure 6-27**.

Edit the circular pattern you just created. In the **Parameters** rollout, uncheck the **Equal spacing** check box. Change the instance angle to 45 degrees. There are still four occurrences, but they are not spaced *within* the 45 degree angle. Instead, the bodies are 45 degrees apart. See **Figure 6-28**. When the **Equal spacing** check box is checked, the instances are equally spaced throughout the instance angle.

Figure 6-26.
First, a single ear was created on this part. A circular pattern was then created to place the other two ears.

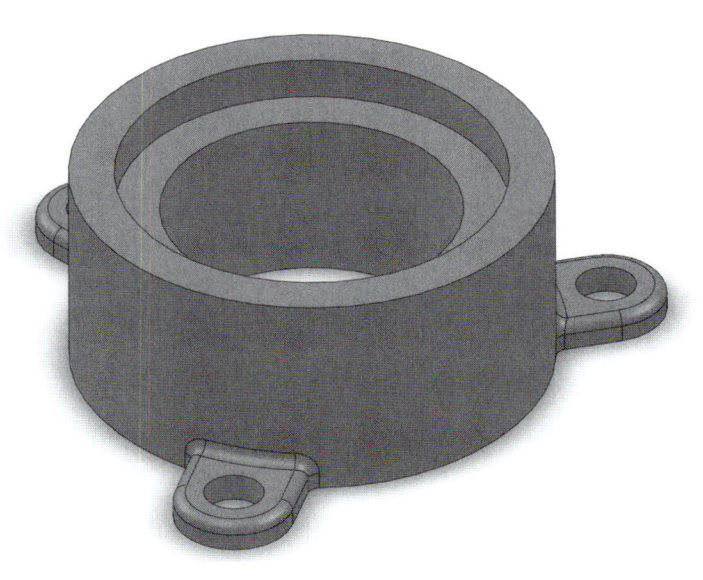

Figure 6-27.
This circular pattern of four instances was created by selecting the original body as the item to pattern and the reference axis as the axis of revolution for the pattern.

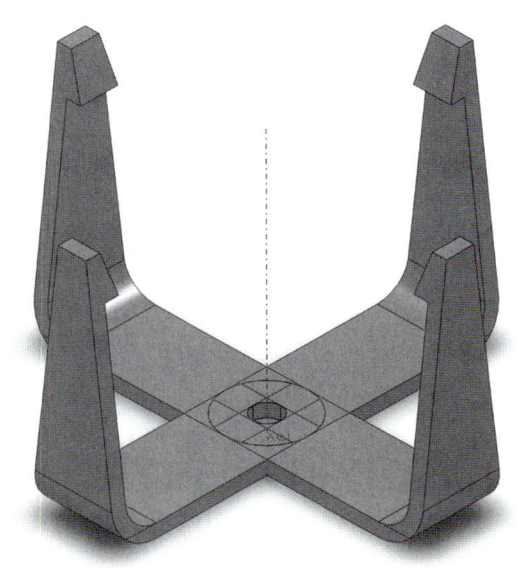

Chapter 6 Adding Features

Figure 6-28.
Instead of equally spacing the instances over a specified angle, you can specify that each instance is a set angle from the previous instance.

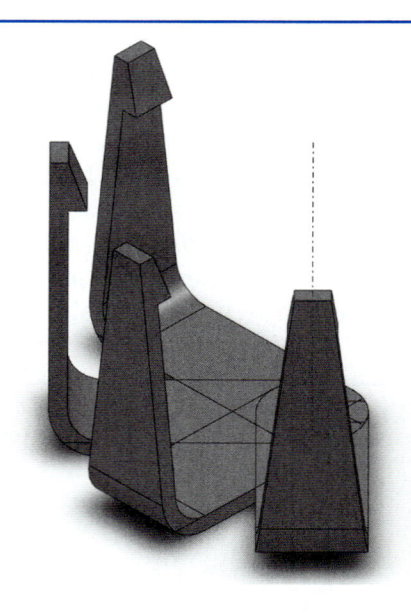

Mirror Tool

The **Mirror** tool mirrors features about a reference plane, flat face on the part, or a planar face. It performs much the same function as the sketch **Mirror** tool. Open Example_06_15.sldprt. This part is similar to the one used earlier to create a circular pattern, except the visibility of the right plane has been turned on.

Pick the **Mirror** button in the **Features** tab of the **Command Manager**. The button is located on the main tab, but is also in the flyout below the **Linear Pattern** button. The **Mirror Property Manager** is displayed, **Figure 6-29**.

In the **Features to Mirror** rollout, pick the selection box so it is active (highlighted blue). Then, select all four features that compose the ear. You can select the features in the graphics window or by using the flyout **Feature Manager** design tree. Next, activate the selection box in the **Mirror Face/Plane** rollout. Pick the right plane as the reference plane. Finally, pick the green check mark button to mirror the features. See **Figure 6-30**.

Figure 6-29.
Mirroring a feature.

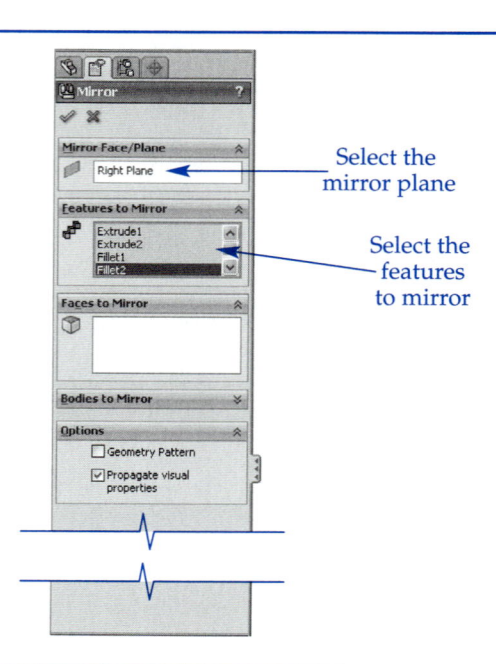

Figure 6-30.
All features in one ear were mirrored to create the second ear.

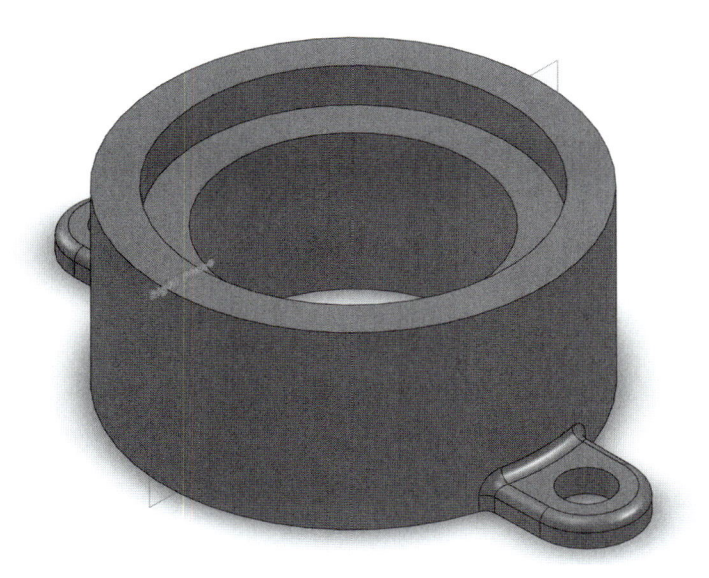

Chapter Test

Answer the following questions on a separate sheet of paper or complete the electronic chapter test on the student website.
www.g-wlearning.com/CAD

1. List four advantages of creating holes using the **Hole Wizard** tool over extruding circles.
2. What are the six termination options for a hole?
3. Briefly describe how to add threads to a hole. Assume you are in the process of creating the hole.
4. What is the purpose of a counterbore?
5. Which tool is used to create a counterbore?
6. How can threads be applied to the outside of a cylindrical feature?
7. Define *fillet*.
8. Define *round*.
9. Which tool is used to create a fillet?
10. Which tool is used to create a round?
11. What is a variable-radius fillet?
12. Define *chamfer*.
13. What are the two basic types of patterns (arrays) that can be applied to features and sketches?
14. Briefly, how can you create a pattern that has one row and four columns?
15. Which tool is used to mirror selected features of a part?

Chapter Exercises

Complete the chapter exercises on the student website.
www.g-wlearning.com/CAD

Exercise 6-1 C Bracket.
Complete the exercise on the student website.

Exercise 6-2 Mounting Bracket.
Complete the exercise on the student website.

Exercise 6-3 Casting.
Complete the exercise on the student website.

Exercise 6-4 Mounting Bracket Casting.
Complete the exercise on the student website.

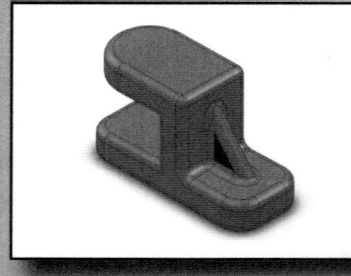

Exercise 6-5 Pin.
Complete the exercise on the student website.

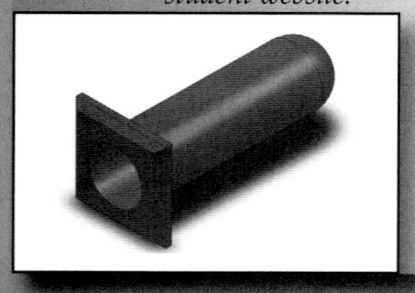

Exercise 6-6 Windshield Wiper Arm.
Complete the exercise on the student website.

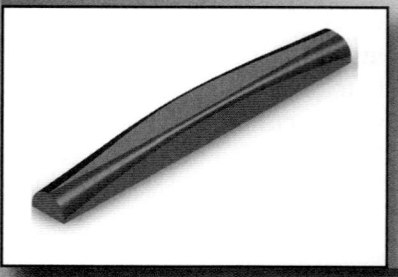

Exercise Circular Flange.

6-7 Complete the exercise on the student website.

Exercise Caulking Gun Rod.

6-8 Complete the exercise on the student website.

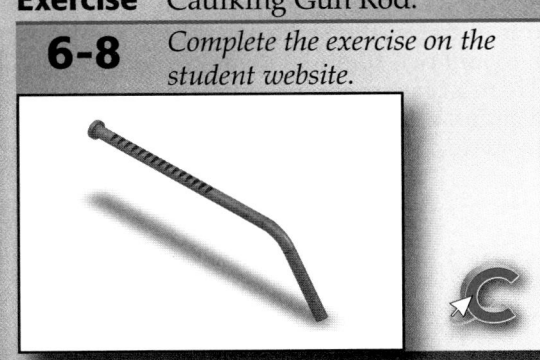

Exercise Coupling.

6-9 Complete the exercise on the student website.

Chapter 6 Adding Features

Splitting faces, covered in Chapter 7, allows you to divide geometry for various purposes. In this example, the **Split Line** tool is used prior to rounding the edges of the nut. First, the top face and two adjoining faces of the part are each "split" by selecting the sketch on each face. Then, a fillet is applied to the adjoining faces. This fillet is applied to all other top edges using a circular pattern. Then, the procedure is repeated on the bottom edges. A center cutout is made to complete the part.

Chapter 7

Adding More Features

Objectives

After completing this chapter, you will be able to:
- Create shelled parts.
- Add ribs and webs to parts.
- Create embossed and engraved parts.
- Create face drafts on parts.
- Create splits.

Shell Tool

The **Shell** tool hollows out parts, turning them into thin-walled parts typical of die cast metal or injection-molded plastic parts. The overall thickness of the wall is specified. In addition, individual faces can have unique thicknesses. Part faces, both flat and curved, can be removed by the shell operation to create open boxes.

Basic Shell Operation

Open Example_07_01.sldprt. This part has eight faces, **Figure 7-1.** Four of these faces will be removed during the shell operation. First, pick the **Shell** button on the **Features** tab in the **Command Manager**. This opens the **Shell***n* **Property Manager**, **Figure 7-2.** With the **Faces to Remove** selection box in the **Parameters** rollout active (highlighted blue), move the cursor over the part. As you move the cursor, the face that will be selected is outlined in orange. Move the cursor over face A, as indicated in **Figure 7-1,** and pick to select it. The face is highlighted in blue and listed in the **Faces to Remove** selection box.

Then, in the **Parameters** rollout, enter .1" in the **Thickness** text box. This thickness will be applied to all faces not removed from the selection. To create the shell, pick the green check mark button. A cavity is created inside of the part. See **Figure 7-3A.** Notice how face A is removed to create an open part. If it was not removed during the operation, the cavity would be completely enclosed.

135

Figure 7-1.
This part will be shelled. The faces indicated here will be removed in various combinations to produce different results.

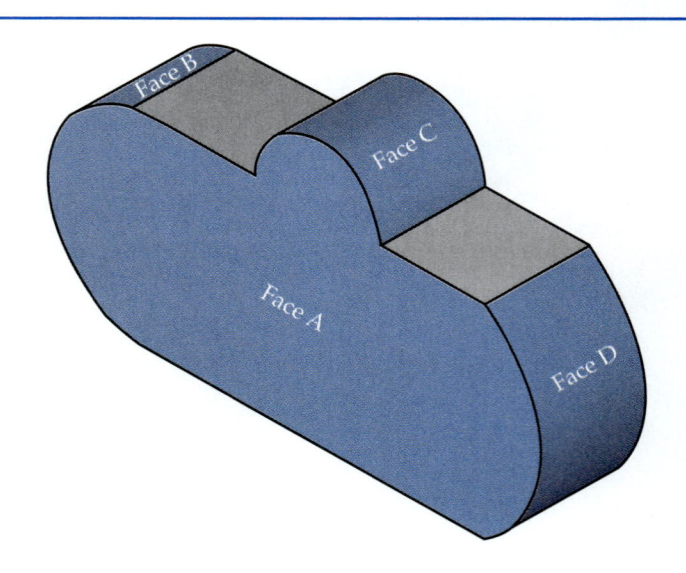

Figure 7-2.
Making settings for the shell operation.

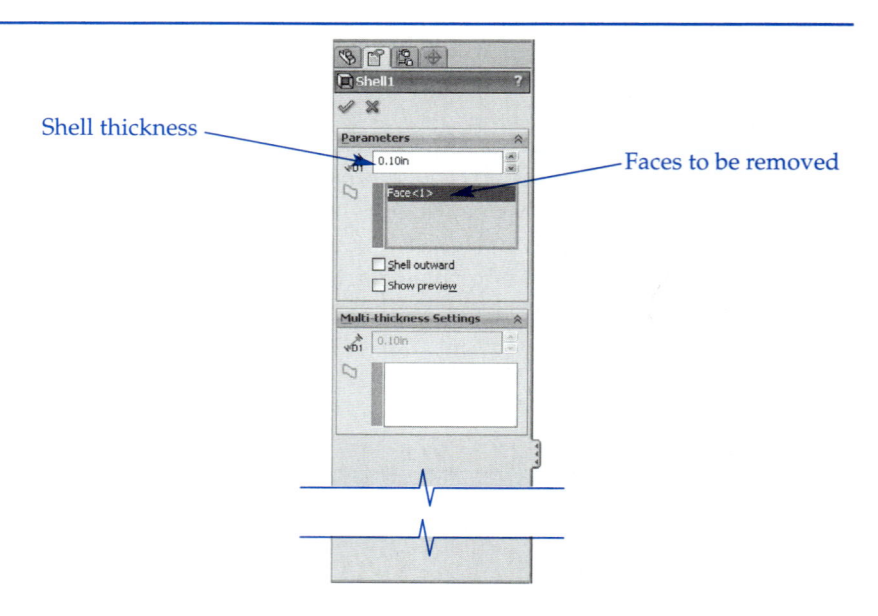

Shell thickness

Faces to be removed

Multiple faces can be removed while using the **Shell** tool. This can be done in the initial operation or by editing the feature. To edit the feature, click on the shell name in the design tree and pick the **Edit Feature** button in the shortcut toolbar. Then, with the **Faces to Remove** selection box active, pick face B on the part. Pick the green check mark button in the **Property Manager** to update the feature. See **Figure 7-3B**.

When editing the feature, you can also remove faces from the exclusion. In other words, you can add the face back onto the part. Edit the feature again. With the **Faces to Remove** selection box active, pick face B to deselect it. You can also right-click on the face name in the selection box and pick **Delete** from the shortcut menu. Then, pick face C to select it. Pick the green check mark button to update the feature. See **Figure 7-3C**.

Edit the feature again and make the changes so faces C and B are retained and faces A and D are removed. See **Figure 7-3D**. Notice the sharp chamfers created by removing face D.

Multiple Shell Thicknesses

The **Shell***n* **Property Manager** has options that determine how the cavity wall is created in relation to the base part. By default, the shell is applied so the outer shape

Figure 7-3.
The shell operation with various faces removed. A—Face A. B—Faces A and B. C—Faces A and C. D—Faces A and D.

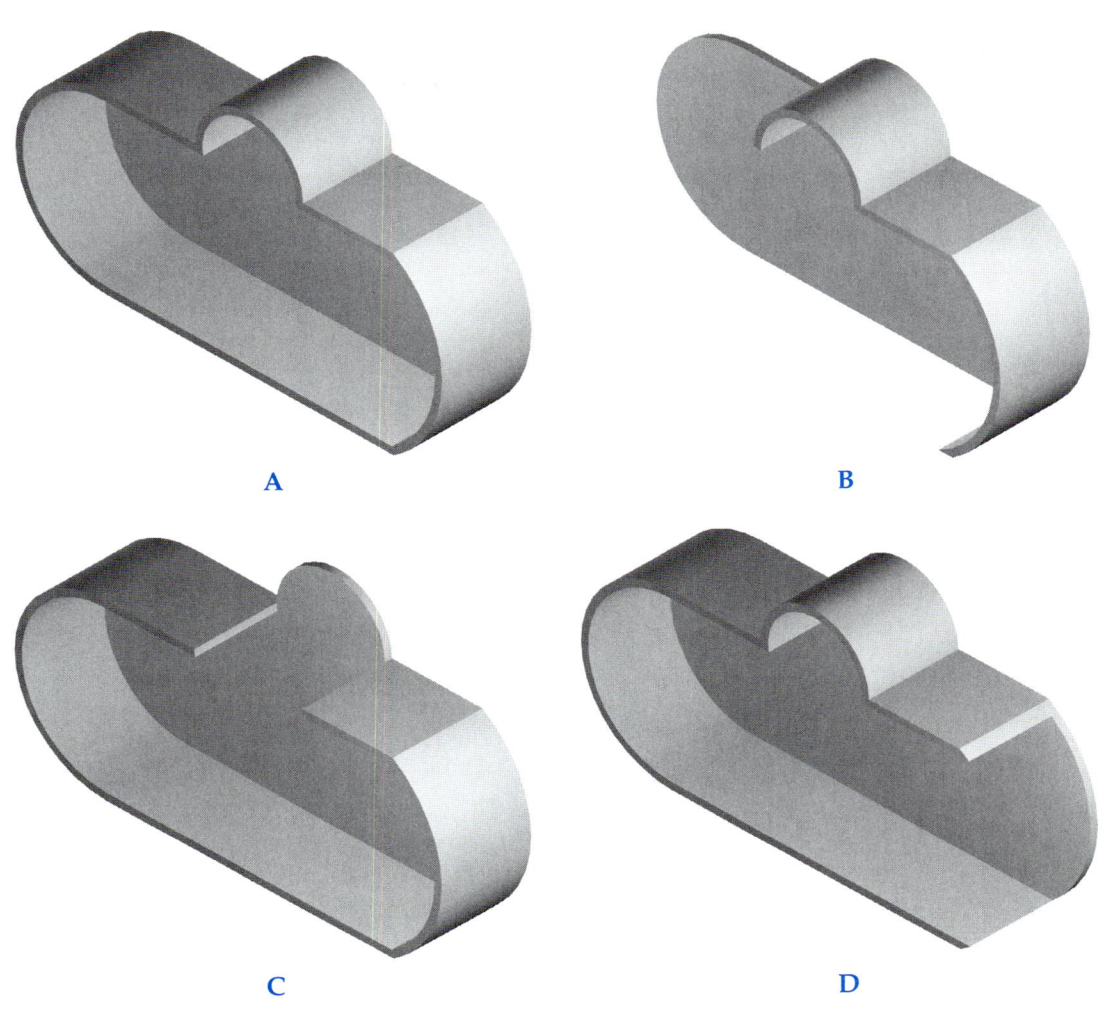

A

B

C

D

of the part remains the same size. In other words, the cavity wall is to the inside of the part. When the **Shell outward** check box is checked, material is added to the outside of the part to create the cavity wall. In this case, the cavity has the dimensions of the original part.

Open Example_07_02.sldprt. See **Figure 7-4A.** Activate the **Shell** tool and remove the large, front face. Also, set the wall thickness to .5″. Make sure the **Shell outward** check box is unchecked and create the shell, **Figure 7-4B.** Edit the feature, check the **Shell outward** check box, and apply the change. Notice how this option makes the hole smaller and the overall size larger. See **Figure 7-4C.**

By default, the same wall thickness is applied to all faces. However, you can apply different wall thicknesses to selected faces. Open Example_07_03.sldprt. This simple box was shelled with a thickness of .1″ and the front face was removed. Edit the shell feature and expand the **Multi-thickness Settings** rollout. Pick the selection box so it is active (highlighted blue) and select the top face of the part. In the **Multi-thickness Settings** rollout, enter .3″ in the **Multi-thicknesses** text box. See **Figure 7-5A.** Finally, pick the green check mark button to update the part. The result is shown in **Figure 7-5B.** You can add multiple settings; each setting can have multiple faces if needed.

Chapter 7 Adding More Features

Figure 7-4.
A—The part before shelling. B—The shelled part without using the **Shell outward** option. C—The shelled part using the **Shell outward** option.

A

B

C

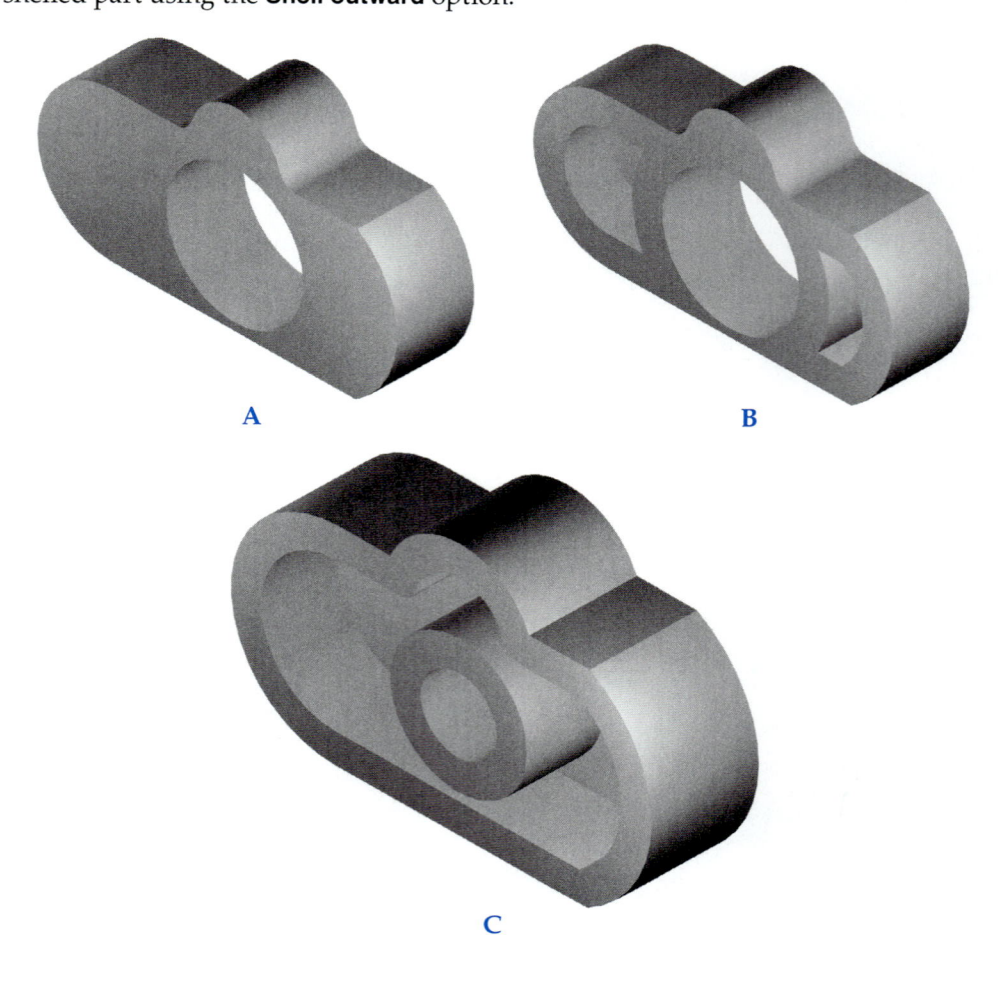

Figure 7-5.
A—Setting multiple thicknesses for the shell operation. B—The wall thickness at the top of the part is different than for the other walls.

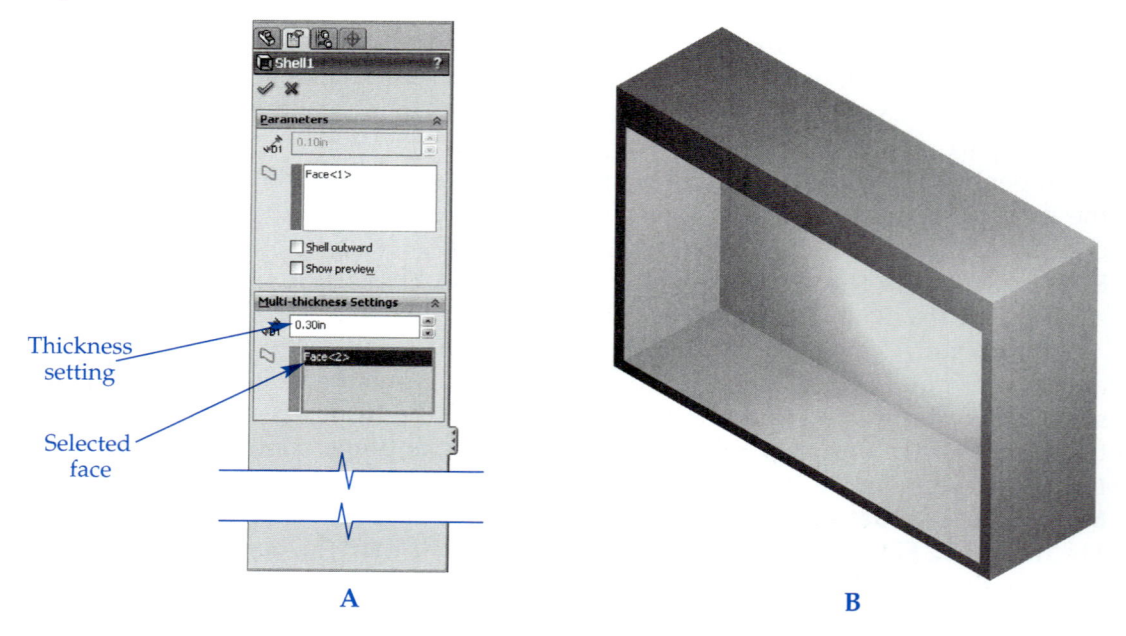

Thickness setting

Selected face

A

B

138 Learning SolidWorks 2009

Shelling Multiple Features and Combining Bodies

Open Example_07_04.sldprt. This part was built with two extruded circles and then shelled with a 2 mm wall thickness. The side and bottom face were removed in the operation. See **Figure 7-6A.** Sketch a 70 mm diameter circle on the top of the part and extrude it 50 mm high. Do not merge the new feature with the existing solid body (uncheck the **Merge result** check box). Shell the new feature to the inside with a thickness of 10 mm and the top face removed. The result is shown in **Figure 7-6B.**

Next, expand the Solid Bodies branch in the design tree. Press the [Ctrl] key, select both bodies in the design tree, right-click, and select **Combine** from the shortcut menu. The **Combine***n* **Property Manager** is displayed. Pick the **Add** radio button in the **Operation Type** rollout and then pick the green check mark button to complete the operation. This merges the two solids into a single solid. Notice that since there is now only one body, the Solid Bodies branch is no longer displayed in the design tree.

CAUTION
If you merge the new feature upon creation and then try to create the shell, you will get an error message.

Rib Tool

Often, features called ribs or webs are added to parts to increase their strength or support a specific feature. The difference between a *rib* and *web* is that ribs are closed and webs are open. See **Figure 7-7.** The **Rib** tool creates ribs from a simple sketch, usually a single line.

Open Example_07_05.sldprt. The visibility of the front plane has been turned on. Pick the **Sketch** button on the **Sketch** tab in the **Command Manager**. Select the front plane as the sketch plane.

Next, project the two red faces onto the sketch plane to create two lines. Pick the **Intersection Curve** button in the **Sketch** tab of the **Command Manager**. It is located in

Figure 7-6.
A—The original shelled part (shown in section). B—An extruded feature is added to the part (shown in section) and a different shell operation performed.

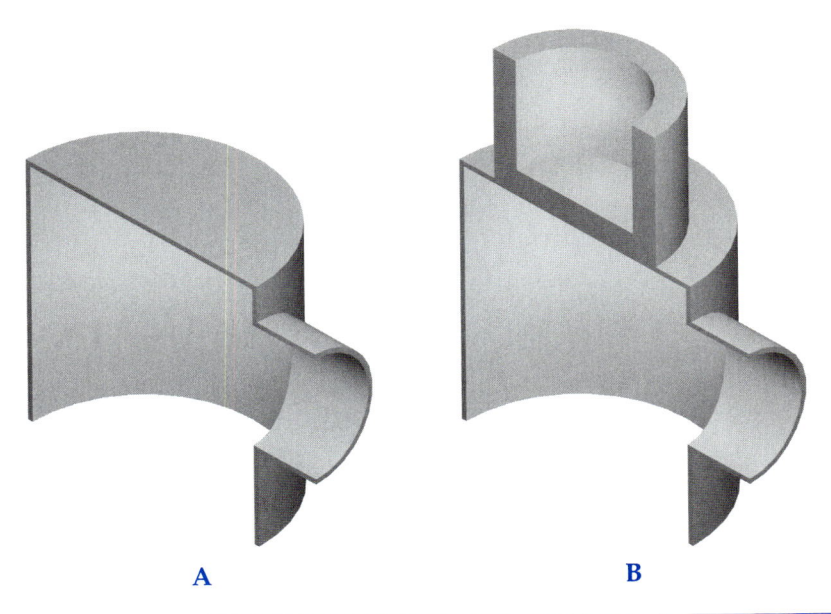

A   B

Chapter 7   Adding More Features

Figure 7-7.
A—A rib is added to the angled bracket. B—This is a web on an angled bracket.

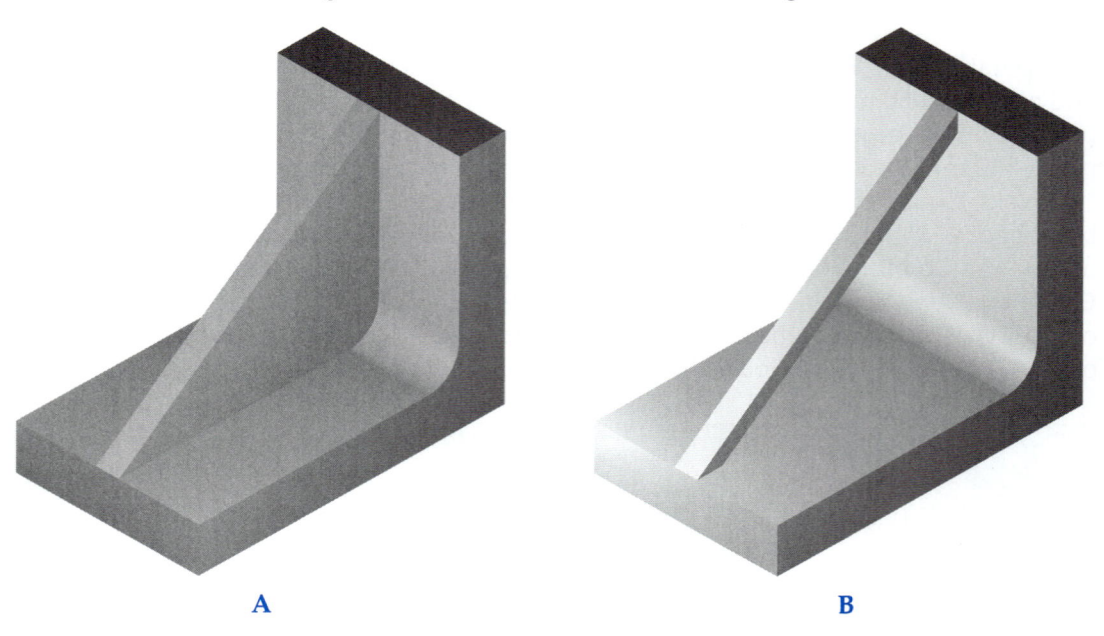

A

B

the flyout below the **Convert Entities** button. Then, with the selection box in the **Select Entities** rollout active, pick the two red faces. Then, pick the green check mark button to project the lines. Press the [Esc] key to end the tool.

Draw a line between the endpoints of the projected lines, as shown in **Figure 7-8.** This line is the profile for the rib (or web). Also, select the two projected lines and turn them into construction lines. This is done by checking the **For construction** check box in the **Options** rollout of the **Line Properties Property Manager**. Finish the sketch.

Pick the **Rib** button on the **Features** tab in the **Command Manager**. Then, pick the sketch. The **Rib Property Manager** is displayed. See **Figure 7-9**. In the middle of the **Parameters** rollout, there are two buttons that set the extrusion direction. If you pick the **Normal to Sketch** button, the extrusion is applied perpendicular to the sketch plane. If you pick the **Parallel to Sketch** button, the extrusion is applied parallel to the sketch plane. In this case, pick the **Parallel to Sketch** button. If the preview arrow is not pointing toward the part, check the **Flip material side** check box.

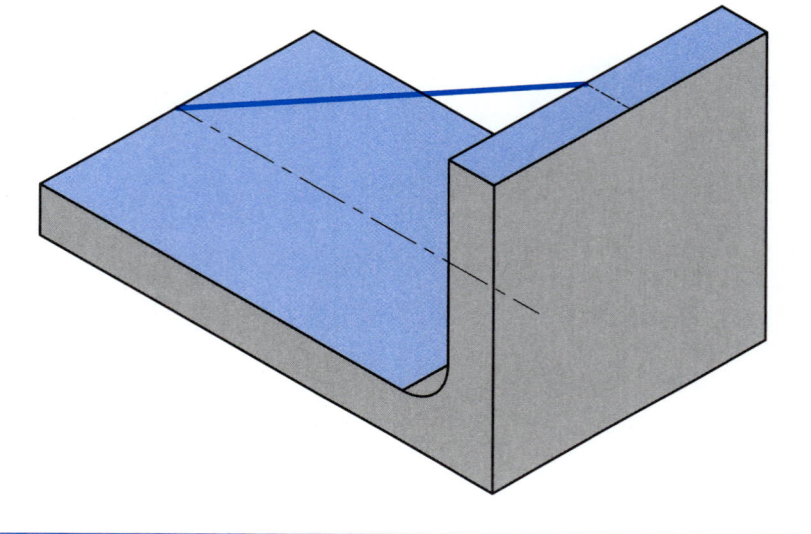

Figure 7-8.
Creating a line to use for the rib operation.

Figure 7-9.
Making settings for the rib operation.

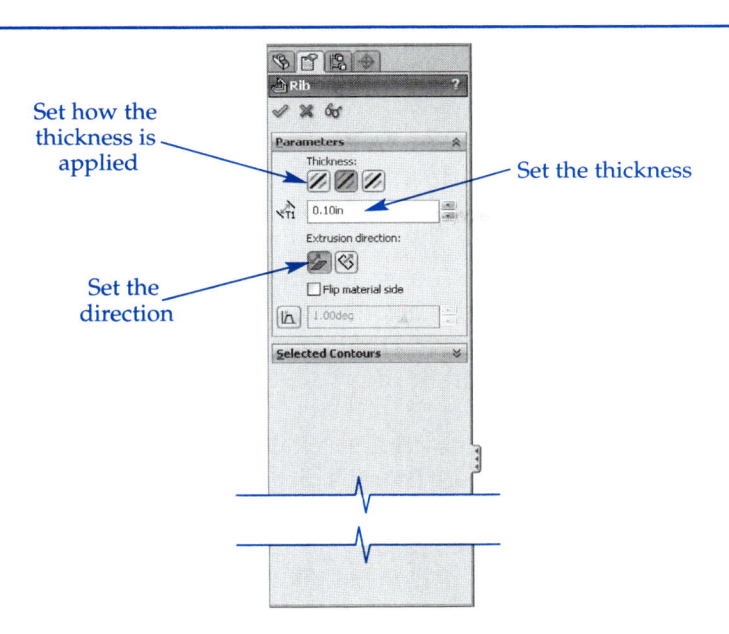

Set how the thickness is applied

Set the thickness

Set the direction

In the **Thickness** area of the **Parameters** rollout, enter .375″ in the **Rib Thickness** text box. This is the width of the rib. Above the **Rib Thickness** text box are three buttons that determine how the width is applied in relation to the sketched line. The width can be applied fully to one side or the other or equally on both sides of the line. For this example, select the **Both Sides** button so that the thickness is equally applied on each side of the line. Finally, pick the green check mark button to create the rib. See **Figure 7-10.**

The sketch curve (line) for a rib does not have to be drawn full length. By default, when using the **Rib** tool, the curve will be extended to the next faces. Open Example_07_06.sldprt. The line was drawn with the top of the box as the sketch plane. The length of the line is arbitrary, but the line passes through the center of the part. Activate the **Rib** tool, pick the line as the profile, and set the thickness to .125″. Pick the **Normal to Sketch** button and make sure

Figure 7-10.
The rib is completed.

Chapter 7 Adding More Features

141

the preview arrow points down toward the part. Next, pick the green check mark button to create the rib. The rib extends from wall-to-wall. Also, notice that the rib is not created inside of the hole. See **Figure 7-11**.

Now, edit the rib feature. In the **Parameters** rollout of the **Rib Property Manager**, select the **Draft On/Off** button so it is on (depressed). This applies a draft angle to the rib. Enter 20 in the **Draft Angle** text box. This value is used for emphasis; a draft angle is typically 1 or 2 degrees. By default, the **Draft outward** check box is checked. This applies the draft angle so the rib gradually gets thicker as it extends toward the part. Pick the green check mark button to update the part.

The **Rib** tool also accepts multiple lines as profiles. Open Example_07_07.sldprt. Five lines are drawn through the centers of the six hole bosses. Note that the lines do not touch the outside walls of the part. Activate the **Rib** tool, select all five lines as the profile, and set the thickness to .1″. Pick the **Normal to Sketch** button and pick the green check mark button to create the ribs. See **Figure 7-12**.

You are not limited to straight lines as the rib profile. Circles, arcs, and splines can also be selected as profiles. **Figure 7-13** shows a part where the ribs were created with a circle and three lines. Open Example_07_08.sldprt. Study this part to see how the profiles were created. Notice that there is only one rib operation listed in the design tree.

Figure 7-11.
A rib is added to the inside of the part. The rib does not pass through the hole.

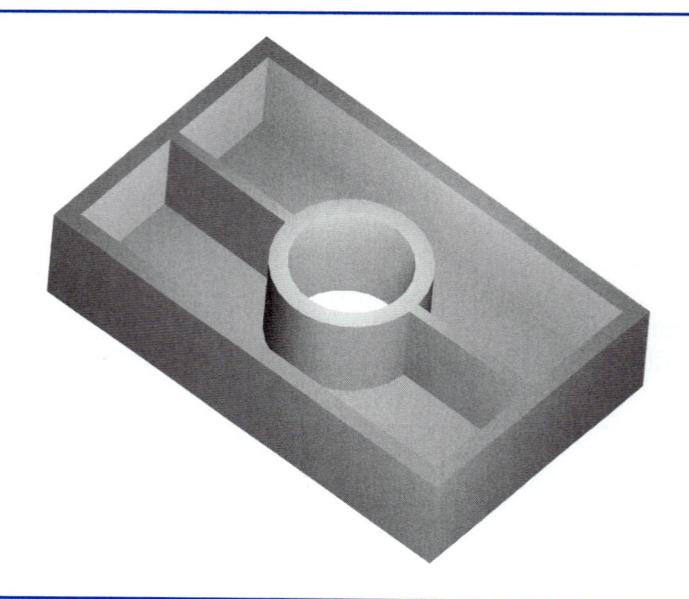

Figure 7-12.
Five lines were used to create the ribs in this part in a single operation.

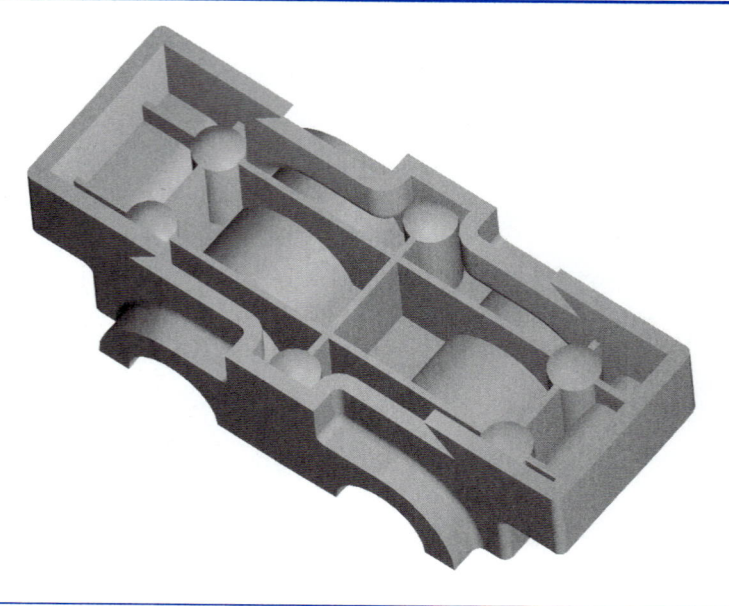

Figure 7-13.
A combination of lines and a circle were used to create the ribs on this part.

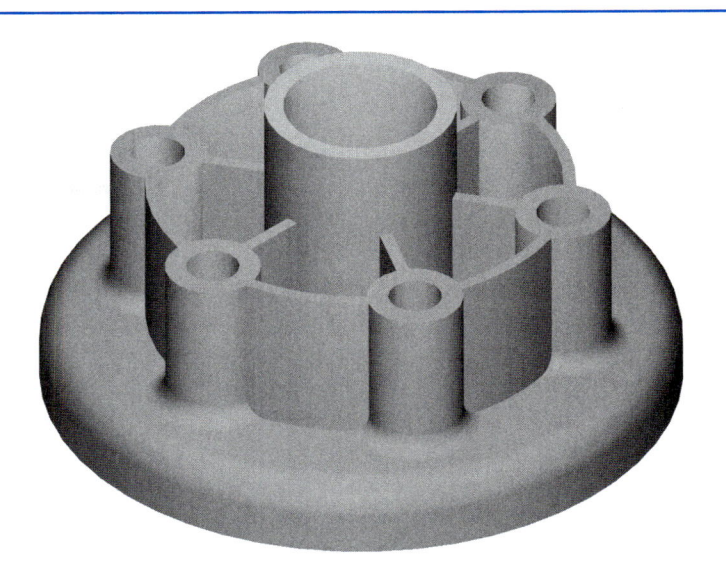

Creating Text

To *emboss* a sketch or its selected contours means to extrude them above a face. To *scribe* a sketch means to cut, or engrave, it into a face. The **Extruded Boss/Base** and **Extruded Cut** tools can both emboss and scribe text created by the sketch **Text** tool. In this section, you will look at adding sketch-based text features to both planar faces and cylindrical surfaces.

Open Example_07_09.sldprt. You will now place text on the top, flat face of the cylinder. Later, you will emboss this text. Pick the **Sketch** button on the **Sketch** tab of the **Command Manager** and select the front face as the sketch plane. Then, pick the **Text** button. The **Sketch Text Property Manager** is displayed, **Figure 7-14.**

Figure 7-14.
Adding text to a sketch.

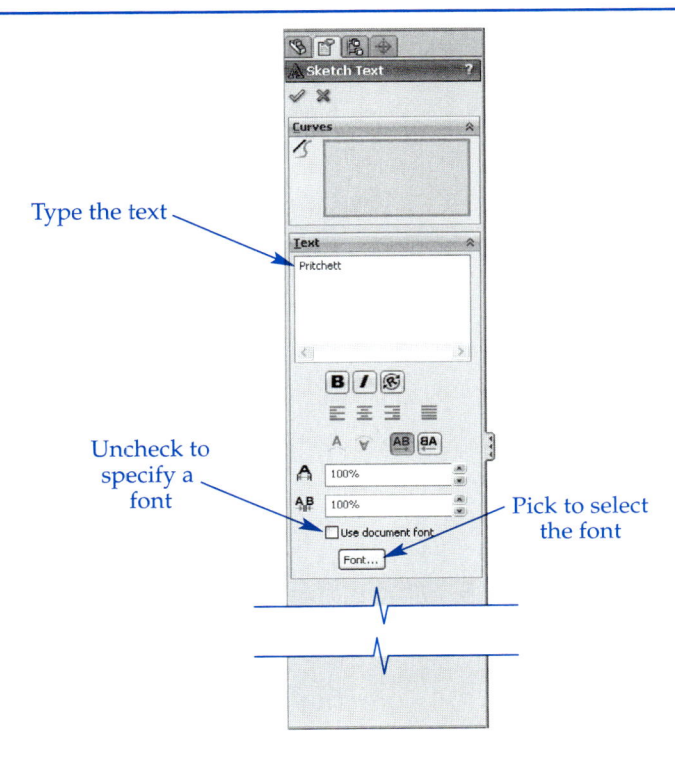

Type the text

Uncheck to specify a font

Pick to select the font

Chapter 7 Adding More Features   **143**

In the **Text** rollout, pick in the large edit box and type your name. To change the font, uncheck the **Use document font** check box. Then, pick the **Font...** button to display the **Choose Font** dialog box. This is a standard Windows font selection dialog box. Choose the font and set the size, then pick the **OK** button. For this example, select Arial in the **Font:** list. Also, pick the **Units** radio button in the **Height:** area and enter 1 in the text box to its right. This sets the text height to 1".

Now, pick the green check mark button in the **Sketch Text Property Manager** to place the text. Next, drag the text so your name is approximately centered on the face. Finally, finish the sketch. You may now use the **Extruded Boss/Base** tool to emboss or **Extruded Cut** tool to engrave the text on the planar surface of a part just as you would any other sketch profile.

PROFESSIONAL TIP

To create rotated text, draw a line at the proper angle. Then, using the selection box in the **Curves** rollout, select the line. The text is aligned with the line.

Wrapping Features onto Non-Planar Faces

Open Example_07_10.sldprt. This part has text created on a reference plane offset from the curved face. The text is Arial font and .625" high. Pick the **Wrap** button on the **Features** tab of the **Command Manager**. Then, select the sketch containing the text as the profile. You will need to use the flyout **Feature Manager** design tree.

In the **Wrap Parameters** rollout, pick the **Deboss** radio button. Then, enter .1" in the **Depth** text box. Pick the selection box in the **Wrap Parameters** rollout so it is active (highlighted blue). Then, pick the curved face on the part. Finally, pick the green check mark button to engrave the text. See **Figure 7-15.** Notice how the edges of the text are engraved perpendicular to the face of the cylinder.

Figure 7-15.
The text is wrapped onto the curved face of the cylinder.

Edit the feature. In the **Pull Direction** rollout, pick the selection box so it is active. Then, pick the reference axis in the graphics window. Update the feature. The text is not wrapped onto the face before being engraved. In this manner, the letters are distorted. The three letters are distorted at the beginning and end of the word. See **Figure 7-16**.

> **PROFESSIONAL TIP**
>
> The **Wrap** tool can be used to wrap any sketched contour onto a face, not just text. You can wrap text to planar or cylindrical faces.

Drafts

Some manufacturing processes, such as casting, forging, and injection molding, require a draft angle on the part. A *draft angle* is an angle on the sides of a part so that the part can be removed from the forming tool. Therefore, the forming tool itself must have corresponding angles on its cavity walls. The actual feature, the angled sides, is called the *draft*. A draft angle can be created on a part when a sketch is extruded or later using the **Draft** tool. This tool can also be used to put a unique draft angle on one or more faces, simplifying the construction process.

Neutral Plane

The **Draft** tool requires several selections and is best explained with a simple part. Open Example_07_11.sldprt. This part file contains two extruded blocks. The left-hand block has two colored faces; one green face and one yellow face. The draft will be applied to the yellow face. Pick the **Draft** button on the **Features** tab in the **Command Manager**. The **Draft Property Manager** is displayed, **Figure 7-17**.

Figure 7-16.
A—Text is engraved in a curved feature, but distorted. B—In a top view, you can see that the lines are parallel, resulting in the distortion of the text.

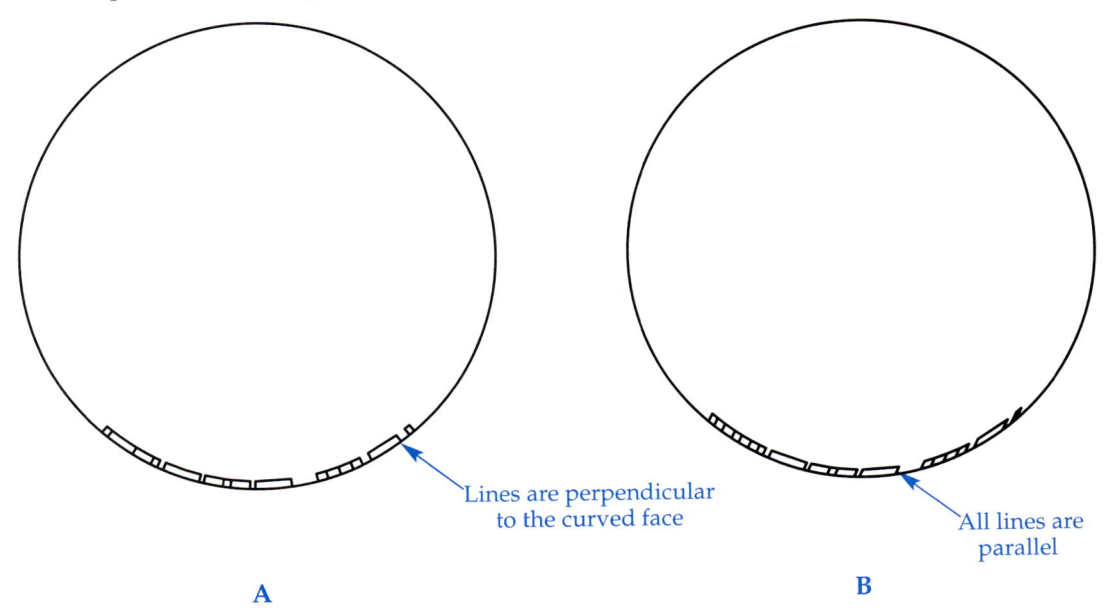

Lines are perpendicular to the curved face

All lines are parallel

A

B

Chapter 7 Adding More Features

Figure 7-17.
Making settings for a draft angle.

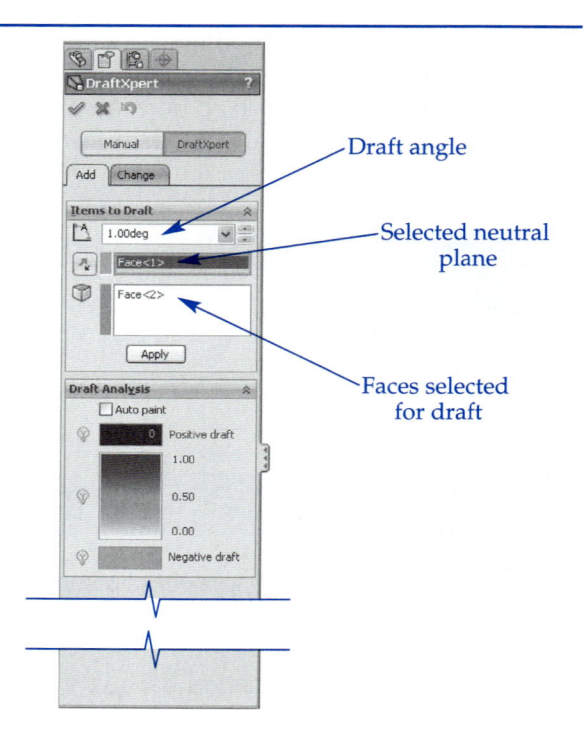

The draft angle is set in the **Draft Angle** text box in the **Items to Draft** rollout. Typically, a draft angle is only 2° to 3°. For this example, a large angle is used to emphasize the effect of the operation. Pick in the text box and enter 20 as the draft angle.

The draft will be applied with a pull direction perpendicular to a neutral plane. If you imagine a mold over the top of this part, the pull direction is the direction the mold is "pulled" to remove the molded part. With the **Neutral Plane** selection box active in the **Items to Draft** rollout, select the green face on the left-hand box. An arrow appears on the face indicating the direction that the mold will be pulled from the part. Make sure that the arrow is pointing up, or away from the part. You can flip the pull direction by selecting the **Reverse Direction** button next to the **Neutral Plane** selection box or by picking the arrow in the graphics window.

Next, you need to select the faces to which the draft angle will be applied. With the **Faces to Draft** selection box active in the **Items to Draft** rollout, pick the yellow face on the left-hand box. If needed, you can pick multiple faces. However, for this example, only select the yellow face. Then, pick the green check mark button in the **Property Manager** to apply the draft angle. See **Figure 7-18.**

The right-hand block will have a draft angle applied using a reference plane to locate the draft. Pick the **Draft** button on the **Features** tab. Enter 20° as the draft angle, if it is not already entered. With the **Neutral Plane** selection box active, pick the reference plane in the middle of the block. An arrow should appear on or near the plane. If the arrow does not point up, reverse the direction. Now, with the **Faces to Draft** selection box active, pick the purple face. Then, pick the green check mark button to apply the draft. The resulting draft is significantly different than the previous one. See **Figure 7-19.** Compare the two methods to see where material was added and subtracted.

PROFESSIONAL TIP

Both methods of adding draft affected the entire face. If the face above or below the work plane needs to remain undrafted, the face has to be split. You will learn how to do this in the Split Tools section in this chapter.

Figure 7-18.
A—The pick point determines which edge is fixed and used to create the draft. The top edge is fixed. B—The resulting draft.

A

B

Figure 7-19.
A—Using a reference plane to create the draft. B—The resulting draft.

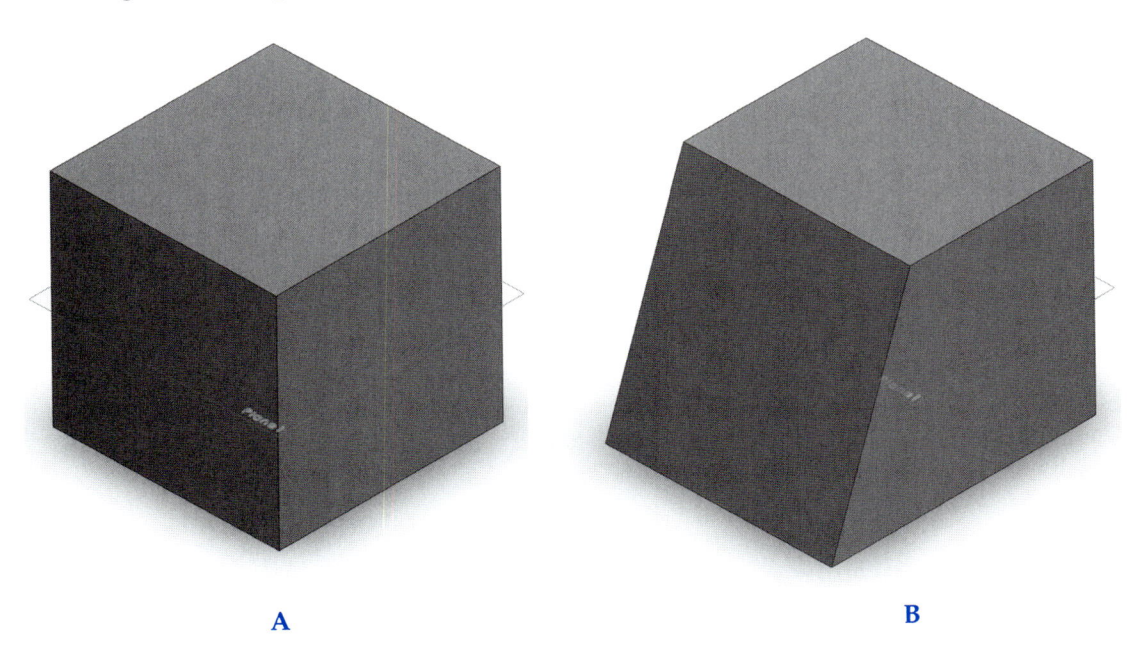

A

B

Other Drafts

Open Example_07_12.sldprt. Two of the cavity's vertical edges are filleted; the other two are square. Because of the adjacent fillets, SolidWorks will not be able to apply a draft angle to just the red face.

Chapter 7 Adding More Features 147

Activate the **Draft** tool. Pick the **Manual** button at the top of the **Draft Property Manager**. In the **Type of Draft** rollout, pick the **Neutral Plane** radio button. In the **Draft Angle** rollout, set the angle to 12° (for emphasis). With the selection box active in the **Neutral Plane** rollout, pick the green face; the arrow should point up out of the cavity. Pick the selection box in the **Faces to Draft** rollout to activate it. Select the red face on the cavity wall.

If you attempt to apply the draft now, SolidWorks will generate an error. This is due to the filleted corners of the cavity that are connected to the red face. In the **Face propagation:** drop-down list at the bottom of the **Faces to Draft** rollout, choose Along Tangent. Notice that the red face, the two filleted corners and the two long side faces are all selected. Finally, pick the green check mark button to create the draft. See **Figure 7-20.** If you look at the top edge of the cavity, you can see that three of the walls have a face draft. The fourth wall, between the square corners, remains straight.

PRACTICE 7-1

Complete the practice problem on the student website.
www.g-wlearning.com/CAD

Split Tools

The **Split** feature and **Split Line** tools are used to divide a part or face based on selected geometry. The split can be along a face, reference plane, or sketched curve. When the **Split** tool is used on a part, one or more areas of the split part may be discarded. When using the **Split Line** tool, which works on faces, all sides of the split are retained. Also, with this tool you can select multiple faces or apply the split to all of the faces on the part. The examples in this section demonstrate the principles of the two split tools. At the end of this section, a practical example is provided.

Figure 7-20.
The face draft is applied to the three walls connected by radii.

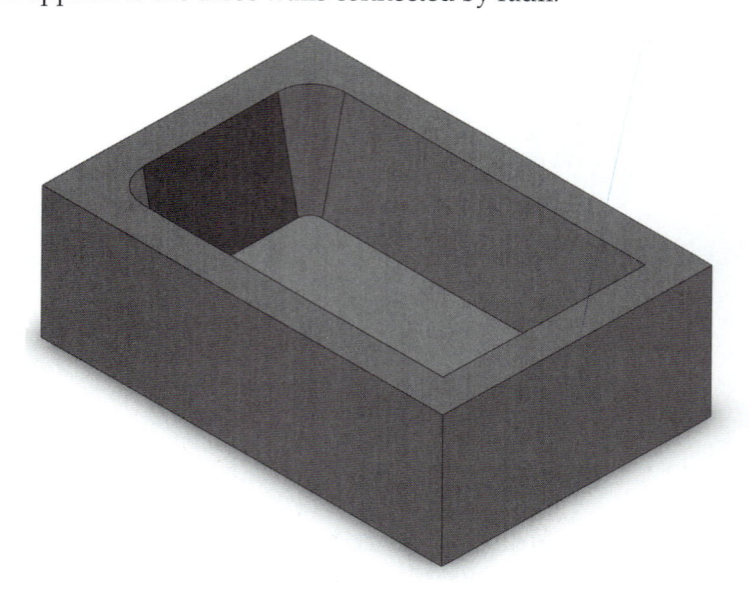

Using the Split Tool

Open Example_07_13.sldprt. There is an unconsumed sketch on the front face consisting of two lines and two arcs. This sketch will be used to split the part. Activate the **Split** tool by selecting **Insert>Features>Split...** from the pull-down menu. The **Split Property Manager** is displayed, **Figure 7-21.** This tool applies the operation to the part, not faces.

Now, activate the selection box in the **Trim Tools** rollout, if it is not already active. Then, select the sketch in the graphics window. Pick the **Cut Part** button in the **Trim Tools** rollout. A preview of the split solid appears in the viewing area. In the **Resulting Bodies** rollout is a small spreadsheet listing the bodies that will result from the split. Picking a row so it is highlighted also highlights the corresponding body in the graphics area. In this example, highlighting row 2 should highlight the top body on the part. Check the check box in that row to indicate the top body will be cut. Then, check the **Consume cut bodies** check box below the spreadsheet. This means the cut body will be removed from the part. Finally, pick the green check mark button in the **Property Manager** to split the part. The top of the part is removed. See **Figure 7-22.**

Using the Split Line Tool

Delete the split operation from the design tree. Do this by right-clicking on the Split branch and selecting **Delete** from the shortcut menu. When asked to confirm the deletion, pick the **Yes** button. Now, pick the **Split Line** button on the **Features** tab of the **Command Manager**. It is located in the flyout below the **Curves** button.

In the **Type of Split** rollout, pick the **Projection** radio button. With the **Sketch to Project** selection box active in the **Selections** rollout, pick the sketch on the part. Next, with the **Faces to Split** selection box active, pick the front face on the part. Finally, pick the green check mark button to split the face.

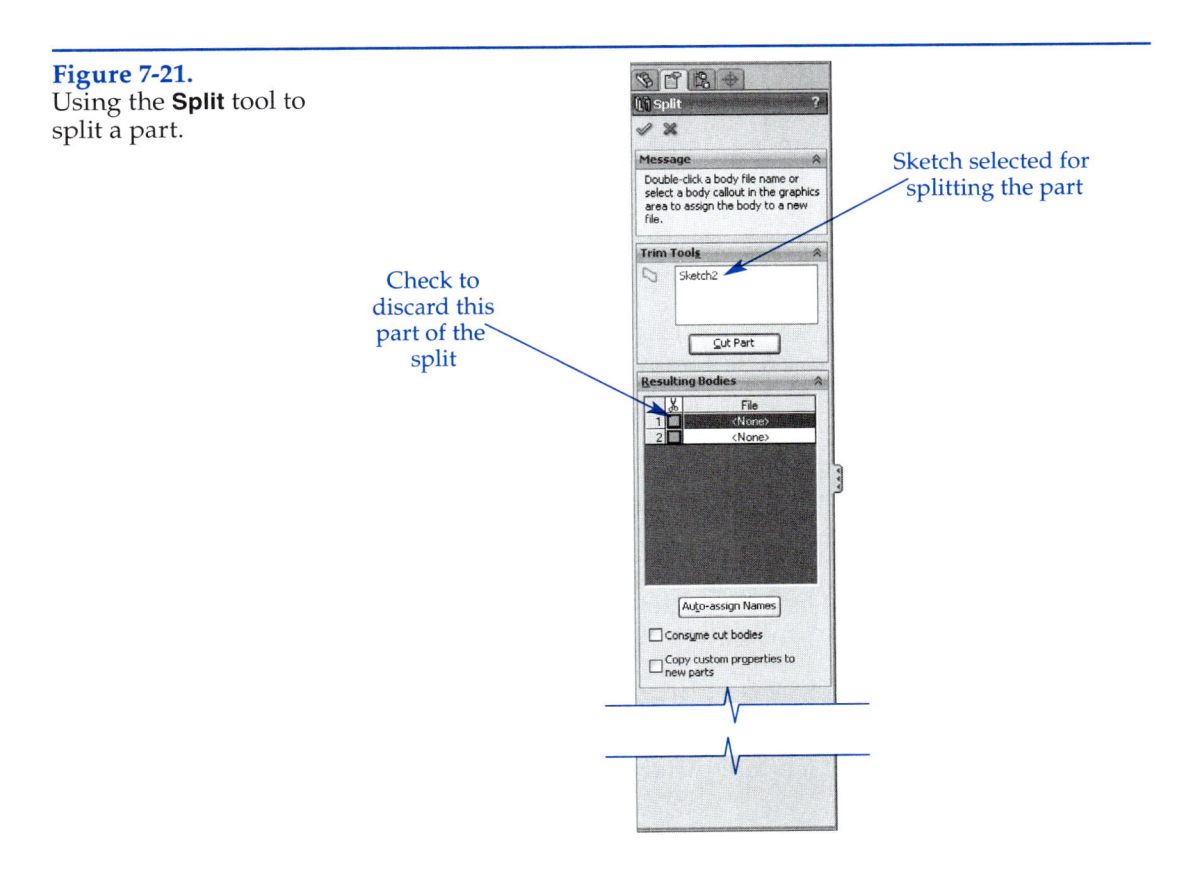

Figure 7-21.
Using the **Split** tool to split a part.

Chapter 7 Adding More Features

149

Figure 7-22.
This part was created by splitting a block.

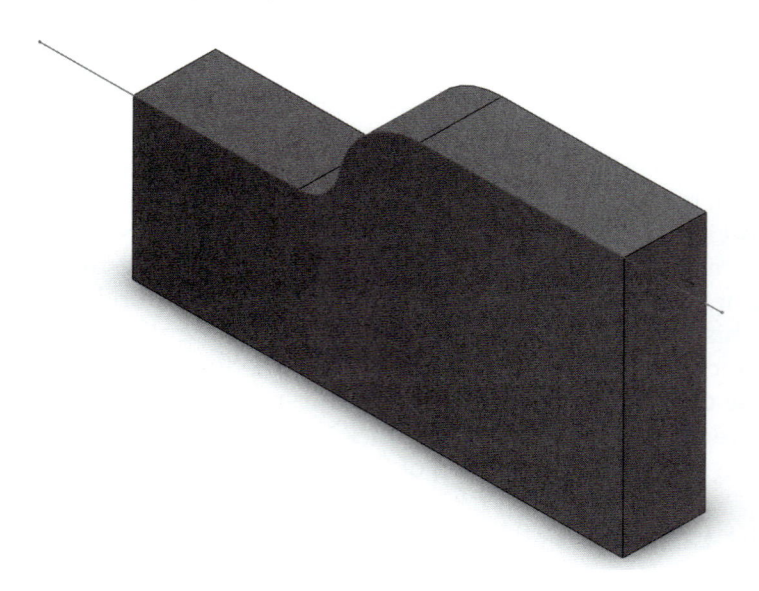

The face is now divided into two parts. Change the color of each face. Right-click on a face and select the **Appearances** drop-down list in the shortcut toolbar. See **Figure 7-23A.** Then, select the face in the drop-down list. The **Appearances Property Manager** appears. See **Figure 7-23B.** In the **Color** rollout, select a color for the face. Then, pick the green check mark button to change the color of the face. The end result is shown in **Figure 7-24.**

Chapter Test

Answer the following questions on a separate sheet of paper or complete the electronic chapter test on the student website.
www.g-wlearning.com/CAD

1. What is the purpose of the **Shell** tool?
2. Why would faces be removed during the shell operation?
3. Which types of faces can be removed during a shell operation?
4. Define *web*.
5. Define *rib*.
6. Which tool is used to create a rib?
7. Which type(s) of objects are used as the path by the tool(s) in question 7?
8. Define *emboss*.
9. Define *scribe*.
10. Which tools can be used to emboss text? Which tool is used to engrave text?
11. Which tool is used to create text in a sketch?
12. Define *draft angle*.
13. Which tool is used to create a draft angle on a part?
14. What is the purpose of the **Split** tool?
15. How does the **Split Line** tool differ from the **Split** tool?

Figure 7-23.
Changing the color of a feature, in this case the face created by the split. A—Selecting what to change. B—Selecting the color for the selected feature.

A

B

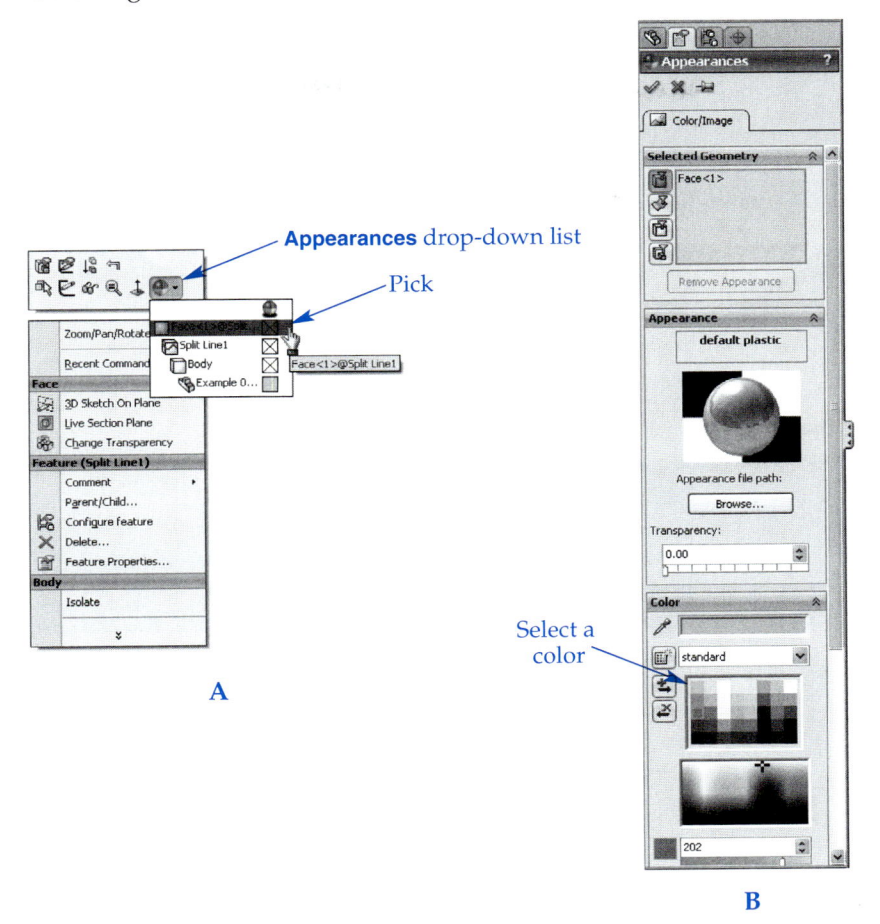

Figure 7-24.
The color of the selected feature has been changed.

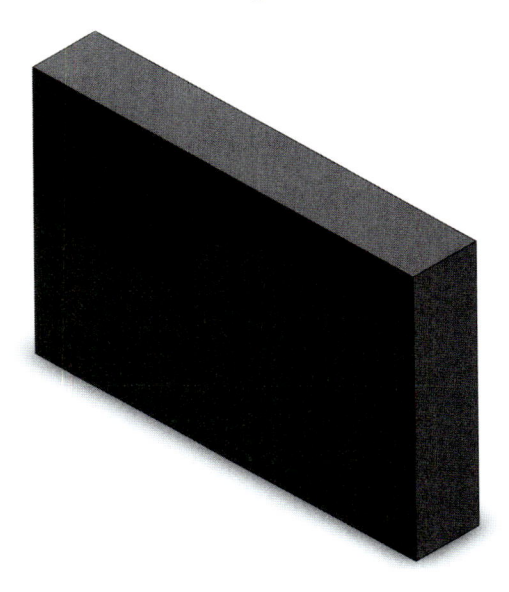

Chapter 7 Adding More Features

Chapter Exercises

Complete the chapter exercises on the student website.
www.g-wlearning.com/CAD

Exercise 7-1 Casting.
Complete the exercise on the student website.

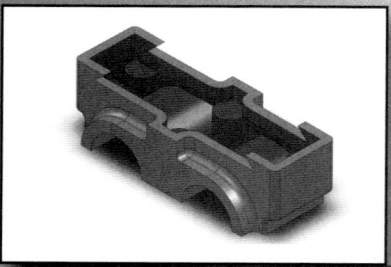

Exercise 7-2 Windshield Wiper Arm.
Complete the exercise on the student website.

Exercise 7-3 Ribbed Collar.
Complete the exercise on the student website.

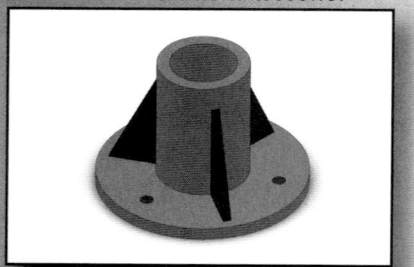

Exercise 7-4 Extruded Text.
Complete the exercise on the student website.

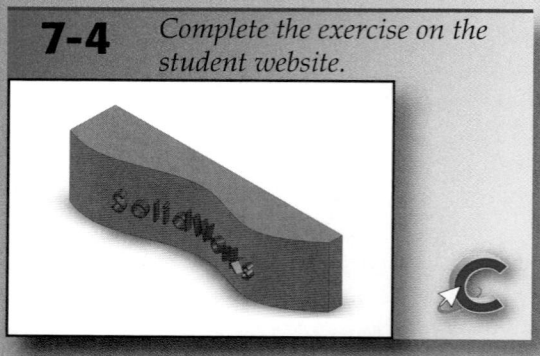

Exercise 7-5 Magnet.
Complete the exercise on the student website.

Learning SolidWorks 2009

Chapter 8

Creating Part Drawings

Objectives

After completing this chapter, you will be able to:
- Create 2D drawings of SolidWorks models.
- Specify drawing sheet size and border.
- Explain the different views that can be created in drawing files and describe how to create them.
- Edit existing drawing views.
- Update drawing views when the part changes.

Creating a 2D Part Drawing

2D engineering drawings can be directly developed from SolidWorks part and assembly files. This chapter explains how to create part drawings and the various types of views. Views created in a drawing are directly related to the part model and any changes in the model are automatically reflected in the drawing. The same functionality applies when creating assembly drawings. Assembly drawings are discussed in a later chapter.

The easiest procedure to create a part drawing is to have the part file open. Open the file **Example_08_01.sldprt**. See **Figure 8-1**. This is a cast and machined part. Notice the part's orientation with respect to the default planes and the direction of the X, Y, and Z axes. Remember, the X axis on the triad is red, the Y axis is green, and the Z axis is blue. This will help you understand the creation of the drawing views. Now, select **Make Drawing from Part/Assembly** from the **New** flyout in the **Menu Bar**.

A new SolidWorks drawing file is opened and the **Sheet Format/Size** dialog box appears, **Figure 8-2**. The **Standard sheet size** radio button is selected by default and allows you to select a predefined sheet format based on the settings in a sheet format file (template file). Sheet format files have a **slddrt** extension. The predefined sheet formats are identified by sheet size and orientation. There are two standard types of sheet sizes available—US customary (for inch drawings) and metric (for drawings made in millimeters). The sheet formats corresponding to the letter sizes A through E

Figure 8-1.
The drawing views of this part will be created in a part drawing.

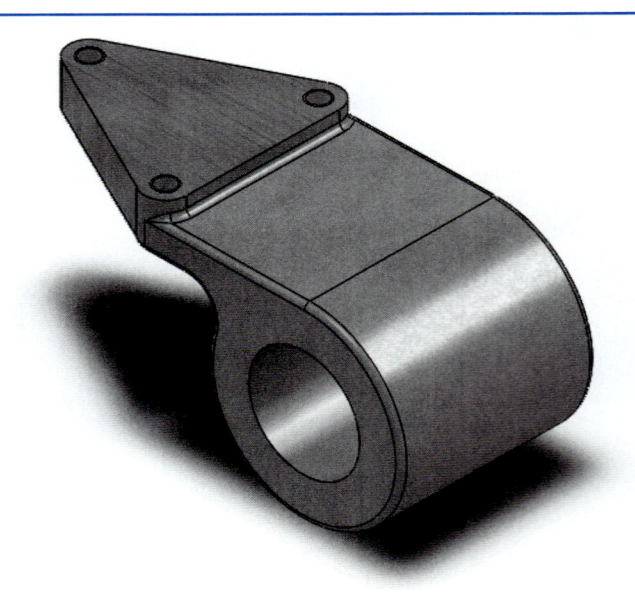

Figure 8-2.
When starting a new drawing file, a predefined sheet format can be selected from the **Sheet Format/Size** dialog box.

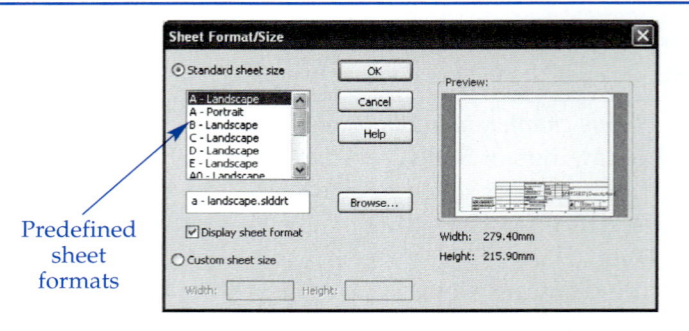

Predefined sheet formats

are for inch drawings. These formats specify that dimensions are in inches in the title block. The sheet formats corresponding to the letter number sizes A0 through A4 are for metric drawings. These formats specify that dimensions are in millimeters in the title block. Since the part for this example is drawn in metric units, we'll create an A2-size drawing. Select A2-Landscape in the **Sheet Format/Size** dialog box and pick **OK**.

PROFESSIONAL TIP

New files you create are set to default units based on the default SolidWorks settings on your system. The unit settings for a document can be found in the **Document Properties** tab of the options/properties dialog box. Documents based on US customary units are set to IPS (inch, pound, second). Documents based on metric units are set to MMGS (millimeter, gram, second). If you need to use more than one unit format for new drawings, you can set up template files with different unit settings and use them to start new files. A template can be used to start a new file by picking the **Advanced** button in the **New SolidWorks Document** dialog box and selecting the desired template. When using this method, the template must be stored in the SolidWorks Template folder. Templates for part, assembly, and drawing files have the characters dot in the file extension. A template drawing file has the file extension drwdot. A template file can be created by opening an existing file or template file, making the appropriate settings, and then saving the file as a template using the appropriate file option in the **Save As** dialog box.

The new drawing appears and the **View Palette** is displayed on the right side of the screen. See **Figure 8-3**. The new drawing consists of a sheet, border, and title block. The *sheet* is the beige drawing area. It determines the size of the border and the title block. For example, if you change the size of the sheet, the border and title block change with it. The *border* consists of the outer rectangles with the alphanumeric zone labels. The *title block* is located in the lower-right corner of the border and consists of areas for the drawing title, date, designer's initials, sheet size, and other information.

> **NOTE**
>
> You can make changes to the title block and border of a sheet by editing the sheet format. The sheet format is edited by right-clicking on the sheet name in the design tree and selecting **Edit Sheet Format** from the shortcut menu. This is discussed in Chapter 9.

The **View Palette** shows preview images of the views of the part. It is used to drag views into the drawing. Picking anywhere on screen closes the **View Palette**. You can redisplay it by picking the **View Palette** tab on the task pane.

Notice in the title block that the drawing's current sheet size is A2. Suppose a larger size sheet (such as A1) is needed. To change the sheet size, right-click on Sheet1 in the design tree and select **Properties...** from the shortcut menu. This opens the **Sheet Properties** dialog box, **Figure 8-4**. In the **Sheet Format/Size** area, select a different

Figure 8-3.
A new SolidWorks drawing file with the default border and title block.

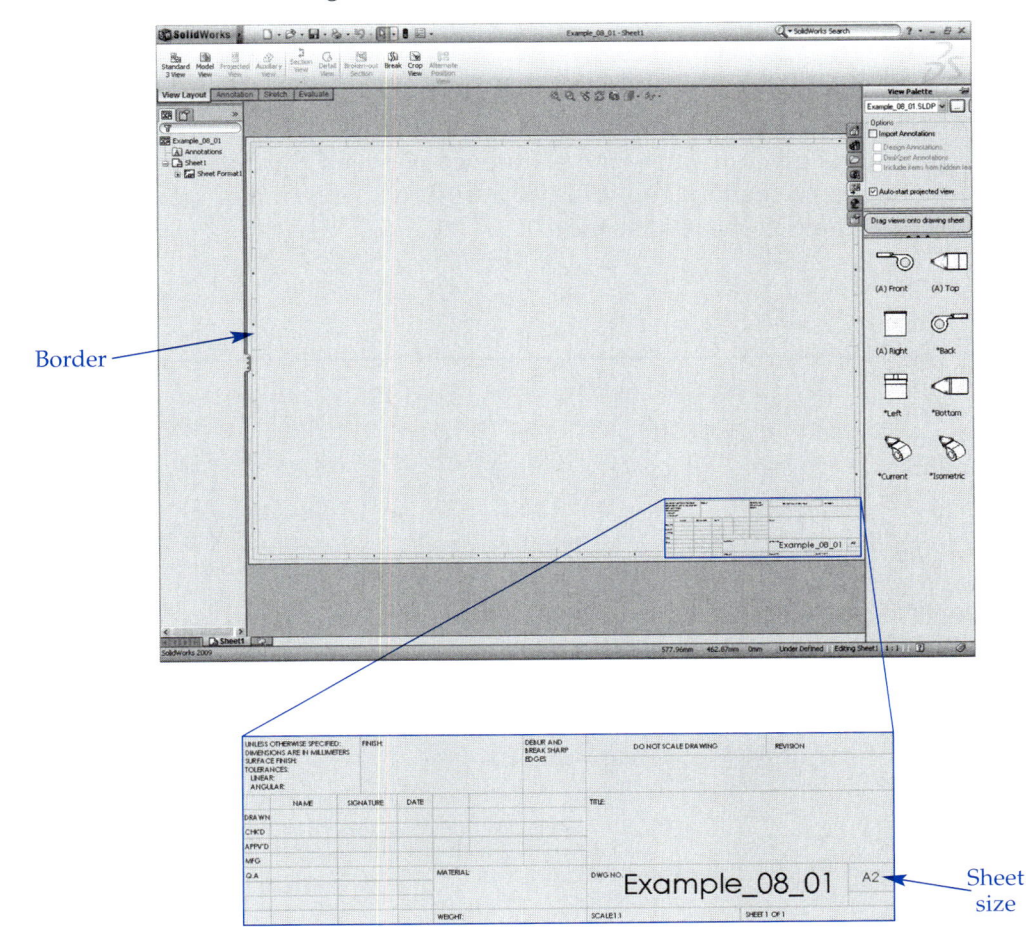

Chapter 8   Creating Part Drawings

Figure 8-4.
The **Sheet Properties** dialog box is used to change the sheet size, rename the sheet, and change the type of projection.

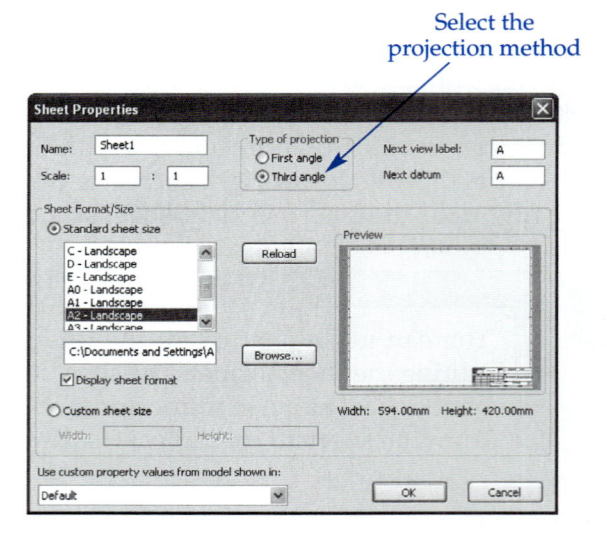

sheet size. Pick **OK** to exit the dialog box. In the graphics window, the larger sheet is displayed, the border expands to fill the new sheet, and the title block text indicates the sheet size. Now, reopen the **Sheet Properties** dialog box. Notice the options in the **Type of Projection** area. These options control how the drawing views are projected. First-angle projection is used in Europe, and third-angle projection is used in the United States. For this example, select the **Third angle** radio button in the **Type of Projection** area and make sure the sheet size is set to A2-Landscape. A comparison of different view projections is shown in **Figure 8-5**.

> **NOTE**
>
> In Figure 8-5, the top view of the part is selected as the front orthographic view. This orientation is used for illustration purposes only and is given to show the difference between third-angle and first-angle projection. You will use a different selection of views for the example in the next section.

Figure 8-5.
A comparison between third-angle projection and first-angle projection. For the examples shown, the top view of the part is selected as the front orthographic view. A—Third-angle projection. This type of projection is common in the United States. B—First-angle projection. This type of projection is common in Europe.

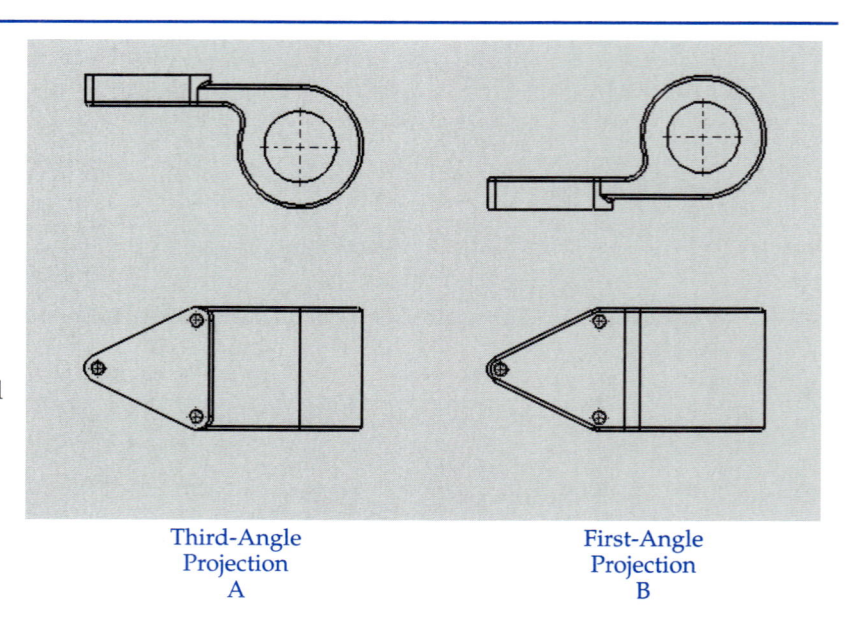

Third-Angle Projection
A

First-Angle Projection
B

156   Learning SolidWorks 2009

Creating the Drawing Views

As a 2D drawing layout is created, you are actually working on a separate drawing file. However, when drawing views of a part are created, the part file is linked to the drawing file. This means that any future changes made to the part are automatically updated in the drawing file. This also works the other way. If you change a dimension in a drawing view within the drawing file, the part file updates to reflect the new values.

Save the new drawing you created as Example_08_01.slddrw. Now, pick the **Window** pull-down menu and notice that there are two SolidWorks files open. The SLDPRT file—Example_08_01.sldprt—is the part file for this example and the SLDDRW file is the 2D drawing that you are creating.

PROFESSIONAL TIP

More than one part file can be used to create drawing views in a single drawing layout. For example, you may need to create a sheet of details that contains views of many parts.

Creating a Base View

The next step is to create drawing views. Start by creating a *base view,* from which others will be generated. For the base view, select the view that is most representative of the shape or contour of the part and the one that will show the least number of hidden lines. How the view is named in SolidWorks depends on the plane selected for the first part sketch and on how the part was constructed.

The most straightforward way to create the base view is to drag and drop it from the **View Palette**. See **Figure 8-6**. For this part, pick the Back view and drag it to the left side of the drawing. In this example, the back view of the part will be used as the

Figure 8-6.
Using the **View Palette** to insert the base view of the drawing.

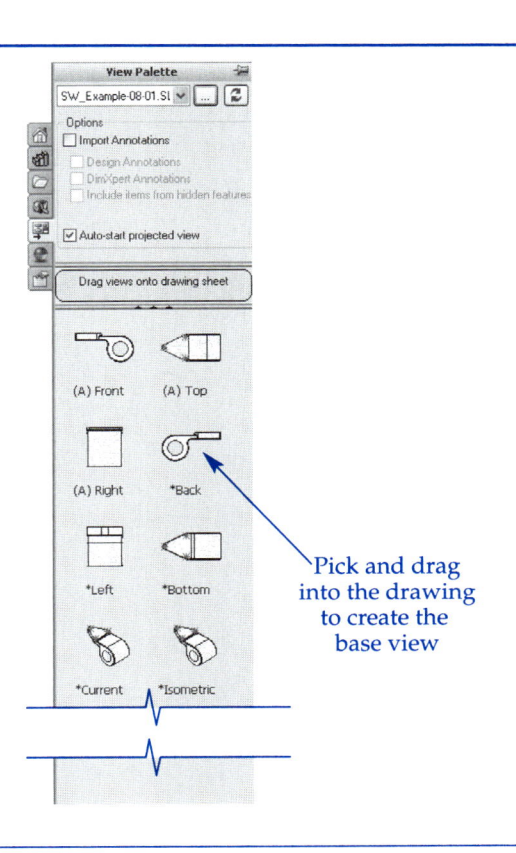

Chapter 8   Creating Part Drawings

front view in the orthographic drawing. This orientation will show fewer hidden lines in the drawing. Dragging the view from the **View Palette** into the drawing inserts the view and activates the **Projected View** tool. This tool allows you to "project" additional views into the drawing from the base view. Before you project the remaining views, you will set the scale of the base view and rename it. Pick the green check mark button in the **Projected View Property Manager** to exit the **Projected View** tool.

Next, move the cursor over the base view until the dashed view border is highlighted and pick on the border. This opens the **Drawing View Property Manager**. See **Figure 8-7**. In the **Scale** rollout, select the **Use custom scale** radio button and select a scale of 1:1 from the drop-down list. All other views created from the base view inherit this scale.

The options in the **Display Style** rollout determine how hidden lines are displayed and whether or not the part is shaded in the view. When the Wireframe option is selected, all visible and hidden lines of the part are shown. When the Hidden Lines Visible option is selected, visible lines are shown as solid lines and hidden lines are shown as dashed lines. When the Hidden Lines Removed option is selected, only visible lines are shown. When the Shaded With Edges option is selected, the part is shaded and edges are visible. When the Shaded option is selected, the part is shaded but edges are not visible. The Shaded styles are often used for an isometric view, which you will create later in this example. A shaded view also helps in visualizing the shape of the final part. For the base view, select the Hidden Lines Visible option. Then, pick the green check mark button to close the **Drawing View Property Manager**.

In the drawing file, the base view is listed as Drawing View1 in the design tree. Left-click two single times (do not double-click) on the name of the view and rename it Front View. Also, look at the title block. The drawing number is automatically entered as the part file name.

Figure 8-7.
The **Drawing View Property Manager** is used to set the scale, orientation, and display style of the view.

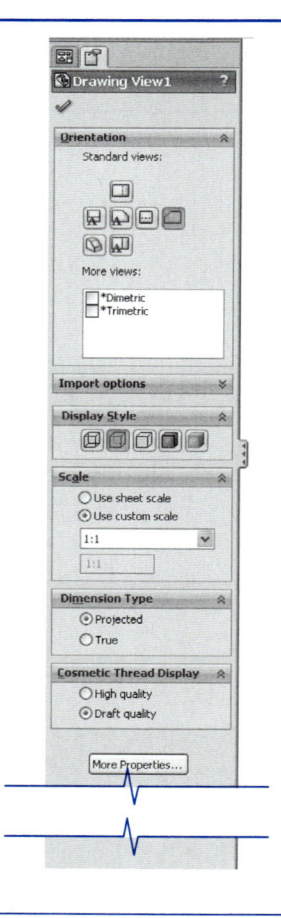

The base view could also be created by picking the **Model View** button in the **View Layout** tab of the **Command Manager**. This displays the **Model View Property Manager**. The **Part/Assembly to Insert** rollout shows the opened part model as the source for the 2D drawing layout. All open part files will be available in this rollout. Double-click on the name of the part from which you want to add a view. If no part file is open, you can specify any part file as the source by picking the **Browse…** button in the rollout. After selecting the part file, the **Model View Property Manager** is redisplayed with additional options. You can now select the views to create and set other options, such as scale and display style.

> **PROFESSIONAL TIP**
>
> Line weight and style settings for drawing file geometry are available in the **Document Properties** tab of the options/properties dialog box. These settings control line thickness and type and can be accessed by selecting Line Font on the left side of the dialog box. These are local settings that affect the currently open drawing file only.

Projecting Views

Now, three views will be projected from the base view (front view): top, right side, and isometric. Pick the **Projected View** button in the **View Layout** tab of the **Command Manager** and select the base view in the drawing. The **Projected View Property Manager** is opened and a line appears in the graphics window that originates from the base view and follows the cursor. Move the cursor directly above the front view and pick a point. A new view appears in the drawing. Now, move the cursor to the right of the front view and pick to create a right-side view. Another new view appears in the drawing. Next, move the cursor to the upper-right corner of the drawing sheet and pick to create an isometric view. Now, pick the green check mark button to close the **Projected View Property Manager** or press the [Esc] key to exit the **Projected View** tool.

Isometric views generally look better if the scale is less than that of the corresponding orthographic views. Sometimes, isometric views are also shaded. Select the isometric view in the drawing. In the **Drawing View Property Manager**, select the **Use custom scale** radio button and select User Defined from the drop-down list. Then, enter a scale of 1:1.2 in the text box below the drop-down list. Also, pick the **Shaded With Edges** button to shade the view. Pick the green check mark button to close the **Drawing View Property Manager**.

Views can be moved after they have been placed. Move the cursor over the view until the view border is highlighted. Then, pick on the border and drag the view to a new location. The top and right-side views can only be moved in a straight line from the base view. This is because they are constrained to the base view from which they were derived. However, the isometric view can be moved to anywhere on the drawing.

You have now seen how to set up a basic orthographic drawing of a part. In the next section, you will learn how to create other types of drawing views. Save and close both Example_08_01.sldprt and Example_08_01.slddrw.

> **PROFESSIONAL TIP**
>
> If you hold down the [Ctrl] key while placing the view, you will break the aligned relationship between the views and you can place the view anywhere you want on the drawing.

Creating Other Views

SolidWorks can be used to create a number of other views using the base view. These views include full sections, half sections, aligned sections, auxiliary views, detail views, broken-out section views, broken views, and relative views. The following sections describe these views.

Full Section View

Open Example_08_02.sldprt and Example_08_02.slddrw. In the drawing file, zoom in to the top view on the sheet using the **Zoom to Area** tool. Then, pick the **Section View** button in the **View Layout** tab of the **Command Manager**. Follow the steps listed below to define two points of the section line to create a full section view. Select your mouse picks carefully.

1. Hover over the center of the top view until the center point is acquired, but do *not* pick.
2. Move the cursor straight to the left until it is beyond the view border. Keep a straight projection line as you do this. A dotted line gives you visual feedback that you are keeping the line straight. Once the cursor is at a point beyond the border and the projection line is straight, pick that point. This is the start of the section line.
3. Move the cursor in a straight line to the right until it is beyond the border on the right side of the view. Pick that point.
4. Pick a point below the top view and the section view is created. See **Figure 8-8**.
5. After the view is created, the **Section View Property Manager** is displayed. See **Figure 8-9**. In the **Section Line** rollout, make sure that A is entered in the **Label** text box and not anything else, such as A-A or B. Also, select the **Use custom scale** radio button in the **Scale** rollout and select 1:2 from the drop-down list. Notice the **Flip direction** check box in the **Section Line** rollout. This option is used in case the section is oriented in the wrong direction.

This is a full section view of the part. If needed, you can just display the faces that are cut by checking the **Partial section** check box in the **Section View** rollout. The display style can be changed by using the options in the **Display Style** rollout.

Figure 8-8.
The cut line and the resulting section view. The display style for the section view is set to Hidden Lines Removed.

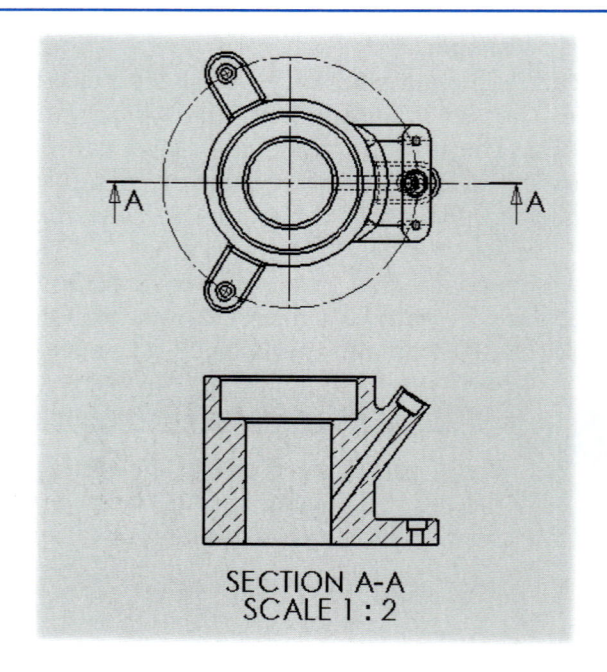

Figure 8-9.
The **Section View Property Manager** is used to define the orientation, view label, scale, and display style of the view.

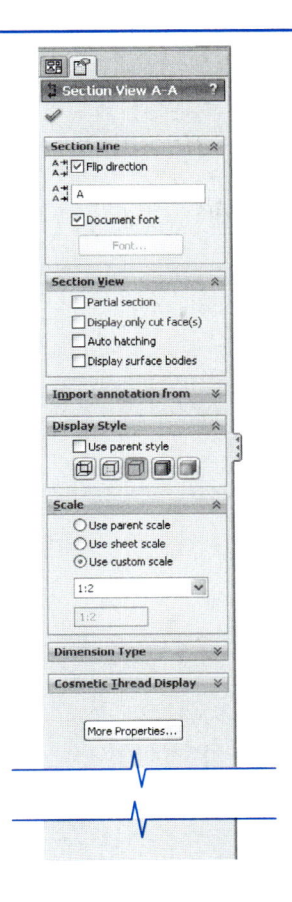

Create another section view. This time, do not select the center of the part—just sketch a straight line through the part. Then, pick and drag the cutting-plane line. Notice how the section view is redefined by dragging it to a new location.

These two section views are not fully descriptive according to drafting standards. Delete both of the section views you've just created by picking their borders and pressing the [Del] key. Then, continue to the next section.

Half Section View

A half section view is created by drawing two section lines that pass through the part and form a right angle. To create this type of view, you must first create a sketch that defines the "cut." Select the top view and pick on the **Sketch** tab. Using the **Line** tool, draw two construction lines by picking points as shown in **Figure 8-10**. The two lines must be selected before you start the **Section View** tool, so use the **Select** tool and the [Ctrl] key to pick the lines. Pick the vertical line first, then the horizontal line. Now, pick the **Section View** button in the **View Layout** tab of the **Command Manager** and pick a location below the top view.

Try moving the cutting-plane line for the section view in the top view. You will find that you will not be able to because of the way it was defined. As the points were picked, SolidWorks placed relations on the lines. They are, in essence, "nailed down" to the part's features. Delete the view and continue to the next section.

Partial Section

Create another section view and this time draw a horizontal section line from the center point of the top view to a point on the right outside of the view. A SolidWorks alert box appears and asks whether you want to create a partial section. Select **Yes** and locate the view below the top view. See **Figure 8-11**. Delete the view and continue to the next section.

Chapter 8 Creating Part Drawings

Figure 8-10.
The cut line and the resulting half section view.

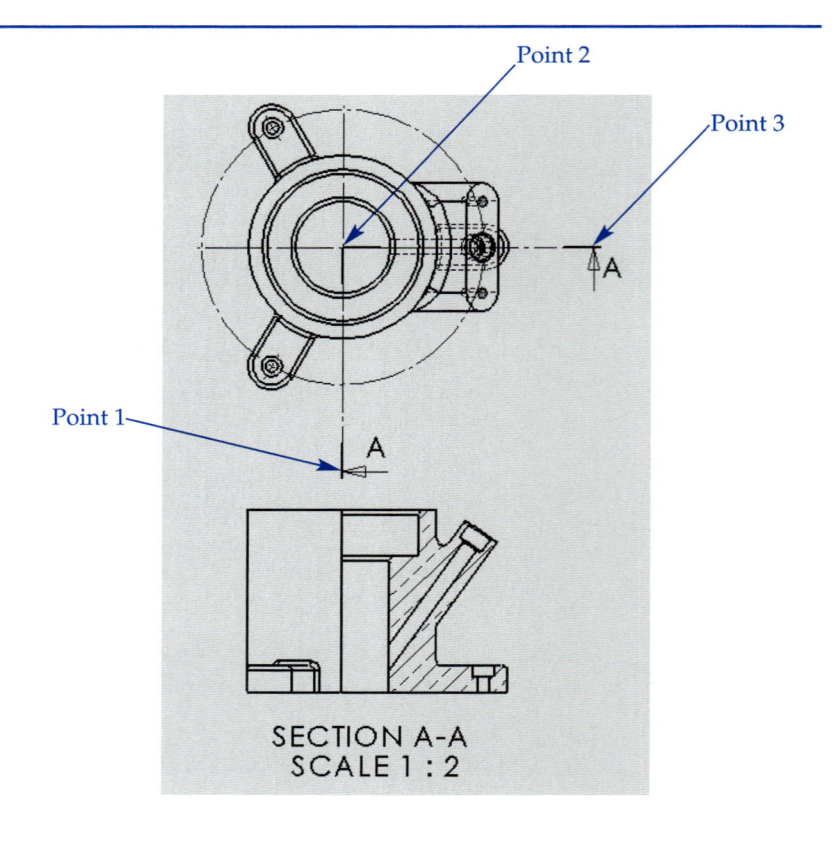

Figure 8-11.
Creating a partial section view.

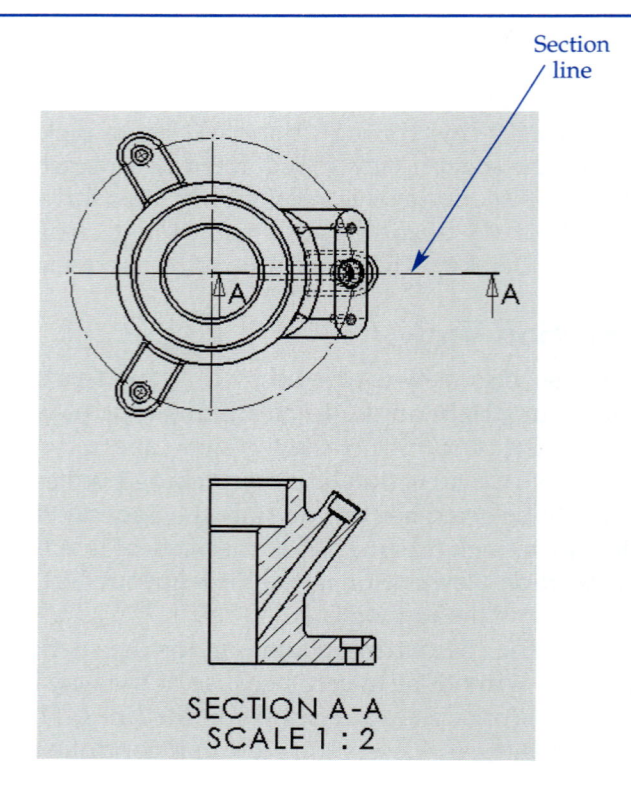

Aligned Section View

Drafting standards require the full section view to show the left mounting foot as if it were in the plane of the section line. This will require an aligned section view. In an *aligned section view*, features lying in a different plane are revolved into the

cutting plane. To create this type of view, pick on the **Section View** pull-down menu in the **View Layout** tab of the **Command Manager** and select **Aligned Section View**. You are prompted to draw two lines to define the section. Continue as follows.
1. Draw a line from the center point of the top view through the center of the lower-left foot. Refer to line 1 in **Figure 8-12**.
2. Right-click and select **End chain** from the shortcut menu.
3. Draw a second line from the center point to the right side of the view. Refer to line 2 in **Figure 8-12**. The order of drawing these lines is important as the section view is perpendicular to the second line you draw.
4. Move the cursor down below the top view and pick to generate the section view. You may have to flip the view using the **Flip direction** check box in the **Section Line** rollout of the **Section View Property Manager**. When finished, save and close both Example_08_02.sldprt and Example_08_02.slddrw.

PROFESSIONAL TIP

You can rename the view by entering a different letter in the **Section Line** rollout of the **Section View Property Manager**.

Auxiliary Views

An *auxiliary view* can be used to project a true representation of any inclined or oblique face on a part. Open Example_08_03.sldprt and Example_08_03.slddrw. The angled feature in this part requires an auxiliary view to show the inclined face so it can be dimensioned. A section view cannot be used to create an auxiliary view; therefore, you will project an auxiliary view from the front view in the Example_08_03.slddrw drawing file.

Pick the **Auxiliary View** button in the **View Layout** tab of the **Command Manager**. You are prompted to select a reference edge. Pick the edge view of the top face of the inclined boss in the front view. See **Figure 8-13**. Then, pick to position the new view.

Figure 8-12.
Creating an aligned section view.

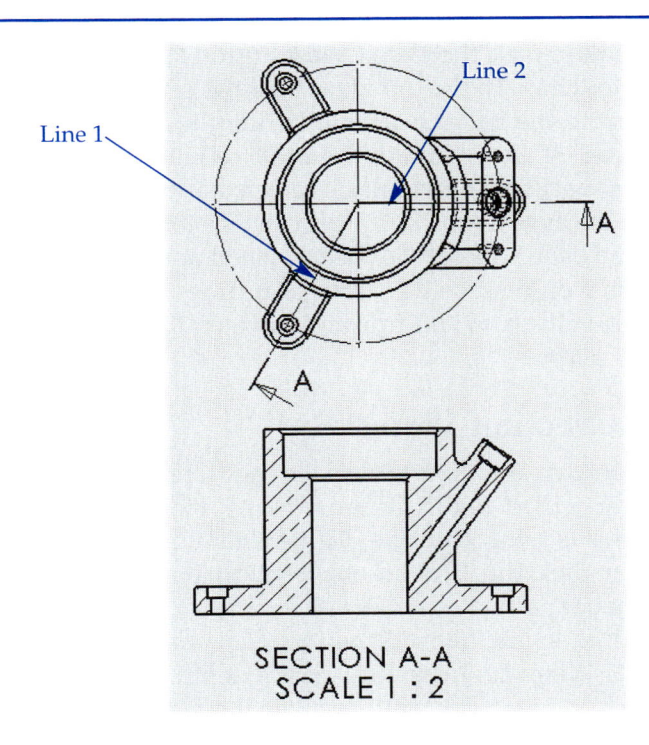

Chapter 8   Creating Part Drawings

Figure 8-13.
Creating an auxiliary view.

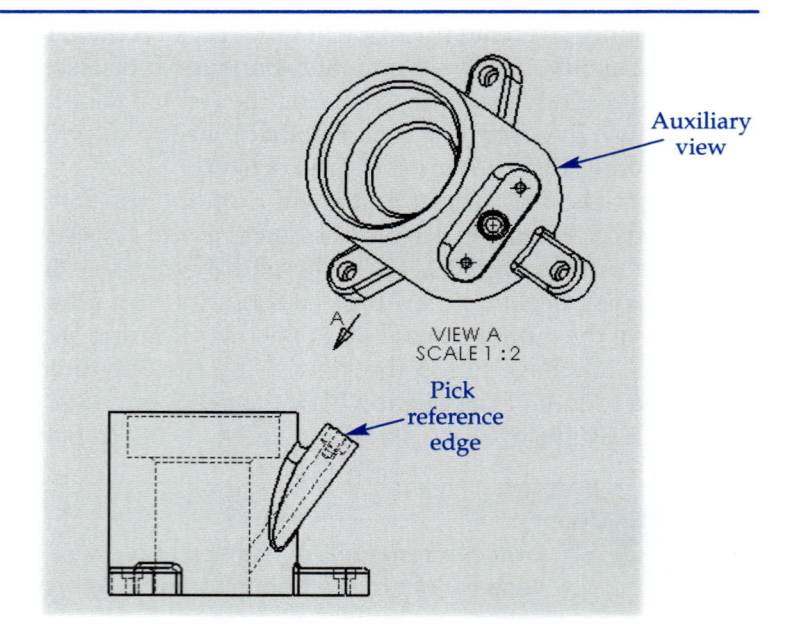

Generally, the entire part is not shown in auxiliary views. Usually, the auxiliary view shows only the feature in question. Cropping views is discussed later in this chapter.

Detail Views

A *detail view* focuses on a small feature of the part that cannot be properly shown or dimensioned in a drawing view. The detail view is typically drawn at a larger scale—think of it as zooming in on the feature. The scale for detail views is set in the system options. To change it, open the **System Options** tab of the options/properties dialog box and pick on Drawings on the left side. The **Detail view scaling:** option appears near the bottom of the dialog box and the default setting is 2.

The top view will be the source for the detail view in this example and it will focus on the end of the upper-left foot. Zoom in on the top view. In the **View Layout** tab of the **Command Manager**, pick the **Detail View** button. You'll now draw a circle around the area you want to detail. In the top view, pick the center of the hole in the upper-left foot. Move the cursor to the left and pick to define the detail circle. Then, place the view as shown in **Figure 8-14**. Even though the **Scale** rollout in the **Detail View Property Manager** shows the **Use sheet scale** radio button selected and a scale of 1:1, the detail view is twice the sheet scale because of the setting in the system options. You could select the **Use custom scale** radio button and the User Defined option to input the scale of your choice, such as 2:1. This would make the detail four times the sheet scale. For this example, use the default scale setting. When finished, save and close both Example_08_03.sldprt and Example_08_03.slddrw.

Broken-Out Section Views

The **Broken-out Section** tool does not create a new section view but cuts a section at a specified depth in an existing view to display interior details. Open Example_08_04.sldprt and Example_08_04.slddrw. Select the front view named Drawing View2 and then pick the **Broken-out Section** button in the **View Layout** tab of the **Command Manager**.

Draw a closed spline around the inclined projection on the right side of the view. See **Figure 8-15**. When prompted to set the depth, select a horizontal hidden line near the center of the top view. This entity will be named Silhouette Edge<1> in the **Broken-out**

Figure 8-14.
Creating a detail view.

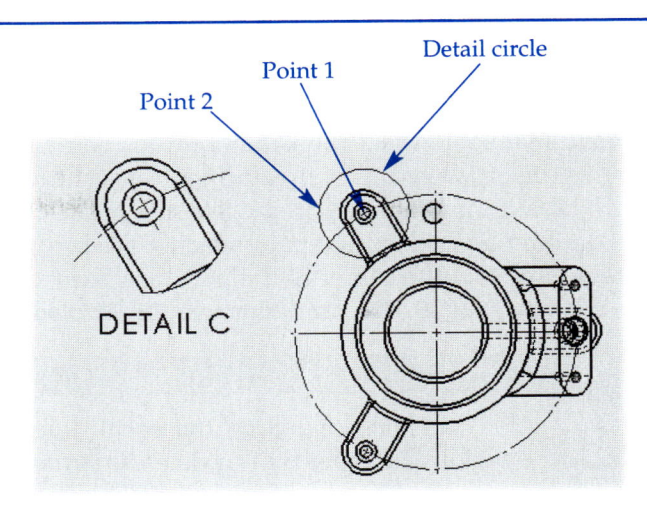

Figure 8-15.
Creating a broken-out section view. A—A closed spline is sketched to define the section in the front view. The depth of the section is specified in the top view by selecting a horizontal hidden line near the center of the part. B—The resulting section view.

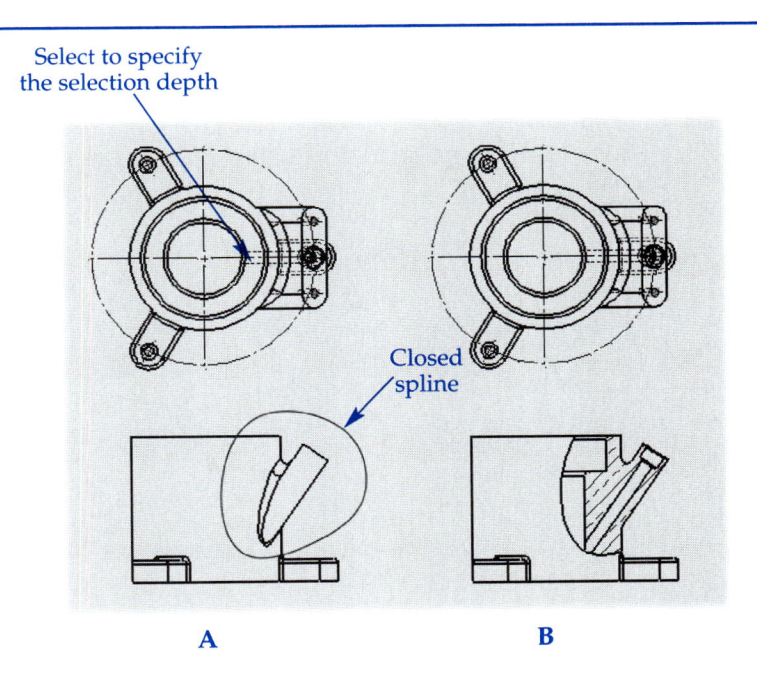

Section Property Manager. Check the **Preview** check box to see the results and then pick the green check mark button. When finished, save and close both Example_08_04.sldprt and Example_08_04.slddrw.

Broken Views

A *broken view* is used on long parts where a large section of the part contains no features and does not need to be shown. In effect, a broken view shortens the part so the view will fit on the drawing sheet. Open the file Example_08_05.sldprt. This is a part file containing a long angle iron with features at both ends and the center. Since this part was drawn in metric units, you will create an A1-size part drawing.

Select **Make Drawing from Part/Assembly** from the **New** flyout in the **Menu Bar**. In the **Sheet Format/Size** dialog box, select the A1-Landscape sheet format. The **View Palette** appears. Drag and drop the Left view into the drawing, as this view shows the fewest hidden lines. SolidWorks will fit the view to the drawing by setting the scale to 1:4. Press the [Esc] key to exit the **Projected View** tool. For this example, set the display style of the view to Hidden Lines Removed. Also, select the **Use custom scale** radio button in the **Scale** rollout of the **Drawing View Property Manager** and set the view scale to 1:1. Now,

Chapter 8   Creating Part Drawings   165

the view is larger than the drawing. Pick the **Zoom to Fit** button in the view tools at the top of the graphics window to view the entire drawing. See **Figure 8-16**. You will now create a broken view to fit the view onto the drawing sheet. In the **View Layout** tab of the **Command Manager**, select the **Break** button. You are prompted to place the break line segments. Place two pairs of break lines, one on each side of the center hole. Place the first two break line segments on the left side of the part. See **Figure 8-17**. Repeat the procedure on the right side of the part, spacing the break lines evenly in relation to the first two segments and the center of the part. See **Figure 8-18**. When finished, save and close both Example_08_05.sldprt and Example_08_05.slddrw.

> **PROFESSIONAL TIP**
>
> You can pick and drag the break lines to adjust the gap between breaks. The view will update dynamically after you drag the break lines. You can also set the break line style in the **Broken View Settings** rollout in the **Broken View Property Manager**.

Figure 8-16.
The view runs off of the sheet before the broken view is defined.

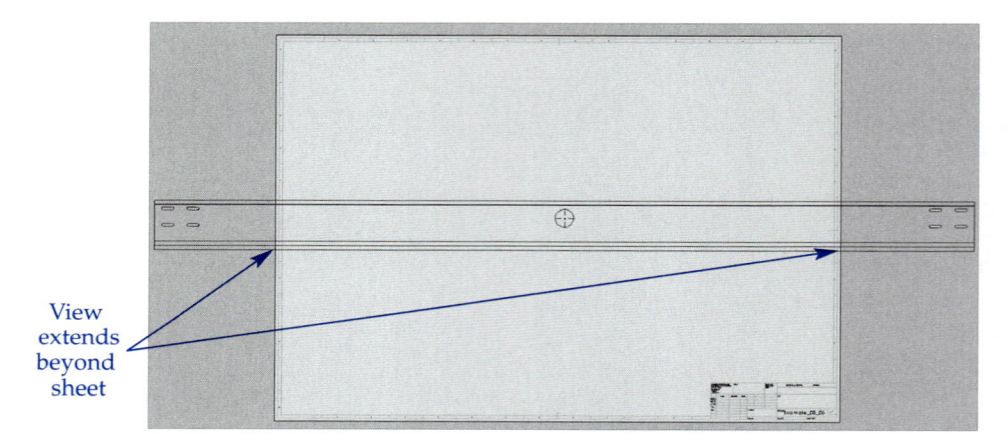

Figure 8-17.
Two points are used to place the break lines. These points define the break on the left side of the part.

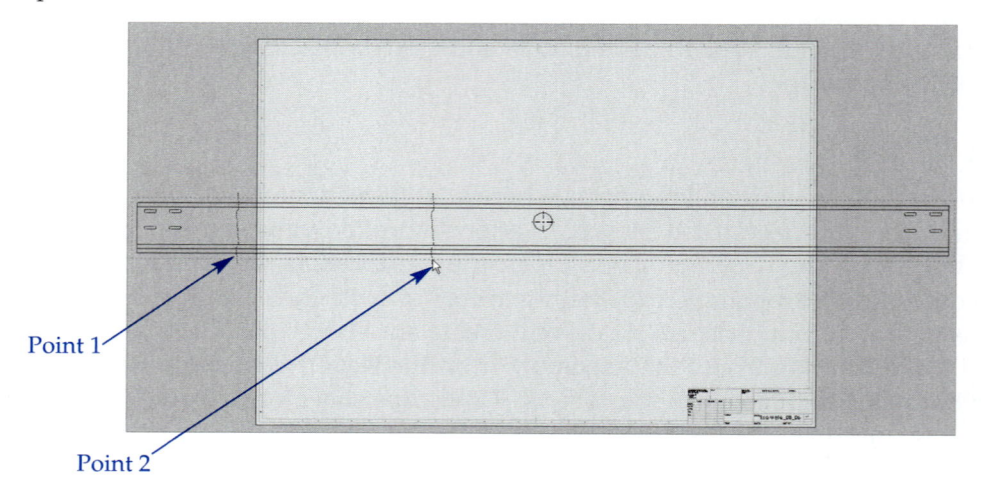

Figure 8-18.
The resulting broken view.

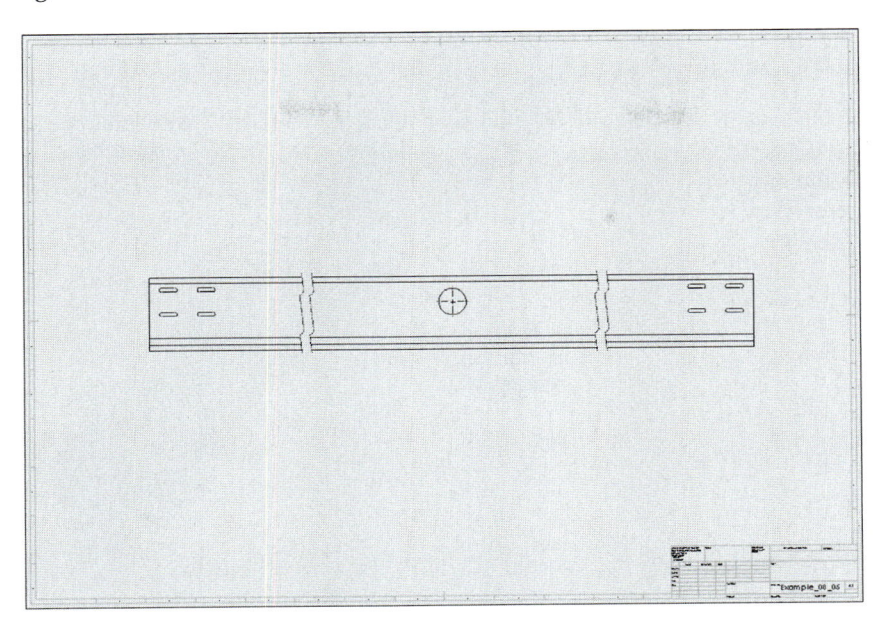

Relative Views

A *relative view* is an orthographic view that represents a viewing orientation established by a face or plane in the model. This type of view is useful when you want to use an orientation that differs from that of the default views generated from the part. For example, you may want to select a certain face of the part and orient it as the front view in the orthographic drawing. A relative view is created by selecting two orientation references in the part file and specifying the desired orientation in the orthographic drawing. It is easiest to have the part and drawing files open and tiled when selecting reference entities.

Open the file Example_08_06.sldprt. Notice that the top surface of the part is constructed on the top plane. You will create an orientation of views in which this surface is shown as the front view on the drawing. Since this part was drawn in US customary units, you will create a B-size part drawing.

Start a new drawing file from the part file and select the B-Landscape sheet format. Tile the two files horizontally by selecting **Window>Tile Horizontally**. Then, activate the **Relative To Model** tool by selecting **Insert>Drawing View>Relative To Model**. You are prompted to select a face of the model. Select the top surface of the horizontal center section in the part file. See **Figure 8-19**. The **Relative View Property Manager** appears in the part file and lists the surface you just selected as the first orientation reference entity in the **Orientation** rollout. In the First drop-down list, select Front. Now, select the second orientation reference. Select the adjacent face of the horizontal center section. In the Second drop-down list in the **Orientation** rollout, select Top. Pick the green check mark button to close the **Relative View Property Manager**.

Now, maximize the drawing file and pick on the drawing sheet to place the front view. Then, use the **Projected View** tool to place the top view above the front view. Set the display style of the top view to Hidden Lines Visible. When finished, save and close both Example_08_06.sldprt and Example_08_06.slddrw.

Chapter 8   Creating Part Drawings

Figure 8-19.
Two orientation references are selected from the model to create a relative view. In this example, the first orientation reference defines the front view and the second orientation reference defines the top view.

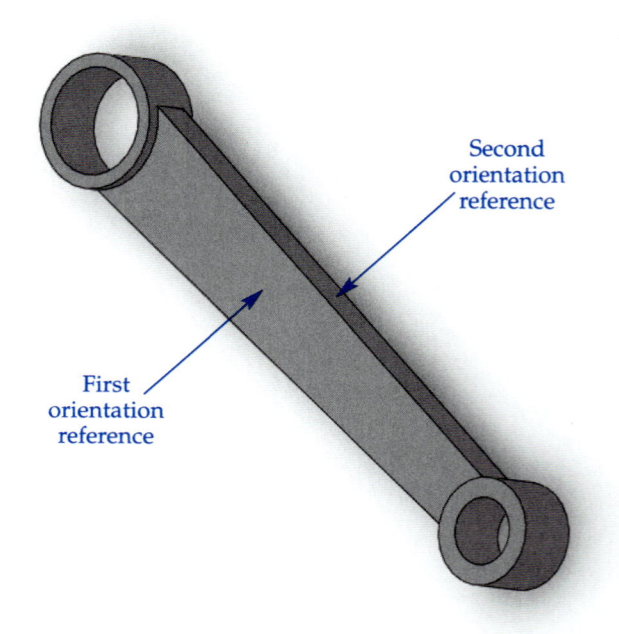

Cropping Views

You can crop a drawing view to remove a portion that you do not want to display. Cropping a view is useful when you want to modify an existing view without creating a new view. To crop a view, first sketch a closed shape, such as a circle, around the area you want to keep in the view. Then, select **Insert>Drawing View>Crop**. The area outside the shape is hidden. You can restore the uncropped view by right-clicking on the view and selecting **Crop View>Remove Crop** from the shortcut menu. You can also edit the cropped view by selecting **Crop View>Edit Crop** from the shortcut menu. This option is used to edit the closed shape defining the crop.

Creating Sketches in Drawing Files

You can create sketches in drawing files using the same tools that are used when creating sketches in part files. A sketch is created in a drawing file when 2D geometry needs to be created on the drawing sheet, but there is no 3D model to form the basis for the 2D geometry. In other words, it must be manually created. You can create the sketch so that it is contained within a drawing view by first creating an *empty view*. This is an empty drawing view used to serve as a container for the sketch. By first creating an empty view, you can move or scale the entire sketch as a unit on the drawing sheet.

Open the file Example_08_07.slddrw. This is a blank drawing file with a C-size drawing sheet. You will create a sketch of a simple connecting rod shape in the drawing. See **Figure 8-20**. First, create an empty view by selecting **Insert>Drawing View>Empty**. A blank view with a dashed border appears on screen and follows the cursor. Pick to place the view on the sheet. Do not be concerned with the size of the view; it will adjust as you create the sketch. Now, use the **Line** tool and the two dimensions shown in **Figure 8-20** to create the sketch. The 2D geometry is now in the drawing. It can be relocated on the sheet as needed. If desired, you can also rename the view from Drawing View1 to reflect the contents of the sketch. When you are finished, save and close Example_08_07.slddrw.

Figure 8-20.
The drawing used to create the sketch in the drawing file.

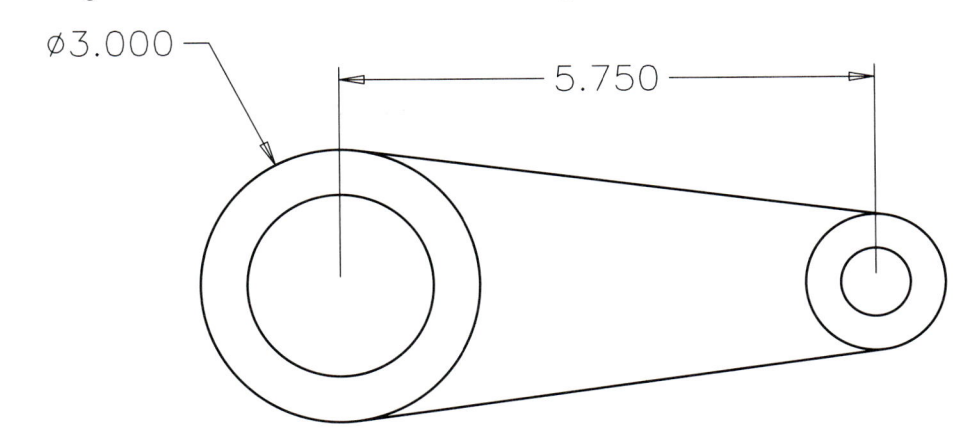

Editing Drawing Views

You now know how to create drawing views, but it is important to know how to edit them as well. Open Example_08_08.slddrw. This drawing consists of a base view and a number of drawing views. Click on any drawing view to display the **Drawing View Property Manager**. The options that are enabled or grayed out depend on the view type.

The **Drawing View Property Manager** can be used to "clean up" drawing views so that they are more presentable and comply with standards. Edit the views in this drawing as follows.

1. Open the **Drawing View Property Manager** for the isometric view. Change the display style. Uncheck the **Use parent style** check box and pick Shaded with Edges. Then, change the display style to Shaded and note the differences.
2. Open the **Drawing View Property Manager** for the auxiliary view. Change the display style to Hidden Lines Removed. Also, enter D in the **Label** text box. Change the scale to a custom scale of 1:1. Pick on the note VIEW D in the drawing and drag the text closer to the view.
3. Pick on the top view and right-click. In the shortcut menu, select **Tangent Edge>Tangent Edges Removed** from the shortcut menu. This makes the view more readable.
4. Any line in a view can be hidden. Pick one of the lines in the top view, right-click, and select **Hide Edge** from the shortcut menu.

Rotating Views

You can change the angular orientation of a drawing view using the **Rotate View** tool. This tool rotates the view in its 2D plane. To rotate a view, select the **Rotate View** button in the view tools at the top of the graphics window. When the **Rotate Drawing View** dialog box appears, enter a rotation angle in the **Drawing view angle:** text box. You can also rotate the view dynamically by picking on the view and dragging. If you want to return the view to its default orientation, right-click on the view border and select **Alignment>Default Rotation** from the shortcut menu.

Chapter 8 Creating Part Drawings

Changing the Model

SolidWorks is capable of *bidirectional associativity*. This means the drawing will follow any changes made to the part, or the part will follow any changes made to the drawing. Open Example_08_08.sldprt and, if not already open, Example_08_08.slddrw. In the part file, change the extrusion height of **Extrude5** to 10 mm. Without saving the part, switch to the drawing file. There will be a pause as the drawing changes to reflect the alteration made to the part. Close both files without saving the changes.

This illustrates the concept of bidirectional associativity. Conversely, you could change a model dimension in the drawing and thereby affect changes to the part. In Chapter 9, you will learn how to place dimensions and other types of annotations on a drawing.

PRACTICE 8-1

Complete the practice problem on the student website.
www.g-wlearning.com/CAD

Chapter Test

Answer the following questions on a separate sheet of paper or complete the electronic chapter test on the student website.
www.g-wlearning.com/CAD

1. From which type of file is a SolidWorks drawing created?
2. What is the purpose of the **Sheet Format/Size** dialog box?
3. How can you change the size of the current sheet after creating a drawing file?
4. What is the purpose of the **View Palette**?
5. What is a *base view*?
6. Briefly describe how to create a base view.
7. How can you move a view on the drawing sheet after it has been placed?
8. What are the five display styles for a view?
9. Briefly describe how to create a full section view.
10. What is the difference between a *broken-out section view* and a *broken view*?
11. What is the purpose of an *empty view*?
12. How are drawing views updated when the part is edited?

Chapter Exercises

Complete the chapter exercises on the student website.
www.g-wlearning.com/CAD

Exercise 8-1 Beam. *Complete the exercise on the student website.*

Exercise 8-2 Bevel Gear. *Complete the exercise on the student website.*

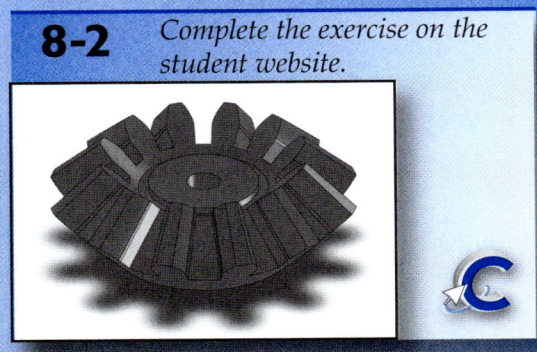

Exercise 8-3 Tubular Brace. *Complete the exercise on the student website.*

Chapter 8 Creating Part Drawings

Part drawings are linked to the model from which they are generated. Since the drawing is parametrically linked to the model, any time the model is changed, the drawing will update to match.

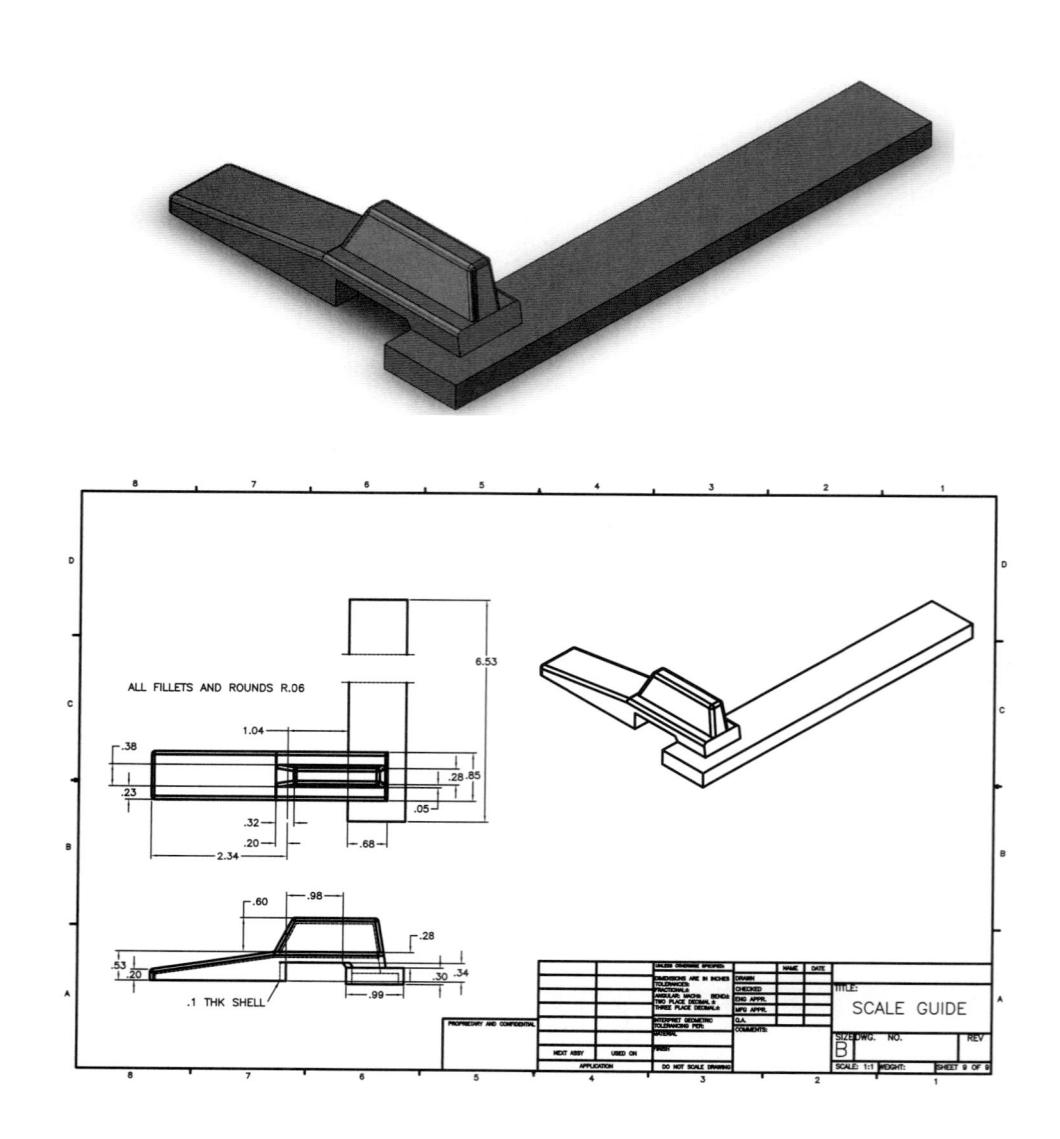

Chapter 9

Dimensioning and Annotating Drawings

Objectives

After completing this chapter, you will be able to:
- Specify a drafting standard.
- Create a custom drafting standard.
- Dimension drawing views.
- Apply different annotations to a SolidWorks drawing.
- Define a title block and input title block data.
- Create a revision table.

Preparing to Annotate a Drawing Layout

Open **Example_09_01.sldprt** and examine the part. This is a simple part with chamfers, fillets, through holes and a tapped hole. Notice the part's orientation to the coordinate system and note the location of the default planes. Also, open **Example_09_01.slddrw**. This is the completed three-view orthographic drawing with an isometric view. Notice in the front view that the centerlines for the through holes and the note for the tapped hole were automatically created with the front view. Pick the note and move it above the front view. In this chapter, you will continue working on this drawing.

Drafting Standards

This section explains drafting standards and how they are implemented in SolidWorks. Understand that *all* of the annotations used in this chapter are governed by a drafting standard. In the United States, the ***American National Standards Institute (ANSI)*** drafting standards are most commonly used and we'll use the ANSI standard for this drawing. However, many engineering firms also work on international projects. SolidWorks provides several other drafting standards for use with other countries, including the ISO, DIN, JIS, BSI, GOST, and GB standards. The ***International Standards Organization (ISO)*** oversees the ISO standards, which are used throughout the world.

The *German Institute for Standardization* oversees the *DIN (Deutsches Institut fur Normung)* standards. The *Japanese Industrial Standard (JIS)* is used in Japan. The *British Standards Institution (BSI)* oversees national standards in Britain. The *Gosstandart (GOST)* standards are used in Russia and neighboring countries. The *Guobiao (GB)* standards are used in China.

To access the drafting standards, open the **Document Properties** tab of the options/properties dialog box in the drawing file and pick on Drafting Standard. See **Figure 9-1**. In this drawing, the ANSI drafting standard is set current and is displayed in bold in the **Overall drafting standard** drop-down list. The **Document Properties** tab is used to make changes to a drafting standard. If you make changes to a drafting standard, a new modified drafting standard called a *custom standard* is created in the document to prevent overwriting the original standard.

Be careful when making changes in this dialog box. If you make changes and save the edits, a custom standard is created and made current. If you want to restore the default standard, pick on Drafting Standard and select the standard from the **Overall drafting standard** drop-down list. Custom standards are useful in certain situations. For example, custom standards may be required when certain drafting conventions are used based on company or industry practice. One of the advantages to using a custom standard is that it can be saved to an external file and used in multiple documents.

Pick on Dimensions and change the primary precision to 2 places. A note appears indicating that the standard has been changed to ANSI-MODIFIED. See **Figure 9-2**. Pick on Drafting Standard and you can rename, copy, or save the standard to an external file. For this example, rename the standard to Chapter_9 and also save it to an external file named Chapter_9.sldstd. This will make it available to other drawings.

Figure 9-1.
A—The **Document Properties** tab of the options/properties dialog box is used to select a drafting standard, make changes to a standard, or create a custom standard based on an existing standard.

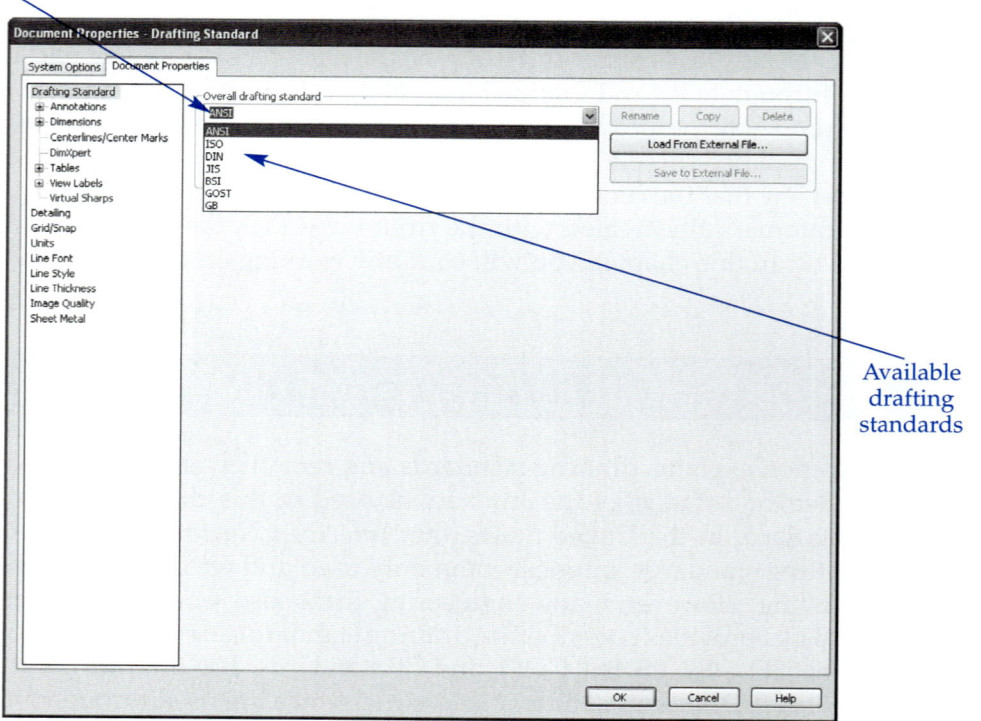

Figure 9-2.
After changing the primary precision setting, a custom drafting standard is created and made active.

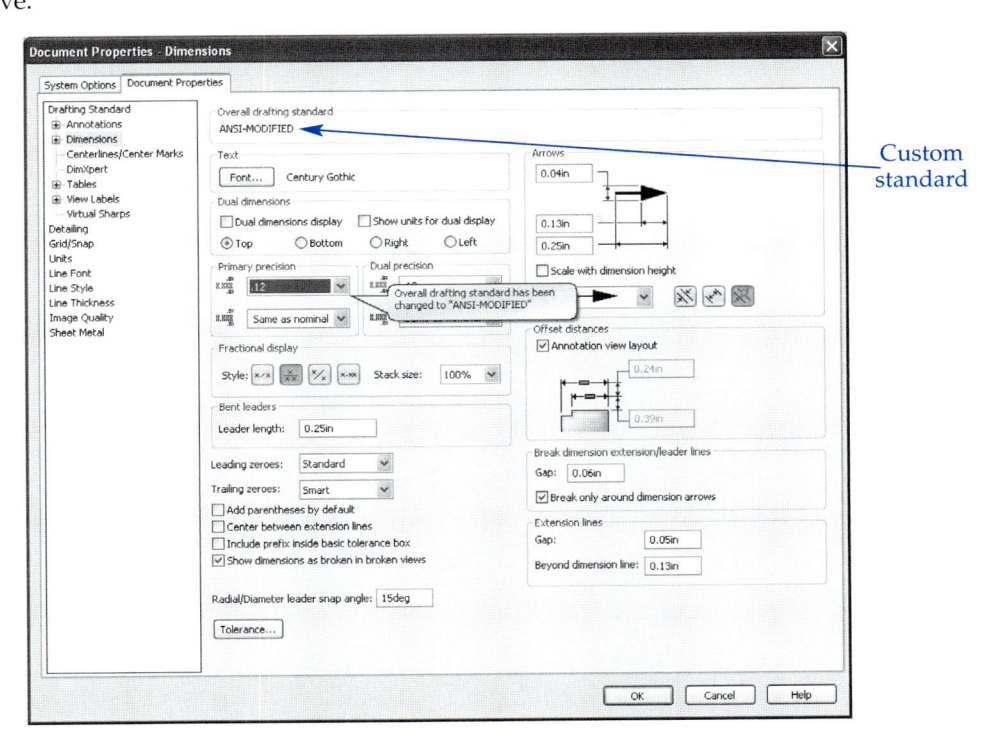

Adding Centerlines

Every circular feature in a drawing view usually has a centerline. The only exceptions are fillets or small, design radii. The **Centerline** tool is used to add centerlines to drawing views. After accessing this tool, pick the two line segments representing the sides of the hole. You can also pick a drawing view to add the centerlines in the view in a single step.

Notice in **Figure 9-3A** that the front view has centerlines applied automatically. You will add two centerlines in the top view and three in the right view. First, hide the lines representing the features that will coincide with the centerlines in both views. Then, pick the **Centerline** button in the **Annotation** tab of the **Command Manager**. Select the required entities to place the centerlines in each view.

Notice that the hole shown as a circle in the top view has centerlines, but they do not extend past the view. Pick and stretch the ends of the lines to extend them. The completed view should look like **Figure 9-3B**.

> **PROFESSIONAL TIP**
>
> Center marks can also be added to views using the **Center Mark** tool. The default option allows you to place a single center mark by selecting a circle or arc. As an alternative to creating center marks and centerlines manually, you can have them inserted automatically upon creating the views. To create center marks and centerlines automatically, pick Detailing in the **Document Properties** tab of the options/properties dialog box and check the corresponding check boxes in the **Auto insert on view creation** area.

Chapter 9 Dimensioning and Annotating Drawings

Figure 9-3.
Adding centerlines to the drawing views. A—The existing views. B—The drawing after adding and modifying centerlines.

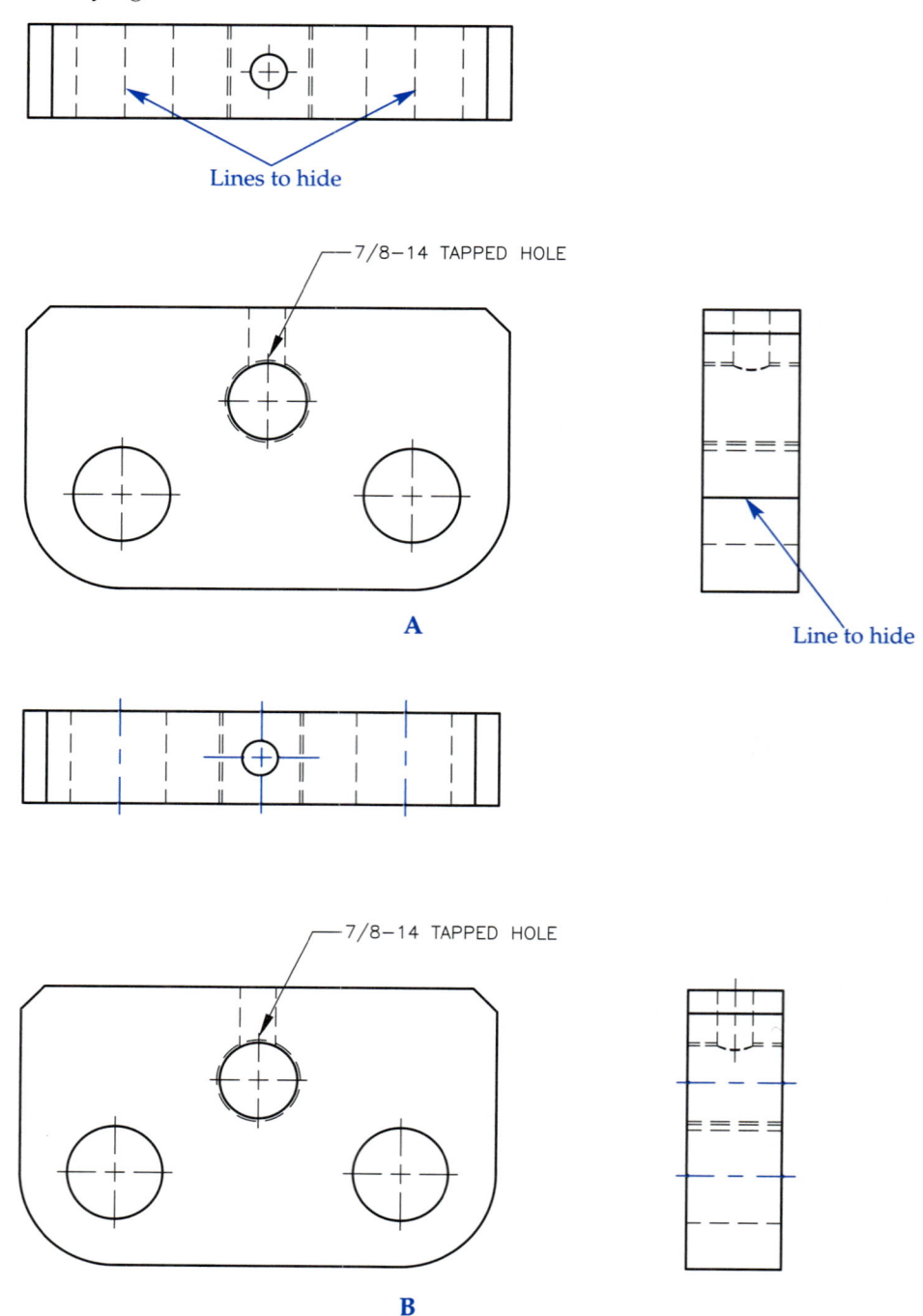

Dimensioning in SolidWorks

The two types of dimensions used in SolidWorks are model and reference. *Model dimensions* are those placed on the sketches of the part. These dimensions are *parametric dimensions*. When you create a drawing file, model dimensions can be displayed on a drawing view. If they are changed either on the part or the drawing, both part and drawing geometry change. In other words, this is a bidirectional relationship. *Reference dimensions,* on the other hand, are added to the drawing views manually. They are driven by the part geometry. That is, if the part changes, the reference dimensions change in the drawing. However, reference dimensions do not drive the part. Changing a reference dimension from the default value in the drawing file does not change the part.

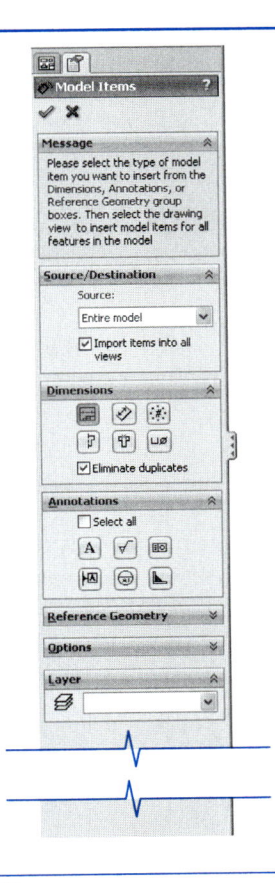

Adding Model and Reference Dimensions

Now, you will insert dimensions in the Example_09_01.slddrw drawing file. First, you will add model dimensions (the dimensions from the part file). The **Model Items** tool is used to insert model dimensions. In the **Annotation** tab of the **Command Manager**, select the **Model Items** button. The **Model Items Property Manager** appears. In the **Source/Destination** rollout, select Entire model from the **Source:** drop-down list and make sure the **Import items into all views** check box is checked. In the **Dimensions** rollout, pick the **Marked for drawings** button. See **Figure 9-4.** When finished, pick the green check mark button. Annotations will be placed on the front and top views.

In the front view, pick the 5.00 dimension and move it up above the dimension for the chamfer. Also, move any other dimensions that overlap in the front view.

Next, you will create two reference dimensions. In the **Annotation** tab of the **Command Manager**, select the **Smart Dimension** button and place a vertical reference dimension on the right view. This is a duplicate of the 3.00 dimension in the front view. Pick the green check mark button. Now, in the drawing, pick on the 3.00 reference dimension. The **Dimension Property Manager** is displayed. In the **Primary Value** rollout, checking the **Override value:** check box allows you to override the default value. Remember, overriding the value will only change the reference dimension in the drawing, not the part. Which dimensions you use in your drawings depends on your design intent, but most designers make model changes in the part file, not the drawing file. Press the [Esc] key to close the **Dimension Property Manager**. Using the **Smart Dimension** tool, place a reference dimension in the right view to locate the tapped hole vertically. See **Figure 9-5.**

Figure 9-4.
The settings for generating the model dimensions in the drawing.

Chapter 9 Dimensioning and Annotating Drawings

177

Figure 9-5.
Adding model dimensions and reference dimensions to the drawing views.

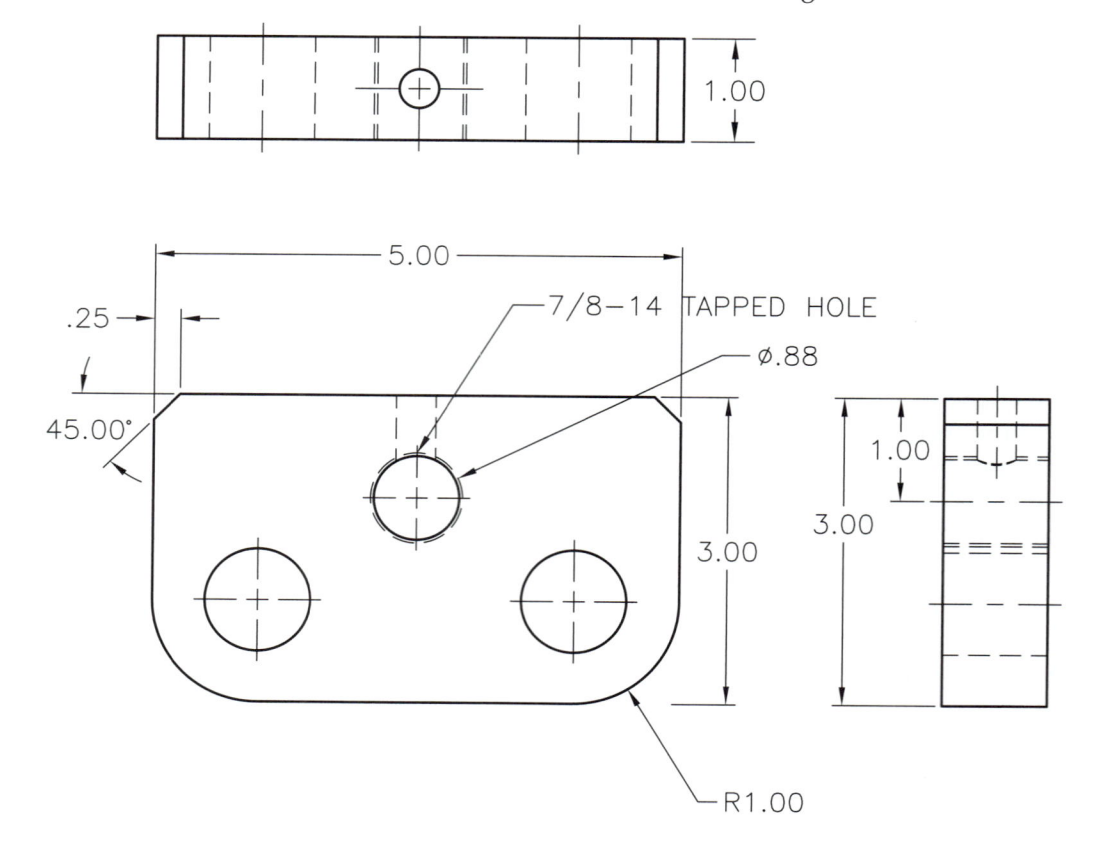

> **NOTE**
>
> Model dimensions are black in the drawing views. Reference dimensions are gray.

We'll now change a parametric dimension that will change the model. In the front view, double-click on the 3.00 vertical dimension. In the **Modify** dialog box, change the value to 4.00 and press [Enter]. All the views are highlighted; pick the **Rebuild** button in the **Menu Bar** or press [Ctrl][B] and the part and drawing are changed. Now, double-click on the 4.00 dimension, change the value back to 3.00, and rebuild the part again to restore the original dimension.

Dimension Styles

Dimension styles can be created to control the appearance of dimensions on drawing views. For example, you might want to use a certain font for dimensions and notes. A dimension style can be created by picking on a dimension, setting the desired options in the **Dimension Property Manager**, and picking the **Add or Update a Style** button in the **Style** rollout. Various dimension settings are available in the **Value**, **Leaders**, and **Other** tabs of the **Dimension Property Manager**. When you create a dimension style, the style is named and can be applied to any dimension in the drawing. The dimension style can also be saved to an external file. Dimension styles appear in the **Set a current style** drop-down list in the **Style** rollout of the **Dimension Property Manager**. By default, this drop-down list displays <NONE>. A dimension style can be applied to a dimension by picking it and selecting the style from the **Set a current style** drop-down list.

178 Learning SolidWorks 2009

Layers

Layers can be used for organizing annotations and controlling line properties in drawings. If you pick on the hole note in the front view, the **Layer** rollout appears at the bottom of the **Note Property Manager**. If you pick on the **Layer** drop-down list, you'll see that there's only one predefined layer named FORMAT. You can create a layer by using the **Layer Properties** tool. To access this tool, select **View>Toolbars>Layer** to display the **Layer** toolbar and select the **Layer Properties** button. This displays the **Layers** dialog box, which you can use to create a new layer and set the layer properties. See **Figure 9-6.** Pick the **New** button to create a new layer. To change a layer property, pick on the associated column header and use the controls. You may have to adjust the width of the column headers to display all of them in the dialog box. For this example, create a new layer named Hole Notes, leave it turned on, change the color to red, and leave the linetype and thickness unchanged. Pick on the layer name to highlight it and close the dialog box. Now, access the **Smart Dimension** tool. If you have Hole Notes selected in the **Layer** drop-down list in the **Layer** rollout of the **Dimension Property Manager**, annotations are automatically placed on that layer as you annotate the drawing views. Close the **Dimension Property Manager** and select NONE in the **Layer** drop-down list of the **Layers** toolbar.

You can change an existing object in the drawing to a different layer by selecting the object and changing the layer setting in the **Layer** drop-down list. Try this on the hole note in the front view and it should turn red.

Adding Hole and Thread Notes

A *hole note* describes the properties of a given hole. For example, a hole note indicates the depth of a drilled hole; whether the hole is countersunk, counterbored, or spotfaced; and the type of threads (if the hole is tapped). The part in Example_09_01.slddrw contains four parametric hole features. Only one of these is tapped. You will add hole callouts for the holes in the front and top views using the **Hole Callout** tool.

In the **Annotation** tab of the **Command Manager**, pick the **Hole Callout** button. Insert hole callouts for the hole in the top view and one of the 1" holes in the front view. Also, insert a new hole callout for the tapped hole in the front view. Hide the red dimension and the .88" diameter dimension. See **Figure 9-7**.

We'll now change the 3/8" hole in the top of the part to a tapped hole and see how that changes the drawing. In the part file, right-click on 3/8 Diameter Hole1 in the design tree and select **Edit Feature** from the shortcut toolbar. This activates the **Hole Wizard** tool. Pick on the Tap hole type in the **Hole Type** rollout. This will change all specifications and conditions. Change the hole specification to 3/8-24 and change the end condition to Up To Next. In the **Options** rollout, pick the **Cosmetic thread** button

Figure 9-6.
The **Layers** dialog box.

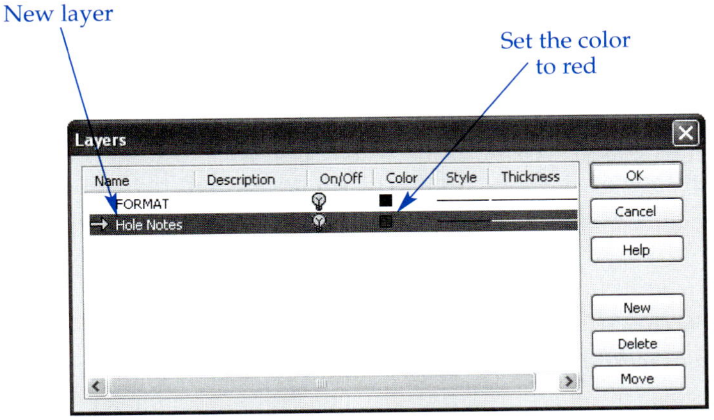

Figure 9-7.
Adding hole callouts to the drawing views.

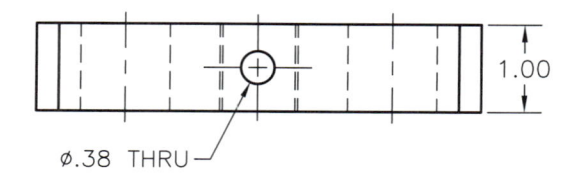

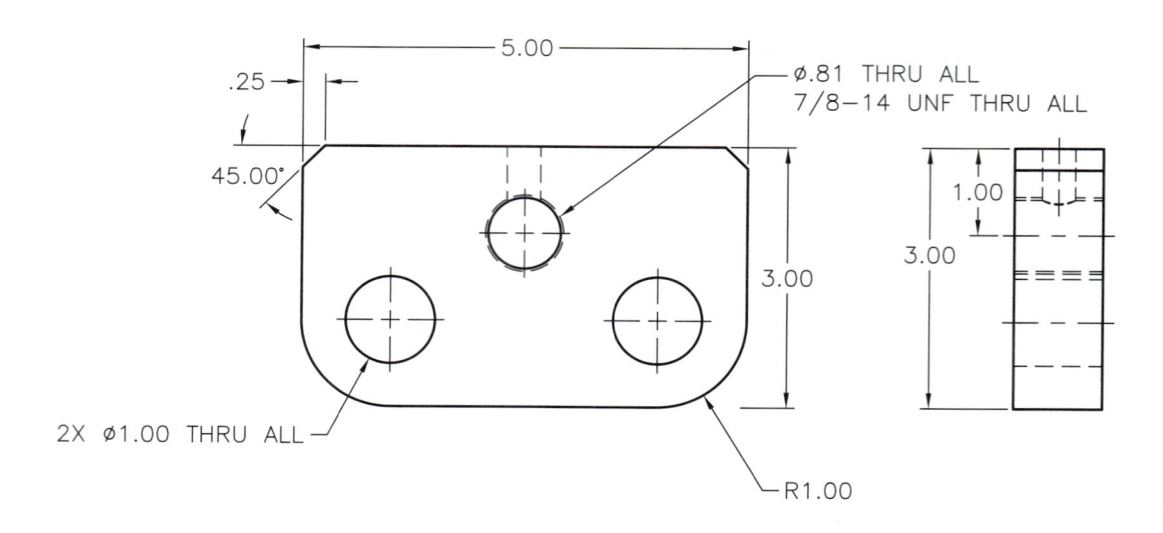

and check the **With thread callout** check box. Pick the green check mark button. Return to the drawing and the hole callout will be updated to a thread note.

Return to the part file and undo the previous operation. This will also remove the thread note from the drawing.

Adding Surface Texture Symbols

Surface texture symbols are typically used to describe the quality of the machined finish on a given face or surface. In this example, the top face of the part is to be finish ground. The quality of the machined surface is indicated on the drawing by a surface texture symbol. A thorough study of surface textures and related terminology is beyond the scope of this textbook. However, you will learn how to place surface texture symbols on a drawing using the **Surface Finish** tool.

Zoom in on the front view. In the **Annotation** tab of the **Command Manager**, pick the **Surface Finish** button. Then, pick a point on the line that represents the top surface. The **Surface Finish Property Manager** appears. See **Figure 9-8**. The **Symbol** rollout is used to specify the type of symbol created. The **Symbol Layout** rollout is used to define the properties associated with the symbol. The **Format** rollout is used to specify the font for the symbol text. The **Angle** rollout is used to set the angular rotation of the symbol. The **Leader** rollout is used to select a leader style when you want to place a leader or multiple leaders with the symbol. For this example, enter .0005 as the maximum roughness value, specify Grind as the production method, and select Circular as the lay direction in the **Symbol Layout** rollout. Leave all of the other settings at their defaults, and pick the green check mark button to place the symbol. See **Figure 9-9**.

Adding Text

Everyone working with prints eventually learns that what is written on a drawing is as important as what is drawn. The **Note** tool is used to place text in the drawing.

Figure 9-8.
The **Surface Finish Property Manager** is used to define a surface texture symbol.

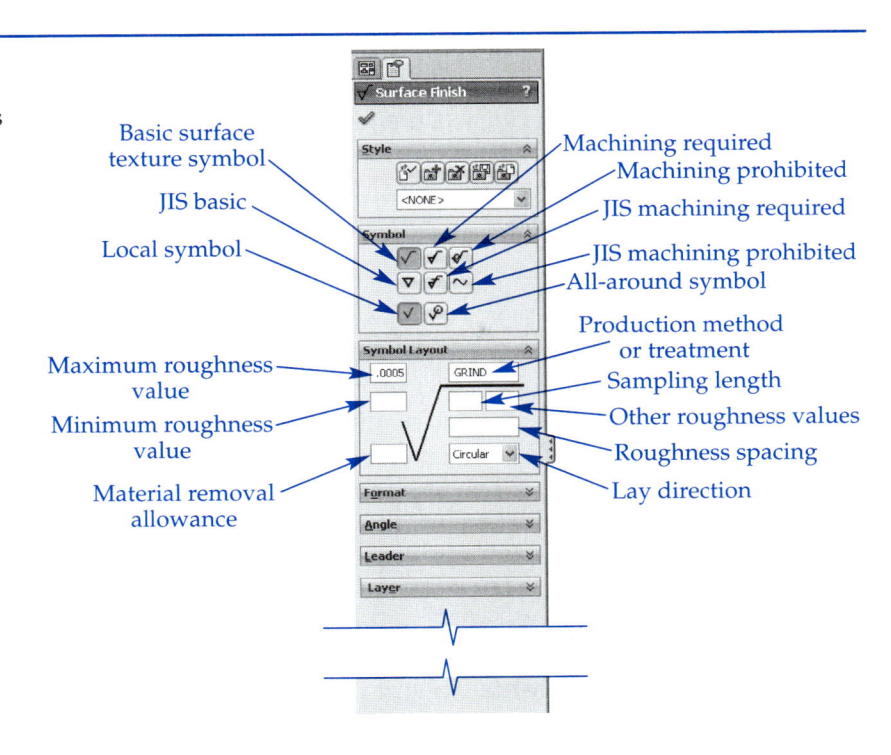

Callouts: Basic surface texture symbol, JIS basic, Local symbol, Maximum roughness value, Minimum roughness value, Material removal allowance, Machining required, Machining prohibited, JIS machining required, JIS machining prohibited, All-around symbol, Production method or treatment, Sampling length, Other roughness values, Roughness spacing, Lay direction

Figure 9-9.
The drawing after adding the surface texture symbol.

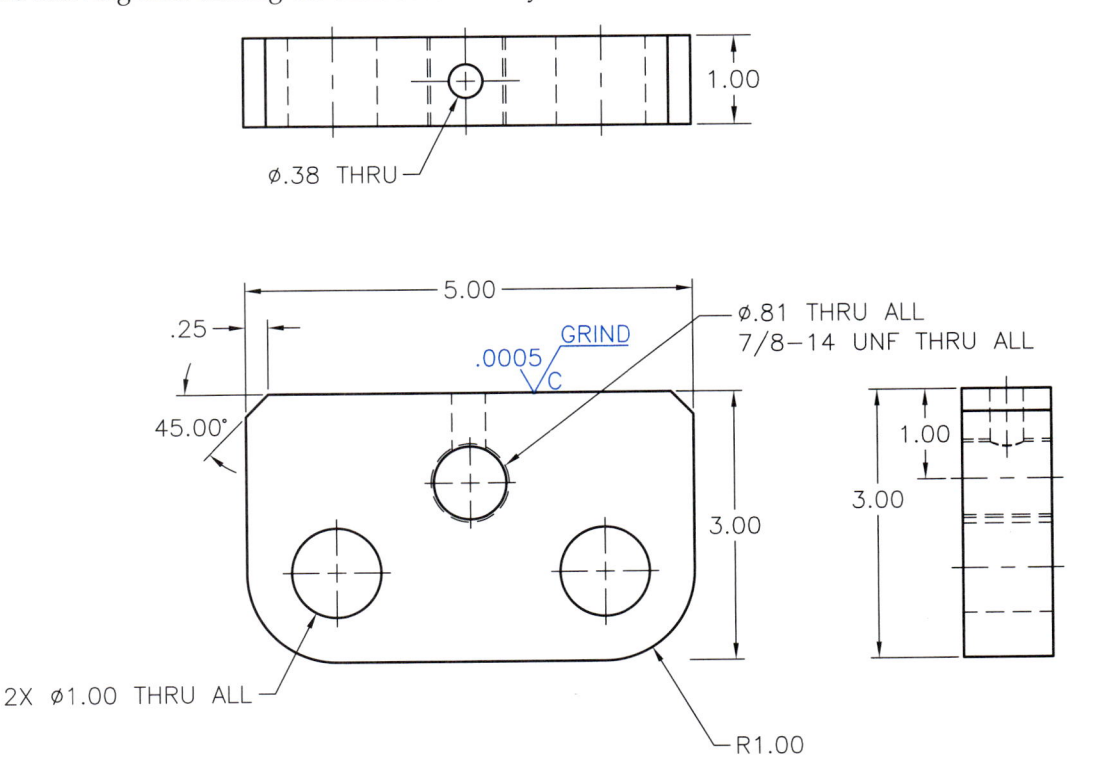

By default, text is created using the Century Gothic font and a height of .125″. These settings can be changed for an individual note in the **Note Property Manager** or for the entire drawing by accessing the **Document Properties** tab of the options/properties dialog box. Select Annotations>Notes to access the settings for note text.

Keep in mind, notes can be used in many situations—on sketches, on drawing borders, in title blocks, etc. In this example, we'll input a general part note and we'll

Chapter 9 Dimensioning and Annotating Drawings

also put it on its own layer. Using the **Layers** toolbar, create a new layer named Notes and make it active.

In the **Annotation** tab of the **Command Manager**, select the **Note** button and click and drag on the drawing above the top view to establish a text box. The **Formatting** toolbar appears. See **Figure 9-10**. For this note, we'll accept the default settings. In the text box, input the following:

NOTE:
1. REMOVE ALL BURRS
2. BREAK ALL SHARP EDGES 0.01 MAX
3. DIMENSIONS APPLY AFTER PLATING

When you begin a line of text with a number or letter character followed by a period, then type the text, and press [Enter], list formatting is automatically applied. While the **Note** tool is active, you can also use the **Note Property Manager** to set options for the text. See **Figure 9-11**. The **Style** rollout is used to create a note style and apply it to notes. Creating a note style is similar to creating a dimension style. The **Text Format** rollout is used to control the text alignment and rotation. This rollout is also used to insert symbols for geometric tolerances, surface finish specifications, and datum features. The **Leader** rollout is used to insert a leader with the note. A variety of shapes and arrowhead styles are available. The **Leader Style** rollout is used to set the leader style and thickness. The **Border** rollout is used to select a geometric shape for the note border. The **Layer** rollout is used to assign the note to a layer. Picking the green check

Figure 9-10.
The **Formatting** toolbar is used to specify font, alignment, and formatting settings when entering text.

Figure 9-11.
The **Note Property Manager**.

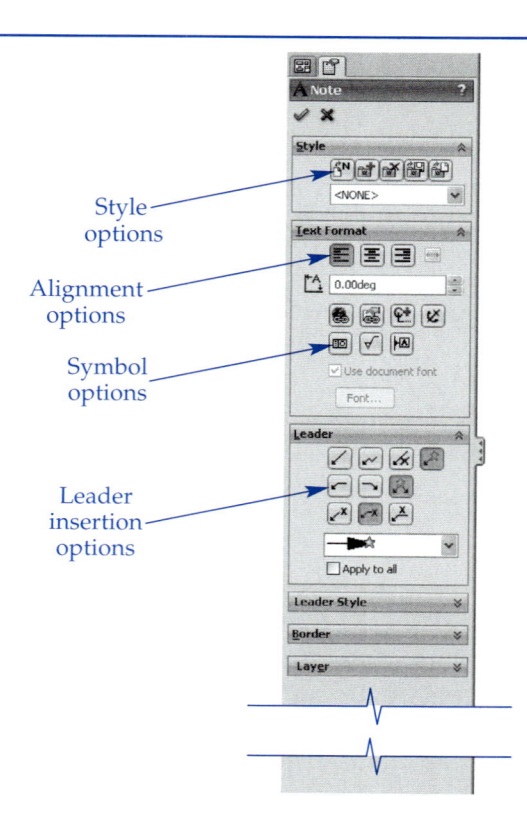

mark button above the **Style** rollout closes the **Note Property Manager** and places the note on the drawing. See **Figure 9-12.**

In the Example_09_01.slddrw file, there is a note under the front view. The text font for this note is set to Times New Roman. You can use the **Format Painter** tool to copy the font (and style) of that note to the note you just typed in. Zoom out so you can see both notes. In the **Annotation** tab of the **Command Manager**, pick the **Format Painter** tool, pick the note under the front view, and then pick on the note that you entered. When you are finished, save and close both Example_09_01.sldprt and Example_09_01.slddrw.

Baseline Dimensions and Ordinate Dimensions

Baseline dimensions and ordinate dimensions can be added to a drawing in Solid-Works. Baseline dimensioning and ordinate dimensioning are both forms of datum dimensioning. In these systems, dimensions originate from a *datum*. In *baseline dimensioning*, dimensions originate from a *baseline* selected to establish the datum. An edge or vertex is selected as the baseline. In *ordinate dimensioning*, one horizontal and one vertical extension line establish an origin called the *zero ordinate*. The extension lines define the X and Y datum axes. The entire view is dimensioned from the zero ordinate, which is usually located at the view's lower-left corner. The zero ordinate is identified with zeroes placed at the ends of the extension lines. Distances along the X and Y axes to other features are specified using other extension lines, with the distances placed numerically at their ends.

Figure 9-12.
Adding a general note to the drawing.

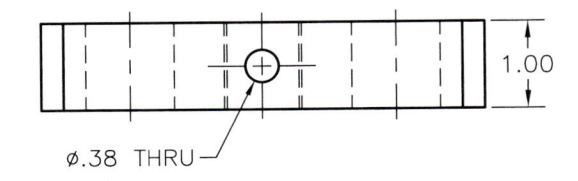

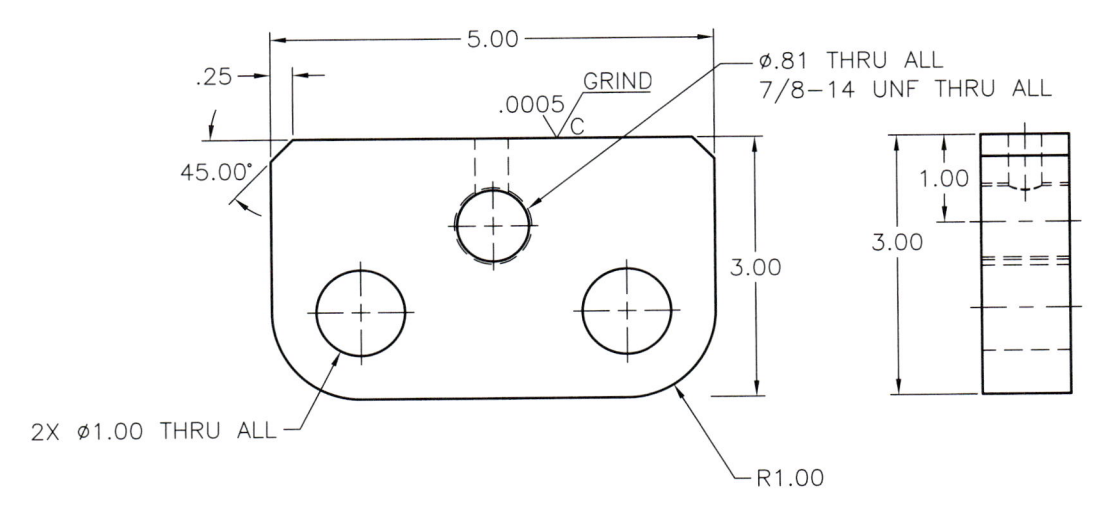

Chapter 9 Dimensioning and Annotating Drawings

183

Open the drawing file **Example_09_02.slddrw**. In the **Annotation** tab of the **Command Manager**, pick on the **Smart Dimension** drop-down list and select **Horizontal Ordinate Dimension**. Pick the lower-left corner of the front view to define the zero ordinate. Move the cursor down and pick to set the length of the extension line. Then, pick the endpoints indicated in **Figure 9-13**. Also, pick the center point of the hole. You can pick the points out of order. Note that the dimension precision is set to 3 places after the decimal. This is the default document setting.

Repeat the process using the **Vertical Ordinate Dimension** tool to place vertical dimensions. Refer to **Figure 9-13**.

Baseline dimensions are shown in the top view of the part. They are all automatically lined up and measured from the same baseline (datum).

Chamfer Dimensions

The part in this example includes a large chamfer. We'll use the **Chamfer Dimension** tool to dimension this chamfer in the front view. When using this tool, the order of picking is important. In the **Annotation** tab of the **Command Manager**, pick on the **Smart Dimension** drop-down list and select **Chamfer Dimension**. Pick the inclined line labeled AB and then the vertical line labeled BC and place the dimension. See **Figure 9-14**. Line AD would have worked just as well for the second pick. The points for these lines in the drawing file are labeled with note text. Point D is labeled with an automatic leader generated by the **Note** tool.

Figure 9-13.
Creating horizontal and vertical ordinate dimensions. The top view is dimensioned using baseline dimensions.

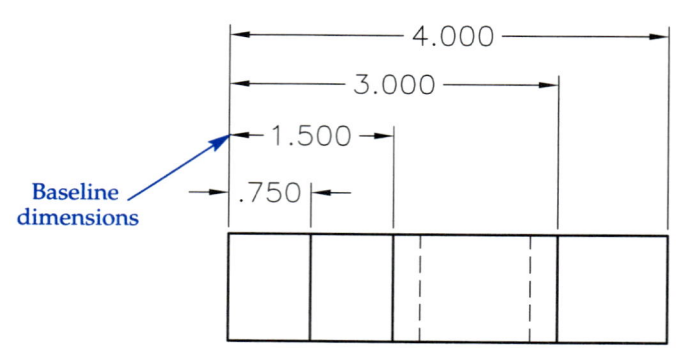

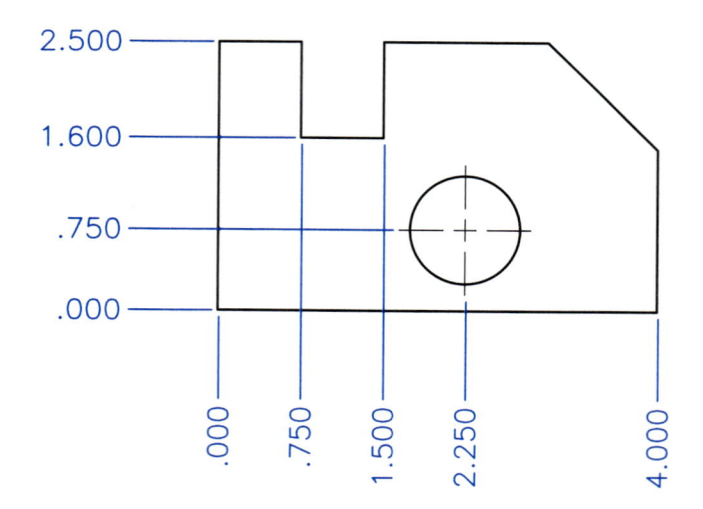

Figure 9-14.
Creating the chamfer dimension. The labeled points in the front view are shown for illustration purposes only.

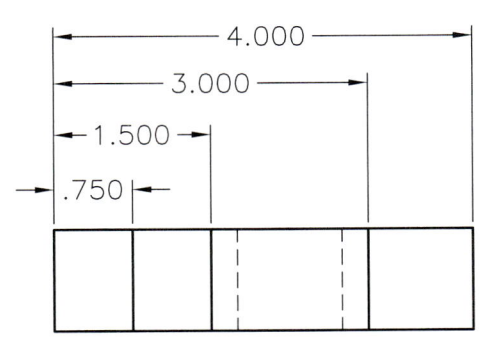

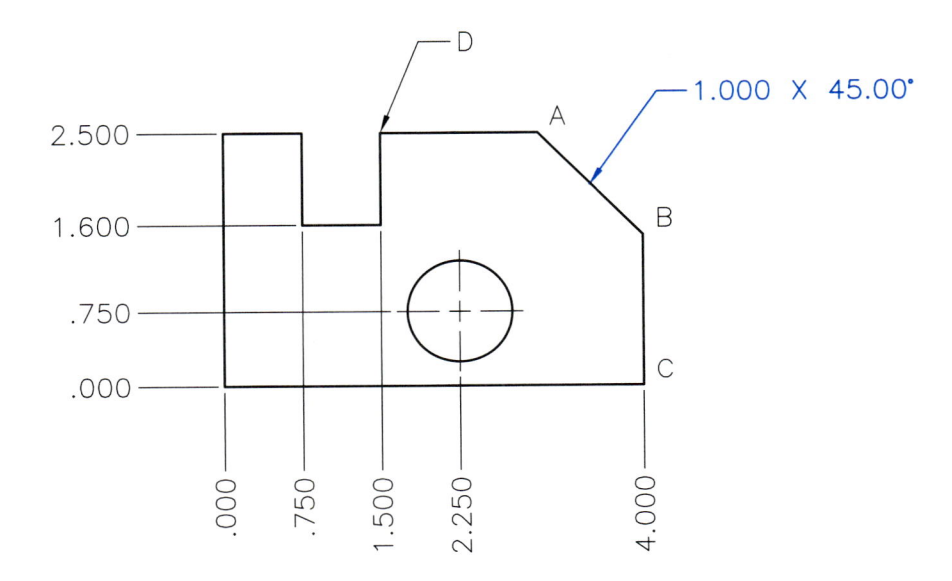

Dimensioning Isometric Views

Reference dimensions on an isometric view are shown correctly by using true length dimensions. Depending on how the isometric view was created, you may have to set the correct dimensioning type for the view in the **Drawing View Property Manager**. Pick on the view and make sure the **True** radio button is selected in the **Dimension Type** rollout. This setting creates true dimensions in the view. If the **Projected** radio button is selected, dimensions show the incorrect foreshortened values. Close the **Drawing View Property Manager**. Then, place the reference dimensions with any of the dimension tools. A correctly dimensioned isometric view is shown in **Figure 9-15**. Save and close both Example_09_02.sldprt and Example_09_02.slddrw.

Editing the Title Block

Open Example_09_03.slddrw and zoom in on the title block in the lower-right corner of the drawing. The drawing number (under the heading DWG. NO.) is set by default to the name of the file. As you can see, the text size is too large. In the design tree, right-click on Sheet Format1 and select **Edit Sheet Format**. All the drawing views will disappear and you can edit the drawing number by double-clicking on it. Change the text size to .125" and make it bold. See **Figure 9-16**. Then, pick the green check mark

Figure 9-15.
True length dimensions are used for dimensioning isometric views.

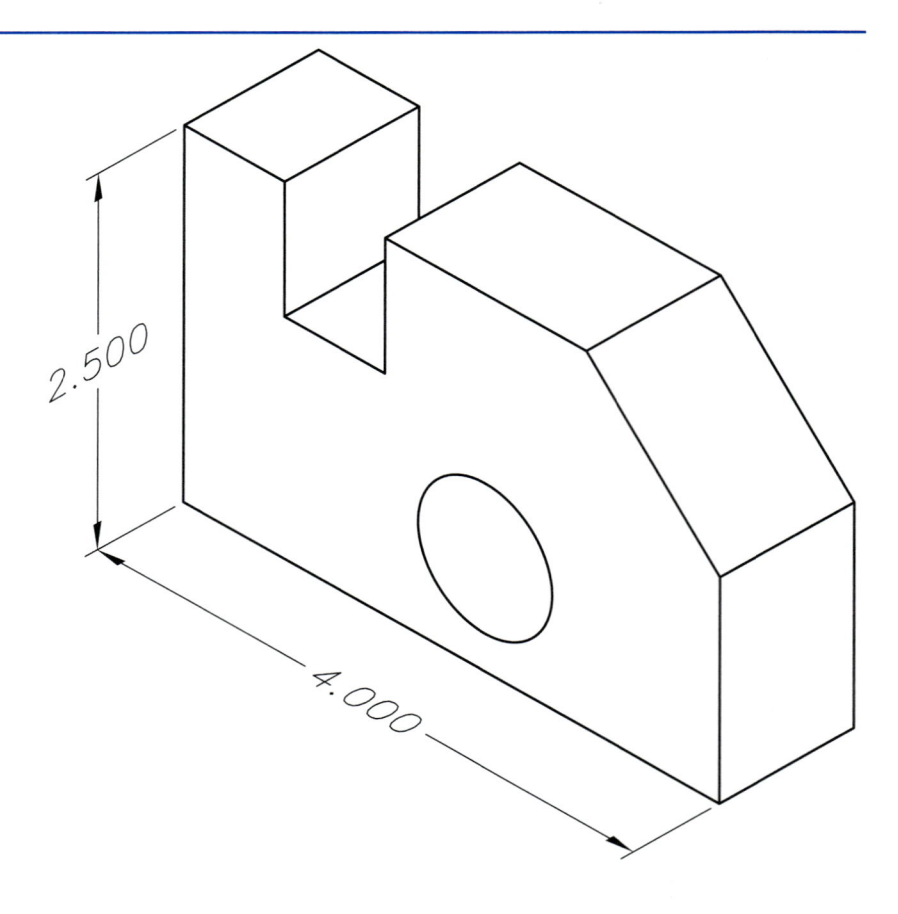

Figure 9-16.
Editing text for the drawing number in the title block.

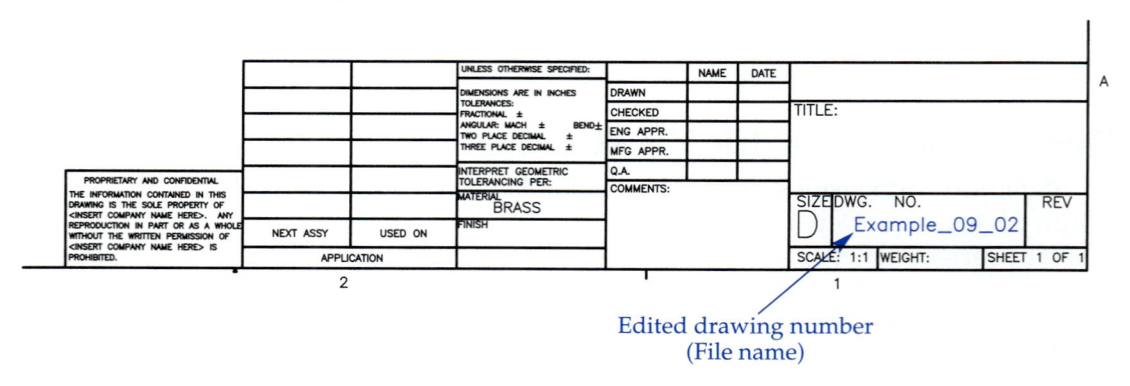

Edited drawing number (File name)

button in the **Note Property Manager**. To make the views visible, right-click again on Sheet Format1 and pick **Edit Sheet**. This exits the sheet format editing environment.

Expand Sheet Format1 in the design tree and notice that there are no choices for the title block. To set the note fields that can be input and edited in the block, such as who checked the drawing and when, you must first "define" these fields.

Right-click on Sheet Format1 and select Define Title Block. Once again, the views disappear. A large rectangle, a border, is displayed; drag the upper-left corner and position and size this border around the title block as shown in **Figure 9-17**. This border is used to define the area where users will enter title block data. Now zoom in again on the title block. The note fields that may be made editable are shown by boxes with an X inside. If you click on any one of them, such as the box under Title:, it will turn blue and its name will be listed in the **Text Fields** rollout in the **Title Block Property Manager**.

Figure 9-17.
Editing the title block. After the border area is defined for entering title block data, the note fields to be made editable are selected.

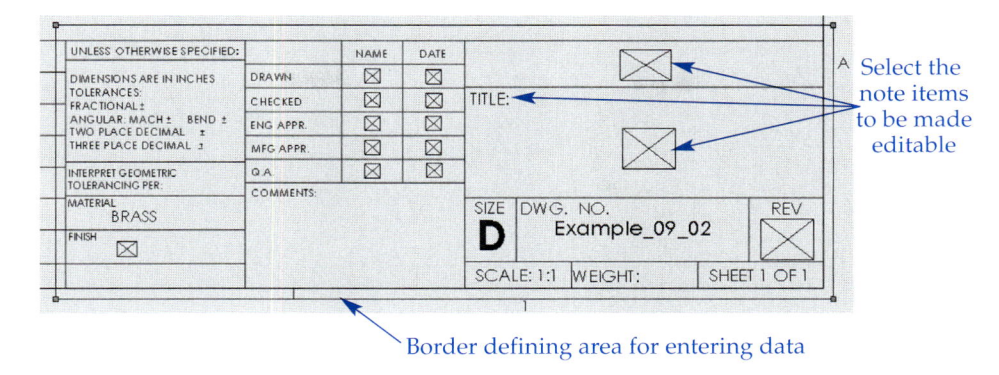

Also click on the box above the title, where we'll input the company name. In addition, you can click on any text in the title block to make it editable, such as the word Title. Refer to **Figure 9-17**. After you are done selecting, pick the green check mark button in the **Title Block Property Manager**. Now, the entry Title Block1 will appear under Sheet Format1 in the design tree.

Now, right-click on Title Block1. There are three title block options in the shortcut menu. The **Edit Title Block** option will take you back to defining the notes to make editable (the environment you just exited from). The **Enter Title Block Data** option allows you to put text into the selected notes. The **Delete Title Block** option will delete the notes you selected to be editable, but not the entire title block.

Select **Enter Title Block Data** and change the word Title to Part Name. Press the [Tab] key to advance to the next field and enter the name Adapter. Press the [Tab] key again and enter the company name of your choice in the corresponding field. See **Figure 9-18**. Pick the green check mark button in the **Title Block Data Property Manager**. When finished, save and close Example_09_03.slddrw.

PROFESSIONAL TIP

You can edit the geometry making up the title block when editing the sheet format. When the sheet format editing environment is active, the title block geometry is displayed in blue. You can use the sketch tools to modify the existing geometry, or you can add new geometry as needed. A sheet format can be saved to a template file (SLDDRT file) so that it can be used in other drawing files. To save a sheet format to a template file, select **Save Sheet Format…** from the **File** pull-down menu. In the **Save Sheet Format** dialog box, name the file and specify where the file will be saved. The sheet format template file can be accessed in the **Sheet Format/Size** dialog box when starting a new drawing file, or when you display the **Sheet Properties** dialog box for a selected sheet.

PRACTICE 9-1

Complete the practice problem on the student website.
www.g-wlearning.com/CAD

Figure 9-18.
The title block after entering the data.

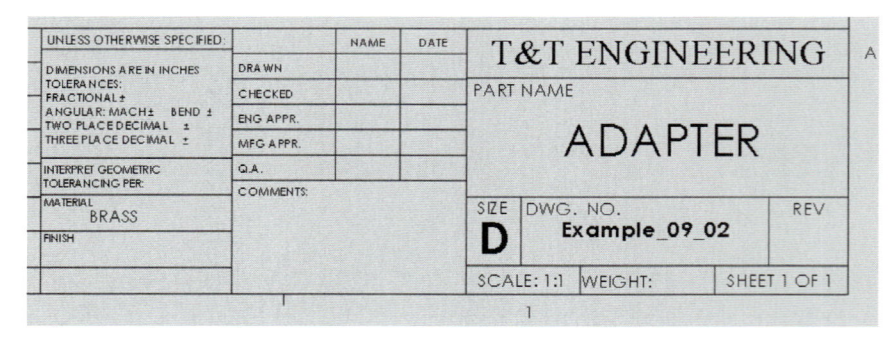

Creating a Revision Table

The *revision table* is used to document the revisions that have been made to a drawing. It is typically located in the upper right-hand corner of the drawing border, but it can be located in any of the corners.

Open Example_09_04.sldprt and Example_09_04.slddrw. The diameter of the large 1.500" hole needs to be revised to 1.350". This is a model dimension (parametric dimension), so you can change it in the drawing file. Double-click on the dimension and change the value to 1.350 in the **Modify** dialog box. The dimension is changed and the view is highlighted; pick the **Rebuild** button in the **Menu Bar** or press [Ctrl][B]. This will change both the drawing and the part. This change now needs to be documented in a revision table.

In the **Annotation** tab of the **Command Manager**, pick on the **Tables** drop-down list and select **Revision Table**. The **Revision Table Property Manager** is displayed. See **Figure 9-19**. The default values will place the table in the upper-right corner of the

Figure 9-19.
The **Revision Table Property Manager**.

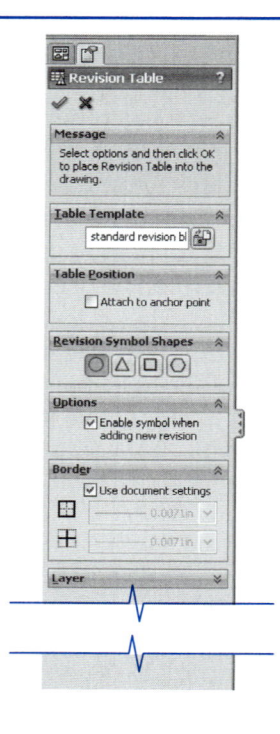

drawing, use a circle for the revision symbol, and automatically require you to locate the revision symbol when a change is entered in the table. Pick the green check mark button and the empty revision table is placed in the corner.

Now, you will add the revision symbol to call out the change on the drawing. Right-click on the table and select **Revisions>Add Revision** from the shortcut menu. The revision symbol, a small circle, appears on the drawing. Hover over the circumference of the revised 1.350″ circle to highlight it. A leader will appear attached to the revision symbol. Pick on the circumference and then place the circle to the upper right of the view. Pick the green check mark button in the **Revision Symbol Property Manager**. To input the description of the change, double-click on the Description box in the new row and input DIA. OF BORED HOLE CHANGED FROM 1.500 TO 1.350. Click on any place in the drawing to accept the input. Using the same process, put your initials in the Approved box. See **Figure 9-20**. When finished, save Example_09_04.sldprt and Example_09_04.slddrw.

PRACTICE 9-2

Complete the practice problem on the student website.
www.g-wlearning.com/CAD

Figure 9-20.
The completed drawing after adding the revision table and revision symbol.

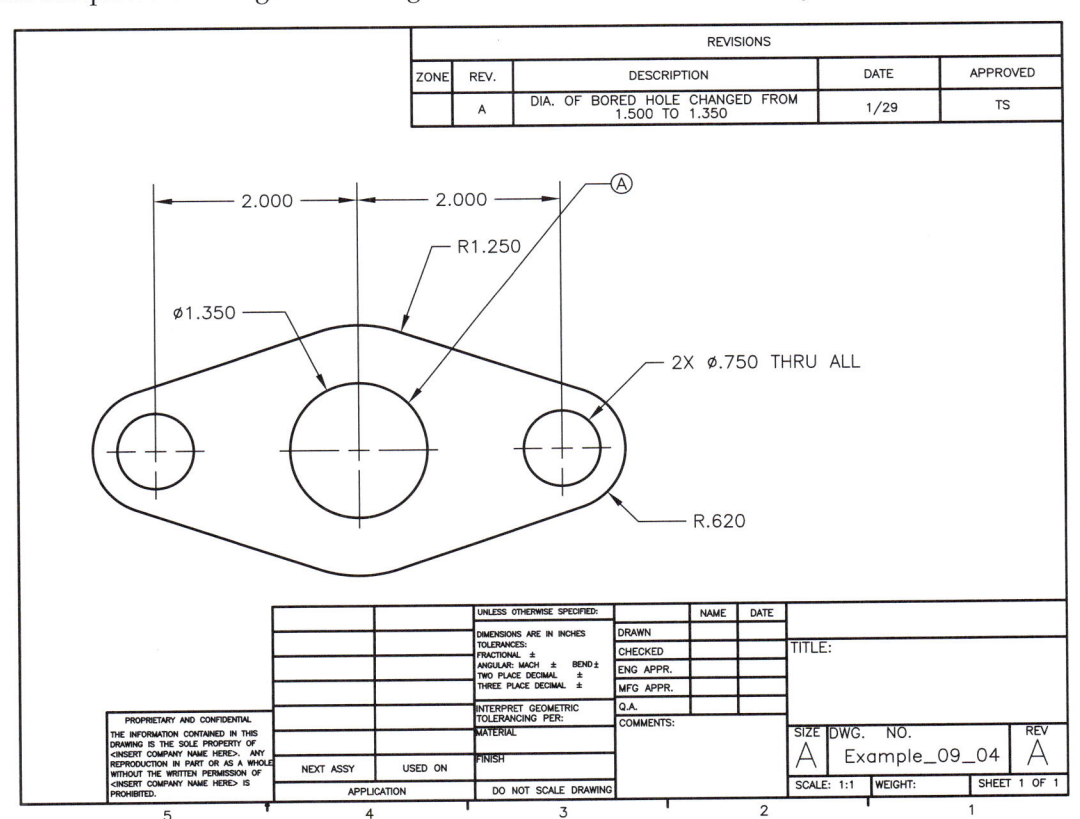

Chapter 9 Dimensioning and Annotating Drawings   **189**

Chapter Test

Answer the following questions on a separate sheet of paper or complete the electronic chapter test on the student website.
www.g-wlearning.com/CAD

1. How do you access a drafting standard and set it current in a SolidWorks file?
2. Explain how to create a custom drafting standard and save it to a file.
3. What is the difference between a *model dimension* and *reference dimension*?
4. Explain how to create a dimension style.
5. What is a *hole note*?
6. Which tool is used to create a hole note?
7. What is a *surface texture symbol*?
8. Briefly explain how to create a note using the **Note** tool.
9. In ordinate dimensioning, what point serves as the origin for measuring dimensions along the X and Y axes?
10. Briefly explain how to define note fields in a title block for use in entering title block data.
11. What is a *revision table*?
12. Explain how to create a revision symbol and enter a related description in a revision table.

Chapter Exercises

Complete the chapter exercises on the student website.
www.g-wlearning.com/CAD

Exercise 9-1 Support Beam. *Complete the exercise on the student website.*

Exercise 9-2 Mass-Produced Part. *Complete the exercise on the student website.*

Exercise 9-3 Precision Part. *Complete the exercise on the student website.*

Chapter 10

Sweeps and Lofts

Objectives

After completing this chapter, you will be able to:
- Explain the difference between an extrusion, sweep, and loft.
- Explain the process for creating a sweep.
- Create 3D sketches.
- Create 2D and 3D sweeps.
- Create lofts.

Sweeps and Lofts

As you have seen, many complex parts can be created using extrusions and revolutions. However, SolidWorks has two other modeling techniques that are very powerful—sweeps and lofts. A *sweep* is a solid object created by extruding, or "sweeping," a profile along a path. With the **Extruded Boss/Base** tool, the path is an implied straight line the length of which is set by the extrusion's end condition (Blind, Up to Vertex, Up to Surface, Offset from Surface, Up to Body, or Mid Plane). A *loft* is similar to a sweep except that you can use multiple profiles to create a solid of varying cross sections. In lofts, a curve called a *guide curve* can be used to deform the lofted profiles. There may be multiple guide curves or none at all.

Creating Swept Features

Swept features are typically created for piping or tubing, but are not limited to these uses. You may be able to quickly create a feature as a sweep that would take much longer to create as an extrusion. For example, a picture frame with mitered corners is best modeled as a sweep. Sweeps have a variety of applications in modeling piping, tubing, and similar parts.

Creating a Sweep Path

The first step in creating a sweep is to create the *path*. The path is simply a sketched curve. It is dimensioned and constrained just like any other sketch and may be open or closed, depending on the shape of the final part. For example, if the part is piping, then the path will be open. If the part is a picture frame, then the path is closed.

Open Example_10_01.sldprt and examine the two sketches. Select the Sketch for Path branch in the design tree so the sketch is highlighted in the graphics window. Notice that the path lies on a plane. Therefore, it is considered a *2D path*. The path was created on the top plane, but any sketch plane can be used. Later in this chapter, you will learn about 3D paths and the ways of creating them.

Example_10_01.sldprt is an example of piping. In this type of application, it is best to plan the path so that it originates at a known point. In this case, the path originates at the origin.

Creating a Cross-Sectional Profile

Like the path, the *cross-sectional profile* is a sketch that is dimensioned and constrained. However, the profile sketch must be separate from the path sketch. In order to use the **Swept Boss/Base** tool, there must be two unconsumed sketches—the path and the profile. In this example, the profile was sketched on the front plane. Pick the Sketch for Profile branch in the design tree so the sketch is highlighted. The sketch is of two concentric circles centered on the origin. Since the path is on the top plane and starts at the origin, this ensures that the cross section is at the start of the path and intersects the path. SolidWorks requires that the starting point of the path be on the same plane of the cross section.

Creating the Sweep

With the path and the profile created, it is time to create the sweep using the **Swept Boss/Base** tool. Pick the **Swept Boss/Base** button in the **Features** tab of the **Command Manager**. The **Sweep Property Manager** is displayed. See **Figure 10-1**. With the **Profile** selection box active in the **Profile and Path** rollout, pick the profile in the graphics window. Select the sketch with the two concentric circles (Sketch for Profile). Next, with the **Path** selection box active in the **Profile and Path** rollout, select the path in the graphics window. The path is the S-shaped line (Sketch for Path).

You may have noticed when you selected the path and profile that a preview of the sweep appears along the path. Notice how the profile follows the path, adjusting its orientation so it is always perpendicular to the path. There are many options you can set for the sweep. For this example, accept the default settings by picking the green check mark button. The sweep is created. See **Figure 10-2**.

Profile Not Perpendicular to the Path

In the previous example, the cross section was sketched perpendicular to the path. To see the importance of this, open Example_10_02.sldprt. The path is the same as in the previous example. The profile is also the same; however, notice that the sketch is *not* perpendicular to the path. The profile sketch is angled at 30° to the plane on which the path lies. Using the same procedure described above, create a sweep of the profile.

Notice that the resulting cross section of the part is *elliptical,* **Figure 10-3A**. If you rotate the view, you can clearly see the end of the pipe is elliptical, **Figure 10-3B**. This is because the circular profile is projected onto a plane that is perpendicular to the path plane. When a circle is viewed at an angle, it appears as an ellipse. Since the circular profile is not perpendicular to the path plane, the projected profile is an ellipse, which is then extruded along the path. It is important to remember this as you sketch paths and profiles.

Figure 10-1.
The **Sweep Property Manager** is used to make the settings for a sweep.

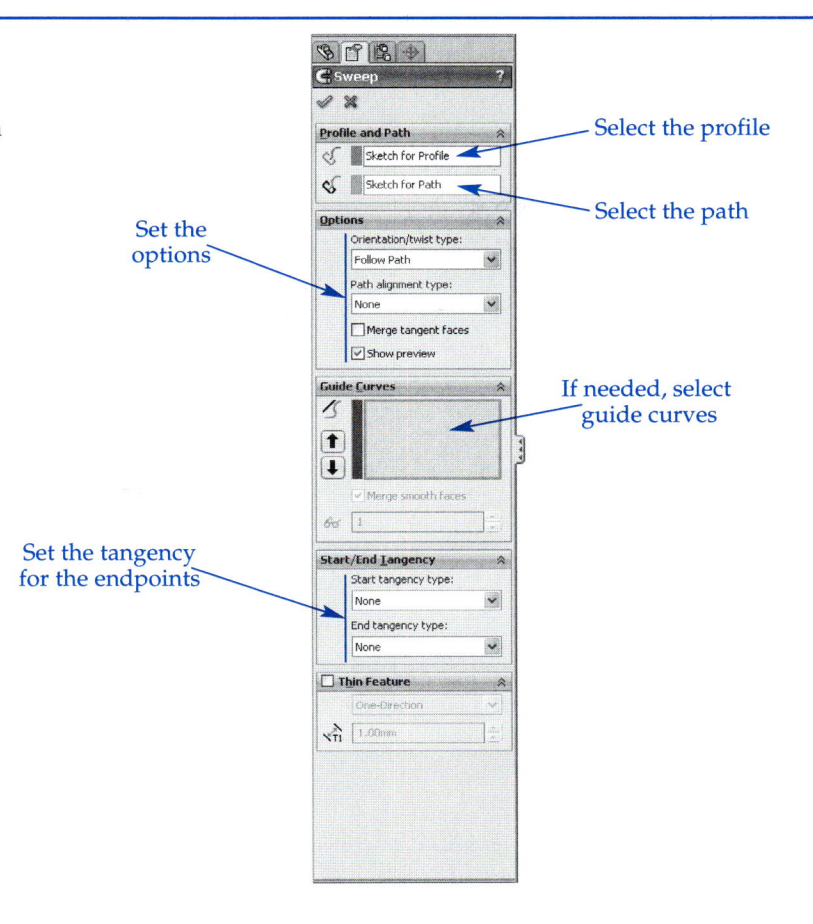

Select the profile

Select the path

Set the options

If needed, select guide curves

Set the tangency for the endpoints

Figure 10-2.
Two concentric circles were swept along a path to create this pipe run.

Chapter 10 Sweeps and Lofts

193

Figure 10-3.
A—If the circle profile is not perpendicular to the path, an elliptical cross section is created.
B—Rotating the view clearly shows the elliptical shape.

A   B

Closed Paths

In the previous examples, the paths were open. However, the path can be closed. Open Example_10_03.sldprt. This file contains two unconsumed sketches—a profile and a path. Notice that the path is a rectangle; in other words, it is closed. Use the **Swept Boss/Base** tool to create the part as a solid. The resulting part is picture frame molding. Pay particular attention to how the profile is extruded ("swept") around the corners. Sharp corners are created. Even if a circle is swept on this path, sharp corners are created because the path has sharp corners.

Practical Example of Sweeps

Look at **Figure 10-4.** This is a guard used in an industrial application to prevent large debris from entering a pipe inlet. Now, open Example_10_04.sldprt. The two bottom rings are already created in the file. The front plane has been made visible. Also, the file contains a reference plane and two reference axes. Plane for Arc Height is parallel to the rings and 8" above the top ring. Vertical Axis is coincident to the Y axis of the coordinate system. Horizontal Axis is coincident to the X axis of the coordinate system. You will now model one of the spokes as a sweep, create a circular pattern for the remaining spokes, and create the cap.

Creating the Sweep Path

1. Start a new sketch on the front plane.
2. Expand the Rings branch in the design tree to show the consumed sketch used in its construction.
3. Right-click on the Sketch for Rings name in the design tree and pick the show button in the shortcut toolbar.

194   Learning SolidWorks 2009

Figure 10-4.
This is a guard for a pipe inlet. A single spoke was created as a sweep, then a circular pattern was created. A—A top, isometric view. B—A bottom, isometric view.

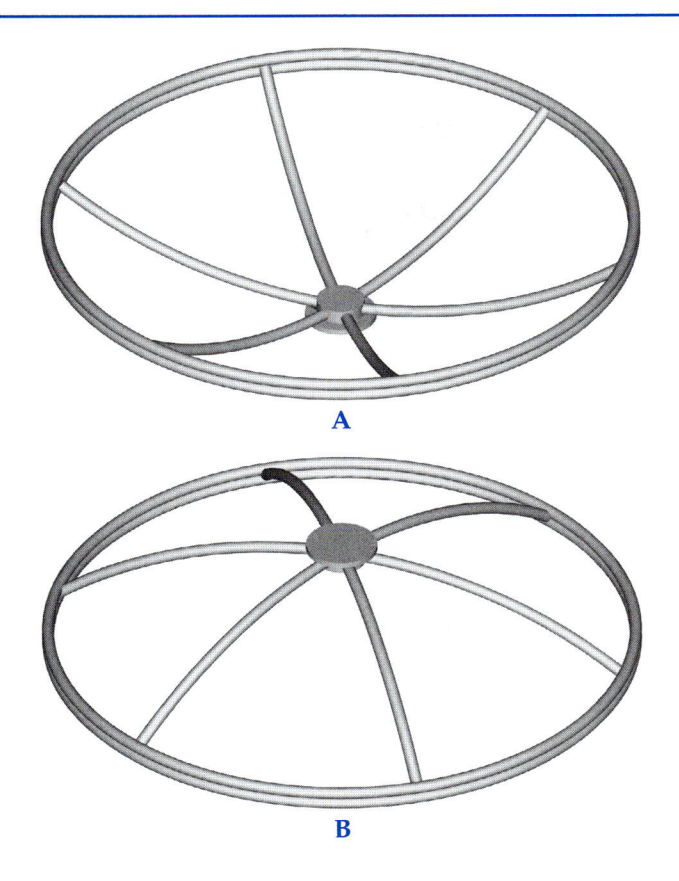

A

B

4. Zoom in on the lower-right corner so the two circles in Sketch for Rings and the vertical reference axis are visible in the graphics window.
5. Holding down the [Shift] key, select both circles in Sketch for Rings. Then, pick the **Convert Entities** button in the **Sketch** tab of the **Command Manager**. This projects the two circles into the new sketch.
6. Select the two projected circles and turn them into construction lines by checking the **For construction** check box in the **Options** rollout of the **Properties Property Manager**.
7. Draw a vertical construction line and constrain it collinear to the vertical reference axis.
8. Draw a horizontal construction line and constrain it collinear to the horizontal reference axis.
9. Pick the **Mirror Entities** button on the **Sketch** tab of the **Command Manager**. Select both circles as the entities to mirror and the vertical construction line as the centerline. Mirror the circles and zoom out so the entire part is visible.
10. Pick the **Three Point Arc** button in the **Sketch** tab of the **Command Manager**.
11. Select the start point of the arc as the center point of the top, left-hand circle.
12. Select the endpoint of the arc as the center point of the top, right-hand circle.
13. Place the third point on the arc tangent to the horizontal construction line.
14. This arc is the path for a sweep. See **Figure 10-5**. Finish the sketch.

Creating the Cross Section

The sketched profile to be swept does not have to be at the end of the path. In this example, it is easiest to create the cross-sectional profile at the midpoint of the path.

1. Display the isometric view.
2. Start a new sketch on the right plane by right-clicking on Right Plane in the design tree and picking the **Sketch** button in the shortcut toolbar.

Chapter 10 Sweeps and Lofts

Figure 10-5.
The path for one spoke. Project it into the sketch for the cross section to locate the profile.

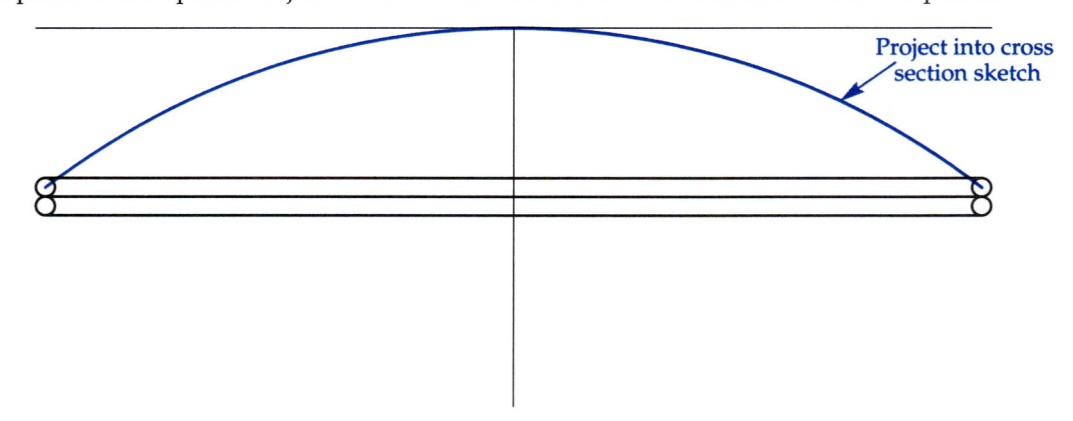

3. Select the path arc created earlier and pick the **Convert Entities** button to project it onto the sketch plane. This results in a line. Change this line into a construction line.
4. Draw a circle with its center at the top endpoint of the projected line. Dimension the diameter of the circle as 1.0″. This is the cross-sectional profile.
5. Finish the sketch.

Completing the Part

1. Pick the **Swept Boss/Base** button in the **Features** tab of the **Command Manager**.
2. Select the circle as the profile.
3. Select the arc as the path.
4. Pick the green check mark button to create the sweep.

Notice that the sweep is only from the center of the rings to one end, not along the entire length of the arc. This is because the profile is in the middle of the path. If the profile was at one end of the path, the sweep would be created along the entire length of the path.

5. Pick the **Circular Pattern** button in the **Features** tab of the **Command Manager**.
6. Pick the sweep as the feature and the vertical reference axis as the pattern axis. Create a pattern of six items over 360 degrees.
7. To create the center cap, start a new sketch on the front plane.
8. Draw and dimension the sketch of the cap as shown in **Figure 10-6**. Constrain the lines to the reference axes as shown. Then, finish the sketch.
9. Use the **Revolved Boss/Base** tool to create the center cap. Use the vertical reference axis as the axis of revolution.

The part is now complete. Among other things, this example shows the reasons for building parts about the origin and in line with the basic reference planes.

PRACTICE 10-1

Complete the practice problem on the student website.
www.g-wlearning.com/CAD

Figure 10-6.
The sketch for the button, which is created as a revolution.

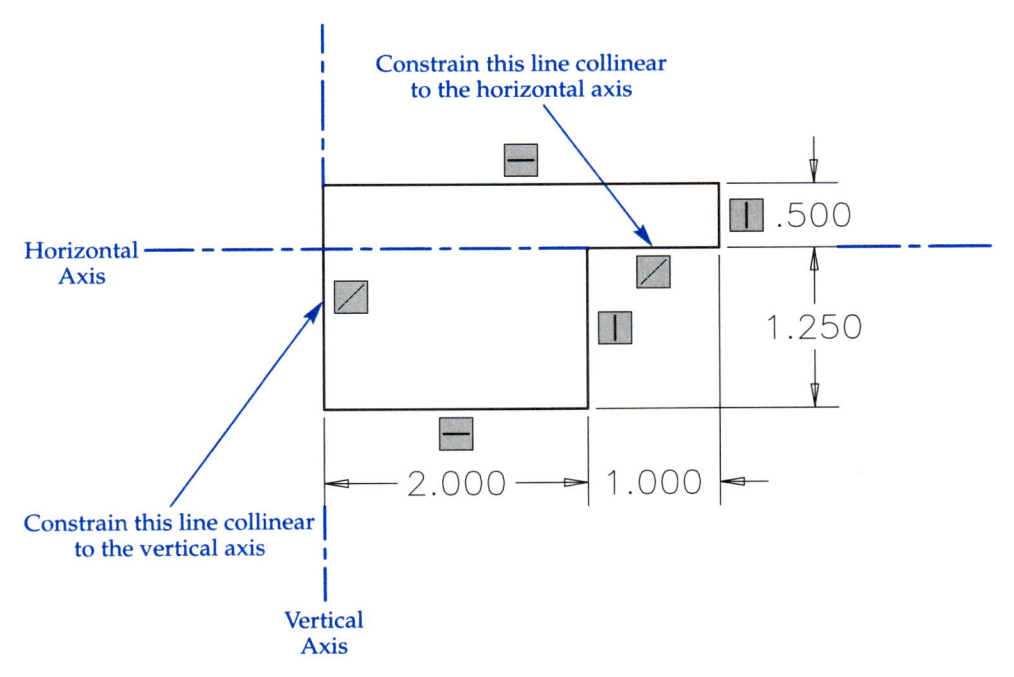

3D Sweeps

Two-dimensional planar sweeps have many applications, but there are also times when more-complex, nonplanar 3D sweeps are required. Examples of these situations are pipe or tubing runs and wire harnesses. In order to create a 3D sweep, the path must be created as a 3D sketch. To start a new 3D sketch, pick the **3D Sketch** button in the **Sketch** drop-down list on the **Sketch** tab of the **Command Manager**. The 3D sketch environment is started.

A 3D sketch can be composed of 3D lines/curves or a 3D spline. Existing points or reference points can be selected to create these curves. The same tools in the **Sketch** tab of the **Command Manager** are used for creating 2D and 3D sketches, though some tools are unavailable in the 3D sketching environment.

The next example is a pipe run. Open **Example_10_05.sldprt**. A pipe tee has been created. You will create the pipe run as a sweep from the top of the tee.

1. Start a 2D sketch on the top face of the tee.
2. Select the two circles representing the pipe OD and ID, then pick the **Convert Entities** button to project them into the sketch. These will be used as the cross section for a sweep. Also, the center point of the circles will be used to start a 3D path.
3. Finish this 2D sketch.
4. Display the isometric view and zoom out so the tee fills about 1/8 of the graphics window. It helps to create 3D sketches in the isometric view.
5. Start a 3D sketch by picking the **3D Sketch** button in the drop-down list below the **Sketch** button on the **Sketch** tab of the **Command Manager**.
6. Activate the **Line** tool.

Chapter 10   Sweeps and Lofts

Next to the cursor, the symbol XY appears. This denotes that the line segment will be created parallel to the XY (front) plane, but not necessarily *on* the XY plane. To switch between XY, YZ, and ZX orientations, press the [Tab] key. The symbol next to the cursor always indicates the current orientation. Remember, the orientation is parallel to the indicated plane, but the curve you are drawing may not be *on* the indicated plane. Refer to **Figure 10-7** as you continue.

7. Pick the center point of the stub as the starting point for the 3D sketch. Make sure the XY orientation is current, as indicated by the cursor symbol. Then, draw a line along the positive Y axis about 6″ in length. Leave the **Line** tool active.
8. In the XY orientation, draw a line along the positive X axis approximately 42″ in length.
9. Press the [Tab] key until the ZX symbol (or YZ symbol) is shown next to the cursor. Draw a line along the negative Z axis about 36″ in length.
10. Press the [Tab] key until the XY symbol is shown next to the cursor. Draw a line along the positive Y axis about 54″ in length.
11. Draw a line along the negative X axis about 36″ in length.
12. Press the [Tab] key until the ZX symbol is shown next to the cursor. Draw a line along the negative Z axis about 30″ in length.
13. Pick the green check mark button in the **Line Properties Property Manager** or press the [Esc] key to end the **Line** tool.
14. Using the **Smart Dimension** tool, dimension each line segment to the exact values indicated above.
15. Using the **Sketch Fillet** tool, create a 5″ fillet at each corner.
16. Finish the sketch by picking the **3D Sketch** button in the drop-down list below the **Sketch** button.

To finish the pipe run, use the **Swept Boss/Base** tool. Select the sketch with the two concentric circles on the top of the tee as the profile. Select the 3D line as the path. See **Figure 10-8**. Expand the part tree for the sweep. Notice the structure. It contains two sketches, just as a 2D sweep would.

Figure 10-7.
The 3D path for the pipe run is completed.

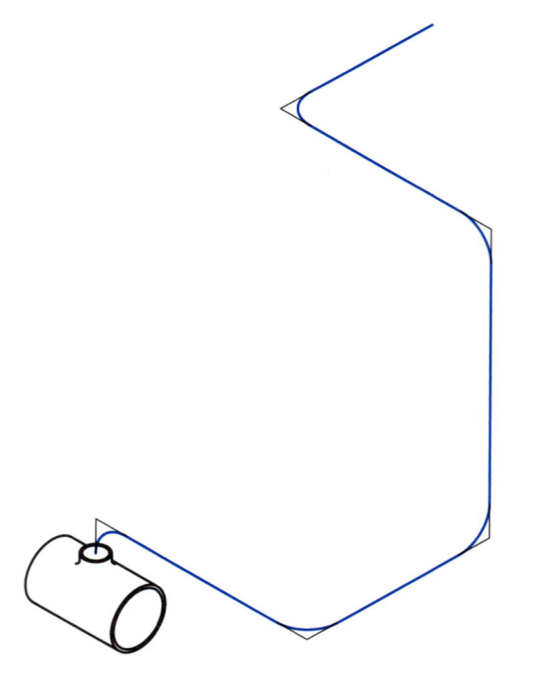

Figure 10-8.
The completed pipe run.

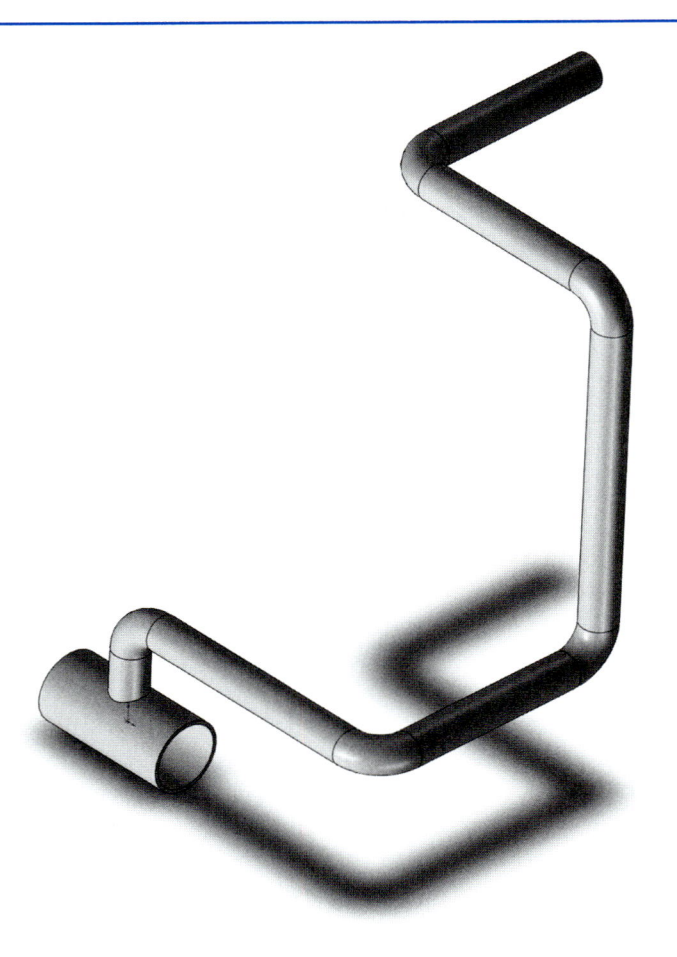

> **PROFESSIONAL TIP**
> When drawing a line in a 3D sketch and the line is close to being parallel to the X, Y, or Z axis, SolidWorks snaps the line to that axis and constrains the sketch entity as being along that axis.

Editing a 3D Sweep

Editing a 3D sweep mainly involves editing the sketches used for the sweep—the path and the profile. Entities created in a 3D sketch and used for profiles can be edited and constrained in the same ways as 2D sketch entities. In this manner, you can constrain the sweep to other features in the part. Additionally, if you right-click on the name of the sweep in the design tree and pick the **Edit Feature** button in the shortcut toolbar, the **Sweep Property Manager** is displayed. This allows you to select a different profile or path or change the output or creation method.

Lofts

A *loft* is a solid or surface generated from a series of cross sections. The cross sections are created as sketches and do not need to be parallel to one another. Note that

Chapter 10 Sweeps and Lofts *199*

the cross sections for lofted solids should be closed profiles. The path for a loft is called a *guide curve.* The process of creating a loft is called *lofting.* Lofting is usually done to create organic shapes or parts with very complex, compound curves. Examples of where lofting is useful include a car body, ship hull, ergonomic mouse, or human hand. Other applications include modeling transitions between two known geometric shapes, such as a square-to-round transition found in HVAC ductwork.

Basic Loft

Open the file Example_10_06.sldprt. There are two reference planes parallel to the front plane, all of which are visible. Each of the visible planes contains a sketch. The sketches are centered on the origin.

Pick the **Lofted Boss/Base** button in the **Features** tab of the **Command Manager**. The **Loft Property Manager** is displayed, **Figure 10-9.** With the **Profile** selection box active in the **Profiles** rollout, pick the three sketched shapes in order from left to right (or right to left). The preview reflects those sketches selected.

The shape of the loft can be adjusted using the handles, or *connectors,* that appear as green dots in the preview. Pick and hold on a handle and drag it to a new location. When you release the mouse button, the preview changes. Controlling the shape of a loft using the connectors is known as *loft synchronization* and is often required to fine-tune the shape of the loft. The location where you pick the cross sections determines where the connector is displayed on the profile.

To display more connectors, right-click in the graphics window and choose **Show All Connectors** in the shortcut menu. The additional connectors are displayed in light blue. The number of connectors displayed is equal to the maximum number of vertices on the start or end profile of the loft. Once you have selected all of the profiles and fine-tuned the loft shape as needed, pick the green check mark button in the **Loft Property Manager** to create the loft. See **Figure 10-10.**

Right-click on the loft name in the design tree and pick the **Edit Feature** button in the shortcut toolbar. Expand the **Start/End Constraints** rollout in the **Loft Property**

Figure 10-9.
The **Loft Property Manager** is used to select the profiles for the loft. If needed, you can use a guide curve to control the shape of the loft.

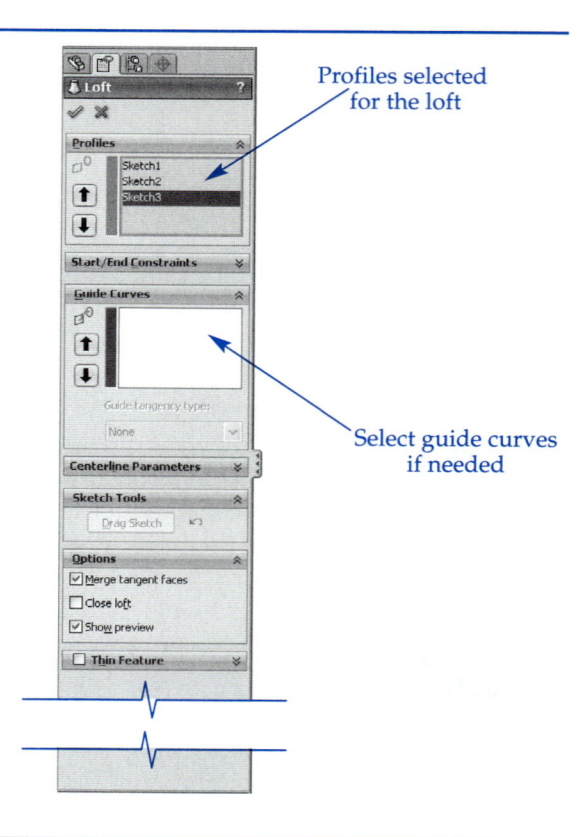

Figure 10-10.
A simple loft consisting of three cross-sectional profiles.

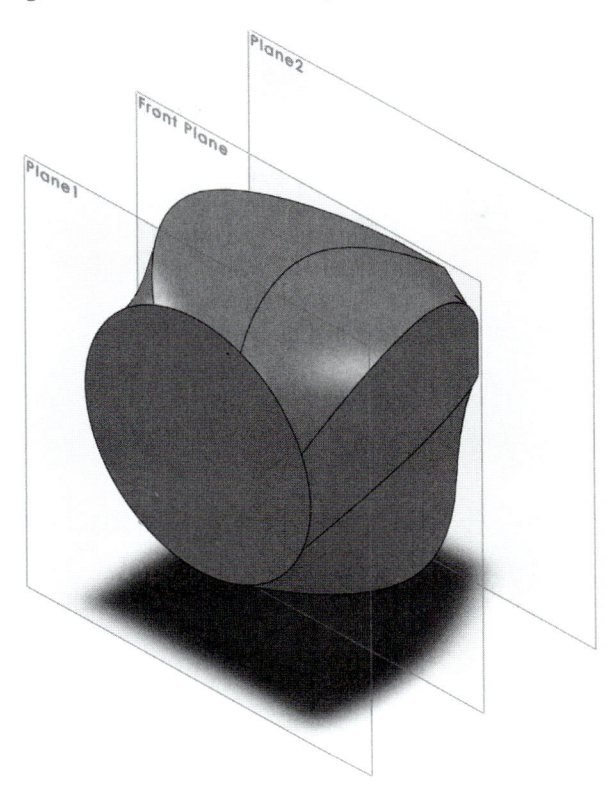

Manager. The options in this rollout are used to define the constraints at the start and end sections of the lofted part. In the **Start constraint:** drop-down list, select the Normal to Profile. Notice how the preview changes. Also notice that additional options are displayed in the rollout. In the **Start Tangent Length** text box, enter a value of 2. This value controls how far the loft maintains the shape of the starting profile before it begins to transition into the next profile. The higher the value, the longer the loft maintains the shape of the starting profile. See **Figure 10-11.**

Loft with Guide Curve

The sketches used for a loft do not have to be in parallel planes. Complex shapes can be created using *guide curves* to guide the shape from one sketch to another. Open Example_10_07.sldprt. Sketch1 is the closed spline on the left and Sketch2 is on the right. Sketch 3 is a spline that will be used as the guide curve. The sketch entity must intersect each shape at one point order to be used as a guide curve. Also, notice how the two reference planes are not parallel.

Pick the **Lofted Boss/Base** button in the **Features** tab of the **Command Manager.** Pick the two closed shapes as profiles. Notice how the feature preview goes straight from one shape to the other. In the **Guide Curves** rollout, activate the **Guide Curves** selection box. Then, select the spline in Sketch3 as the guide curve. Note how the loft is warped or pushed by the guide curve. See **Figure 10-12.**

PROFESSIONAL TIP

Fillets and rounds can be applied to the edges of a loft.

Chapter 10   Sweeps and Lofts   **201**

Figure 10-11.
A—The default shape of the loft. B—By adjusting the tangent at the starting cross section, the shape is altered.

A

B

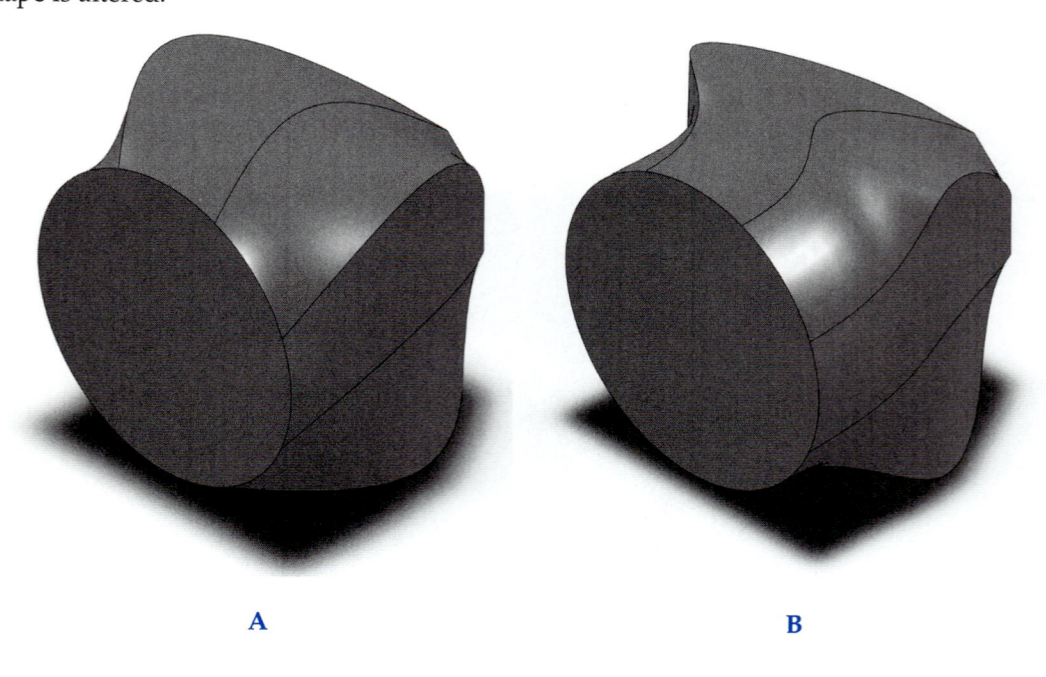

Figure 10-12.
Using a guide curve to control a loft. A—Without a guide curve, the loft extends in a straight line between the two profiles. B—By adding a guide curve that is not a straight line, the loft is deformed to match the shape of the guide curve.

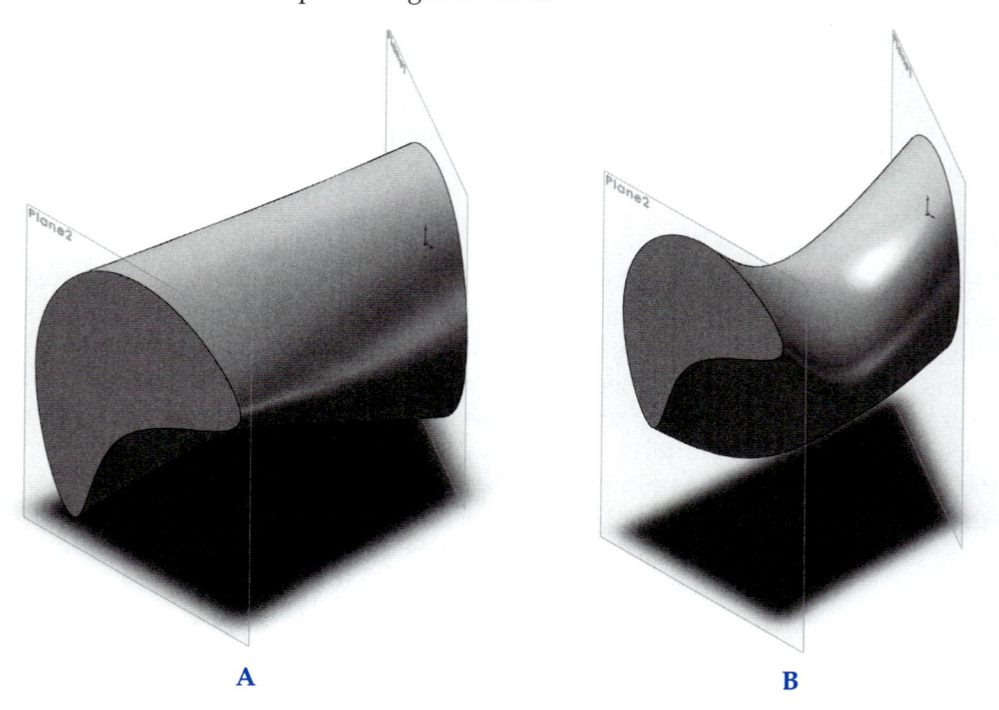

A

B

PRACTICE 10-2

Complete the practice problem on the student website.
www.g-wlearning.com/CAD

Closed-Loop Loft

The two previous examples are open-loop lofts. An *open-loop loft* does not begin and end at the same point. A *closed-loop loft*, which begins and ends at the same point, can also be created. Closed loops are typically used in sheet metal applications, such as the airplane engine cowling shown in **Figure 10-13.** This is a closed-loop loft created from multiple, closed spline sections.

Open Example_10_08.sldprt. There are 10 visible sketches on 10 different reference planes. The sketches were created in order and, thus, appear in order in the design tree. Move the cursor over the first visible sketch (Sketch3) in the design tree to see which profile is highlighted in the graphics window. Then, pick the **Lofted Boss/Base** button. Starting with the first visible sketch, select each profile in order (counterclockwise). Pick each profile at the same corresponding point, such as one of the square corners. Selecting the same corresponding point is important so the connectors will be appropriately placed. Once all sketches are listed in the **Profile** selection box, pick the green check mark button to create the loft, **Figure 10-14A.**

Notice the gap at the top of the loft. Edit the loft feature. In the **Options** rollout, check the **Close Loft** check box. This check box must be checked to connect the first and last cross sections. If it is not checked, this segment is not added and an open-loop loft is created. Then, pick the green check mark button to update the feature. See **Figure 10-14B.**

PROFESSIONAL TIP

By default, the **Merge Tangent Faces** check box in the **Options** rollout is checked when creating a loft. When checked, an edge is not created between segments whose faces are tangent. This eliminates an undesirable seam between the segments.

Figure 10-13.
This is a closed-loop loft. It begins and ends at the same point.

Chapter 10 Sweeps and Lofts

Figure 10-14.
A—By default, the loft is not closed. B—Checking the **Close loft** check box tells SolidWorks to create a closed-loop loft.

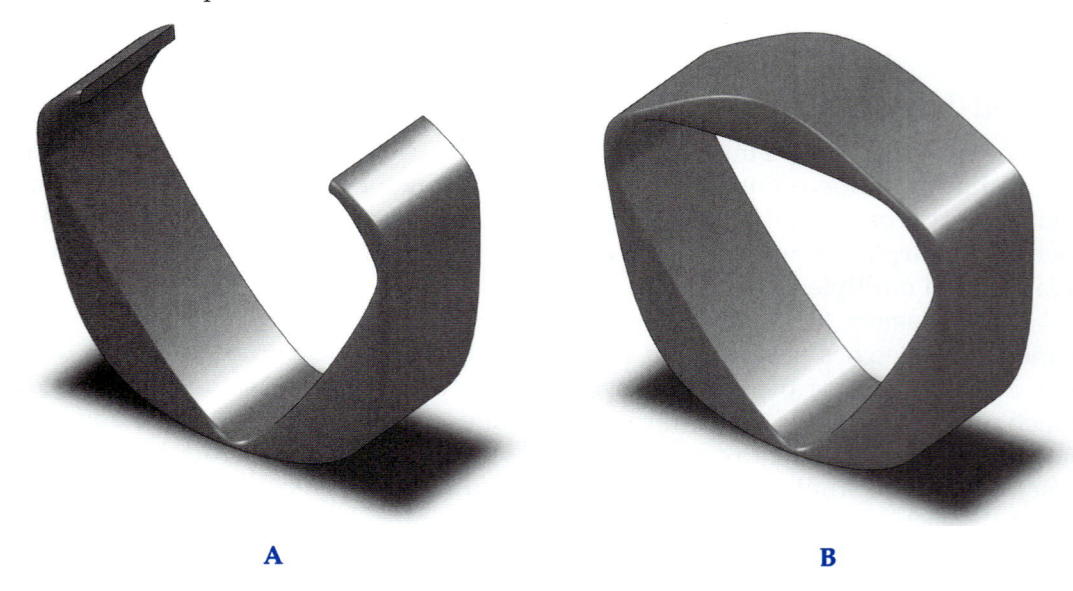

A   B

PRACTICE 10-3

Complete the practice problem on the student website.
www.g-wlearning.com/CAD

Editing a Loft Feature

A loft can be edited in basically the same way as a sweep. Editing the reference planes on which cross-sectional sketches are created will alter the loft's shape. The individual sketches can also be edited, which may have the most effect on the final shape and appearance. If you right-click on the loft name in the design tree and pick the **Edit Feature** button in the shortcut toolbar, the **Loft Properties Manager** is displayed. You can then alter the settings used to create the loft. For example, if you forgot to check the **Close loft** check box, edit the feature and check it. Editing the transitions by adjusting the connectors is usually done after the cross sections are lofted. In this way, you can see which transitions need adjustment.

Chapter Test

Answer the following questions on a separate sheet of paper or complete the electronic chapter test on the student website.
www.g-wlearning.com/CAD

1. What is the difference between an *extrusion* and a *sweep*?
2. What is the difference between a *sweep* and a *loft*?
3. What is a *guide curve*?
4. What is the difference between a *2D path* and a *3D path*?
5. What happens if you sweep a circle along a path if the circle is *not* perpendicular to the path?
6. If a circle is swept around a square corner, what shape does the corner have on the finished part?
7. What is the difference between a *2D sweep* and a *3D sweep*?
8. When are lofts typically created?
9. Explain the difference between an *open-loop loft* and a *closed-loop loft*.
10. When a curve is used to control the shape of a loft, what is the curve called?

Chapter Exercises

Complete the chapter exercises on the student website.
www.g-wlearning.com/CAD

Exercise 10-1 Mating Part. *Complete the exercise on the student website.*

Exercise 10-2 Hitch Pin. *Complete the exercise on the student website.*

Exercise 10-3 Handwheel. *Complete the exercise on the student website.*

Chapter 10 Sweeps and Lofts

A very powerful aspect of modeling with SolidWorks is the ability to create assemblies. In assembly modeling, parts are added to the assembly file. Mates are added to position and constrain parts in relation to each other. (Image courtesy of DS SolidWorks Corp.)

Chapter 11
Building Assemblies with Mates

Objectives

After completing this chapter, you will be able to:

- Create an assembly from existing parts.
- Apply mates using various options.
- Edit mates placed in an assembly.
- Edit parts in place within an assembly.
- Place standard fasteners into an assembly.

Creating an Assembly

In this chapter, you will learn how to create an assembly. An *assembly* is a collection of parts and subassemblies that shows how parts fit together to create the final product. For example, the assembly file shown in **Figure 11-1** contains four different parts—11E01_Base_Plate, 11E01_Bearing_Block, 11E01_Bushing, 11E01_CR_Locating Pin, and a standard cap screw selected from SolidWorks' fastener library. Some of these parts, such as the cap screw, are placed in the assembly file multiple times. When a part is placed in an assembly file, it is called an *instance* of the part. All parts are positioned in an assembly with respect to each other using parametric relations called *mates.*

Building the Assembly

Select **New...** from the **File** pull-down menu, pick the **New** button on the **Menu Bar**, or press [Ctrl][N]. In the **New SolidWorks Document** dialog box, pick the **Assembly** button to specify a new assembly file and then pick the **OK** button. A new, "blank" assembly file is started. Now, you are ready to build the assembly by placing the parts and adding assembly mates.

When a new assembly file is started, the **Begin Assembly Property Manager** is automatically displayed, **Figure 11-2**. The **Open documents:** list box in the **Part/Assembly**

207

Figure 11-3.
Using the triad to rotate the part into a more appropriate orientation.

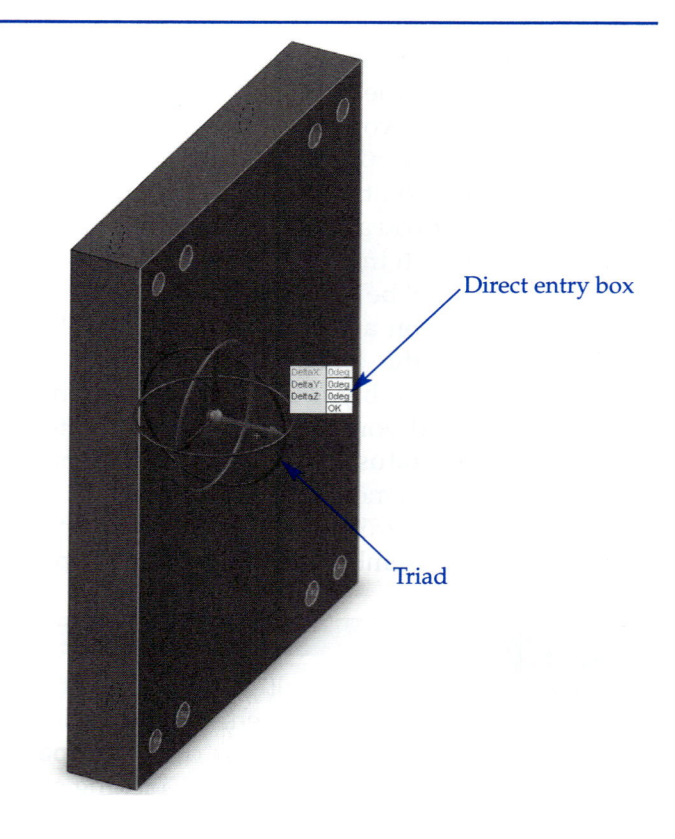

Direct entry box

Triad

Figure 11-4.
The part has been rotated to a more appropriate orientation.

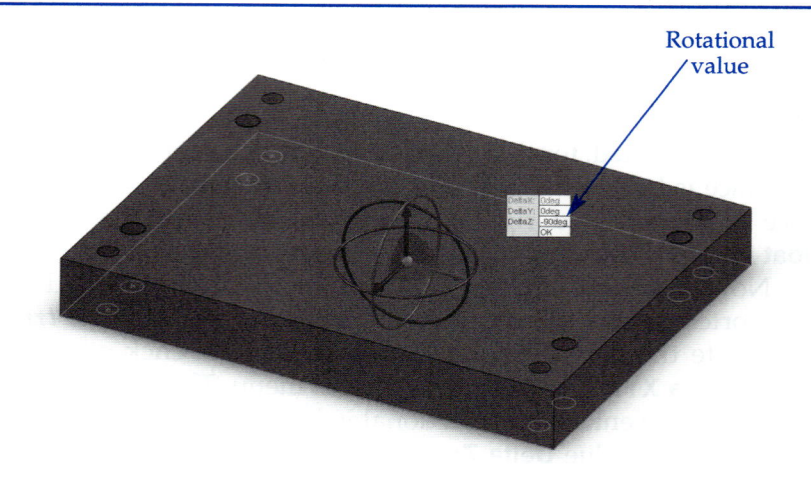

Rotational value

Removing Degrees of Freedom Using Mates

When a part is placed in an assembly, except the first part (which is automatically fixed), it has six degrees of freedom. It can rotate about each of the X, Y, and Z axes. It can also move along each of these axes. Putting it another way, it would take three coordinates (X, Y, and Z) and three angles to specify exactly where the part is in space and its orientation. By applying mates, these degrees of freedom can be removed so the part is fully constrained.

For example, a mating constraint applied face-to-face removes one linear and two angular degrees of freedom. SolidWorks offers many types of assembly mates and separates them into three categories:
- Standard mates.
- Advanced mates.
- Mechanical mates.

The use of various standard mates is examined in this chapter. The later chapters cover advanced and mechanical mates.

Coincident Mate

Note the red face on the short end of the base plate. This face will be aligned with the right plane using a *coincident mate.* Pick the **Mate** button in the **Assembly** tab of the **Command Manager**. The **Mate Property Manager** is displayed, **Figure 11-5.** With the **Entities to Mate** selection box active in the **Mate Selections** rollout, select the red face by clicking on it in the graphics window. Then, select the right plane using the flyout **Feature Manager** design tree. If the **Show Preview** check box is checked in the **Options** rollout (which it is by default), the base plate moves into alignment so the red face and the right plane are coincident to each other.

SolidWorks assumes you want to create a coincident mate, which you do in this case. The **Coincident** button is selected in the **Standard Mates** rollout and on the shortcut toolbar that is displayed. However, the rollout and toolbar display all mates that can be applied to the selections. To apply a different mate, pick the appropriate button. With the **Coincident** button selected, pick the green check mark button in the **Property Manager** or the toolbar to apply the mate. The **Mates** rollout in the **Mate Property Manager** now lists the mate you just applied. All mates in the assembly are listed in this rollout. Pick the green check mark button to close the **Property Manager**.

Notice the Mates branch in the design tree. The Coincident1 mate is listed under the Mates branch. This branch displays all mates in the assembly. The mate can also be found in the Mates in *file name* branch of the 11E01_Base_Plate<1> branch. This branch displays all mates applied to the base plate.

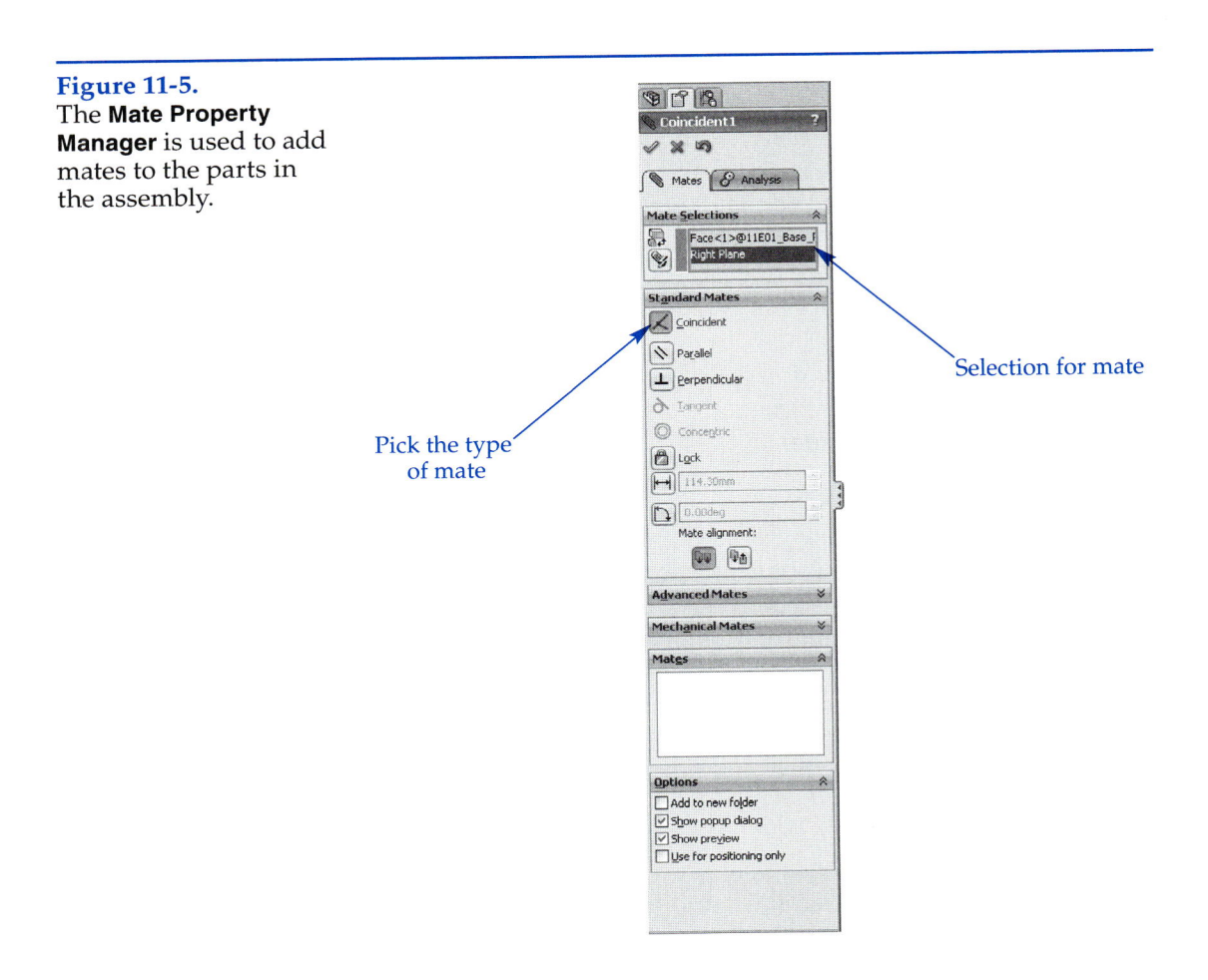

Figure 11-5.
The **Mate Property Manager** is used to add mates to the parts in the assembly.

Chapter 11   Building Assemblies with Mates

This one mate removes three degrees of freedom from the base plate—one translational and two rotational. There are still three more degrees of freedom to remove for the assembly to be fully constrained.

> **PROFESSIONAL TIP**
>
> You can rename mates in the design tree just as you can rename features and sketches. This can be useful. Even in a small assembly you can quickly add many of the same type of mates.

Distance Mate

Now, a *distance mate* will be used to line up the green face on the part with the front plane. Once again, pick the **Mate** button. With the **Entities to Mate** selection box active in the **Mate Selections** rollout, select the green face on the base plate and the front plane (using the flyout **Feature Manager** design tree).

SolidWorks will likely automatically choose a coincident mate and display a preview. However, in this case, a distance mate needs to be applied. Pick the **Distance** button in the **Standard Mates** rollout or the shortcut toolbar.

Next, type .5 in the **Distance** text box next to the **Distance** button in the **Standard Mates** rollout. Only positive numbers are accepted when specifying values for mates. Checking the **Flip Dimension** check box under the **Distance** text box is equivalent to specifying a negative distance.

At the bottom of the **Standard Mates** rollout are two buttons under the **Mate alignment:** heading. These buttons act like radio buttons. Picking the **Aligned** button forces the positive normal of each selection to point in the same direction. Picking the **Anti-Aligned** button causes the positive normals to point in opposite directions. The coincident mate also has these alignment buttons.

For this example, uncheck the **Flip Dimension** check box. Also, pick the **Aligned** button. Then, pick the green check mark button in the **Property Manager** to apply the mate. Pick the green check mark button again to close the **Property Manager**. The base plate is now oriented so its red face is flush with the right plane and its green face is parallel to the front plane, but .5″ below it on the negative Z axis.

If you select the distance mate in the design tree, the corresponding face and plane are highlighted in the graphics window. See **Figure 11-6**. There is also a dimension between the face and the plane. To change the distance, pick on the dimension, enter a new value in the text box that is displayed, and press [Enter]. You can also right-click on the branch in the design tree and pick **Edit Feature** in the shortcut toolbar to edit the mate in the **Property Manager**.

Fully Constraining the Part

Pick on the part and drag it in the graphics window. Now, the base plate can only be moved up and down; there is only one degree of freedom left. To fully constrain the part, a coincident mate will be placed between the blue face on the part and the top plane.

Pick the **Mate** button on the **Assembly** tab. With the **Entities to Mate** selection box active in the **Mate Selections** rollout, select the blue face on the part and the top plane. Pick the **Coincident** button and adjust the alignment if needed to position the part below the plane. Then, apply the mate. The base plate is now fully constrained with no degrees of freedom.

Concentric Mate

The next parts in the logical order of assembly are the locating pins. The geometry in the part file complies with standards and has a flat on one side. Pick the **Insert Components** button on the **Assembly** tab of the **Command Manager**. The **Insert Component Property**

Figure 11-6.
Changing the value for the distance mate. This mate controls how far the face is below the front plane.

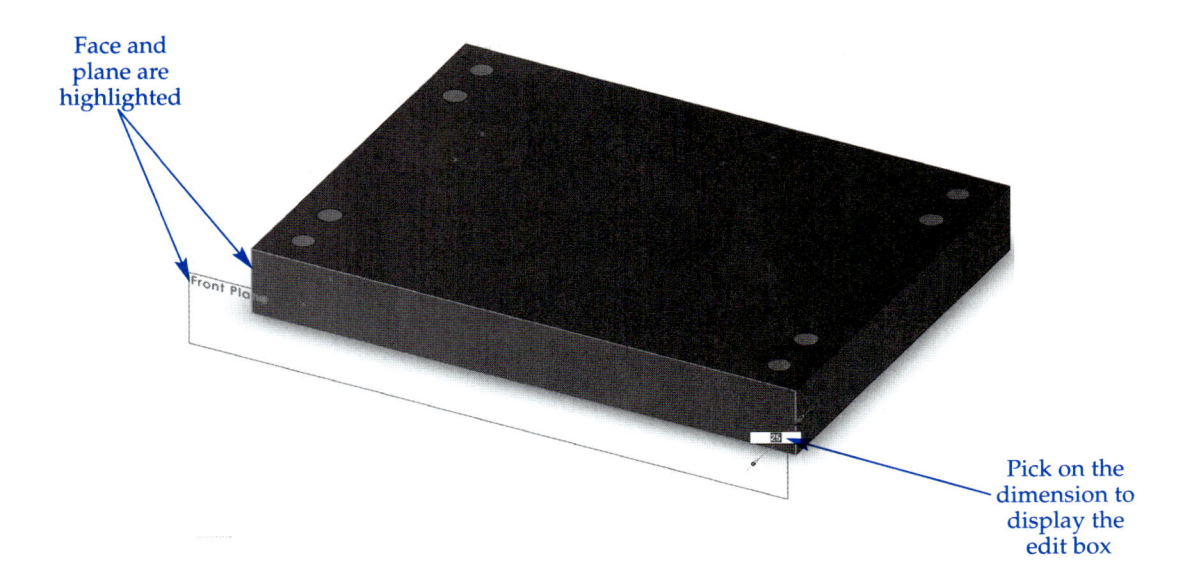

Manager is displayed, which has the same options as the **Begin Assembly Property Manager**. Using the **Browse...** button in the **Part/Assembly to Insert** rollout, locate and open the file 11E01_CR_Locating_Pin.sldprt. Select the pushpin button at the top of the **Insert Component Property Manager**. Then, place four instances of the part into the assembly, one near each corner of the base plate. The exact location is not important because mates will be used to precisely locate the pins. When the four instances are placed, pick the green check mark button to end the "place" tool. See **Figure 11-7.**

The first pin is located by mating the cylindrical surfaces of the pin and the hole with a *concentric mate*. Then, the top of the pin is mated to the top face of the base plate using a distance mate with an offset. Zoom in on the lower-right corner of the base so the hole and pin are visible.

Pick the **Mate** button on the **Assembly** tab. With the **Entities to Mate** selection box active in the **Mate Selections** rollout, select the cylindrical surface of the pin and the inner surface of the hole. The hole for the pin is closest to the edge. The other hole will later receive a bolt.

SolidWorks will likely assume that a concentric mate is to be created. This is the type of mate you need to apply. Be sure the **Concentric** button is selected. If not, pick it. A preview of the pin aligned with the hole is displayed. **Figure 11-8** shows a wireframe display of the pin location. The pin may have a different vertical location in your file. Pick the green check mark button in the **Property Manager** to place the mate. You can leave the **Mate Property Manager** open.

Four degrees of freedom are removed by the application of this mate. The remaining degrees of freedom are movement along and rotation about the axis of the pin. If you pick the pin in the graphics window, you can drag it up and down along the centerline of the hole. You can also rotate the pin within the hole. However, you cannot move the pin perpendicular to the red or green faces on the base plate.

Now, apply a distance mate between the end of the pin and the top, blue face on the base. If the **Mate Property Manager** is still open, make sure the selection box is active in the **Mate Selections** rollout. Then, select the faces. Since the blind hole in the base plate is .5″ deep, enter .5 in the **Distance** text box. If needed, check the **Flip dimension** check box in the **Standard Mates** rollout. The pin should extend .5″ into the hole and partially

Chapter 11   Building Assemblies with Mates

Figure 11-7.
Four instances of the locating pin have been inserted into the assembly file. By applying mates, the pins will be constrained in their matching holes.

Figure 11-8.
The centerline of the pin has been aligned with the centerline of the hole using a concentric mate. While the pin extends into the hole, this depth is not constrained.

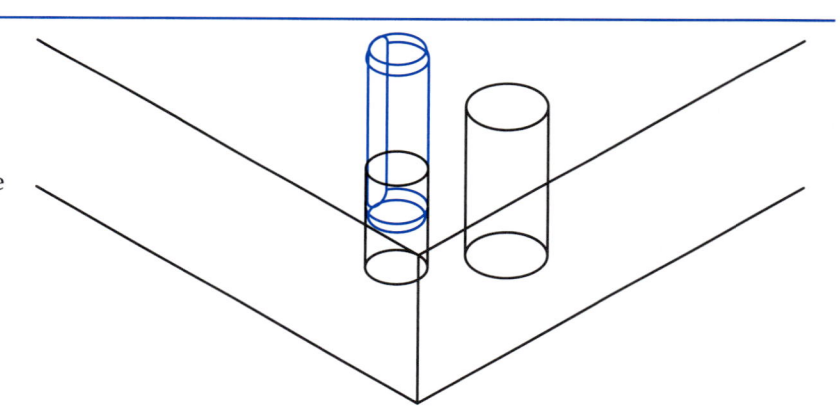

extend out of the hole. See **Figure 11-9.** There is still one rotational degree of freedom left. Removing it is not necessary as the orientation of the flat in the hole is not critical for this example. Close the **Property Manager**.

Applying Smart Mates

The *smart mates* placement option allows a designer to drag a part from its current position to a new one while simultaneously adding a mate. The concentric mates of the remaining three locating pins will be applied using the smart mate feature. Zoom out so the entire assembly is visible. Then, continue as follows.
1. Choose the **Move Component** button in the **Assembly** tab of the **Command Manager**.
2. In the **Move Component Property Manager** that is displayed, pick the **Smart Mates** button in the **Move** rollout. Notice that the **Smart Mates Property Manager** has replaced the **Move Component Property Manager**.

Figure 11-9.
A distance mate is applied between the end of the pin and the top face of the base. An offset was specified so the pin extends into the hole.

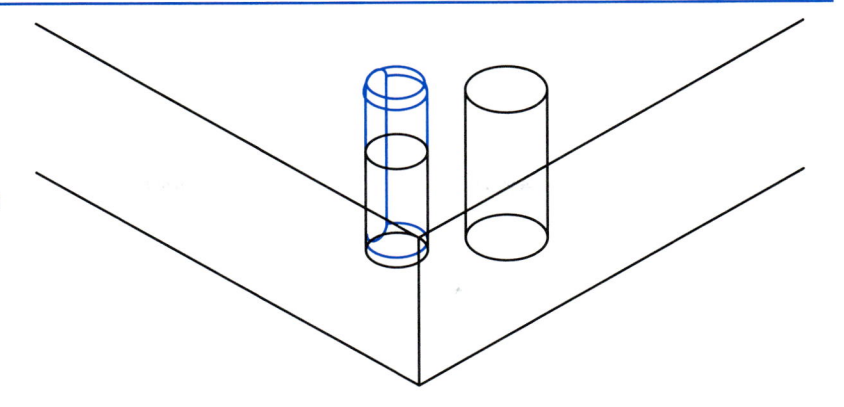

3. Double-click on the cylindrical face on one of the unconstrained pins. Notice that the part becomes translucent.
4. Pick and hold on the translucent pin, then drag it to one of the blind holes in the base plate. When the pin is dragged over one of the blind holes, the smart mates concentric icon appears next to the cursor.
5. Release the left mouse button. The shortcut toolbar appears.
6. In the shortcut toolbar, make any adjustments to the mate type or alignment, then pick the green check mark button to place the mate. For this example, apply a concentric mate.
7. Repeat this for the remaining two pins.

PROFESSIONAL TIP

To save even more time, the smart mates feature can be applied without activating the **Move Component** tool. With nothing selected, hold down the [Alt] key, pick and hold on the cylindrical surface of the locating pin, and drag the pin over a blind hole in the base plate. Then, continue as described above.

Multiple-Mate Mode

SolidWorks allows mating relations to be added to multiple entities at one time to speed up the process of building assemblies. Since the axial position of the first locating pin was constrained with a distance mate, it can be used to locate the remaining three pins. A coincident mate will be applied between the top surface on the first pin and the top surfaces on the remaining pins.

1. Pick the **Mate** button to display the **Mate Property Manager**.
2. In the **Mate Selections** rollout, pick the **Multiple mate mode** button. Notice additional options are available in the rollout, **Figure 11-10**.
3. With the **Common Reference** selection box active in the rollout, select the top face of the first locating pin (the one with the distance mate).
4. With the **Component References** selection box active in the rollout, select the top faces of the three other pins. Zoom and pan as needed to ensure you are selecting the top faces.
5. In the shortcut toolbar, pick the **Coincident** button.

Notice the **Create multi-mate folder** check box in the **Mate Selections** rollout. When this is checked, the three mates you are applying are added to a Multi-Mates branch (subfolder) in the Mates branch of the design tree. This is a nice organizational option for large assemblies, but unnecessary for this simple assembly.

6. Make sure the **Create multi-mate folder** check box is unchecked.

Chapter 11   Building Assemblies with Mates

Figure 11-10.
Using multiple-mate mode to apply coincident mates between the top surfaces on the three remaining pins and the top surface on the first pin.

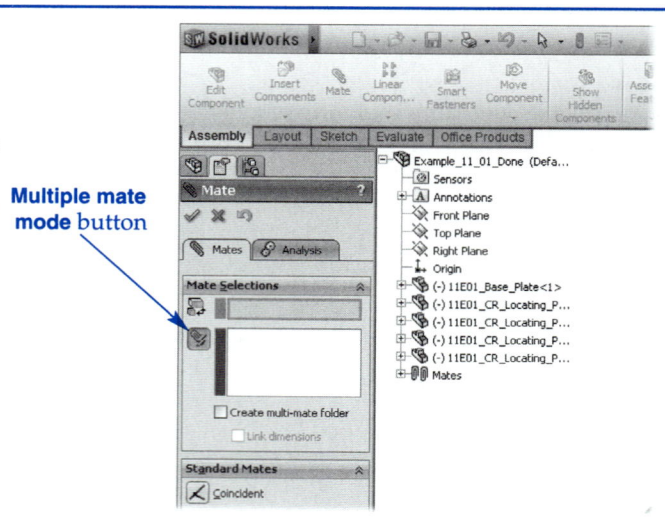

Multiple mate mode button

7. Pick the green check mark button in the **Property Manager** or on the shortcut toolbar to place the mates.
8. Close the **Mate Property Manager**.

Now, if the distance mate on the first pin is edited to change the distance it extends above the base plate, the other pins will follow. This is because the three other pins have their top surfaces constrained coincident to the top surface of the first pin. In effect, the top surface of each pin is constrained to a common elevation.

Placing the Bearing Block

Zoom out so that the entire assembly is visible. This can be done quickly by pressing the [F] key. Now, place one instance of the part 11E01_Bearing_Block.sldprt into the assembly. Remember, its exact location is not important at this point. The bearing block has one red and one green face that will eventually line up with the faces on the base plate of same color. You may need to rotate the view to see the colored faces. The way a technician or assembler would install the bearing block is to place it over the pins and then press it down. This is exactly how you will do it using mates.

Pick the **Mate** button to display the **Mate Property Manager**. Pick the cylindrical face of the locating pin and the cylindrical surface of the blind hole in the bearing block, as shown in **Figure 11-11**. Rotate the view as needed to see the pin and hole. Make sure the **Concentric** button is selected and pick the green check mark button to place the mate. Do not be concerned if the bearing block is out of position at this point. If it is, the next mate will move the block to the correct position. Now, put the same type of mate on the other pin and the hole in the bearing block.

Finally, the bottom of the bearing block needs to be constrained to the top of the base plate. Apply a coincident mate between the top face of the base plate and the bottom face of the bearing block. All degrees of freedom have been removed from the bearing block. See **Figure 11-12**.

Placing the Bushing Using the Pre-Selection Method

The *pre-selection method* entails selecting the entities to be acted on before choosing the tool to be used. This can help speed up the process of building assemblies. This method will be used to apply a coincident mate and a concentric mate to constrain a bushing into the hole in the bearing block.

Place one instance of the part 11E01_Bushing.sldprt into the assembly. Then, continue as follows to constrain the bushing into the hole.

Figure 11-11.
Constraining the bearing block on the pins.

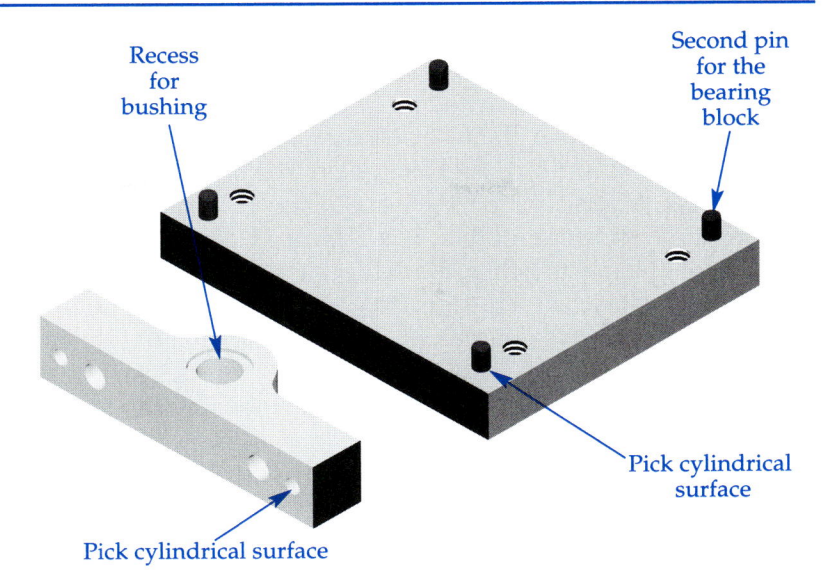

Figure 11-12.
The bearing block is completely constrained. Notice that the colored faces line up.

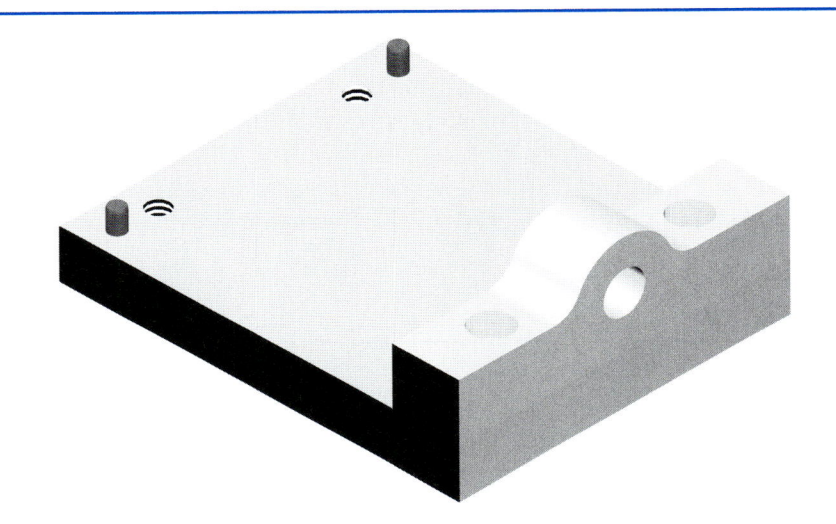

1. Holding the [Ctrl] key, select the back face of the bushing flange (colored yellow) and the counterbored face of the bearing block (also yellow.) The [Ctrl] key can be released once both faces have been selected.
2. Pick the **Mate** button on the **Assembly** tab of the **Command Manager**.
3. Make sure the **Coincident** button is selected.
4. Pick the green check mark button to apply the mate.

Since the **Mate Property Manager** is still open, it is most efficient to apply the next mate. However, to gain practice using the pre-selection method, close the **Mate Property Manager** before continuing.

5. Hold the [Ctrl] key and select the outer cylindrical face of the bushing and the cylindrical face of the hole in the bearing block that will receive the bushing.
6. Pick the **Mate** button.
7. Make sure the **Coincident** button is selected.
8. Pick the green check mark button to apply the mate.
9. Close the **Mate Property Manager**.

Rotate the view. Notice that the bushing is centered in the hole and flush to both sides of the bearing block.

Chapter 11 Building Assemblies with Mates

Determining the Cap Screw Specifications

Before inserting the cap screws that hold down the bearing block, the thread specifications on the threaded holes in the base need to be checked. There are two choices for accessing the base plate—open the part file or edit it in place within the assembly. To edit the part in place, right-click on 11E01_Base_Plate<1> in the **Feature Manager**. You can also right-click on the part in the graphics window. Then, pick the **Edit Part** button in the shortcut toolbar. See **Figure 11-13.**

All of the parts other than the base plate are displayed as wireframes in the graphics window. The 11E01_Base_Plate<1> branch appears in blue in the design tree. Expand this branch to display the part tree for the base plate. See **Figure 11-14.**

Right-click on the 3/8-24 Tapped Hole1 branch in the design tree and pick **Edit Feature** in the shortcut toolbar. The **Hole Specification Property Manager** is displayed. In the **Hole Specifications** rollout, the pitch is indicated as 3/8-24, which is a 3/8 diameter and fine thread with 24 threads per inch. This is correct for this example. Record this information; you will need it to select the correct cap screw. In the **End Condition** rollout, verify that the termination is set to Through All and the thread is set to Through All. Pick the red X button to close the **Hole Specification Property Manager**.

In this case, the feature name correctly indicates the thread. However, do not rely on this. If the feature name has been altered or the feature specifications changed, the name will not match the feature. Always verify the feature settings.

Now, you need to determine the proper length for the cap screw. Left-click on Extrude1 in the design tree to highlight the feature in the graphics window. Notice the dimensions in the graphics window. The dimensions specified in the sketch are shown in black and the dimension related to the extrude operation is shown in blue. The extruded height is 1"; record this information.

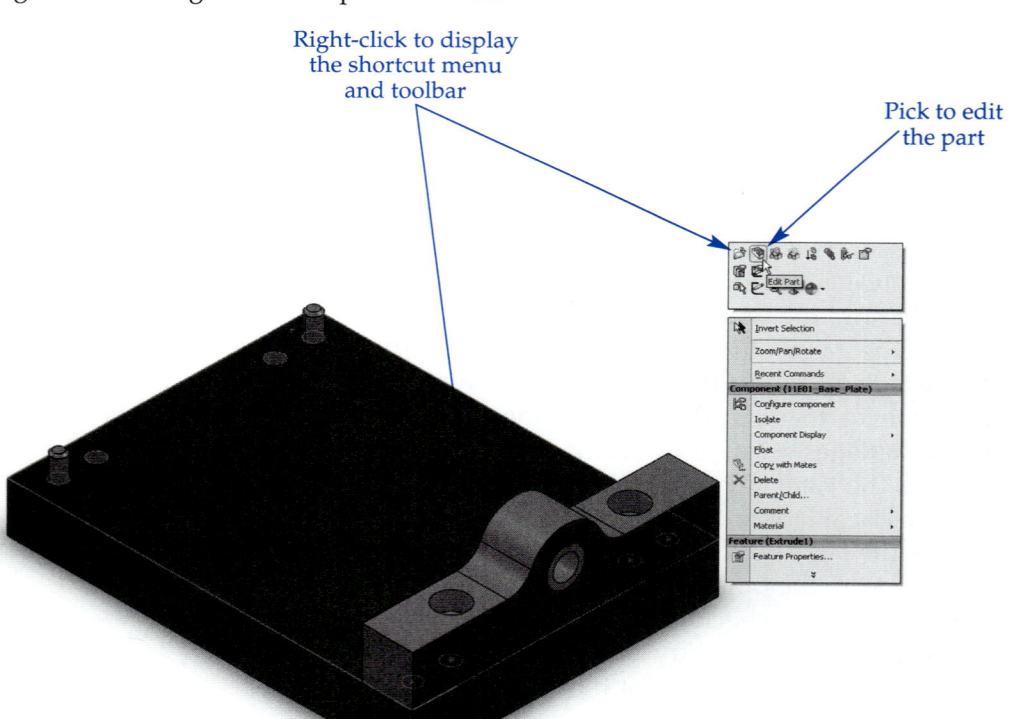

Figure 11-13.
Editing the base using the edit-in-place method.

Figure 11-14.
When editing a part in place, its branch in the design tree and all branches below it are displayed in blue.

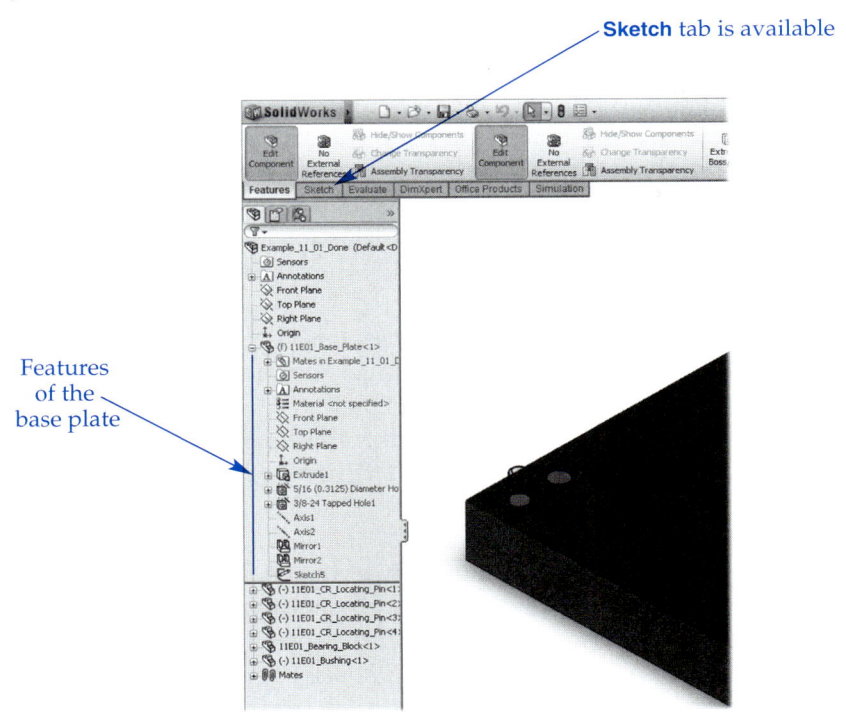

Sketch tab is available

Features of the base plate

Notice the **Edit Component** button on the **Assembly** tab in the **Command Manager** (there are actually two buttons). Currently, the button is depressed. This indicates you are in part editing mode. To return to the assembly, pick the button so it is not depressed. The wireframe display of the features is replaced with the standard shaded view (if the current display is shaded). Also, the 3/8-24 Tapped Hole1 branch in the design tree is no longer displayed in blue.

Using the edit-in-place method, edit the bearing block. Expand the bearing block branch of the design tree, then expand the branch for the counterbored hole. There are two sketches listed under the hole feature. One sketch (Sketch3) contains positioning information and the other (Sketch2) contains the profile revolved to create the hole. Left-click on the Sketch2 branch to show in the graphics window the dimensions of the revolved profile. The counterbore depth is .375" (which may be displayed as .38") and the height of the bearing block is 1". Therefore, the distance from the bottom of the bearing block to the bottom of the cap screws is .625". Record this information.

Looking at the information you recorded, the cap screw must have 3/8-24 thread. Also, the length must be longer than .625" (1 – counterbore depth of .375) but no longer than 1.625" (1 + 1 – .375). Generally, a thread-engagement length equal to at least one diameter is sufficient. In this case, the diameter is 3/8 (.375), so the length should be between .875" (minimum of .5 + one diameter of .375) and 1.625" (maximum length). For this example, you will use 1.25" long cap screws. They provide more thread engagement while not exceeding the maximum length.

> **NOTE**
>
> When editing in place, if you change the part(s) in some way, such as changing the thread size, the referenced files are updated when the assembly is saved.

Chapter 11 Building Assemblies with Mates

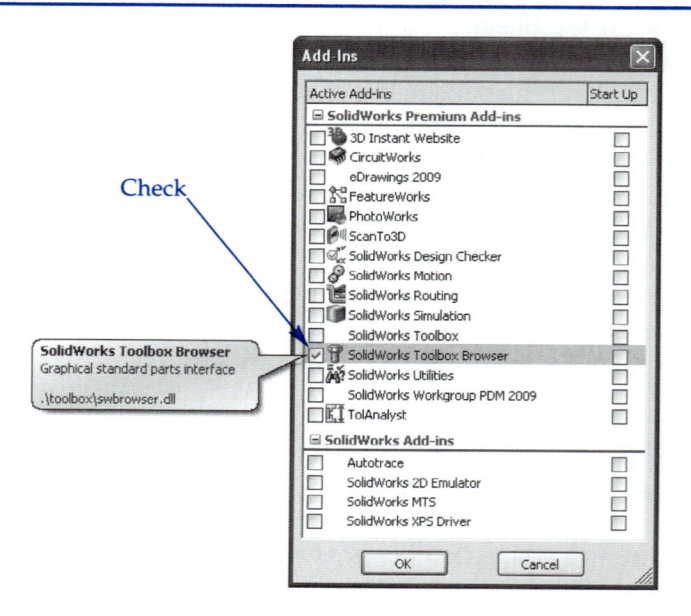

Placing Fasteners from the SolidWorks Toolbox Library

SolidWorks has a library that contains catalogs of a wide variety of standard parts and components. *Standard parts* conform to industry standards for size and other specifications. SolidWorks calls this library the *SolidWorks toolbox library*. Augmented by Internet resources, such as the Thomas Register, these can greatly reduce the time required to build parts for an assembly. The **Smart Fasteners** tool uses the toolbox library to automatically place fasteners into an assembly containing parts with holes designed to accept standard-size fasteners.

The toolbox browser must be enabled to access the library. Select **Tools>Add-Ins...** from the **Menu Bar**. In the **Add-Ins** dialog box that appears, check the **SolidWorks Toolbox Browser** check box, **Figure 11-15**. Then, pick the **OK** button to close the dialog box and enable the browser.

Now, you are ready to place fasteners into the assembly. Pick the **Smart Fasteners** button on the **Assembly** tab of the **Command Manager**. If you receive a warning, pick the **OK** button to dismiss it. Then, continue as follows.

1. With the selection box active in the **Selection** rollout, pick the 3/8 counterbored hole on the bearing block. It can be selected either in the design tree or in the graphics window.
2. Pick the **Add** button in the **Selection** rollout.

SolidWorks determines which fastener may best meet the requirements of the selected hole feature. This may take a few seconds, depending on the speed of your system. The properties of the fastener SolidWorks selects are shown in the **Results**, **Series Components**, and **Properties** rollouts. See **Figure 11-16**. In the **Series Components** rollout, you may add washers or nuts to either the top or bottom stack of the fastener series. For this example, you will not add these. Continue as follows.

3. In the **Properties** rollout, confirm that the calculated fastener has a thread specification of 3/8-24.
4. Adjust the length of the fastener by selecting 1.25 from the **Length:** drop-down list.
5. Select Hex in the **Drive Type:** drop-down list, if not already selected.
6. Pick the green check mark button in the **Property Manager** to create the fastener in the assembly.

Figure 11-15.
Enabling the SolidWorks toolbox browser. This must be enabled to access the SolidWorks toolbox library.

Figure 11-16.
Specifying the fastener to insert from the SolidWorks toolbox library.

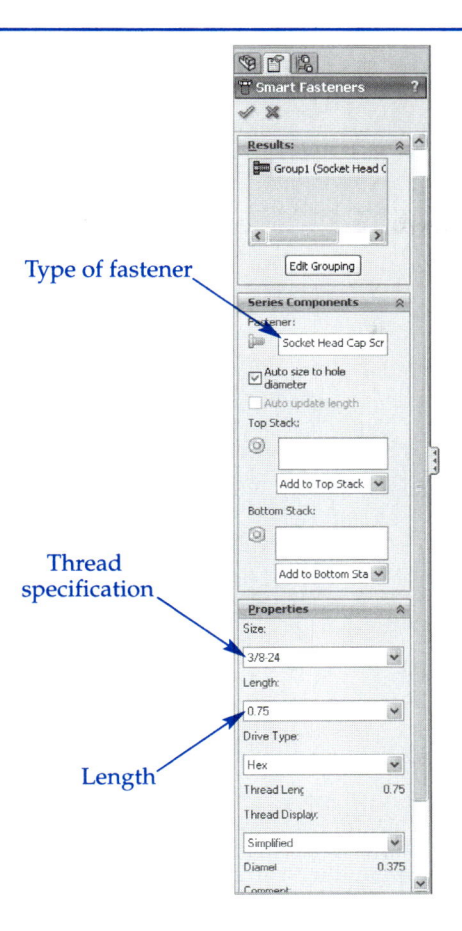

The fastener appears at the bottom of the design tree in the Smart Fastener 1 branch. The new part is automatically constrained using a coincident mate and a concentric mate. These mates appear in the Mates branch of the design tree.

> **PROFESSIONAL TIP**
>
> To change the fastener type, right-click on the **Fastener:** selection box in the **Series Components** rollout and select **Change fastener type...** from the shortcut menu. Then, in the **Smart Fastener** dialog box that is displayed, pick the new fastener type.

Copying an Inserted Part

Now, another cap screw needs to be inserted into the other hole in the bearing block. To do this, you will use the **Copy with Mates** tool. Expand the SmartFastener1 branch in the design tree so you can see the branch for the cap screw. Then, right-click on the cap screw branch and select **Copy with Mates** from the shortcut menu. The **Copy with Mates Property Manager** is displayed, **Figure 11-17**. The mates on the part are displayed in the **Mates** rollout. Using this rollout, you map the mates from the existing part to the location where the copy will be created.

With the **New Entity to Mate** selection box active for the concentric mate, select the matching small-diameter portion of the second hole. Notice that with the selection box active, the corresponding features on the existing part are highlighted. Next, with the **New Entity to Mate** selection box active for the coincident mate, pick the flat surface in the second hole on which the cap screw will bear. Finally, pick the green check

Figure 11-17.
Copying the first instance of the cap screw using the **Copy with Mates** tool.

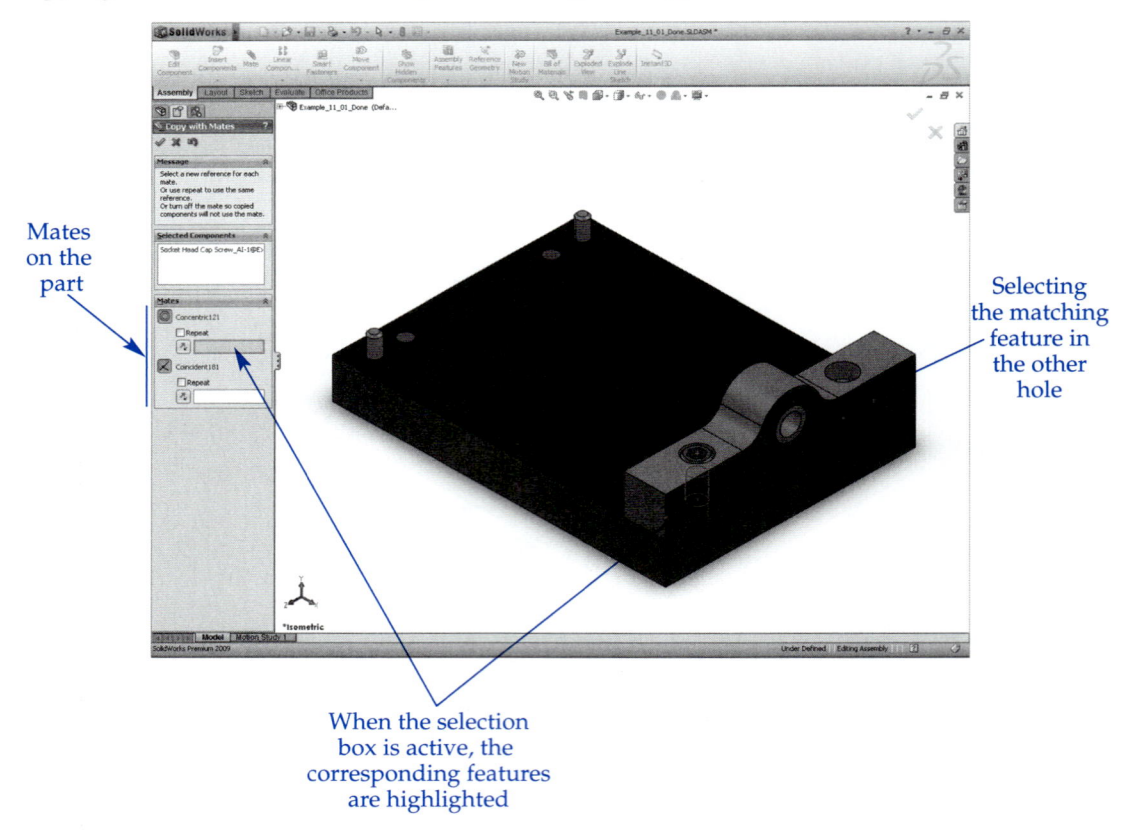

Mates on the part

Selecting the matching feature in the other hole

When the selection box is active, the corresponding features are highlighted

mark button to create and constrain the copy. Then, close the **Property Manager**. The assembly is now complete. Save the file.

PROFESSIONAL TIP

The use of the **Smart Fastener** tool is best reserved for features created with the **Hole Wizard** tool. However, the **Smart Fasteners** tool can often be used to place fasteners in simple holes created using the **Extruded Cut** or the **Revolved Cut** tools.

Constraining Edges of Parts

Start a new assembly file. Pick the **Insert Components** button in the **Assembly** tab of the **Command Manager**. Add one instance of the part 11E02_Base.sldprt. Pick the green check mark button to place the base at the origin. The part is placed in an orientation that is acceptable for this assembly, as shown in **Figure 11-18.**

Now, place one instance of the part 11E02_Molding.sldprt into the assembly. The part is not properly aligned with the base. However, as mates are applied, the part will be correctly oriented.

Pick the **Mate** button in the **Assembly** tab of the **Command Manager**. Select one of the long edges on the flat, bottom face of the molding. You may need to rotate the view or the part to see the proper face on the molding. Then, pick the long, front edge on the

Figure 11-18.
The base is placed into the assembly.

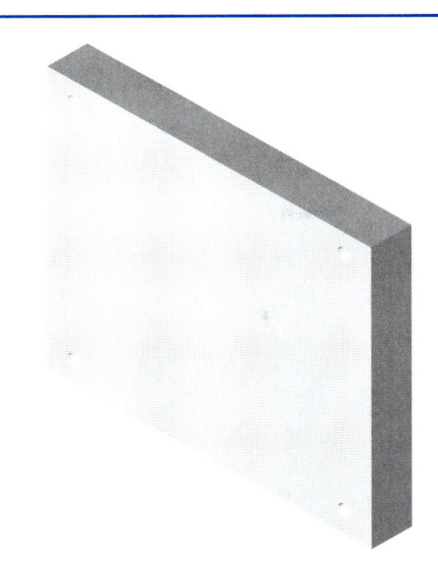

top face of the part. Make sure the **Coincident** button is selected, then pick the green check mark button to apply the mate.

Next, select the straight, outer edge on the green face of the molding. Select the long, vertical edge of the green face on the base. Apply a coincident mate between these edges. The two green faces should be flush and the two red faces should be on top. See **Figure 11-19.** The top edge of the molding's rectangular face is located at the top of the base. Save the assembly file and keep it open for the next section.

Tangent Mate

Now, suppose the upper, curved face (red) of the molding needs to be tangent to the top face of the base (red), instead of the edges being coincident. This can be achieved with the *tangent mate,* which makes two curved faces or one curved and one planar face tangent to each other. Parts can be tangent to the inside or outside of each other. See **Figure 11-20.**

Figure 11-19.
The molding is placed into the assembly and properly constrained. Notice the location of the curved face in relation to the top face of the base.

Chapter 11   Building Assemblies with Mates

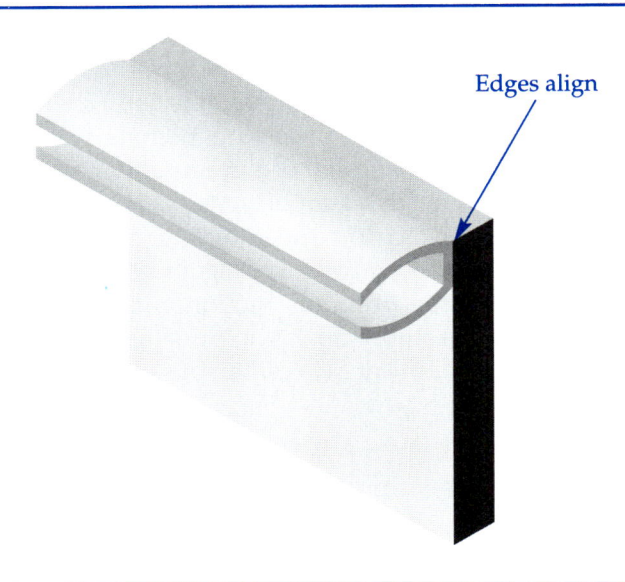

Figure 11-20.
A tangent mate constrains a curved face tangent to either another curved face or a planar face.

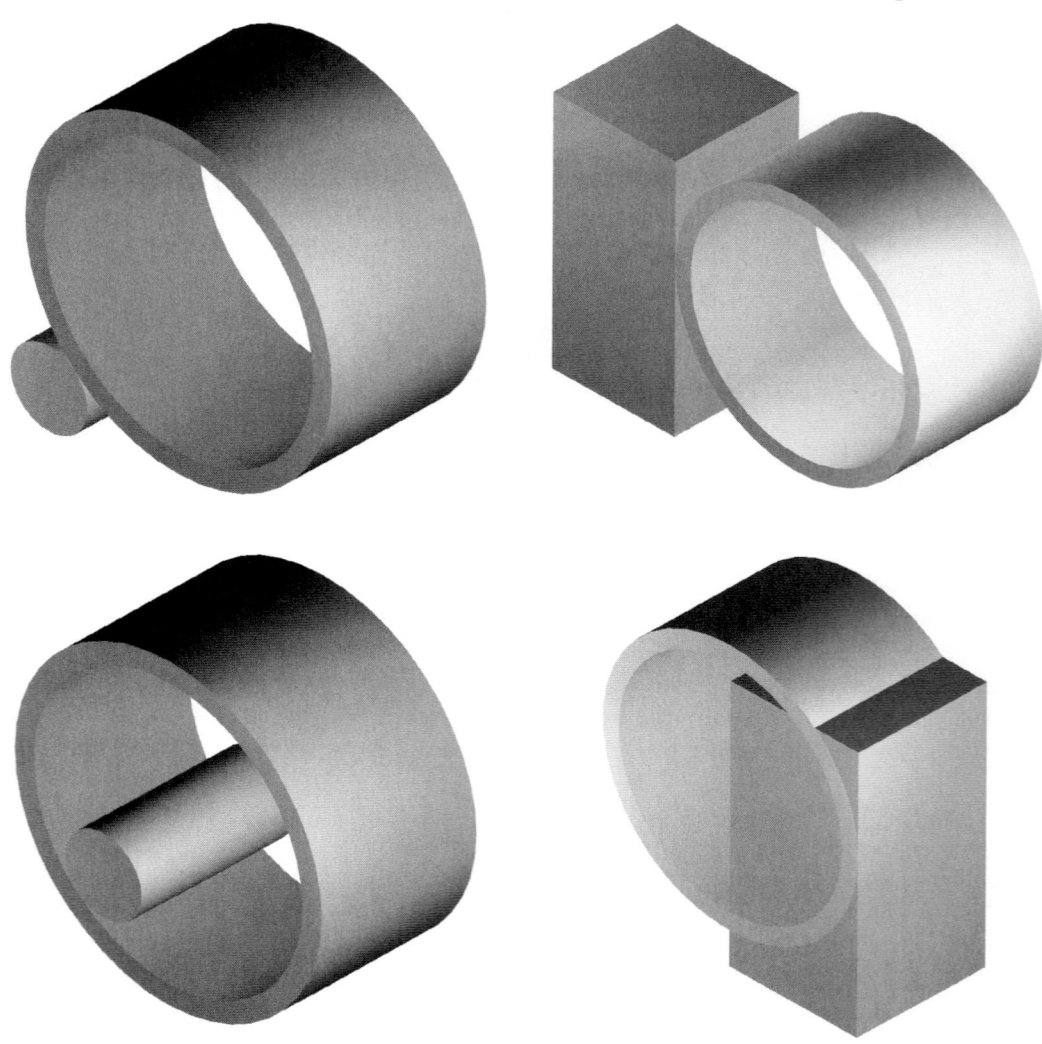

In the **Feature Manager**, right-click on the first mate applied. This is the mate between the two long edges. Select **Delete** from the shortcut menu. In the **Confirm Delete** dialog box that is displayed, pick the **OK** button. If you do not delete this mate, an error will be generated when the tangent mate is applied. Now, you can drag the molding up and down, but it remains constrained to the vertical edge of the base.

Pick the **Mate** button on the **Assembly** tab. Then, select the two red faces. SolidWorks assumes you want to apply a tangent mate, which you do. Make sure the **Tangent** button is selected and then pick the green check mark button to apply the mate. See **Figure 11-21.** Close the **Mate Property Manager**.

Now, the curved face on the molding is tangent to the red face on the base. However, you can still drag the molding about the vertical edge. When the two edges were constrained in the previous section, all degrees of freedom were removed. To fully constrain the assembly now, you must apply one more mate. Apply a coincident mate between the large front face on the base and the rectangular face on the molding. Then, save the file.

Figure 11-21.
The curved surface is constrained tangent to the top face of the base. Compare this to Figure 11-19.

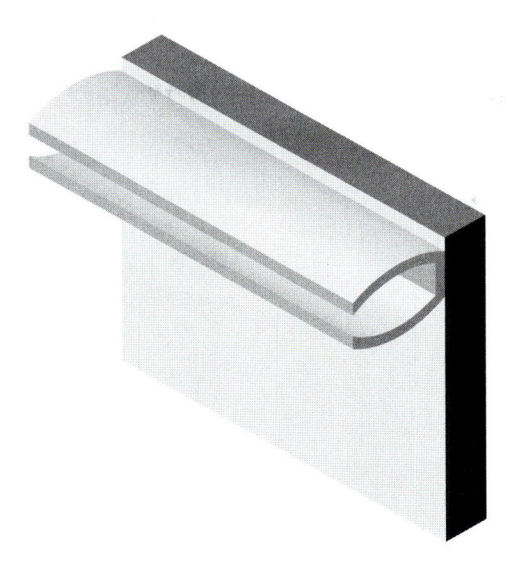

Chapter Test

Answer the following questions on a separate sheet of paper or complete the electronic chapter test on the student website.
www.g-wlearning.com/CAD

1. Define *assembly*.
2. What is an *instance*?
3. What are the parametric relations called that are used to constrain assemblies?
4. What is a *fixed* part?
5. Briefly describe the purpose of the *triad*.
6. When a part is placed in an assembly, how many degrees of freedom does it have?
7. What does the smart mates option do?
8. What is the name of the mode that allows you to apply a mate to more than one part at the same time?
9. Briefly describe *editing in place*.
10. What is a *standard part*?

Chapter Exercises

Complete the chapter exercises on the student website.
www.g-wlearning.com/CAD

Exercise 11-1 Wheel Assembly. *Complete the exercise on the student website.*

Exercise 11-2 Ball Socket Clamp. *Complete the exercise on the student website.*

Chapter 12

Working with Assemblies

Objectives

After completing this chapter, you will be able to:

- Create a part from within the assembly.
- Apply the angle mate.
- Animate mates.
- Constrain reference planes.
- Create adaptive parts containing externally referenced geometry.

Creating Parts in the Assembly View

Using Windows Explorer, look at the folder structure for Example_12_01. The main assembly file is located in the \Example_12_01 folder. This folder also contains a subfolder named \Linkage that contains some of the parts for the main assembly. Contained within the \Linkage folder is a subfolder named \Base_Assembly, which contains the subassembly for the base. SolidWorks searches for parts in the folder containing the assembly file and all subfolders below it. Since the \Linkage and \Linkage\Base_Assembly folders are located below the folder containing the main assembly file, SolidWorks can locate all of the parts.

Open the assembly Example_12_01.sldasm. See **Figure 12-1.** The links in this mechanism have been constrained, but pins need to be inserted through the three joints. So far, you have placed existing part files into an assembly. Now, you will create new parts directly in the assembly view. This is called *top-down modeling*.

Creating the New Part

First, change the units to IPS if needed (**Tools>Options...**). Then, pick the **New Part** button from the drop-down list below the **Insert Components** button in the **Assembly** tab of the **Command Manager**. A green check mark appears next to the cursor. You must select a face or plane on which to position the new part. Pick the right plane. A new part is added to the design tree with the name Part1^Example_12_01. SolidWorks is

227

Figure 12-1.
This is a SolidWorks assembly composed of several parts.

now in edit-component mode. Also, a new sketch has been started on the right plane. Create the new part as follows.
1. Draw a circle at the origin.
2. Dimension the circle to a diameter of .25″.
3. Finish the sketch.
4. Extrude the circle a distance of .5″. Select Midplane in the **End Condition**: drop-down list in the **Direction 1** rollout of the **Extrude Property Manager**.
5. Pick the **Edit Component** button on either the **Features** tab or **Sketch** tab of the **Command Manager** to exit edit component mode.
6. In the design tree, pick on the new part name with two single clicks (not a double click). Rename the part Short_Pin. This name will be used as the file name for the part file.

At this point, the pin is not in the proper location. Also, you may need to rotate the view to see the pin. As you later add mates, the pin will move into the correct location.

To save the new part file, save the assembly file. A dialog box appears indicating that the assembly contains unsaved virtual components. A *virtual component* is simply one created from within the assembly prior to saving it. There are two options for saving the component: within the assembly or external to the assembly. It is recommended to always choose the **Save externally (specify paths)** option. Once you pick this radio button, the dialog box expands, **Figure 12-2**. Select the name of the part (Short_Pin), pick the **Specify Path** button, and browse to the folder where the part file should be saved. For this part, save it in the \Example_12_01 folder. After the path is specified, pick the **OK** button to save the part.

PROFESSIONAL TIP
In this example, since the target folder is the same as the folder containing the assembly file, you could also pick the **Same As Assembly** button to save the new part in that folder.

Constraining the New Part

The new part will have an in-place mate automatically applied to it, constraining it to the plane on which the part was created. To move the new part, this mate will

Figure 12-2.
Saving a part that was created using a top-down approach.

have to be removed. Expand the Short_Pin branch in the design tree, then expand the Mates in Example_12_01 branch below it. Right-click on the mate name in the design tree and select **Delete** from the shortcut menu. Confirm the deletion in the dialog box that appears.

Now, the pin needs to be constrained to the slider. Turn off the visibility of the coupler link to make it easier to see and select the slider. Do this by right-clicking on the component in either the design tree or the graphics area and choosing the **Hide components** button in the shortcut toolbar. You may also want to turn off the display of any visible planes. It may help to drag the pin so it is visible above the base. Then, continue as follows.

1. Place a concentric mate between the pin and the hole in the slider.
2. Place a coincident mate between the front plane of the pin and the right plane of the slider clamp base assembly so the pin is centered. It may be necessary to expand branches of the design tree to locate the desired planes. See **Figure 12-3.**
3. Using the **Insert Component** tool, place another instance of Short_Pin into the assembly. In order to do this, the assembly file and its dependents must have been saved so that the part file for the pin is created.
4. Apply a concentric mate between the second pin and the hole in the input link.
5. Place a coincident mate between the front plane of the pin and the right plane of the slider clamp base assembly so the pin is centered.
6. Turn on the visibility of the coupler link by right-clicking on its name in the design tree and picking the **Show components** button in the shortcut toolbar.

Using this same procedure, create another part called Long_Pin. Make its diameter .25" and its length .75". Apply a concentric mate between the pin and the hole between the base assembly and the input. The end of the pins should be coincident with the outer face. See **Figure 12-4.** Save the assembly file and its dependents.

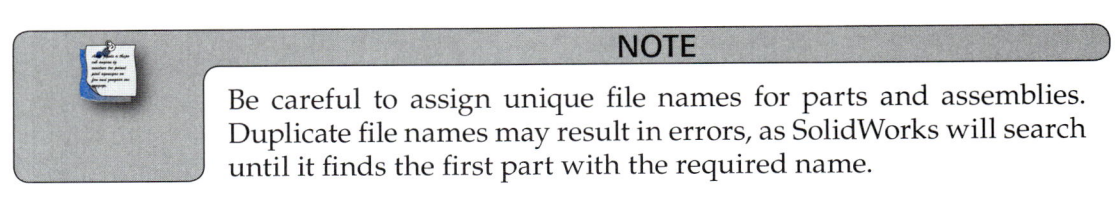

> **NOTE**
>
> Be careful to assign unique file names for parts and assemblies. Duplicate file names may result in errors, as SolidWorks will search until it finds the first part with the required name.

Figure 12-3.
Applying an assembly mate.

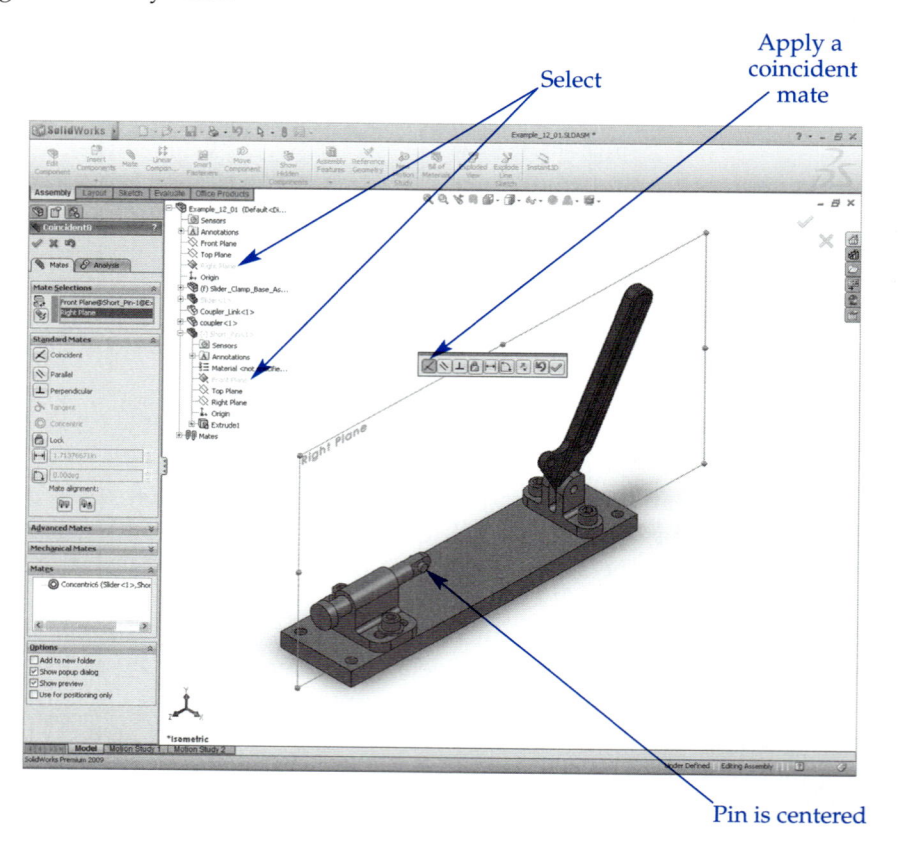

Figure 12-4.
The assembly is complete.

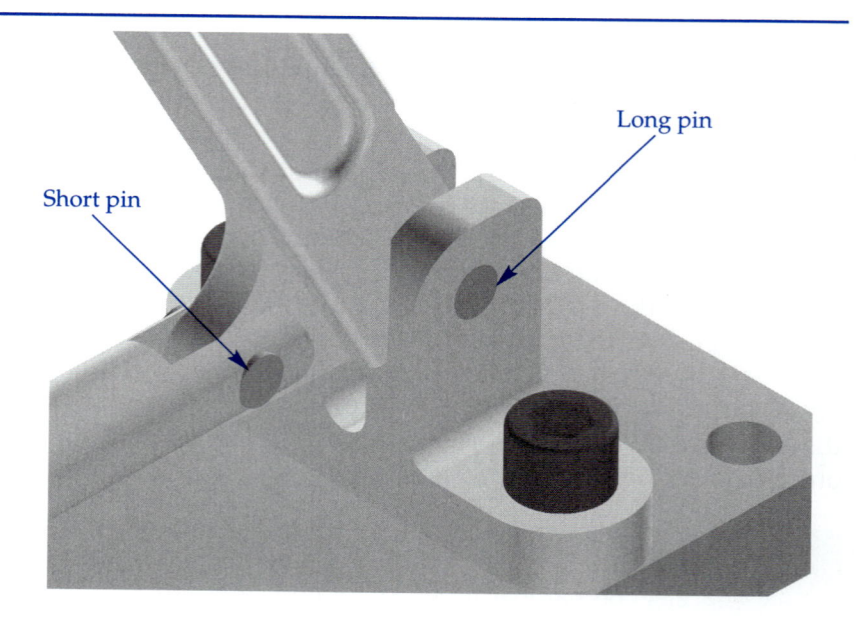

Collision Detection

In the assembly Example_12_01, the input link is free to rotate about its pivot on the base. Try this by picking the input link and dragging. Notice how the coupler link, slider, and the two pins you created are constrained. The input link can also be moved to positions where the parts overlap or interfere with each other, positions that could

230   Learning SolidWorks 2009

never exist in reality. See **Figure 12-5.** SolidWorks has a tool that will prevent parts from moving into these positions. It does this by stopping motion when parts contact each other and, therefore, the process is called *collision detection.*

Pick the **Move Component** button from the **Assembly** tab in the **Command Manager**. In the **Move Component Property Manager**, select the **Collision Detection** radio button in the **Options** rollout. Also, pick the **All Components** radio button and check the **Stop at Collision** check box. Now, drag on the input link in the graphics area. Slowly move it in one direction until SolidWorks detects a collision. The areas of interference are highlighted on the parts. Once you exit the **Move Component** tool, collision detection is turned off.

> **NOTE**
>
> When a collision is detected, SolidWorks may search for an alternate solution to the mate configuration. If the assembly becomes rearranged, it is easily restored to normal by exiting the **Move Component** tool and undoing the operation.

Angle Mate

An *angle mate* works on part edges and faces, reference planes, and reference axes. It sets an angle between any two of these features on two different parts. You will now place an angle mate between the input link and the base.

1. Pick the **Mate** button.
2. Pick the **Angle** button in the **Standard Mates** rollout of the **Property Manager**.
3. With the selection box active in the **Mate Selections** rollout, pick the top face of the rectangular base in the base assembly as the first selection and the narrow, bottom face of the input link as the second selection.
4. Enter 120 in the **Angle** text box in the **Standard Mates** rollout or shortcut toolbar.
5. Apply the mate.

The coupler is now fully constrained and cannot be moved. Save the file and continue to the next section.

Figure 12-5.
Without collision detection enabled, the assembly can be manipulated in a way that results in parts overlapping.

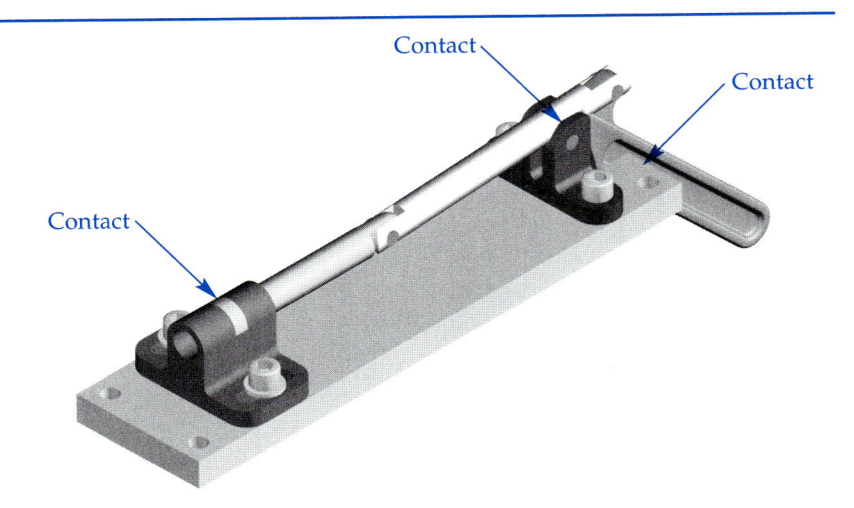

Chapter 12   Working with Assemblies

Introduction to Animation

To *animate* a mate is to "drive" the constrained parts through motion allowed by the mate. By animating the angle mate applied in the previous section, the motion of the mechanism can be simulated. Creating an animation, or *motion study,* is covered in greater detail in a later chapter, but introduced here.

Pick the **New Motion Study** button in the **Assembly** tab of the **Command Manager**. A motion study is started and the animation timeline appears in the **Motion Manager**. See **Figure 12-6**. Notice that the *animation design tree* appears beside the animation timeline. Follow these steps to create a simple animation of the clamp.

1. In the animation design tree, locate the angle mate that constrains the position of the input link relative to the base. It is located in three places in the design tree; any of the three instances can be modified for the animation.
2. With the vertical time bar at the zero position in the timeline, double-click on the name of the angle mate in the animation design tree.
3. In the **Modify** dialog box that appears, enter 130, **Figure 12-7**. This means that at 0:00 seconds (the location of the time bar), the coupler will be at a 130 degree angle from the base.
4. Now, in the timeline area, drag the time bar to the right until it is close to the 3:00 second mark. This mark is halfway between the 2:00 second mark and 4:00 second mark.
5. Double-click on the angle mate in the animation design tree.
6. Enter 60 in the **Modify** dialog box. This means that the coupler will be at a 60 degree angle from the base three seconds into the animation.

Notice that a blue diamond has been placed in the timeline and there are different colored bars spanning the distance between 0:00 seconds and 3:00 seconds. These

Figure 12-6.
Creating a motion study, or animation, of the assembly.

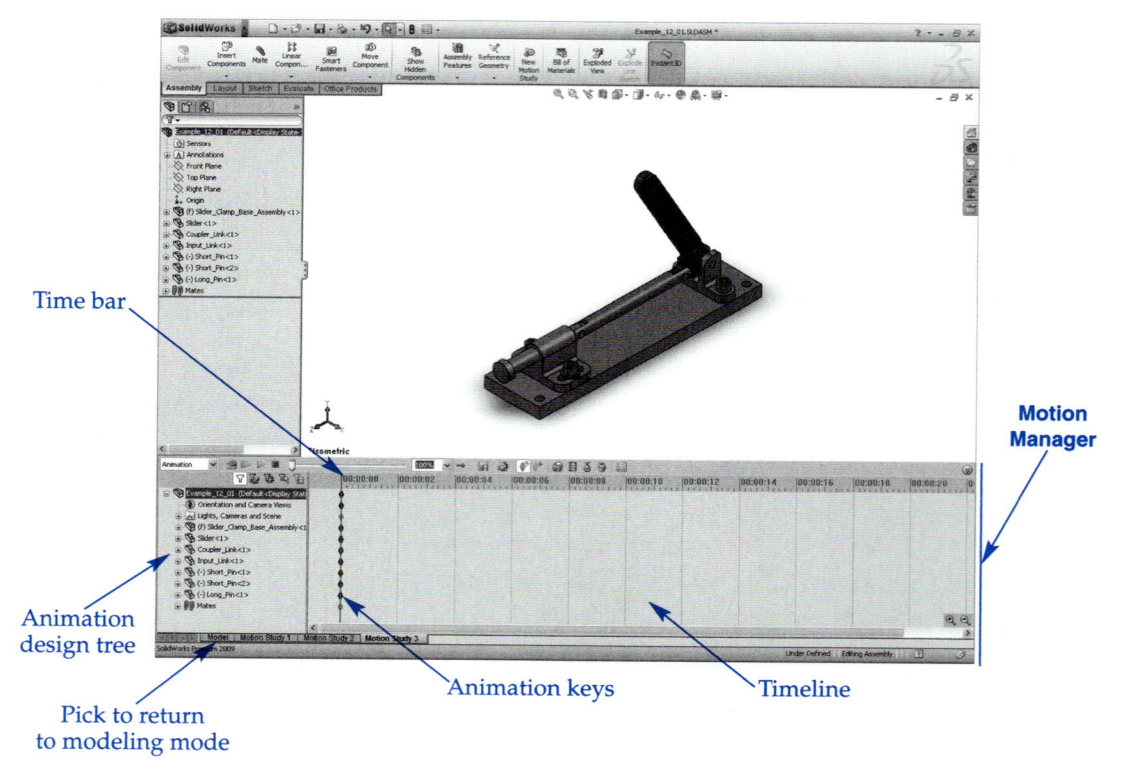

Figure 12-7.
Changing the value in a key.

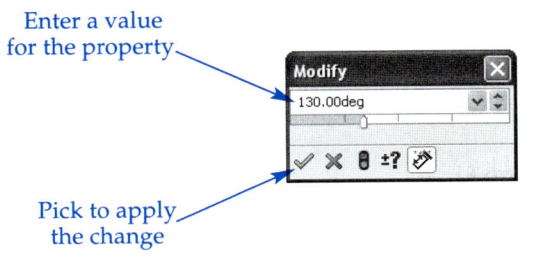

Enter a value for the property

Pick to apply the change

bars represent the movements that SolidWorks will need to solve. The diamond is called an *animation key,* or *key.* A key contains the values for the property at the specified time.

7. Drag the key you just created to the 4:00 second mark. The value contained in the key will now be applied four seconds into the animation, rather than three seconds.
8. Start the animation from the beginning by picking the **Play from Beginning** button from the **Motion Manager** toolbar.

The input link is animated from a closed position to an open position. Notice how all of the parts constrained to the input link also move as allowed by the mates.

9. Return to assembly mode by picking the **Model** tab at the bottom of the screen. To return to the motion study, pick the **Motion Study** tab at the bottom of the screen.
10. Save and close the file.

Any mate that has an offset, such as distance and angle mates, can be animated using this same procedure. With a little creativity, this allows you to create all kinds of sliding animations.

PROFESSIONAL TIP

By picking the **Save Animation** button in the toolbar above the timeline, the motion can be saved to an AVI video file that can be played in Windows Media Player. In this way, you can share the animated part with others who do not have access to SolidWorks.

CAUTION

Save your work before starting a motion study. Also, after starting a motion study it may be best to return the time slider to the 0 second mark before saving the file. If a file containing a motion study is saved with the time slider at a time mark other than the 0 second mark, problems may be introduced into the file.

Constraining Reference Planes and Axes

Mates can be applied to reference planes and axes, as well as part faces. This can simplify the assembly process. In the example in this section, you will be working with a simple model of a one-cylinder engine. All of the parts have reference planes through their centers, which will be used to align the parts.

Open the file Example_12_02.sldasm. This assembly currently includes the engine block and crankshaft (crank). The problem is how to align the center of the crank with the center of the bore without calculating offset values. Notice how the parts were modeled. The block was extruded using the midplane end condition. Its base sketch

Chapter 12 Working with Assemblies

was centered at the origin in the part file. This resulted in a part that is symmetrical about the front and right planes. The crank was modeled so the journal (the area to which the rod connects) is symmetrical about the right plane in the part file.

First, you will constrain two planes to each other to center the crank journal inside of the block. Then, you will constrain the rotational centerline of the crankshaft with the reference axis in the engine block part file. By doing this, the crankshaft is free to rotate and the resulting assembly is much more flexible. For example, if the block dimensions are changed, the crankshaft will remain centered within the bore.

1. Pick the **Mate** button in the **Assembly** tab of the **Command Manager**.
2. In the **Standard Mates** rollout, pick the **Coincident** button.
3. Select the top plane in the crank part file and the front plane in the block part file. Use the flyout **Feature Manager** design tree to select the planes. Also, pick the appropriate alignment button so the end of the crank with the flat is to the left.
4. Pick the green check mark button in the **Property Manager** to apply the mate.
5. Apply a concentric mate between the centerline axis in the crank part file and the rotational axis of the block. Use the flyout **Feature Manager** design tree to select the planes.
6. Close the **Mate Property Manager**.

The crankshaft is now centered under the bore. Also, the rotational centerline of the crankshaft is inline with the centerline of the bearings. See **Figure 12-8**. The crankshaft is free to rotate. Pick and drag to make it rotate.

Now, the connecting rod needs to be placed into the assembly and constrained to the crankshaft. This will be easier to do if you turn off the visibility of the block. Then, place one instance of Con_Rod.sldprt into the assembly. Constrain the large end of the connecting rod to the crankshaft using a concentric mate. The centerline of the large hole should be constrained to the centerline of the journal, not the centerline of the bearing surfaces. See **Figure 12-9**. To center the connecting rod in the journal, apply a coincident mate between the top plane in the connecting rod part file and the top plane in the crank part file.

Using a similar process, place an instance of Piston_Pin.sldprt, constrain the front plane in the pin part file to the top plane in the connecting rod part file, and constrain the centerline of the piston pin to the centerline of the small hole in the connecting rod. Place an instance of Piston.sldprt, constrain the front plane in the piston part file to the front plane in the connecting rod part file, and constrain the centerline of the hole in the piston to the centerline of the pin. See **Figure 12-9**. Your assembly may look slightly different, depending on where you picked planes and centerlines. Continue as follows.

Figure 12-8.
The crankshaft is properly located and constrained.

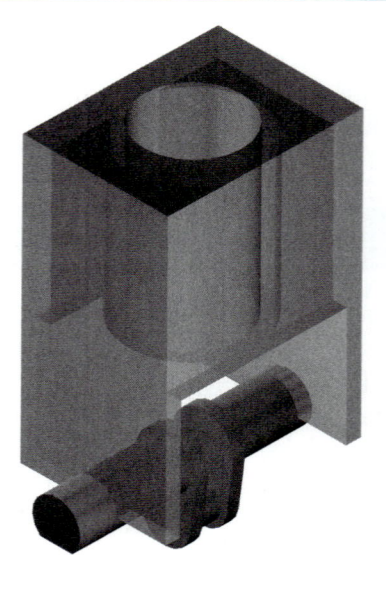

Figure 12-9.
The piston, piston pin, and connecting rod are added to the assembly.

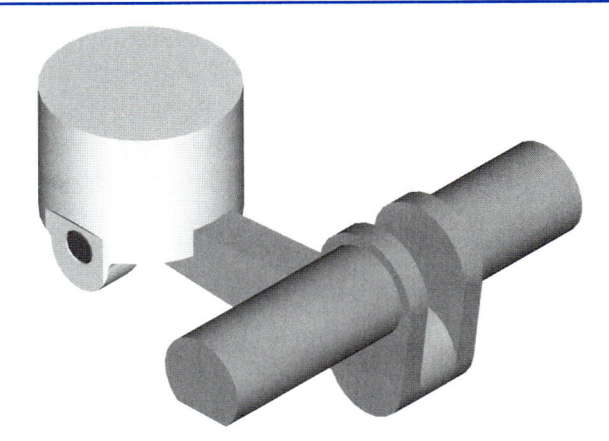

1. Turn on the visibility of the block.
2. Constrain the centerline of the piston to the centerline of the bore using a concentric mate. If the piston is inside of the block in your assembly, you may need to first move the piston in order to acquire the centerline.
3. Place an instance of Flywheel.sldprt into the assembly.
4. Constrain the flat on the flywheel to the flat on the crank. You may need to rotate the view.
5. Constrain the centerlines of the crank and flywheel using a concentric mate.
6. Constrain the end of the flywheel flush to the end of the crank using a coincident mate. The green circle on the flywheel should face away from the engine block.
7. Drag and rotate the flywheel. The piston goes up and down.

Now, automate the motion. Pick the **New Motion Study** button on the **Assembly** tab of the **Command Manager**. On the toolbar above the timeline, pick the **Motor** button. In the **Motor Property Manager** that is displayed, pick the **Rotary Motor** in the **Motor Type** rollout. See **Figure 12-10**. Next, with the selection box active in the **Component/Direction** rollout, pick the outer diameter of the flywheel to specify a center of rotation. In the **Motion** rollout, enter 300 in the text box. Also, make sure Constant speed is selected in the drop-down list. Then, pick the green check mark button in the **Motor Property Manager** to apply the motor. Finally, pick the **Play from Start** button in the animation toolbar to "run the engine." Save the assembly and close all files.

Figure 12-10.
Applying a rotational motor to the assembly.

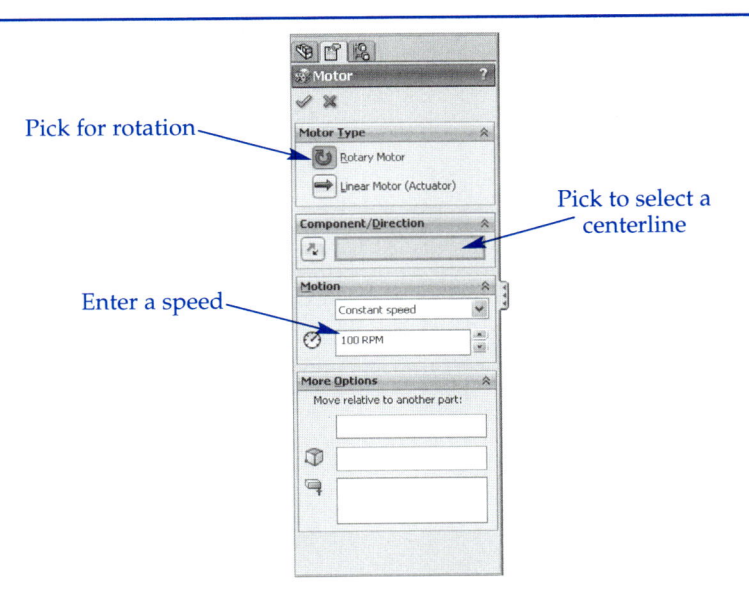

Pick for rotation

Pick to select a centerline

Enter a speed

Chapter 12   Working with Assemblies   **235**

PROFESSIONAL TIP

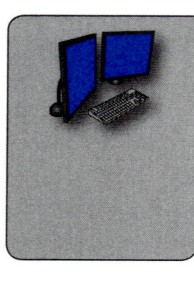

The engine example demonstrates how important it is to create parts according to the design intent. In this example, the parts are designed to fit together in the engine assembly. By carefully analyzing the design intent, the parts were constructed in relation to the origin and front, right, and top planes to allow for easy assembly. If this was not done, it would have been much more difficult to assemble the parts.

Adaptive Parts

A part containing *externally referenced geometry* has unconstrained features, the sizes and locations of which are controlled by another part. For example, you can locate features on a part based on the geometry of a second part. Then, if the second part's features are changed, those on the first part change as well. Parts constructed in this manner are called *adaptive parts.* For instance, the pins created in the Example_12_01 assembly could have been created as adaptive parts. In this way, if the hole size changes, the diameter of the pin changes to match.

Adaptive Location

Open the file Example_12_03.sldasm. This assembly is shown in **Figure 12-11** with the cap moved to expose the six threaded holes in the base. Matching clearance holes need to be placed in the cap. The holes in the base can be projected onto a sketch plane on the cap. Then, holes can be created in the cap, which will be adaptive. The procedure is:

1. Right-click on the cap name in the design tree and pick the **Edit Part** button in the shortcut toolbar.
2. Start a new sketch with the top face of the cap as the sketch plane.

Figure 12-11.
Adaptive clearance holes will be added to the cap. Note: The cap is shown out of place so the threaded holes in the base are visible.

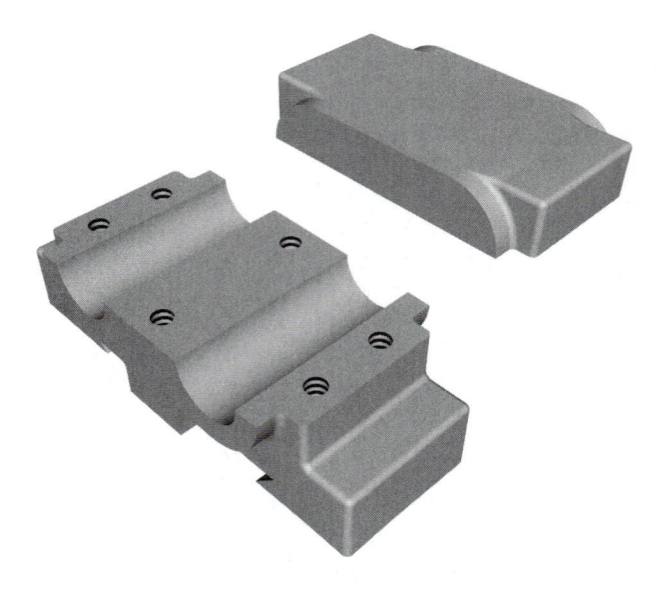

3. Select the circular tops of the six holes in the base. Using the **Convert Entities** tool, project the circles onto the current sketch plane.
4. Finish the sketch.
5. Pick the **Hole Wizard** button in the **Features** tab of the **Command Manager**. Using the **Holes Property Manager**, place clearance holes for 1/2" diameter cap screws at each of the center points. Use the Through All setting. See **Figure 12-12**.
6. Return to the assembly by picking the **Edit Component** button on the **Command Manager**.

Look at the name of the cap in the design tree. An arrow (–>) appears after the name, **Figure 12-13**. This arrow indicates that some feature of the part is adaptive. If you expand the branch for the cap, the arrow appears after the sketch for the holes as well.

Notice the location of the holes in the cap. Now, expand the branch for the base in the design tree. Right-click on Sketch for Hole Locations and pick the **Edit Sketch** button in the shortcut toolbar. Next, edit the sketch in the Hole Feature branch and change the 3" dimension to 1.5". Finish the sketch and then finish the component edit. The corresponding hole in the cap has moved to remain inline with the threaded hole in the base. See **Figure 12-14**. Save the assembly and close all files.

> **PROFESSIONAL TIP**
>
> Experienced users suggest that you leave only a few parts adaptive. When you get the assembly the way you want it, remove adaptivity by right-clicking on the adaptive part and selecting **List External Refs...** from the shortcut menu. A dialog box is displayed that shows all external references in the part. Pick the **Break All** button below the list to remove all external references. When you close the dialog box, the part will no longer be adaptive.

Figure 12-12.
Adding clearance holes to the top part.

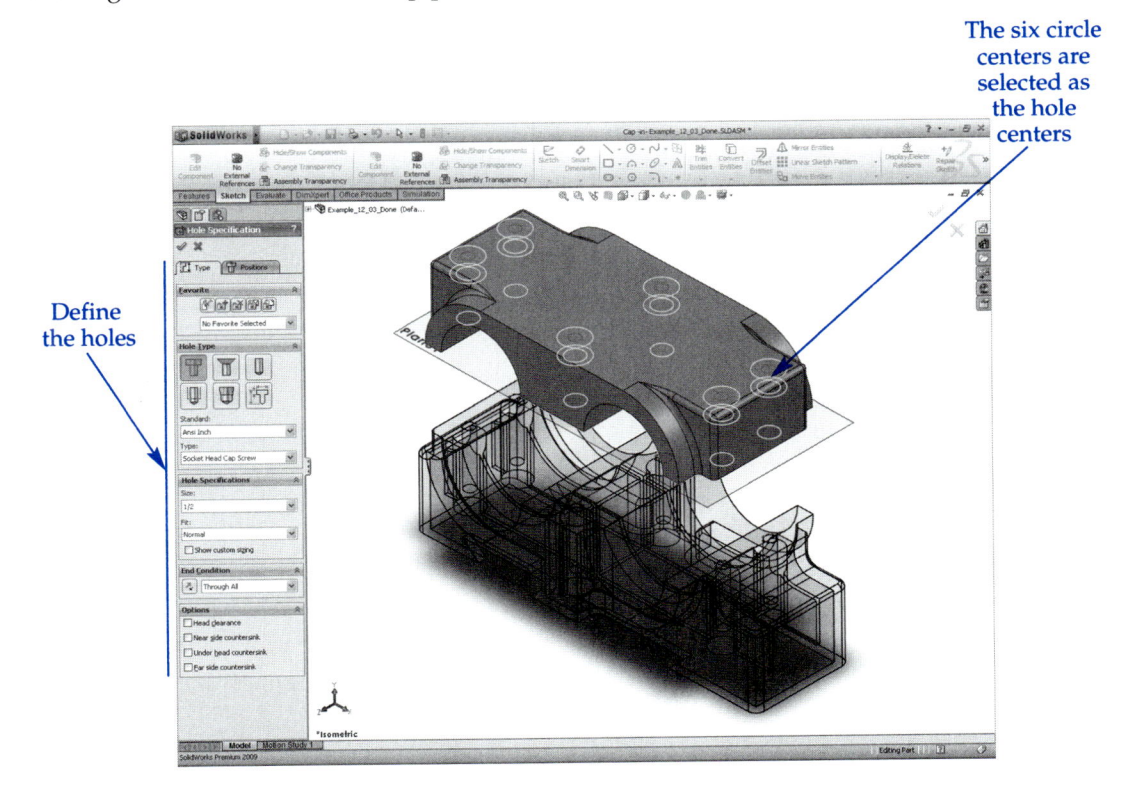

Chapter 12 Working with Assemblies

Figure 12-13.
The part has the adaptive symbol next to its name in the design tree. The sketch for the adaptive feature in the part has the adaptive symbol next to its name in the design tree.

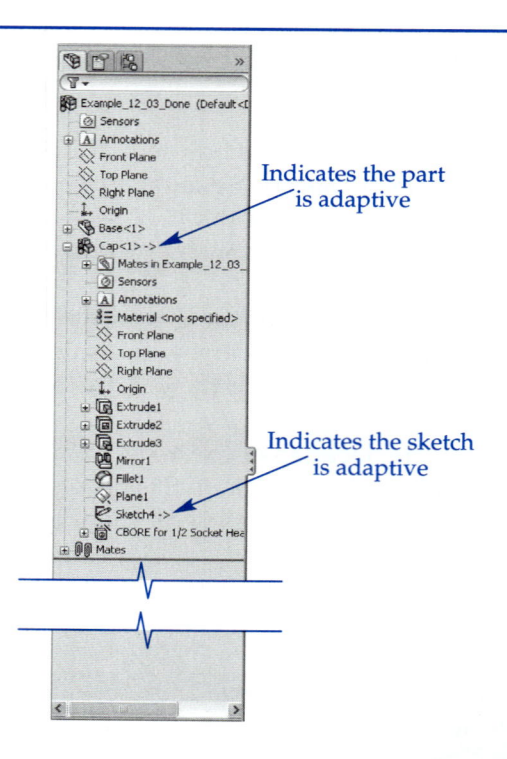

Figure 12-14.
When a threaded hole in the base is moved, the corresponding clearance hole in the cap moves as well.

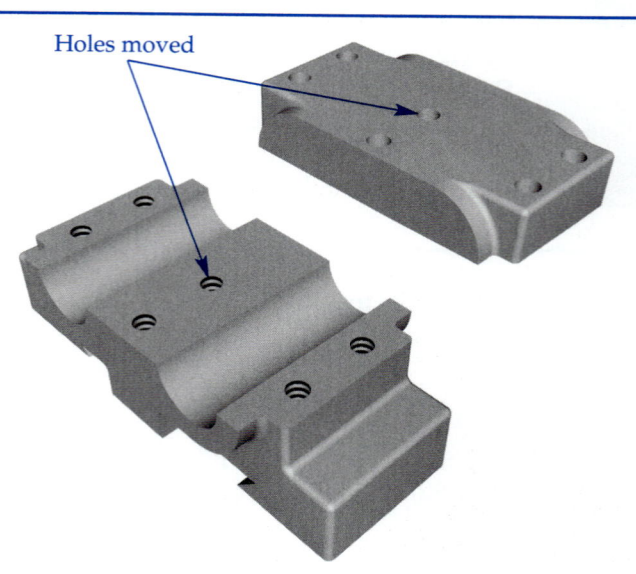

PRACTICE 12-1

Complete the practice problem on the student website.
www.g-wlearning.com/CAD

Adaptive Size

The second application of adaptivity ties the size of features in a part to the size of features in another part in the assembly. For example, the two plates shown in **Figure 12-15** are constrained with a 4″ distance mate. Each post is constrained with concentric and coincident mates to each plate. The length of each post is adaptive. If the 4″ distance is changed to a different value, the posts will automatically change length.

Figure 12-15.
The four posts are adaptive so their length will change as the distance between the two plates is changed.

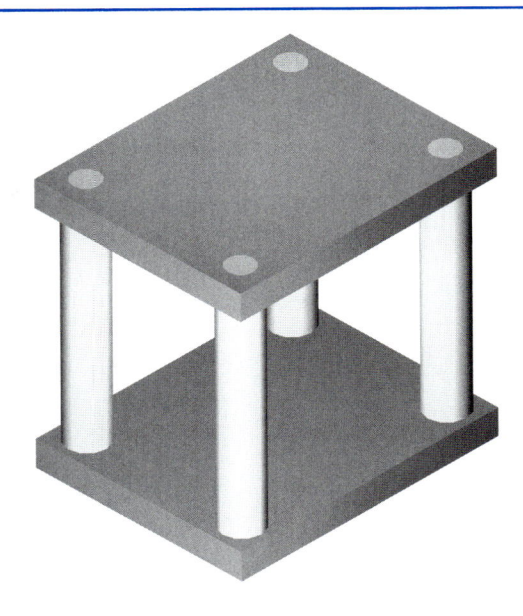

Open the file **Example_12_04.sldasm**. This assembly contains the two plates shown in **Figure 12-15.** You will add the four posts and make their lengths adaptive.
1. Start a new part file. You do not need to close the assembly file. If needed, set the units to IPS.
2. On the top plane, sketch a circle centered on the origin and dimension it to a diameter of .75″.
3. Finish the sketch and extrude the circle 1″ selecting Blind as the end condition.
4. Start a new sketch on one end of the cylinder you just made.
5. Draw a circle at the center of the existing feature. Dimension the circle to a diameter of .5″. Finish the sketch.
6. Extrude this boss .25″, which is the thickness of each plate in the assembly.
7. Create an identical boss on the opposite end of the cylinder.
8. Save the file as Post.sldprt and close the file.
9. In the assembly file, place one instance of Post.sldprt at the lower-right corner.
10. Place a concentric mate between the .5″ diameter boss and the hole in the lower plate.
11. Place a coincident mate between the shoulder on the post and the upper surface of the lower plate. See **Figure 12-16.**
12. Place a concentric mate between the boss on the other end of the post and the corresponding hole on the upper plate.
13. Place three more instances of the post into the assembly. Constrain each in the same way. You can also simplify this process by using the **Copy with Mates** tool.

Now, the second shoulder on each post needs to be constrained to the surface of the second plate. However, the distance between the two plates is 4″, as controlled by a distance mate. If you apply the coincident mate between the second shoulder and second plate, SolidWorks will generate an error. You must first make the posts adaptive so the length of each post will change to match the distance between the plates.
1. Right-click on any instance of the post and pick the **Edit Part** button in the shortcut toolbar.
2. Right-click on the first extrusion feature (not either boss) and pick the **Edit Feature** button in the shortcut toolbar.
3. In the **Direction 1** rollout of the **Extrude Property Manager**, change the end condition from Blind to Up To Surface.

The **Face/Plane** selection box appears in the rollout and is active. This is used to

Chapter 12 Working with Assemblies

Figure 12-16.
The post part file is added to the assembly and inserted into a hole.

select which surface is used as the termination of the extrusion. Since the shoulder on the post should be flush with the underside of the top plate, this surface is used to terminate the extrusion.
   4. Select the face on the underside of the top plate as the termination surface.
   5. Pick the green check mark button to accept the changes made to the feature.
   6. Pick the **Edit Component** button in the **Command Manager** to return to assembly mode.
   7. Display the isometric view.

The assembly should now look like **Figure 12-15.** To see the adaptability of the shafts, edit the distance mate for the plates. Change the distance value to 5" and the posts adapt to the new value. You may need to pick the **Rebuild** button on the **Menu Bar** to update the assembly. The change in the distance mate can also be animated. Save the assembly and close all files.

> **PROFESSIONAL TIP**
>
> Adaptive sizing needs to be used carefully. If the assembly is large and contains multiple adaptive parts, SolidWorks is forced to perform numerous calculations. This will consume system resources and may lead to problems in the assembly.

Chapter Test

Answer the following questions on a separate sheet of paper or complete the electronic chapter test on the student website.
www.g-wlearning.com/CAD

1. What is *top-down modeling*?
2. Which tool allows you to create new parts from within an assembly?
3. What does *collision detection* do?
4. What does the *angle mate* do?
5. When a mate is animated, what occurs?
6. What is a *motion study*?
7. Define *animation key*.
8. What is an *adaptive part*?
9. What are the two types of adaptive parts?
10. How is an adaptive feature indicated in the design tree?

Chapter Exercises

Complete the chapter exercises on the student website.
www.g-wlearning.com/CAD

Exercise 12-1 Linkage. *Complete the exercise on the student website.*

Exercise 12-2 Base and Cap. *Complete the exercise on the student website.*

Mechanical mates, covered in Chapter 13, are very useful when working with assemblies that require motion transfer, such as those involving gears. (Image courtesy of DS SolidWorks Corp.)

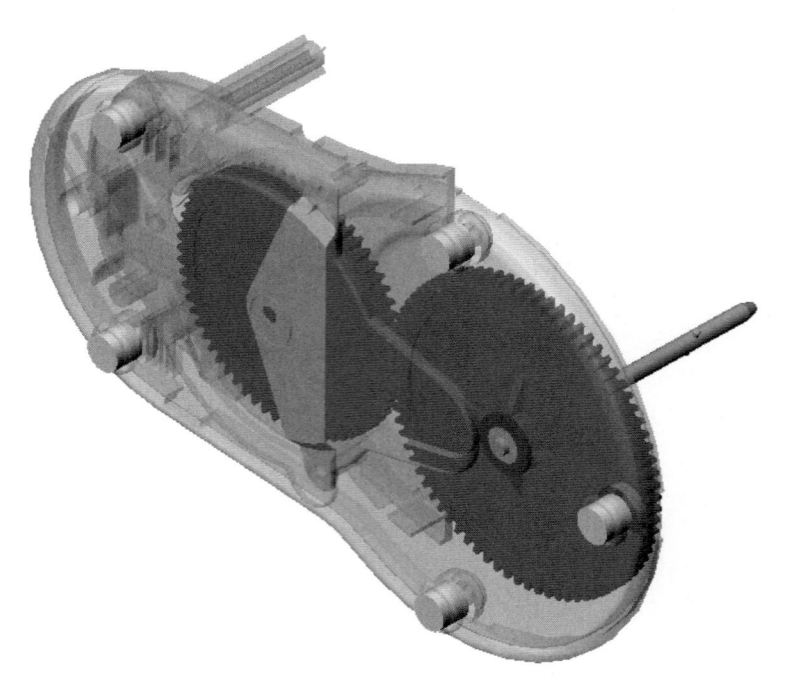

Chapter 13

Mechanical Assembly Mates

Objectives

After completing this chapter, you will be able to:
- Explain the purpose of mechanical mates.
- Use a gear mate.
- Use a rack and pinion mate.
- Use a cam mate.

Mechanical Mates

Besides the assembly mates for positioning components introduced in the last two chapters, there are mates that can relate the relative motion of one component to another. These mates are called *mechanical mates*. When applying a mate, the mechanical mates are found in the **Mechanical Mates** rollout in the **Mate Property Manager**. See **Figure 13-1**. This chapter focuses on the three most useful mechanical mates:
- **Gear mate.** Used for rotating part–to–rotating part, such as a pair of gears. There are two possible solutions when this mate is applied. This mate can be used to simulate a belt drive or gear mesh by changing the direction of the mate.
- **Rack and pinion mate.** Used for rotating part–to–translating part, such as a gear and rack. There are two possible solutions when this mate is applied.
- **Cam mate.** Used for surface contact, such as a cam and follower. There is only one possible solution when this mate is applied.

Gear Mate

A *gear mate* transfers the rotation of one part to another part. Open the assembly file Example_13_01.sldasm. This assembly has two friction wheels that turn together without slipping. This concept is the basis for gear design. The diameters of the wheels represent the pitch diameters of the gears.

Figure 13-1.
SolidWorks has several mechanical mates that are used to constrain motion.

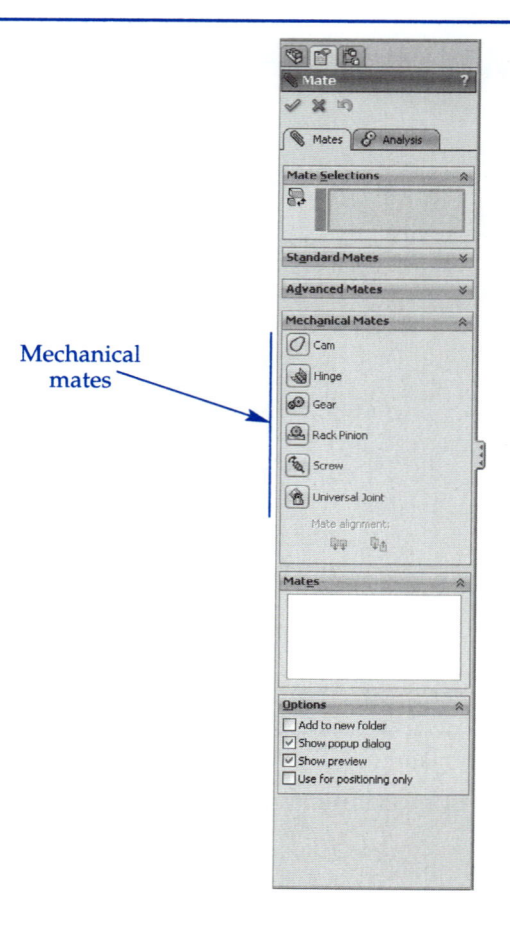

Mechanical mates

Opposite Direction of Rotation

The small wheel has a 2" diameter and the diameter of the large wheel is 4". Since it is twice the size of the small wheel, the big wheel should rotate once for every two rotations of the small wheel. To apply a mate that will do this:
1. Pick the **Mate** button in the **Assembly** tab of the **Command Manager**.
2. Expand the **Mechanical Mates** rollout in the **Mate Property Manager**.
3. Pick the **Gear** button.
4. With the selection box active in the **Mate Selections** rollout, pick the cylindrical surfaces of each wheel. Order is not important.

Since these wheels turn in opposite directions there is no need to check the **Reverse** check box in the **Mechanical Mates** rollout. However, it is always good to check and make sure the mate has been correctly applied. Also, notice in the **Mechanical Mates** rollout that the ratio was automatically calculated. See **Figure 13-2.** This is because the cylindrical surfaces were selected. The flat faces cannot be selected.

Pick the green check mark button to place the mate. The mate appears in the Mates branch of the design tree with the name GearMate*x*. Create a motion study and drive the small gear with a motor. Save and close Example_13_01.sldasm.

Same Direction of Rotation

Open Example_13_02.sldasm. Apply a gear mate between the curved faces of the two pulleys. However, check the **Reverse** check box in the **Mechanical Mates** rollout. Pick the green check mark button to place the mate. In the design tree, expand the tree for Small Wheel. Manually drive the wheels by dragging one of them or create a motion study.

Figure 13-2.
Applying a gear mate to constrain the motion of two engaged wheels.

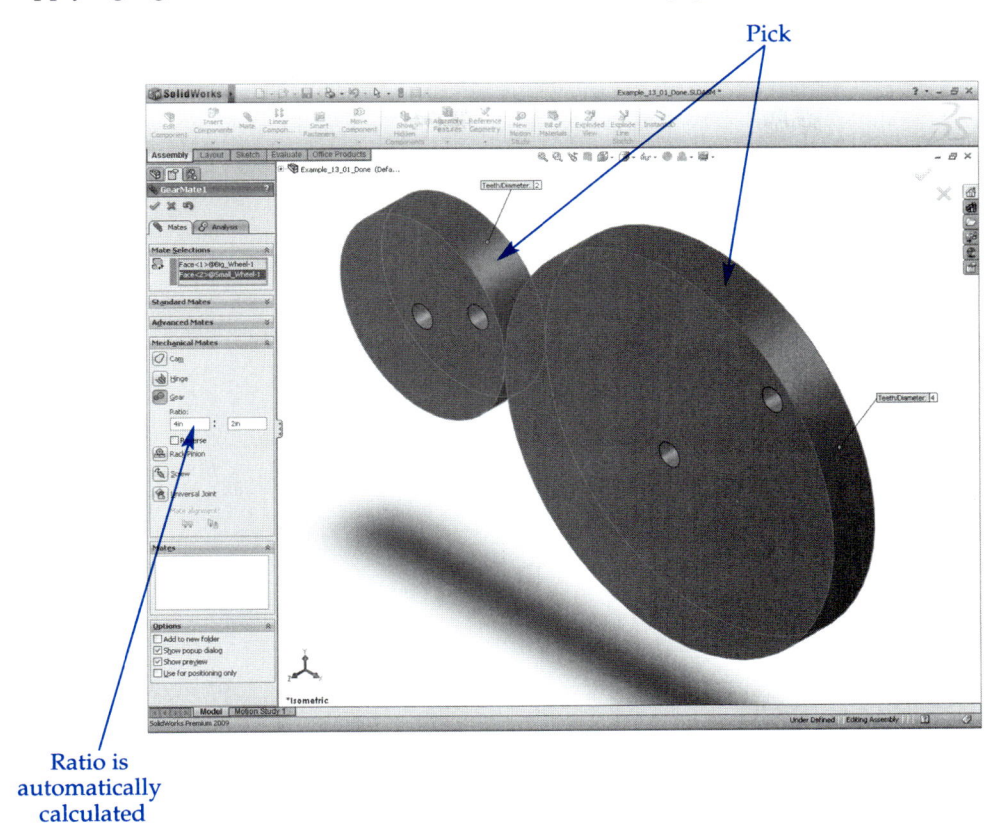

Pick

Ratio is automatically calculated

The small pulley should rotate four times, while the large pulley rotates one time. Save Example_13_02.sldasm and close the file.

Rack and Pinion Mate

Open **Example_13_03.sldasm**. The pinion gear is inserted on the shaft. The rack is constrained to the slide on the frame with two mates. See **Figure 13-3**. A *rack and pinion mate* changes rotational motion into linear motion or linear motion into rotational motion. One will be used to constrain the pinion gear to the rack.

Pick the **Mate** button in the **Assembly** tab of the **Command Manager**. Expand the **Mechanical Mates** rollout in the **Mate Property Manager** and pick the **Rack Pinion** button. In the **Mate Selections** rollout, pick the **Rack** selection box so it is active. Then, pick an edge or axis that is parallel to the direction of motion, such as a long edge of the rack. With the **Pinion** selection box active in the **Mate Selections** rollout, select the circumference of the pinion. Pick the green check mark button to apply the mate.

The value for the relationship between the rotation and translation motions is automatically entered by SolidWorks. The distance is how far the second part (the rack) moves for one rotation of the first part (the pinion). This is equal to the pitch diameter times pi (2 × 3.1416), or 6.28. The value is bidirectional. This means if the rack is driven 6.28 units, the gear will rotate once or if the gear is driven through one rotation, the rack moves 6.28 units.

Now, the rack can be moved back and forth and the gear will rotate. To do this, put a distance mate between the right-hand end of the rack and the inside face of the

Chapter 13 Mechanical Assembly Mates

Figure 13-3.
A rack and pinion mate is used to constrain the rotation of the gear to the rack.

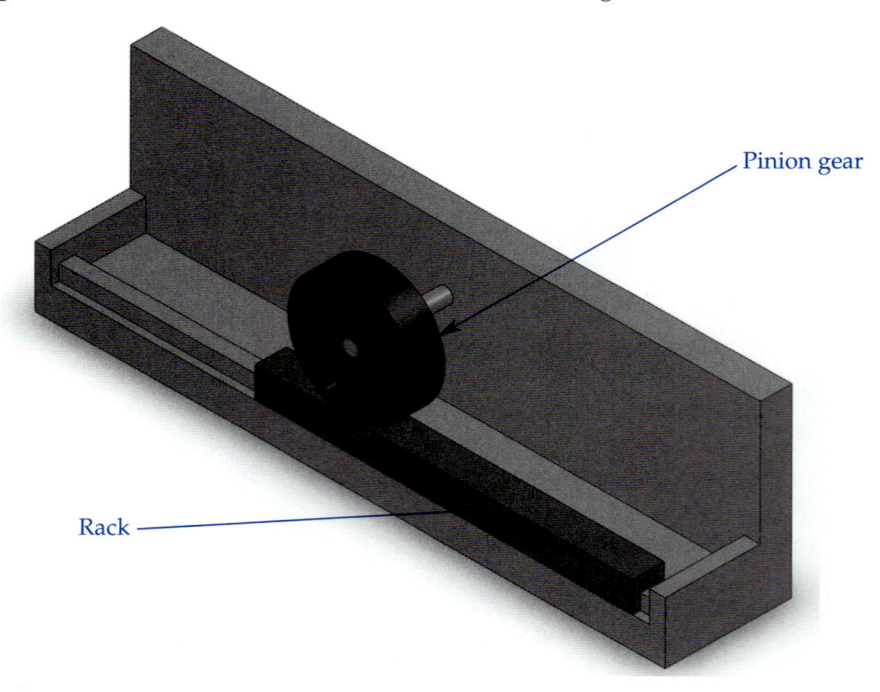

right-hand end of the frame. Rename this mate Drive Me. Then, drive this mate in a new motion study.

> **NOTE**
>
> If the gear is rotating in the wrong direction, edit the rack and pinion mate by right-clicking on its name in the design tree and selecting the **Edit Feature** button in the shortcut toolbar. Then, check the **Reverse** check box in the **Mate Property Manager**.

Rack and Pinion Mate—Second Solution

Open Example_13_04.sldasm. The threaded shaft has right-hand threads and is supported in the frame. See **Figure 13-4**. When the shaft is rotated, the threaded nut moves. If the gear is rotated in a counterclockwise direction (as viewed from the right-hand end of the assembly), the nut moves toward the gear.

Apply a rack and pinion mate to the assembly, picking the gear as the pinion selection and the block as the rack selection. Refer to **Figure 13-4**. The shaft has 12 threads per inch, so pick the **Rack travel/revolution** radio button in the **Mechanical Mates** rollout and enter 1/12 in the corresponding text box. One rotation of the shaft results in 1/12″ of translation (linear movement).

Use a motion study to drive the gear with a motor in a clockwise direction. The block slowly moves toward the gear. Edit the rack and pinion mate and check the **Reverse** check box. This is the correct rotation for left-hand threads. Now, if the gear is driven in the same direction, the block moves away from the gear. Save and close Example_13_04.

Figure 13-4.
A rack and pinion mate is used to constrain the motion of the nut (block) to the rotation of the gear. This simulates the movement of the nut along the threaded rod.

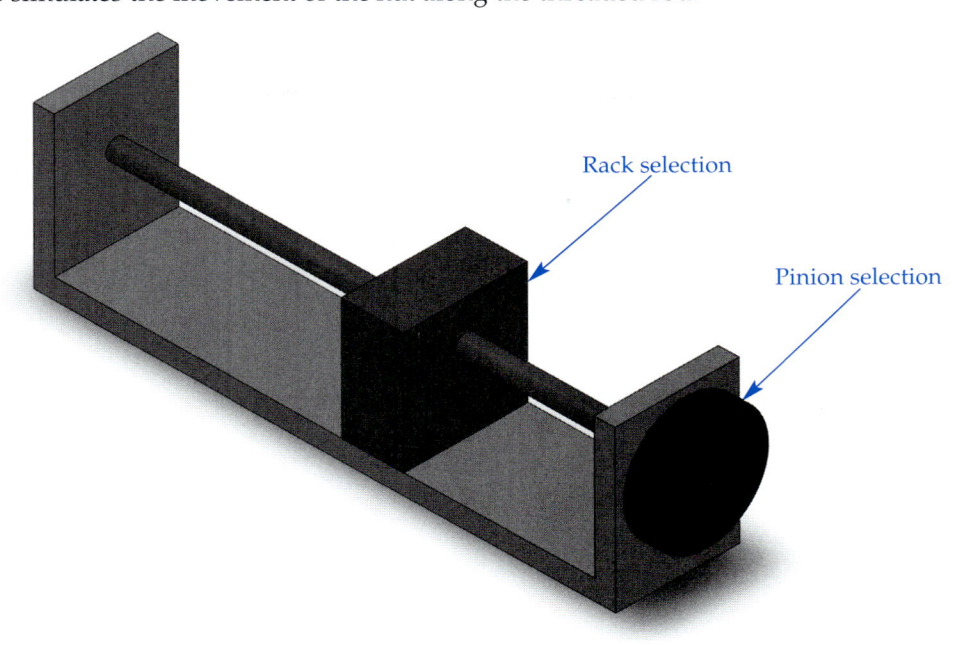

Rack selection

Pinion selection

Cam Mate

The *cam mate* relates the motion of contacting faces on two parts, such as the cam and follower shown in **Figure 13-5.** Open Example_13_05.sldasm. The cam rotates on the shaft, pushing on the follower that slides up and down in the frame. Since there is no return spring, this is a low-speed device. It relies on the weight of the follower to

Figure 13-5.
A cam and follower assembly. A cam mate will be used to constrain the motion of the follower to the rotation of the cam.

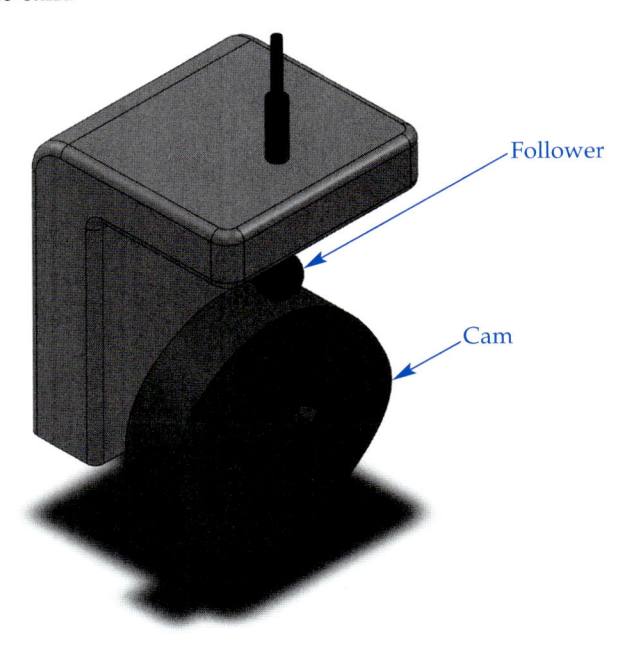

Follower

Cam

Chapter 13   Mechanical Assembly Mates

Figure 13-6.
Pick the cam surface as the entity to mate and the bottom of the follower as the follower.

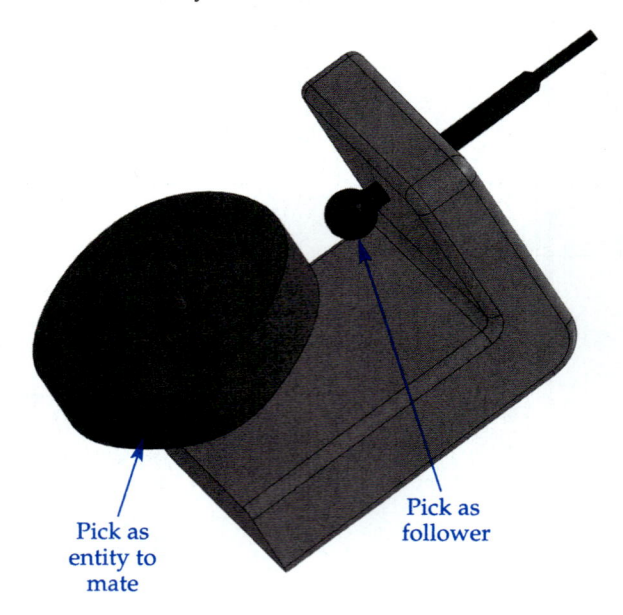

Pick as entity to mate

Pick as follower

maintain contact between the two surfaces. Rotate the view so the bottom cam surface and the bottom face of the follower are visible. You may also need to drag the follower up. See **Figure 13-6.**

Pick the **Mate** button in the **Assembly** tab of the **Command Manager**. Expand the **Mechanical Mates** rollout and pick the **Cam** button. With the **Entities to Mate** selection box active in the **Mate Selections** rollout, pick the contact face of the cam. With the **Cam follower:** selection box active, pick the bottom of the follower. Pick the narrow, cylindrical face. Once this is done, the follower moves down to contact the cam. Pick the green check mark button to apply the mate.

Drag the cam to rotate it. The follower moves up and down, remaining in contact with the face on the cam as it spins. Save Example_13_05.sldasm and close the file.

Chapter Test

Answer the following questions on a separate sheet of paper or complete the electronic chapter test on the student website.
www.g-wlearning.com/CAD

1. List three of the mechanical mates available in SolidWorks.
2. What does a mechanical mate do?
3. The _____ mate is used to transfer the rotation of one part to another part, such as one wheel driving a second wheel.
4. The _____ mate is used to translate the rotation of one part into linear movement of another part, such as a gear driving a rack.
5. The _____ mate is used to maintain contact between two surfaces, such as between a cam and a follower.

Chapter Exercises

Complete the chapter exercises on the student website.
www.g-wlearning.com/CAD

Exercise 13-1 Three Gears. Complete the exercise on the student website.

Exercise 13-2 Four Gears. Complete the exercise on the student website.

Exercise 13-3 Planetary Gear Set. Complete the exercise on the student website.

Chapter 13 Mechanical Assembly Mates

Configurations, covered in Chapter 14, make it possible to manage multiple design variations of parts within a single document. (Model courtesy of DS SolidWorks Corp.)

6 mm Design

10 mm Design

15 mm Design

Figure 13-4.
A rack and pinion mate is used to constrain the motion of the nut (block) to the rotation of the gear. This simulates the movement of the nut along the threaded rod.

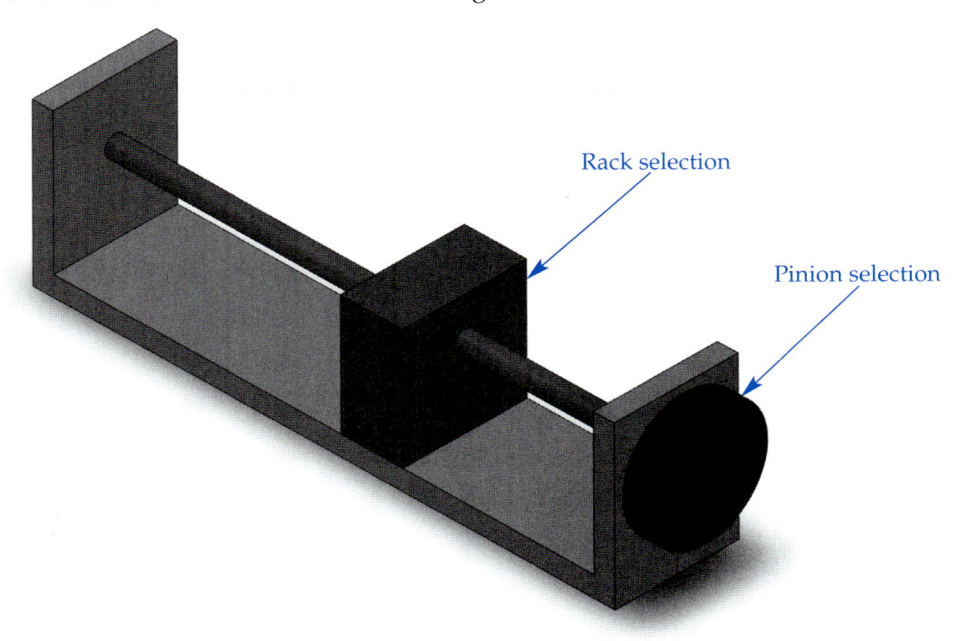

Cam Mate

The *cam mate* relates the motion of contacting faces on two parts, such as the cam and follower shown in **Figure 13-5.** Open Example_13_05.sldasm. The cam rotates on the shaft, pushing on the follower that slides up and down in the frame. Since there is no return spring, this is a low-speed device. It relies on the weight of the follower to

Figure 13-5.
A cam and follower assembly. A cam mate will be used to constrain the motion of the follower to the rotation of the cam.

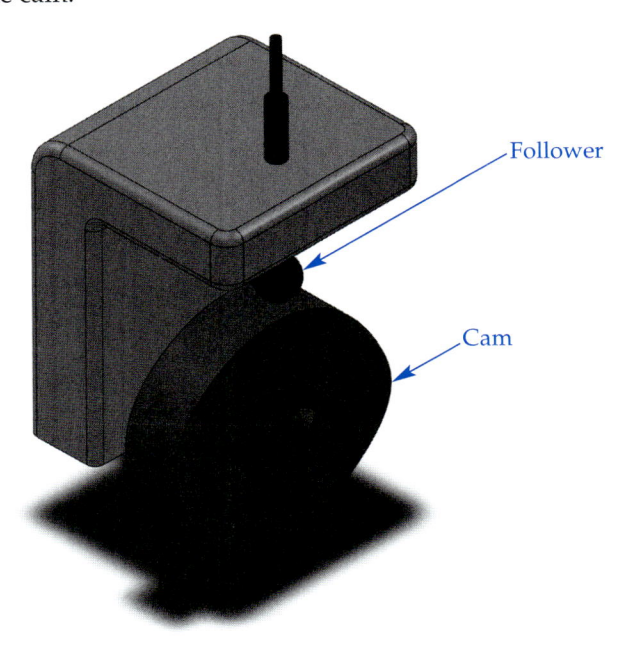

Chapter 13 Mechanical Assembly Mates

Figure 13-6.
Pick the cam surface as the entity to mate and the bottom of the follower as the follower.

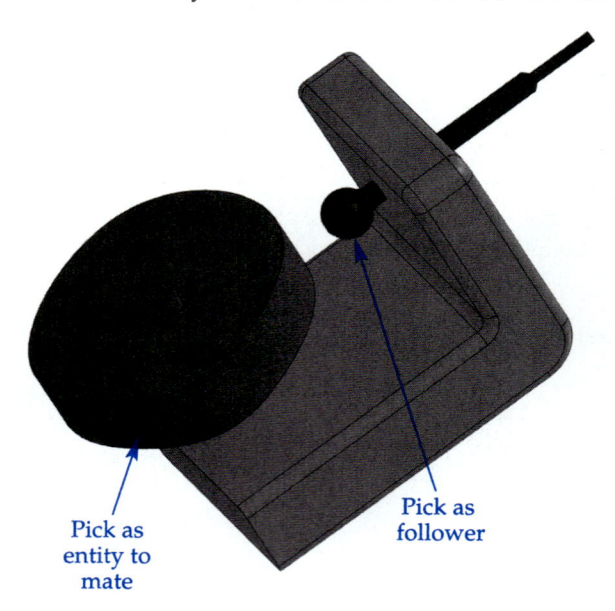

maintain contact between the two surfaces. Rotate the view so the bottom cam surface and the bottom face of the follower are visible. You may also need to drag the follower up. See **Figure 13-6**.

Pick the **Mate** button in the **Assembly** tab of the **Command Manager**. Expand the **Mechanical Mates** rollout and pick the **Cam** button. With the **Entities to Mate** selection box active in the **Mate Selections** rollout, pick the contact face of the cam. With the **Cam follower:** selection box active, pick the bottom of the follower. Pick the narrow, cylindrical face. Once this is done, the follower moves down to contact the cam. Pick the green check mark button to apply the mate.

Drag the cam to rotate it. The follower moves up and down, remaining in contact with the face on the cam as it spins. Save Example_13_05.sldasm and close the file.

Chapter Test

Answer the following questions on a separate sheet of paper or complete the electronic chapter test on the student website.
www.g-wlearning.com/CAD

1. List three of the mechanical mates available in SolidWorks.
2. What does a mechanical mate do?
3. The _____ mate is used to transfer the rotation of one part to another part, such as one wheel driving a second wheel.
4. The _____ mate is used to translate the rotation of one part into linear movement of another part, such as a gear driving a rack.
5. The _____ mate is used to maintain contact between two surfaces, such as between a cam and a follower.

Chapter Exercises

Complete the chapter exercises on the student website.
www.g-wlearning.com/CAD

Exercise 13-1 Three Gears.
Complete the exercise on the student website.

Exercise 13-2 Four Gears.
Complete the exercise on the student website.

Exercise 13-3 Planetary Gear Set.
Complete the exercise on the student website.

Configurations, covered in Chapter 14, make it possible to manage multiple design variations of parts within a single document. (Model courtesy of DS SolidWorks Corp.)

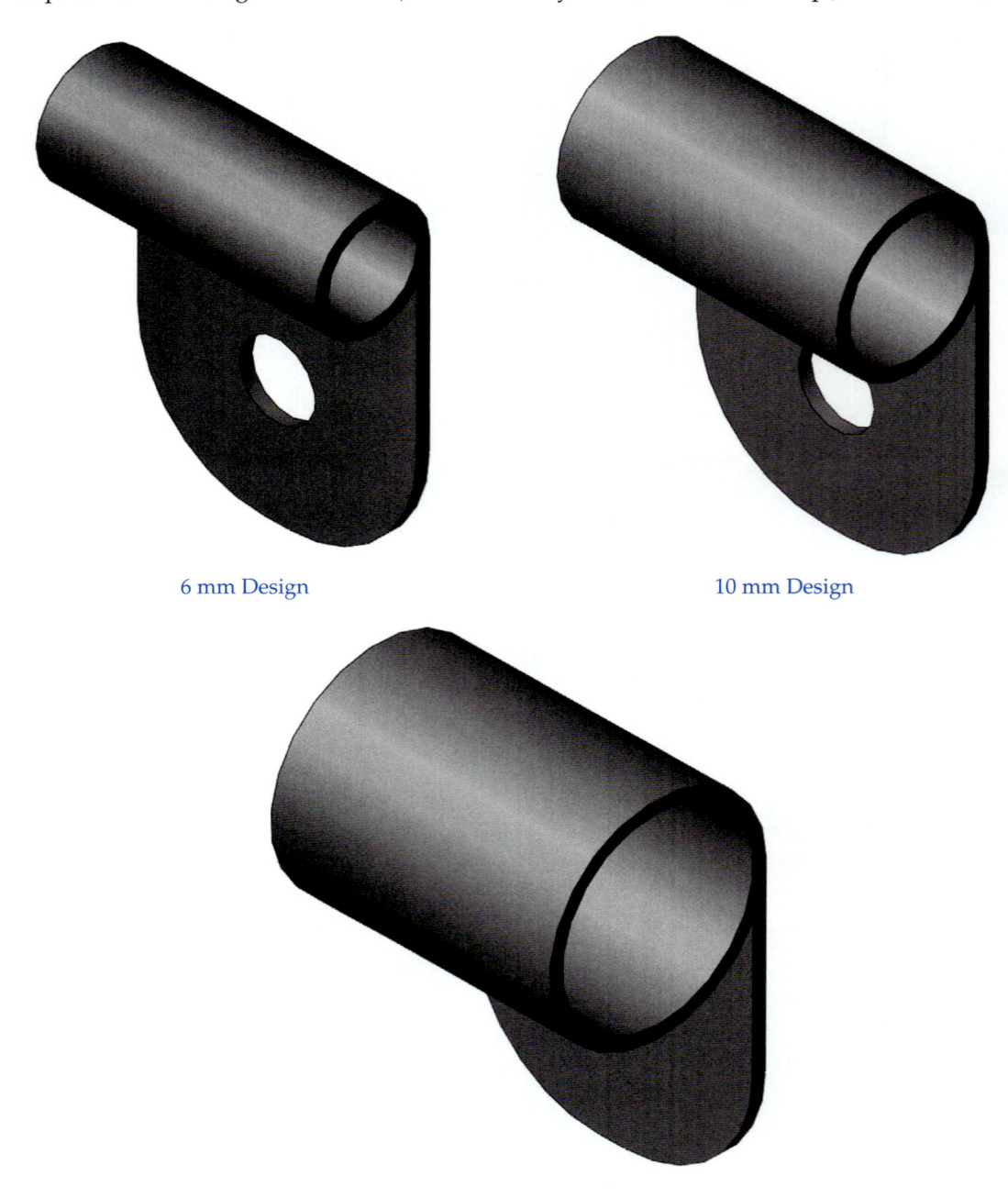

6 mm Design

10 mm Design

15 mm Design

Chapter 14

Configurations and Design Tables

Objectives

After completing this chapter, you will be able to:

- Explain configurations.
- Create multiple configurations.
- Create a design table to control the feature parameters of a part.
- Edit a design table.

Working with Configurations

In this chapter, parts will be modeled with special attention paid to the parametric relationships needed to provide control over the part. With careful planning and attention to detail, sketch dimensions and feature parameters can be modified to easily change the part geometry. A *configuration* is the status of a part with a set of values applied to specific parameters. Various configurations of a part can be handled within a single file using the **Configuration Manager**. Each of these configurations can be modified to suit different applications for a part. For example, multiple sizes for a spacer can be managed as configurations in a single SolidWorks part file.

The examples in this chapter demonstrate the manual creation and modification of multiple part configurations. Design tables will also be used to create and modify multiple configurations.

Creating a New Configuration

Open Example_14_01.sldprt. Right-click on the Annotations branch in the design tree and select **Show Feature Dimensions** from the shortcut menu. Three dimensions, or parameters, are now displayed in the graphics window. You may need to zoom out to see the dimensions. These dimensions are named Inner Diameter, Thickness, and Length. To see the dimension name, hover the cursor over a dimension until the name appears as help text. The Inner Diameter and Thickness dimensions are specified in Sketch1 and the Length dimension is specified in Extrude1. This is also indicated in the help text after the dimension name. See **Figure 14-1.**

Multiple configurations of the spacer need to be made to accommodate different applications. Pick the **Configuration Manager** tab in the **Management Panel** to display the **Configuration Manager**. See **Figure 14-2.**

To create a new configuration, right-click on the file name at the top of the **Configuration Manager** tree. Then, select **Add Configuration** from the shortcut menu. See **Figure 14-3A.** In the **Add Configuration Property Manager** that is displayed, enter the

Figure 14-1.
To see the name of a dimension, hover the cursor over the dimension.

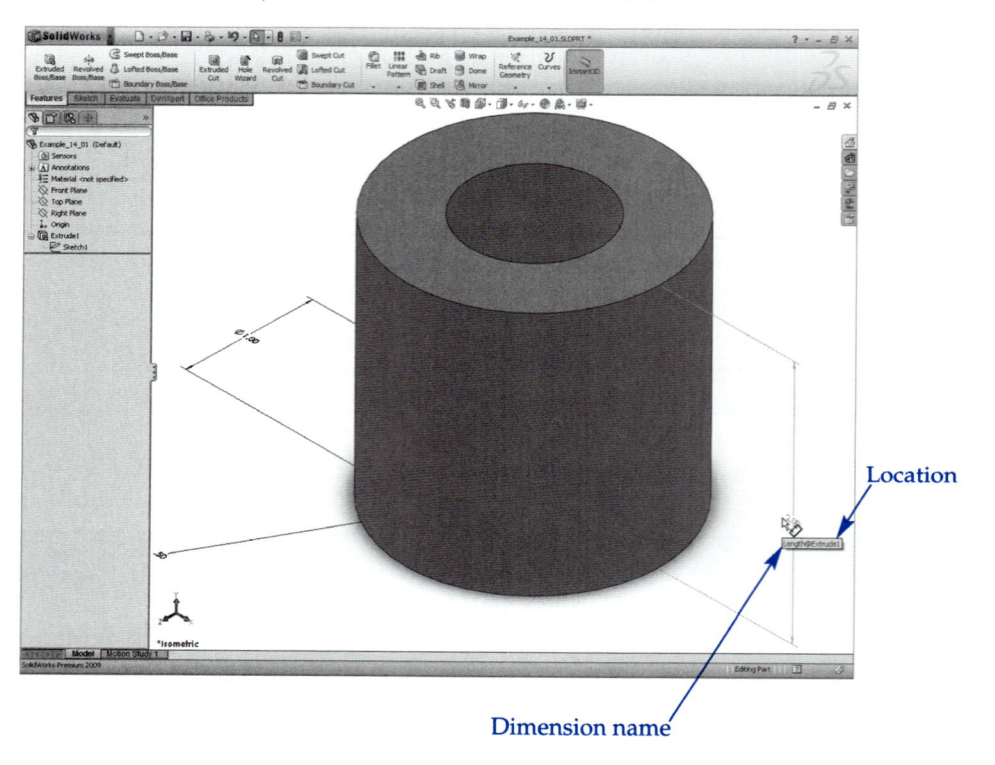

Figure 14-2.
The **Configuration Manager** is used to handle configurations in SolidWorks.

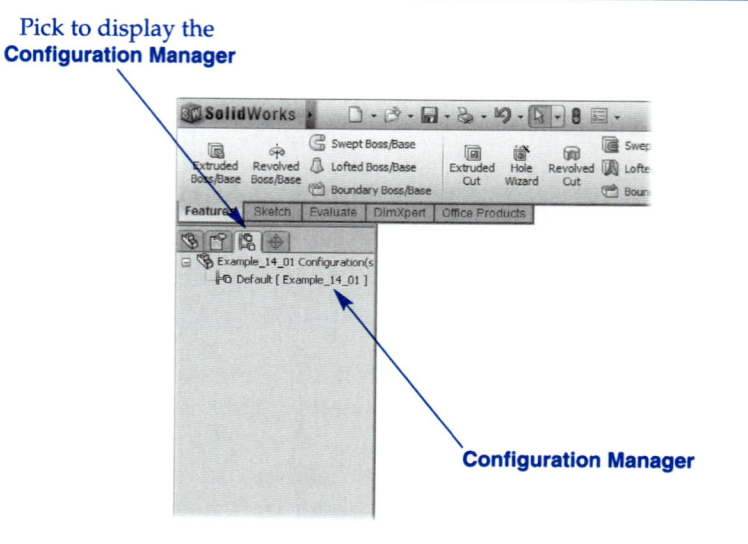

252

Learning SolidWorks 2009

Figure 14-3.
A—Adding a configuration to the part file. B—Entering a name for the new configuration being added to the part file.

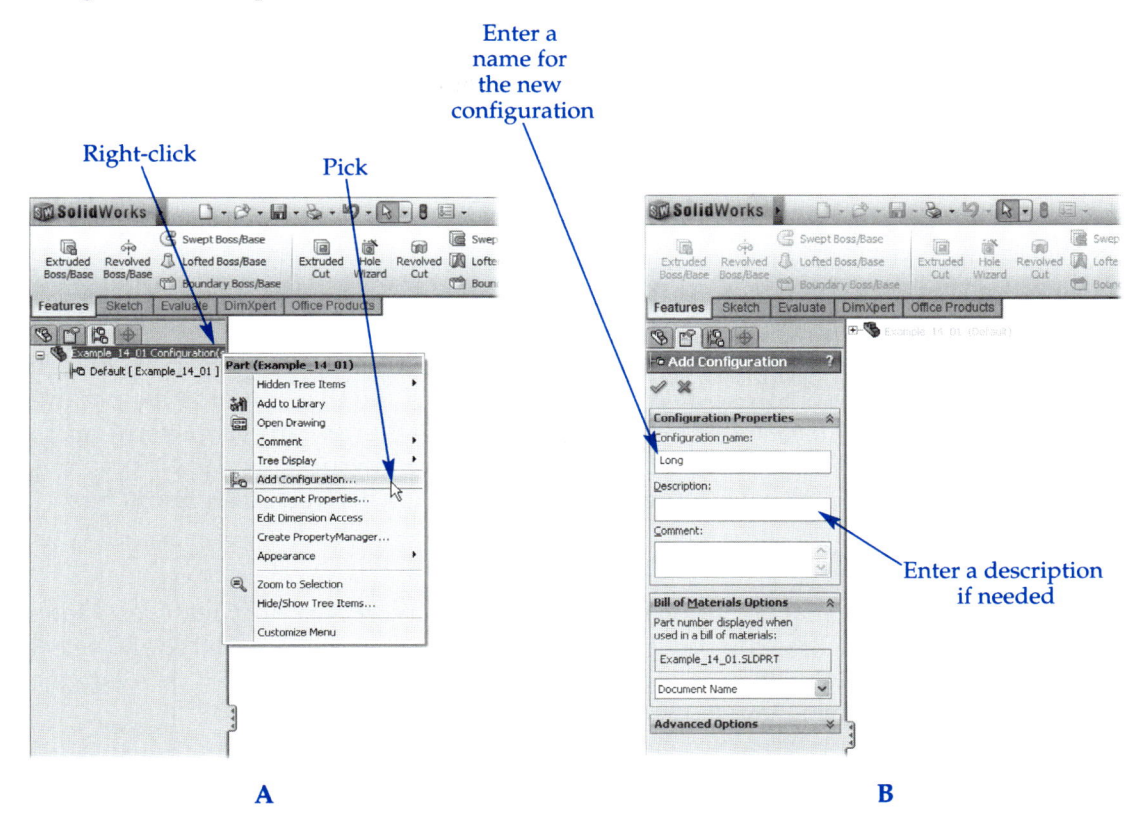

A

B

name Long in the **Configuration name:** text box. See **Figure 14-3B**. Then, pick the green check mark button to close the **Property Manager** and add the new configuration.

Notice that there are now two configurations in the **Configuration Manager**: Default and Long. See **Figure 14-4**. The Long configuration is highlighted and has become the active configuration of the part file. Any changes made to the spacer now will only appear when the Long configuration is active.

In the graphics window, pick on the Length dimension and enter 4 as the new value. Press the [Enter] key or pick anywhere in the graphics window to set the new value. It may be necessary to pick the **Rebuild** button on the **Menu Bar** to update the model. Notice that the length of the spacer has been increased from 2 to 4.

Figure 14-4.
The new configuration has been added to the part file and is automatically active.

Chapter 14 Configurations and Design Tables   253

Now, in the **Configuration Manager**, double-click on the Default configuration to make it active. The spacer returns to the original length of 2. By creating multiple configurations, one part file can contain data for many parts with similar geometry.

Create another configuration of the spacer. First, add a new configuration named Short. With the new configuration active, change the Length dimension to .125″, the Thickness dimension to 1″, and the Inner Diameter dimension to .75″. Notice that the spacer now resembles a washer. Switch between the Default, Long, and Short configurations to see the changes. Then, save the changes and close the part file.

Controlling Configurations with a Design Table

Geometry can be controlled to create multiple configurations by using a design table. A *design table* is a spreadsheet embedded in part file that contains the parameters for the part and corresponding values. Editing a design table is usually much easier than editing the individual parameters in each configuration. Math functions can also be used in the spreadsheet to create relationships between the parameters.

Creating Configurations in a Design Table

The first example is a shelled extrusion of a block with two fillet features. Open Example_14_02.sldprt. Right-click on the Annotations branch in the design tree and select **Show Feature Dimensions** from the shortcut menu. The parameters used to create the model are displayed. You may need to zoom out to see the dimensions.

The Width and Depth dimensions are specified in Sketch1. The Height dimension is specified in Extrude1. The Corner Radius dimension is specified in Fillet1. The Top Radius is specified in Fillet2. The Shell Thickness dimension is specified in Shell1. A design table will be created allowing these feature parameters to be controlled for multiple configurations.

Choose **Insert>Tables>Design Table...** from the pull-down menu. The **Design Table Property Manager** is displayed. In the **Source** rollout, pick the **Auto-create** radio button and leave all other options at their default settings. See **Figure 14-5**. Pick the green check mark button to begin creating the table.

Figure 14-5.
Adding a design table to a part file that does not contain any existing configurations.

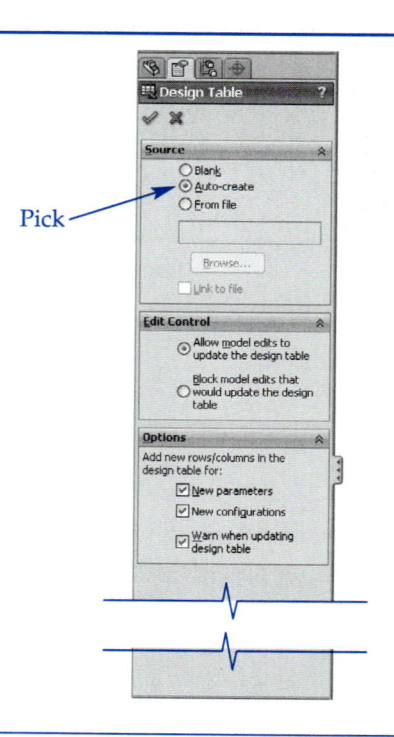

The **Dimensions** dialog box appears after you pick the green check mark button, **Figure 14-6.** Hold the [Ctrl] key and select the parameters you wish to control with the design table. Any skipped parameters will not be driven by the spreadsheet. For this example, select all six parameters and pick the **OK** button to close the **Dimensions** dialog box.

The design table is opened within the drawing area. See **Figure 14-7.** Each parameter selected to be included in the design table has its own column at the top of the spreadsheet. The name of the default configuration appears in cell A3 with the corresponding dimensions making up the rest of the row.

To create a new configuration, select the empty cell below the Default name (cell A4). If you accidentally pick outside of the spreadsheet, the design table will close. Enter your name in the cell. Then, enter 6 in cell B4 under the Width parameter. Also, enter 6 under the Height parameter (cell D4) and change both fillet dimensions to .25 (cells E4 and F4). Next, pick outside of the spreadsheet in the graphics window. The design table is closed and SolidWorks creates a new configuration of the part. A message is displayed indicating a configuration has been added and providing its name.

Figure 14-6.
When adding a design table, you must select which parameters will appear in the design table.

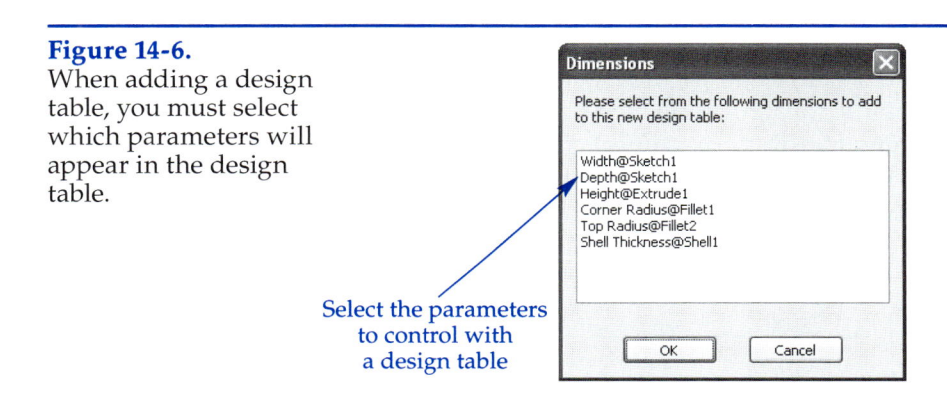

Figure 14-7.
The design table is added to the part file and initially displayed in the graphics window.

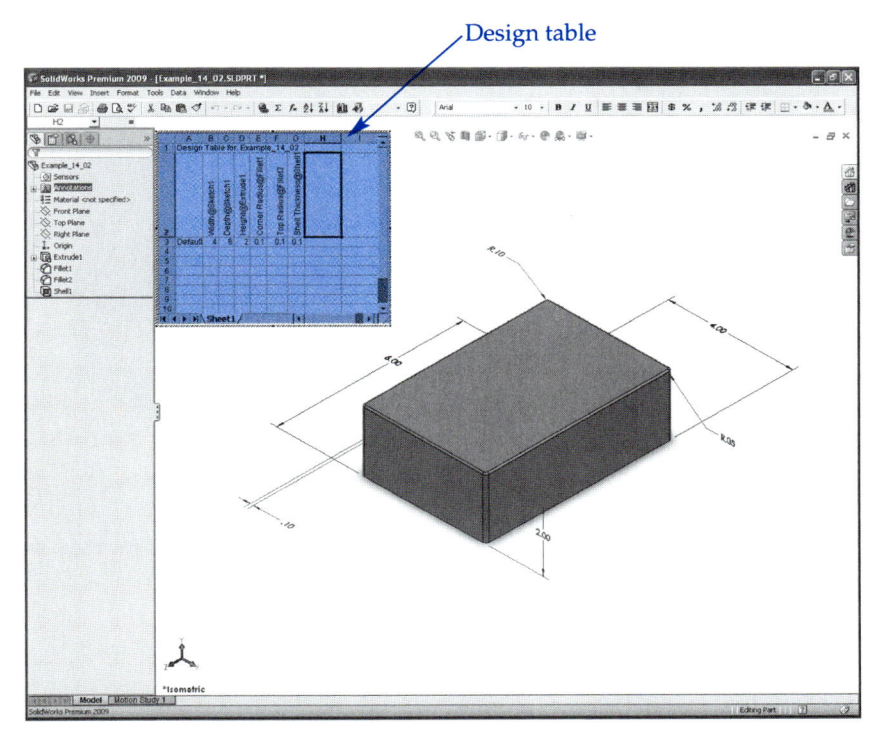

Chapter 14 Configurations and Design Tables   255

Display the **Configuration Manager**. There are now two configurations: Default and the new configuration with your name as the title. Also, the design table appears above the configuration names. Double-click on the new configuration to view the changes to the model. Then, save the file. Leave the file open for the next section.

> **NOTE**
>
> When entering values in a spreadsheet, distances can be specified in inches (in), or millimeters (mm), deg, and so on. If a unit is not specified, then a value will use the default unit value of the part file, such as inches or millimeters.

Editing a Design Table

Right-click on the name of the design table in the **Configuration Manager** and select **Edit Table** from the shortcut menu. The design table is opened and displayed in the graphics window. If you select **Edit in New Window** from the shortcut menu, the design table is displayed in Microsoft Excel.

Notice that the cells left blank while creating the new configuration have assumed the values of the default configuration. See **Figure 14-8.** Now, change the Width, Depth, and Height parameters to 1 in your named configuration. Leave the fillet dimensions as .25. Change the Shell Thickness parameter to .25. The spreadsheet may round the values to one decimal place, depending on the setup of your system.

Figure 14-8.
Editing an existing design table.

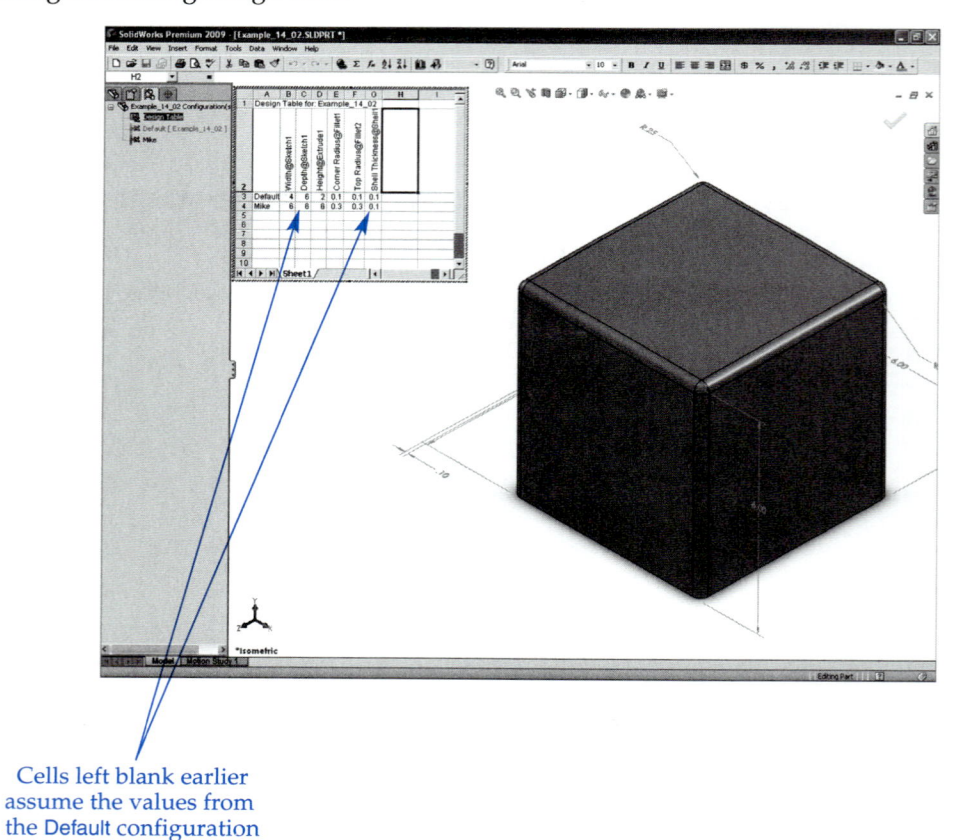

Cells left blank earlier assume the values from the Default configuration

Next, create another configuration named New. Enter the name in the cell below your name (cell A5). In this row, set the Width parameter to 10. Leave all other cells blank. Then, pick in the graphics window to close the design table.

Double-click on your named configuration in the **Configuration Manager** to activate it. Notice the changes. Then, double-click on the New configuration to activate it. Notice how the cells left empty in the design table for the New configuration have assumed the values of the configuration above them in the table, which is your named configuration. This can be seen in the spreadsheet by editing the design table. Save and close the part file.

Creating a Design Table from Configurations

Open Example_14_03.sldprt. Display the **Configuration Manager**. Notice that there are multiple configurations for the part. However, there is no design table in the file. If the file contained a design table, it would be listed above the configurations in the **Configuration Manager**. A design table can be added to a part file even if multiple configurations are already present. The existing configurations can be used to create the design table, which can then be used to add new configurations.

First, display the **Feature Manager**, right-click on the Annotations branch in the design tree, and choose **Show Feature Dimensions** from the shortcut menu. Then, select **Insert>Table>Design Table...** from the pull-down menu. In the **Source** rollout of the **Design Table Property Manager**, pick the **Blank** radio button. Then, pick the green check mark button to begin creating the table. The **Add Rows and Columns** dialog box is displayed, **Figure 14-9**.

Hold the [Ctrl] key and select 20", 24", and 26" in the **Configurations** area. Then, while still holding the [Ctrl] key, select Fork Length, Head Tube Length, and Axle Diameter from the **Parameters** area. Pick the **OK** button to close the dialog box and populate the cells in the design table. Next, in the design table, change the Axle Diameter for the 20" configuration to 12 mm by typing 12mm in the B4 cell. Change the Head Tube Length for the 26" configuration to 7.5". Pick in the graphics window outside of the design table to accept the changes and create the table. Next, in the **Configuration Manager**, double-click on each configuration to see the results. Save the file.

Figure 14-9.
When adding a design table to a part with existing configurations, you must select which configurations and which parameters will appear in the design table.

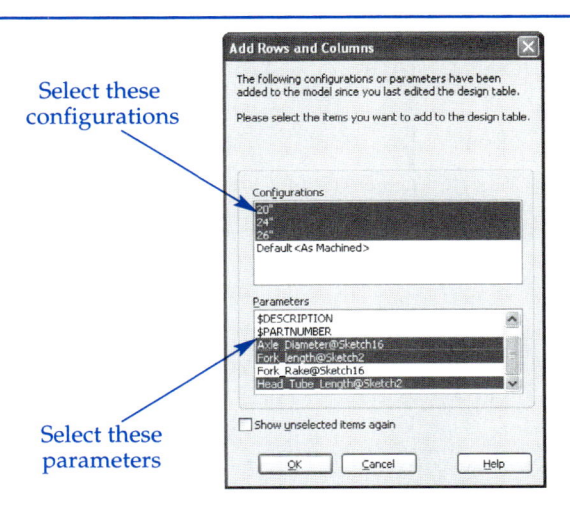

Select these configurations

Select these parameters

Chapter Test

Answer the following questions on a separate sheet of paper or complete the electronic chapter test on the student website.
www.g-wlearning.com/CAD

1. What is a *configuration*?
2. Which feature of SolidWorks in used to handle various configurations?
3. Briefly describe how to add a new configuration to the part file.
4. In a part file with multiple configurations, how do you switch between configurations?
5. What is a *design table*?
6. List two reasons why you might use a design table over manual configurations.
7. Briefly describe how to add a design table to a part file when the file does not contain existing configurations.
8. How do you display a design table for editing?
9. If a cell is left blank for a configuration in the design table, what happens?
10. When adding a design table, what should you pick in the **Source** rollout of the **Design Table Property Manager** to add existing configurations to the design table?

Chapter Exercises

Complete the chapter exercises on the student website.
www.g-wlearning.com/CAD

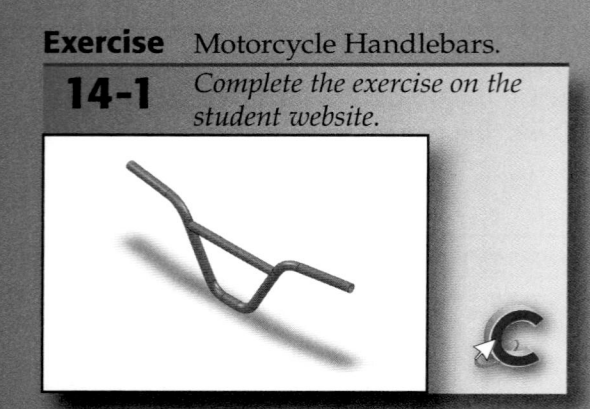

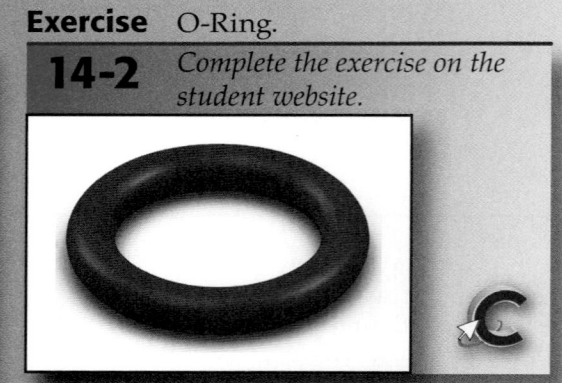

Exercise 14-1 Motorcycle Handlebars. *Complete the exercise on the student website.*

Exercise 14-2 O-Ring. *Complete the exercise on the student website.*

Chapter 15
Surfaces

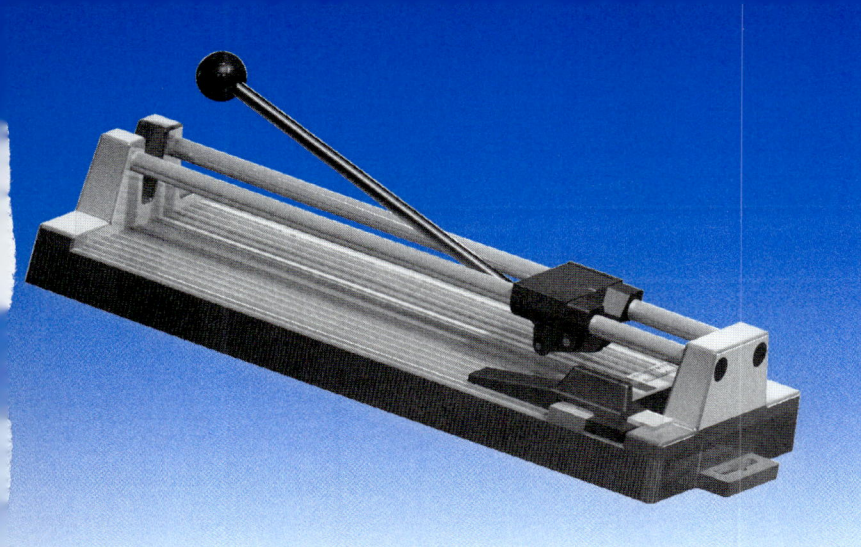

Objectives

After completing this chapter, you will be able to:

- Explain the differences between surfaces and solids.
- Explain the basic process for creating a surface.
- Offset a surface from a solid or surface.
- Use surfaces as construction geometry.
- Stitch surfaces into a quilt.

A *surface* defines the form and shape of an object, but does not have volume. A *solid* also defines the form and shape of an object, but it has volume. SolidWorks is primarily used to create solid objects. However, you can create surfaces to use as construction geometry. In addition, there are some instances where you may want to create the final product as a surface model, such as when sharing a model with software that does not support solid modeling.

The process for creating a surface is basically the same as for creating a solid. First, sketch and constrain the geometry. Then, finish the sketch and select the feature-creation tool you wish to use, such as **Extrude** or **Revolve**. The tools are different from the tools used to create solids, but they look and act much the same. However, you must use the right tool for the job. The tools used for creating surface geometry are found in the pull-down menus, not in the **Command Manager**. Select **Insert>Surface** from the pull-down menu to see the surface-creation tools, **Figure 15-1**.

> **PROFESSIONAL TIP**
> The surface tools can be added to the **Command Manager** for more convenient access. Refer to the SolidWorks documentation for information on customizing the **Command Manager**.

Figure 15-1.
The tools for creating surfaces are located in the **Insert** pull-down menu.

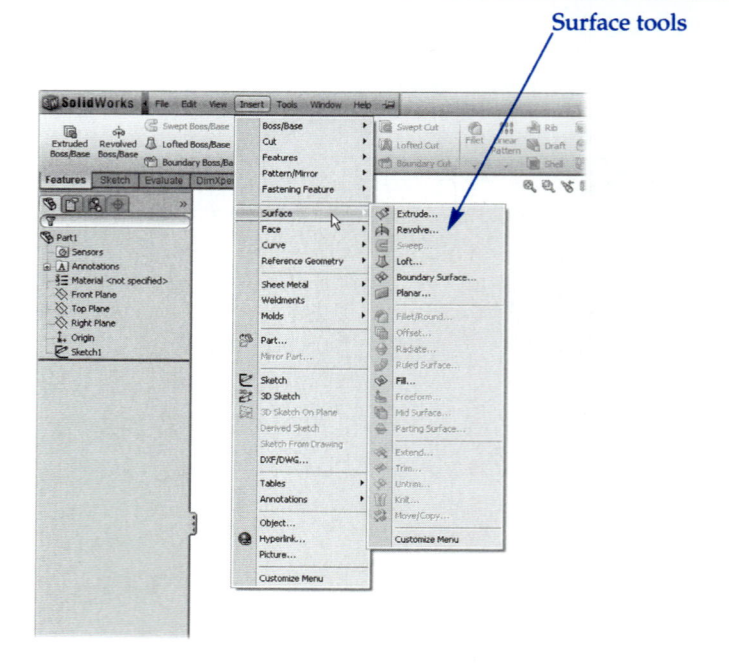

Extruded Surfaces

Open **Example_15_01.sldprt**. This file contains an open, fully constrained sketch composed of a line and an arc. Select **Insert>Surface>Extrude...** from the pull-down menu. Then, select the profile in the graphics window.

Notice that the **Surface-Extrude Property Manager** is nearly identical to the **Extrude Property Manager** used for creating solids. See **Figure 15-2**. In the **Direction 1** rollout, select Blind in the **End Condition** drop-down list. Then, enter 1 in the **Depth** text box in the rollout. Finally, pick the green check mark button to extrude the surface. Notice in the design tree that the feature is named Surface-Extrude1, indicating that the feature is a surface, not a solid.

Revolved Surfaces

Open **Example_15_02.sldprt**. This file contains a sketch that you will revolve into a surface. Like the previous example, the sketch is open. Select **Insert>Surface>Revolve...** from the pull-down menu. Then, select the profile in the graphics window. Since the axis of revolution was drawn as a centerline, it is automatically selected. Otherwise, activate the **Axis of Revolution** selection box in the **Revolved Parameters** rollout and select the axis in the graphics window.

In the **Revolve Type** drop-down list in the **Revolved Parameters** rollout, select One Direction. This specifies that the revolution is in one direction only. You can also choose to have the angle of revolution equally applied about the profile or specify an angle of revolution in each direction from the profile.

Next, enter 270 in the **Angle** text box. See **Figure 15-3**. Notice the preview of the revolution. Finally, pick the green check mark button to create the surface.

Figure 15-2.
Creating a surface extrusion.

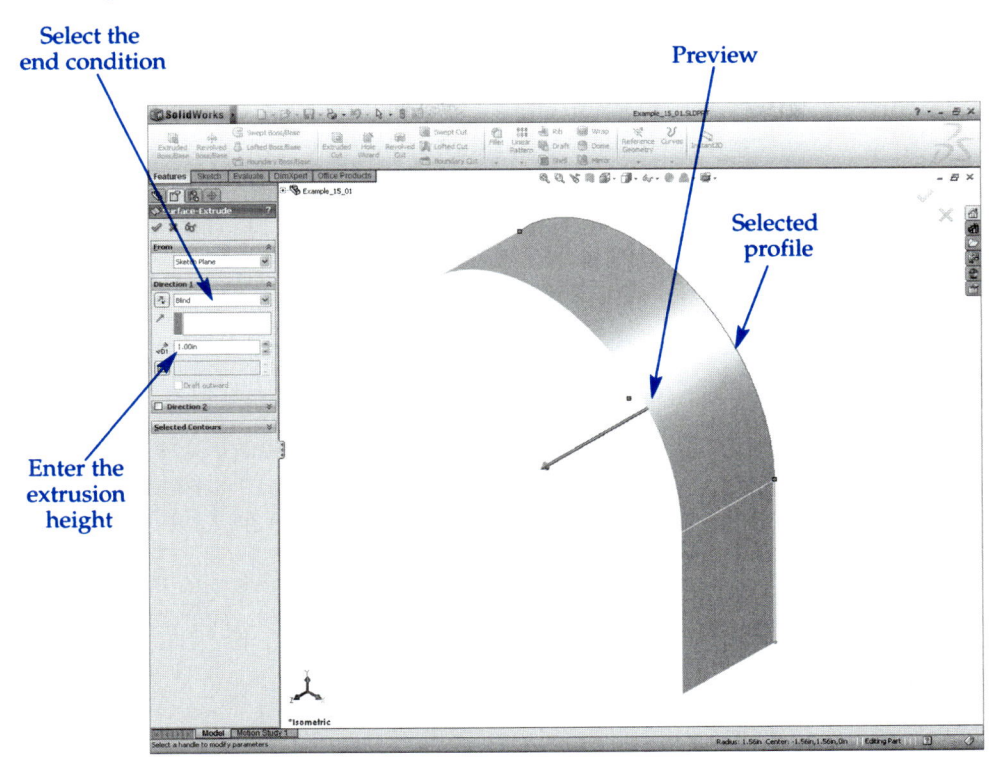

- Select the end condition
- Preview
- Selected profile
- Enter the extrusion height

Figure 15-3.
Creating a surface revolution.

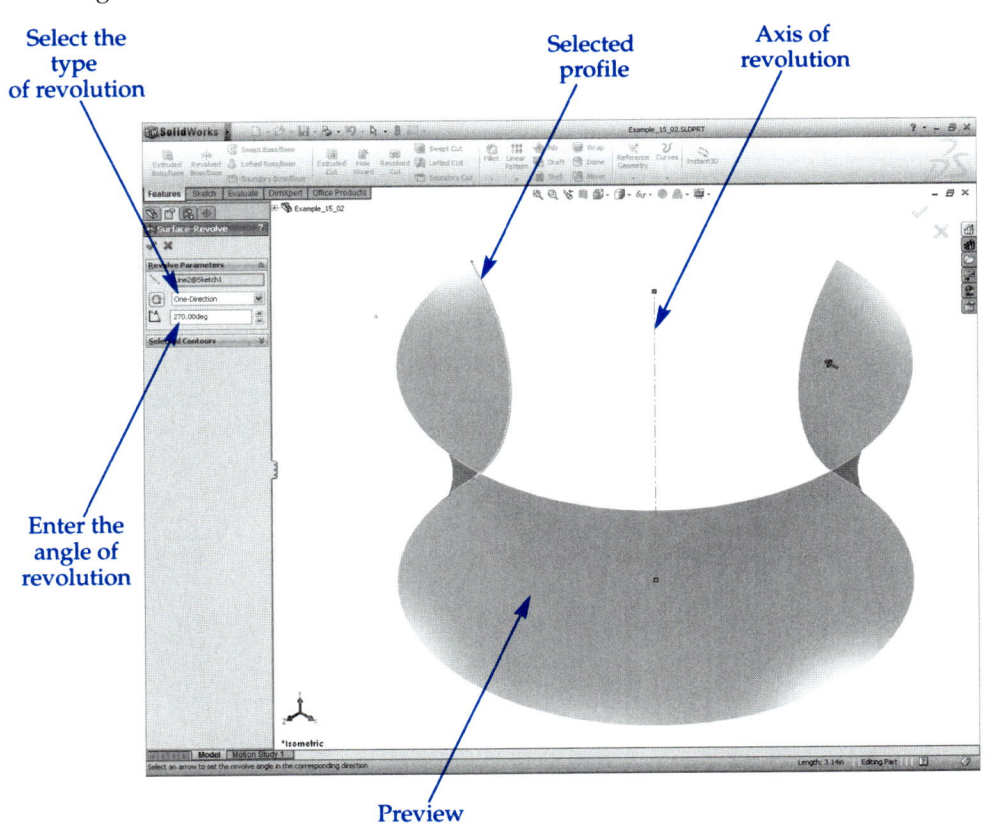

- Select the type of revolution
- Selected profile
- Axis of revolution
- Enter the angle of revolution
- Preview

Chapter 15 Surfaces

Lofted Surfaces

Open Example_15_03.sldprt. This file contains two closed sketches that will be used to create a lofted surface. Select **Insert>Surface>Loft...** from the pull-down menu. Then, select the profiles in the graphics window. Pick the green check mark button to create the loft. A surface is generated between the two sketches. However, notice that the ends—the area of each closed sketch—are open. This is more apparent if the part is rotated to an end view. See **Figure 15-4.** The options explored in Chapter 10 can also be applied to a lofted surface.

Swept Surfaces

Open Example_15_04.sldprt. This file contains two sketches. The curved line will be used as the path for a swept feature. The circle will be the cross section. Select **Insert>Surface>Sweep...** from the pull-down menu. In the **Profile and Path** rollout of the **Sweep Command Manager**, activate the **Profile** selection box. Then, pick the circle in the graphics window. Then, with the **Path** selection box in the **Profile and Path** rollout active, pick the curved line in the graphics window. Finally, pick the green check mark button to create the swept surface. If you rotate the view, it is apparent that this is a tube, not a solid part, **Figure 15-5.**

Thickening and Offsetting Surfaces

The **Thicken** tool allows you to thicken a surface, turning it into a solid. Open Example_15_05.sldprt. This file contains a single lofted surface. If you rotate the view, you will be able to see the interior is hollow. You will use the **Thicken** tool to create a solid out of this surface.

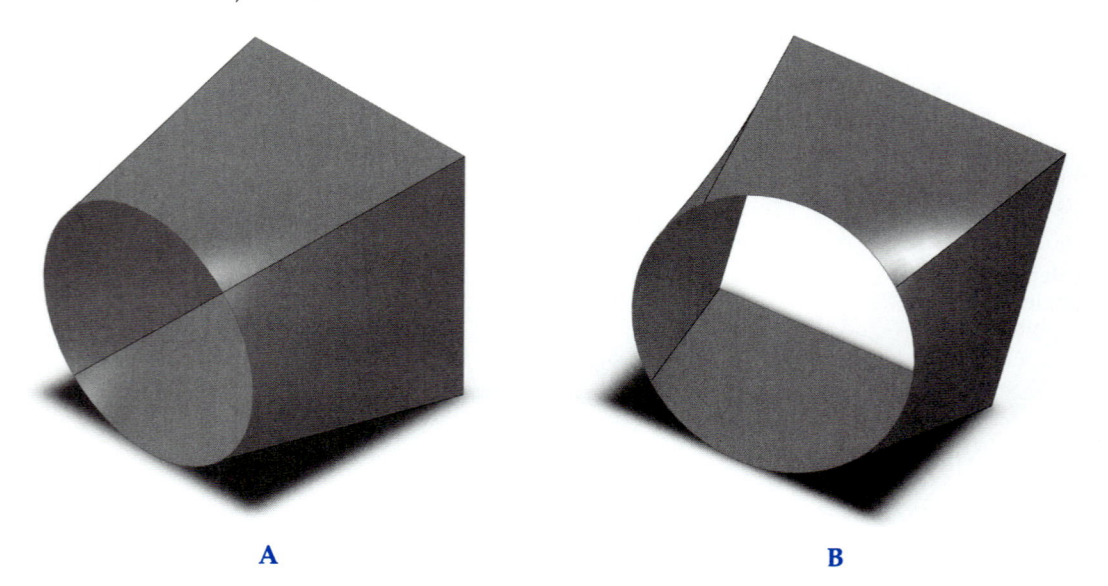

Figure 15-4.
Creating a lofted surface. A—The end result. B—When the view is rotated, you can see a surface was created, not a solid.

A   B

Figure 15-5.
Creating a swept surface. A—The end result. B—When the view is rotated, you can see a surface was created, not a solid.

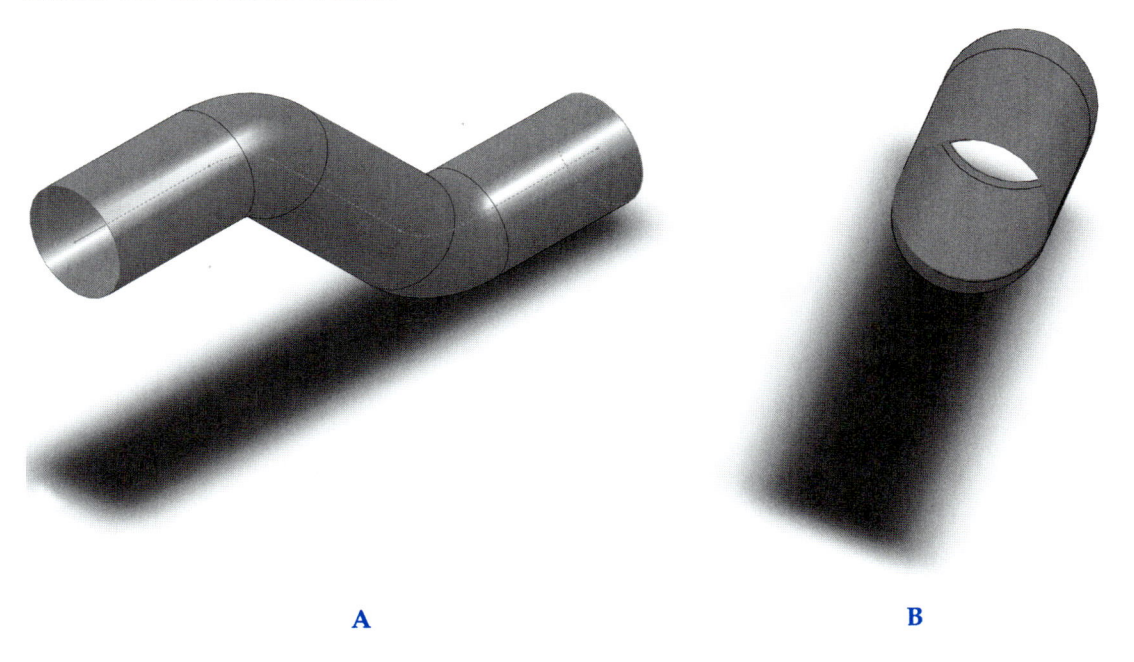

A   B

1. Select **Insert>Boss/Base>Thicken...** from the pull-down menu. The **Thicken Property Manager** is displayed, **Figure 15-6.**
2. With the **Surface to Thicken** selection box in the **Thicken Parameters** rollout active, pick the surface in the graphics window.
3. In the rollout, pick the **Thicken Side 2** button so the preview shows the offset to the inside.
4. Enter .5 in the **Thickness** text box in the rollout.
5. Pick the green check mark button to create the new solid body.

Notice the name of the feature in the design tree is Thicken1.

Undo the operation. Then, select **Insert>Surface>Offset...** from the pull-down menu. The **Offset Surface Property Manager** is displayed. With the **Surfaces or Faces to Offset** selection box in the **Offset Parameters** rollout active, select the surface in the graphics window. Then, enter .25 in the **Offset Distance** text box in the rollout. When you pick the green check mark button, a new surface is created, **Figure 15-7.** In the design tree, the name of the feature is Surface-Offset-1.

A surface can also be offset from a solid part. Open Example_15_06.sldprt, which is a solid part. Next, select **Insert>Surface>Offset...** from the pull-down menu. Then, with the **Surfaces or Faces to Offset** selection box in the **Offset Parameters** rollout active, pick all of the copper-colored faces on the part. You can select a single face or multiple faces. Next, specify a .5″ offset and create the surface. Notice how the new surface matches the contour of the selected faces.

Surfaces as Construction Geometry

As mentioned earlier, surfaces are often used as construction geometry. For example, a surface can be used to terminate an extrusion or revolution. A surface can also be used to split a part. The **Split** tool is discussed in Chapter 7. In this section, a surface will be used to terminate an extrusion. Open Example_15_07.sldprt. This file

Figure 15-6.
Thickening a surface into a solid. Here, the thickness is being applied to the inside of the surface. Thus, the overall exterior size of the part does not change.

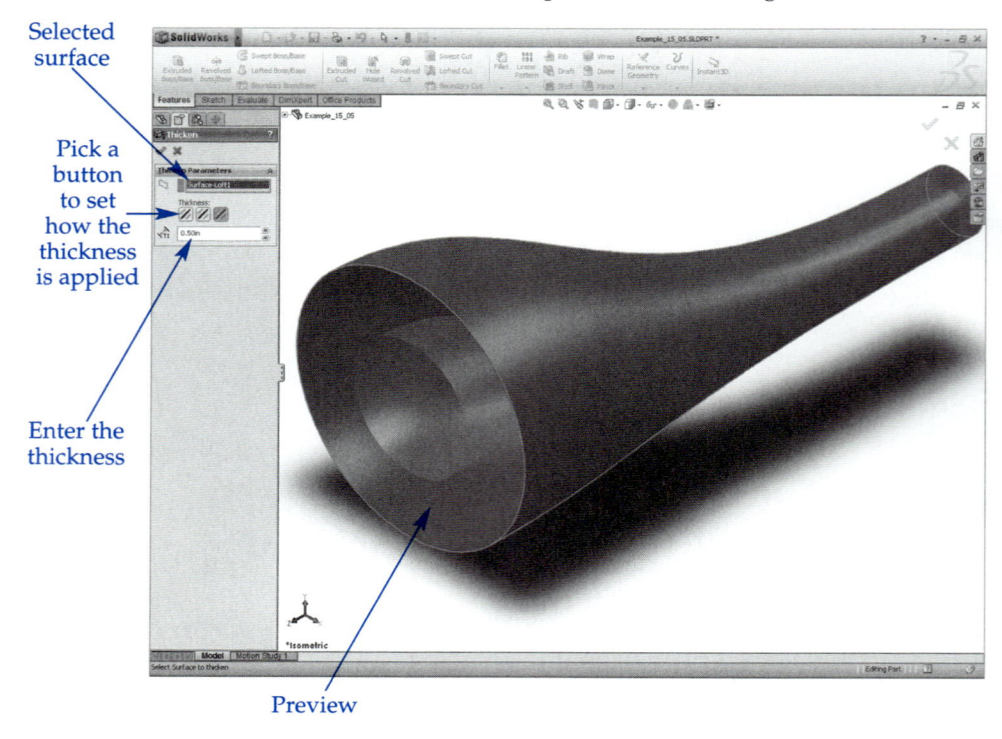

Figure 15-7.
Offsetting a surface from another surface. Here, the new surface is offset to the outside of the original surface.

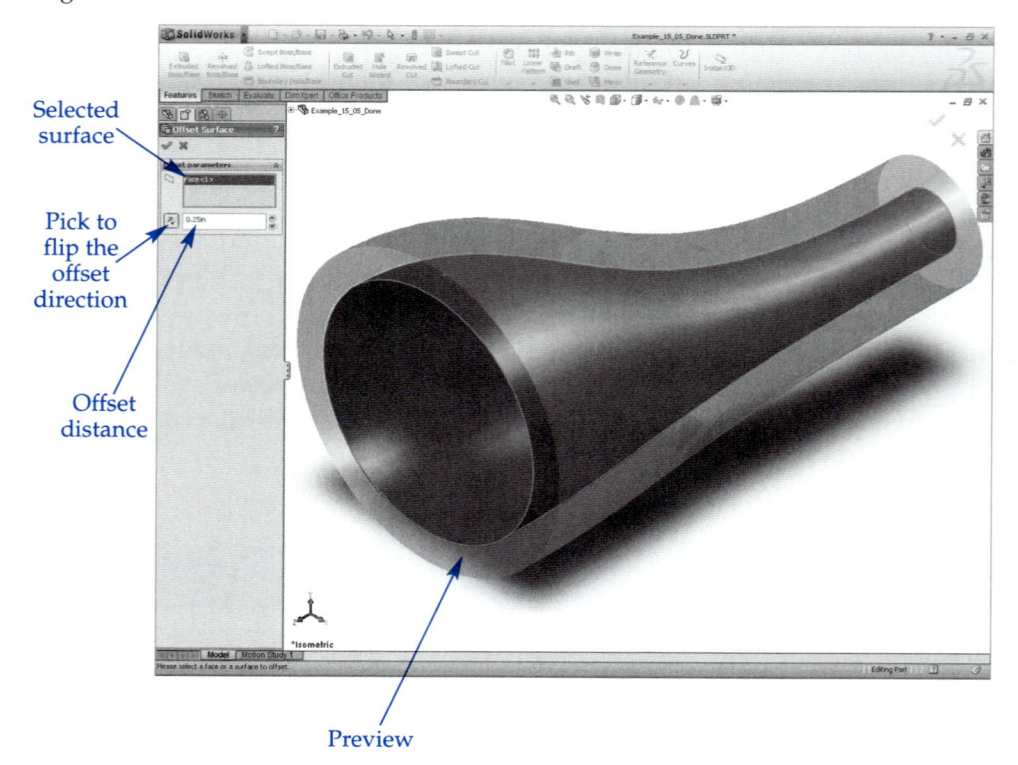

contains a rectangular part and two unconsumed sketches. One sketch will be used to create the construction surface. The other sketch will be extruded as a solid.

First, select **Insert>Surface>Extrude...** from the pull-down menu. Then, extrude the sketch named Sketch for Construction a distance of 1.00" down into the part. See **Figure 15-8A.** Notice that the surface is slightly curved.

Next, pick the **Extruded Cut** button in the **Features** tab of the **Command Manager.** Using this tool, extrude the sketch named Sketch for Subtraction. In the **End Condition** drop-down list in the **Direction 1** rollout, select Up To Surface. Then, with the **Face/Plane** selection box in the **Direction 1** rollout active, select the newly created surface. You may need to select it in the flyout design tree. Finally, pick the green check mark button to create the feature. See **Figure 15-8B.** Notice how the back of the subtracted feature matches the curvature of the surface.

Knitted Surfaces

A *quilt* is a single, continuous surface consisting of two or more faces. The **Knit** tool allows you to "sew" separate surfaces into a quilt. In order for the tool to work, the mating edges of the surfaces to be stitched need to be identical.

1. Open Example_15_08.sldprt.
2. Select **Insert>Surface>Revolve...** from the pull-down menu. Then, revolve Sketch1 90° about the Z axis. If necessary, flip the direction so the revolution extends up and to the left. See **Figure 15-9A.**
3. Select **Insert>Surface>Extrude...** from the pull-down menu. Then, extrude Sketch1 2" extending away from the revolution. See **Figure 15-9B.** You will need to select the sketch in the flyout design tree.

One edge on each surface touches the other surface. Additionally, those two edges are identical. Therefore, these two surfaces can be stitched into a quilt.

Select **Insert>Surface>Knit...** from the pull-down menu. The **Knit Property Manager** is displayed, **Figure 15-10.** With the **Surfaces and Faces to Knit** selection box in the **Selections** rollout active, select both surfaces in the graphics window. Then, pick the green check mark button to knit the surfaces into a quilt. The operation is listed in the design tree as Surface-Knit1.

Figure 15-8.
A—One sketch is extruded into a surface, which will be used as construction geometry to terminate another extrusion. B—The curved back of the cutout feature was used as the terminator for the extruded cut.

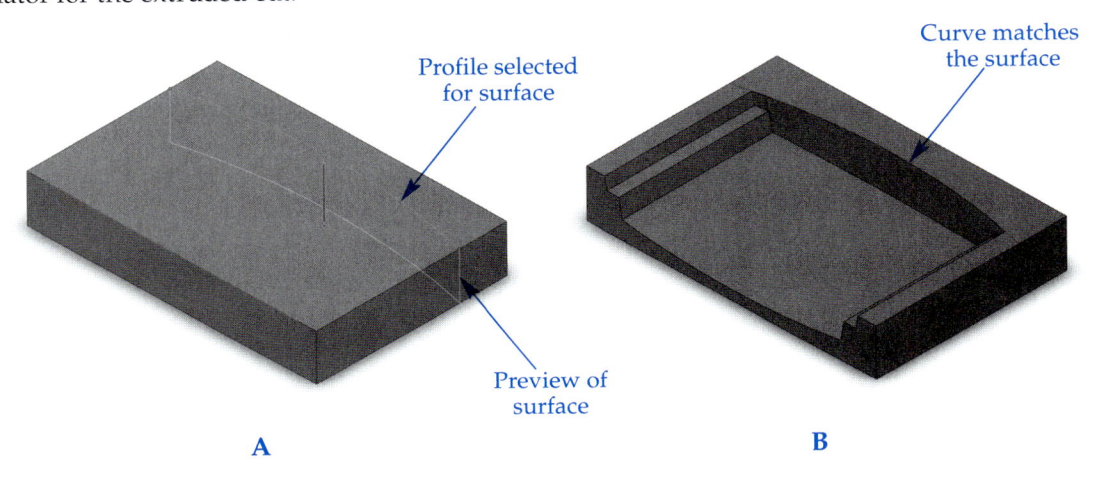

Chapter 15 Surfaces

Figure 15-9.
A—The sketch is first revolved into a surface. B—The sketch is then extruded into a second surface. Since the edges of the two surfaces are identical, the surfaces can be stitched into a quilt.

A

B

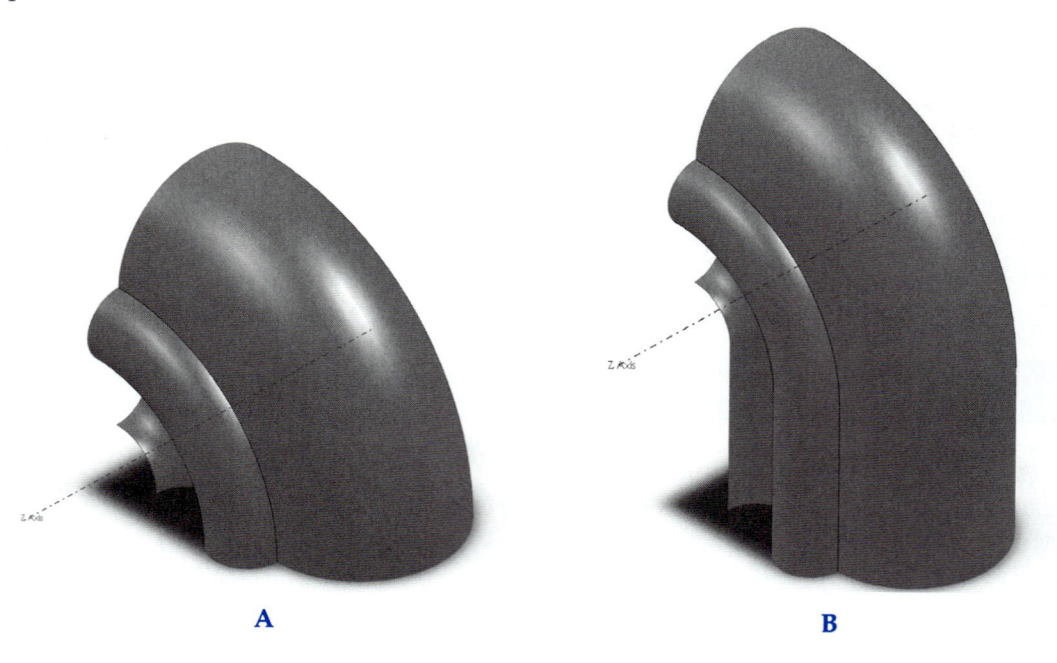

Figure 15-10.
Stitching surfaces into a quilt.

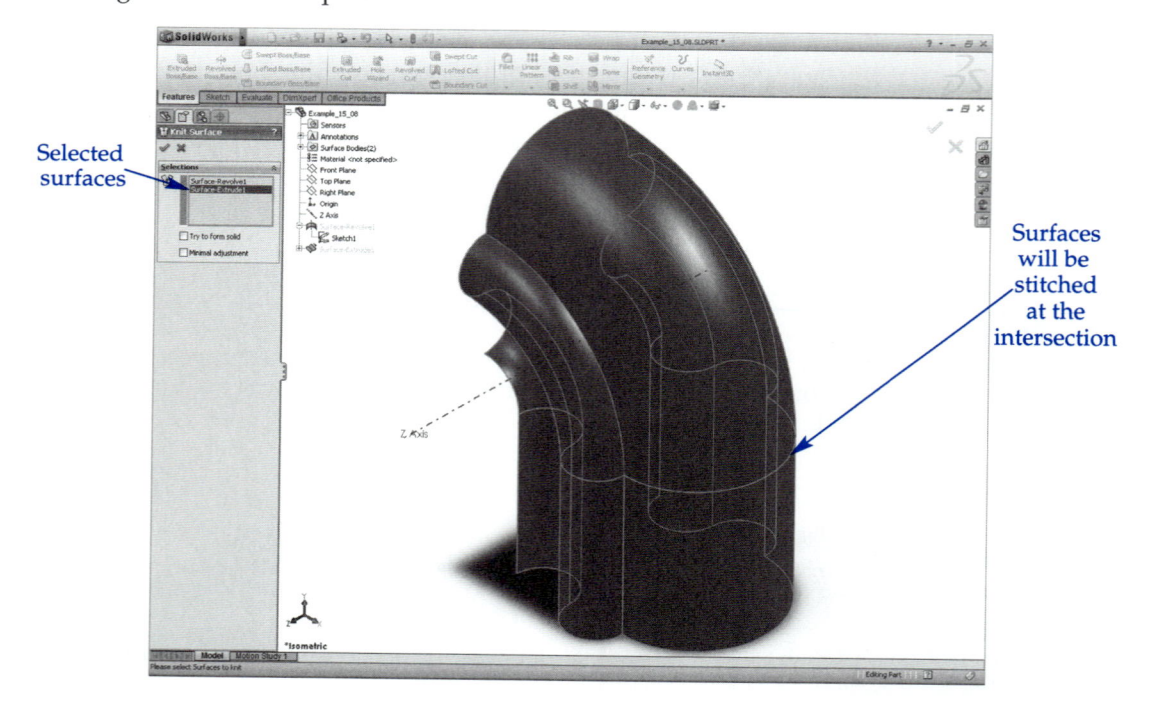

Selected surfaces

Surfaces will be stitched at the intersection

> **PROFESSIONAL TIP**
>
> The quickest way to create the revolved surface described previously is by using the pre-selection method. First select both the Z Axis and Sketch1 sketches. Then, select **Insert>Surface>Revolve…** from the pull-down menu.

Chapter Test

Answer the following questions on a separate sheet of paper or complete the electronic chapter test on the student website.
www.g-wlearning.com/CAD

1. Explain the differences between a *surface* and a *solid*.
2. How does the process for creating a surface differ from the process used to create a solid?
3. Which tool is used to create an extruded surface and where is it located?
4. Which tool is used to create a revolved surface and where is it located?
5. Which tool is used to create a lofted surface and where is it located?
6. Which tool is used to create a swept surface and where is it located?
7. What is the difference between the **Thicken** tool and the **Offset** tool?
8. Define *quilt*.
9. Which tool is used to create a quilt and where is it located?
10. What must be true of two surfaces that are going to be joined using the tool in question 9?

Chapter Exercises

Complete the chapter exercises on the student website.
www.g-wlearning.com/CAD

Exercise 15-1 Offset Surface.
Complete the exercise on the student website.

Exercise 15-2 Revolved Surface.
Complete the exercise on the student website.

Exercise 15-3 Surface Termination.
Complete the exercise on the student website.

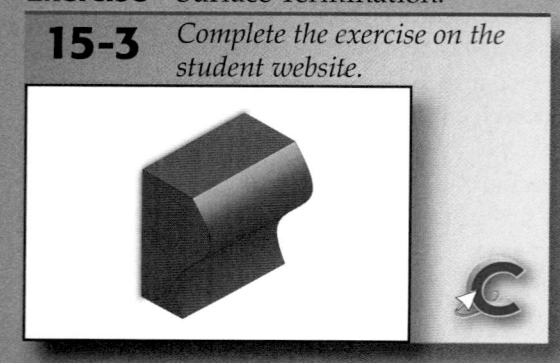

Chapter 16

Assembly Drawings

Objectives

After completing this chapter, you will be able to:
- Create 2D orthographic and section views from assemblies.
- Annotate assembly drawings.
- Create a bill of materials.
- Create balloons to identify parts in an assembly.

Creating Views

Open Example_16_01.sldasm and examine the model to familiarize yourself with the various parts used in the assembly. See **Figure 16-1**. Notice the part's orientation to the coordinate system and note the location of the default planes. This plays a crucial role in specifying the viewing direction for the creation of the drawing views. The view that would best show the faces of both gears would be looking down the X axis, which corresponds to the right side view.

Create a new drawing file. Select **Make Drawing from Part/Assembly** from the **New** flyout in the **Menu Bar**. Specify an E-size sheet and save the file as Example_16_01.slddrw. Right-click on Sheet Format1 in the design tree and select **Properties...** from the shortcut menu. In the **Sheet Properties** dialog box, select the **Third angle** radio button in the **Type of projection** area. Also, set the scale to 1:1. Access the **Document Properties** tab of the options/properties dialog box and make sure the ANSI drafting standard is active. Also, make sure the unit system is set to IPS (inch, pound, second).

Right-click on the drawing and select **Drawing Views>Model...** from the shortcut menu. (Note that the **Standard 3 View** tool will not generate the views we want due to the orientation of the assembly.) Browse and open Example_16_01.sldasm. In the **Orientation** rollout of the **Model View Property Manager**, select the right view. In the **Scale** rollout, make sure the **Use sheet scale** radio button is selected. In the **Display Style** rollout, select Hidden Lines Visible. Then, place the view in the lower-left corner of the drawing. See **Figure 16-2** for the correct orientation and location. Even though the right view orientation of the assembly was selected, it will be the front view (base view) for the

269

Figure 16-1.
An assembly drawing will be created from this assembly.

Figure 16-2.
The correct orientation of the base view.

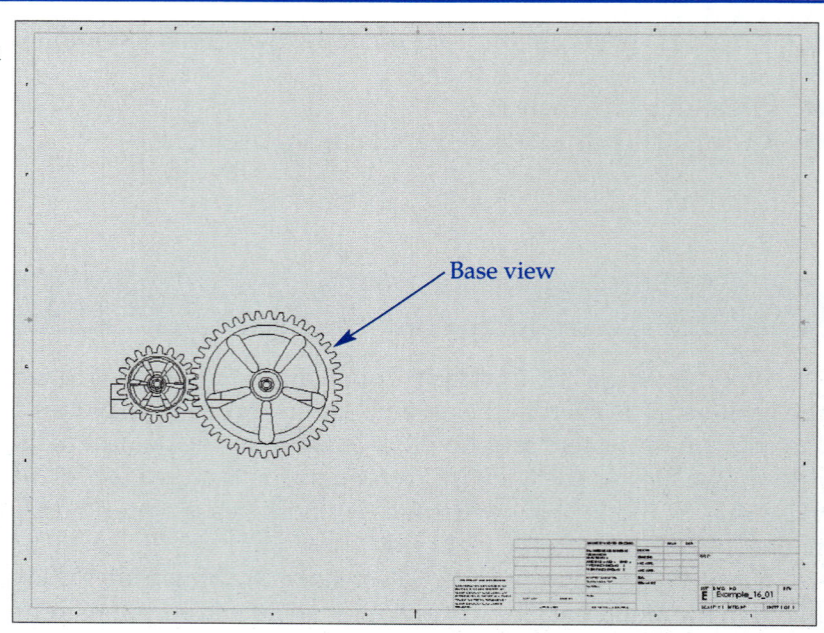

orthographic drawing. You cannot always count on an assembly being properly oriented for the creation of a given view, so you must become comfortable with using the various options available.

Now, create three additional views projected from this front view. The **Projected View** tool should be active after placing the front view. If not, right-click on the front view and select **Drawing Views>Projected view** from the shortcut menu. When the cursor is moved around the drawing, different views appear. Pick a location above the front view and click to place the top view, and then pick a location to the right of the front view and click to place the right view. Finally, pick a location diagonally to the upper right of the front view and click to place the isometric view. Pick the green check mark button in the **Projected View Property Manager**.

270 Learning SolidWorks 2009

Zoom in on the front view showing the faces of the gears. Some of the circles in the gears represent where a fillet blends into a flat face. These are called *tangent edges*. Right-click on the view and pick on **Tangent Edge** in the shortcut menu. You can display the edges (the default), show them in a different line font, or remove them. The *line font* controls the style and thickness of a line based on the type of edge the line represents. Line font options for drawings are set in the document options. Try the options in the shortcut menu and compare the results.

In the design tree, the views are not referred to as Front or Top, but instead have numbers assigned to them. Also, the dependent views (Drawing View2, Drawing View3, and Drawing View4) have a different icon in front of the name than the base view (Drawing View1). See **Figure 16-3.** If you expand Drawing View1 and then expand Example_16_01 you'll see a listing of all the parts in the assembly. Further expanding a part, such as CR_Locating_Pin, details the construction of that part. Right-clicking on the part will let you open it for editing or modification.

Currently, all of the orthographic views inherit the Hidden Lines Visible display style from the front view, the view on which they are based. If you change the display style for the front view, all other views follow suit. To change the display style of just one of the other views, right-click on the view and pick the display style in the **Display Style** rollout of the **Drawing View Property Manager.** Do this for the isometric view. Set the display style to Shaded With Edges, then Shaded. Compare the results of the two styles.

Section Views

Zoom in on the side view. This view does not convey many details of the assembly. A section view through the center of the large gear, revealing interior details, would be more useful. Section views are discussed in Chapter 8. Delete the side view by right-clicking on the view and selecting **Delete** in the shortcut menu. Then, right-click on the front view and select **Drawing Views>Section View** in the shortcut menu. Continue as follows.

1. Hover over the center of the large gear and acquire the center point—do not pick.
2. Slowly move the cursor straight up so a dotted line is being projected from the center of the gear. Pick a point that is outside of the gear and inline with the gear center.
3. Move the cursor straight down through the center past the bottom of the gear and pick that point. Refer to **Figure 16-4.**
4. The **Section View** dialog box appears. This dialog box allows you to exclude components from sectioning, change the direction of the view, and adjust hatching for adjacent parts. You will make these adjustments after placing the view, so pick **OK** to close the dialog box.

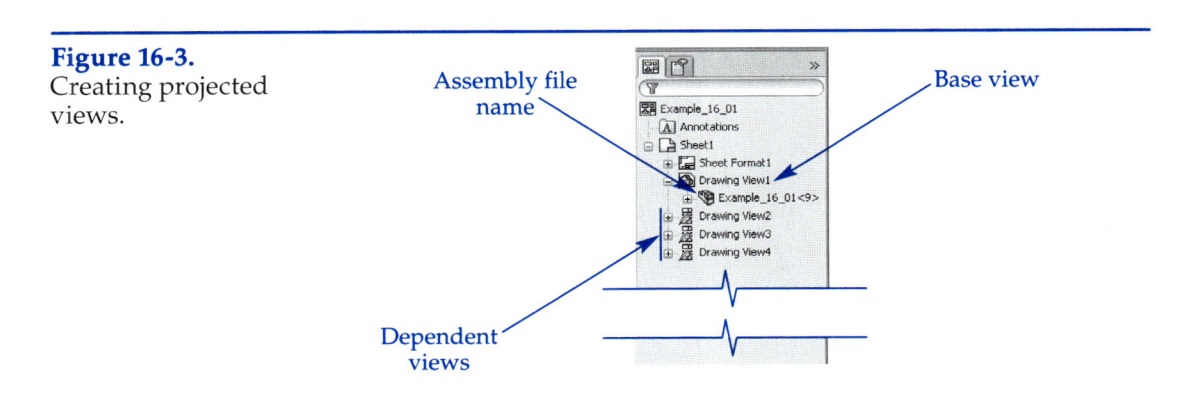

Figure 16-3.
Creating projected views.

Figure 16-4.
Creating a section view.

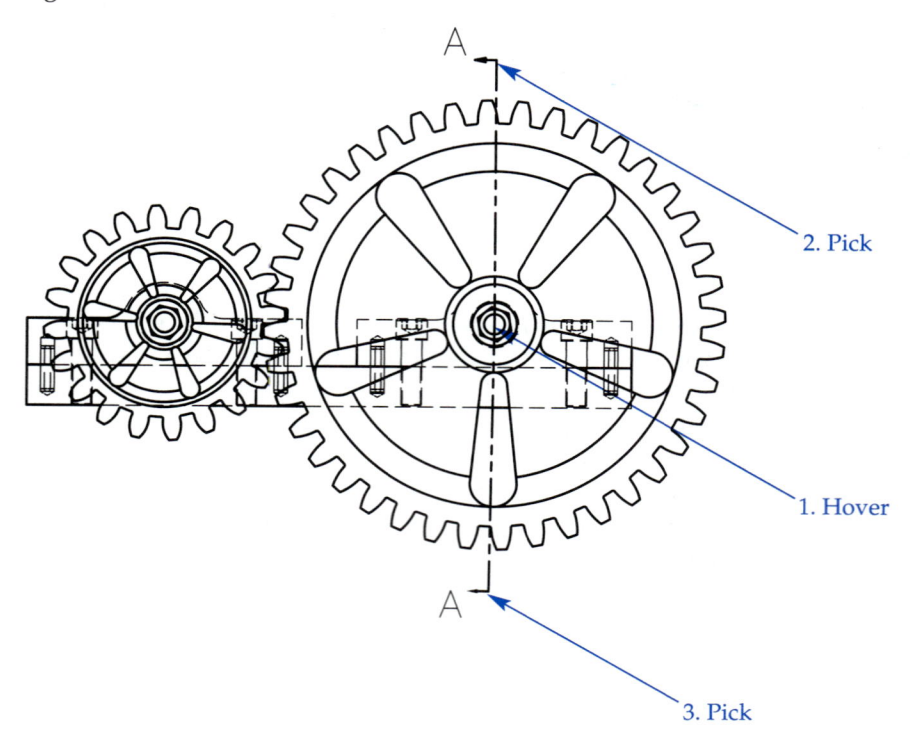

5. Drag the section view to the right of the front view and pick to place it. In the **Section View Property Manager**, check the settings in the **Section Line** rollout. If the section label is anything other than A in the **Label** text box, change it to A. Also, the section line arrows in the front view should be pointing to the left. If not, check the **Flip direction** check box. Next, set the display style of the view to Hidden Lines Removed. Pick the green check mark button to close the **Section View Property Manager**.

Now, zoom in on SECTION A-A. Notice that the section lines in the bearing blocks are in the same direction as the base. Right-click on the view and select **Properties...** from the shortcut menu. When the **Drawing View Properties** dialog box appears, pick the **Section Scope** tab. See **Figure 16-5**. The options in this tab are identical to those in the **Section View** dialog box. Check the **Auto hatching** check box and then pick **OK**. This will change the direction of section lines for adjacent parts.

Also notice that all of the parts in the assembly are sectioned. In accepted drafting conventions, shafts, fasteners, and most standard components are not sectioned. The section lines need to be removed from these parts. Right-click on the view and select **Properties...** from the shortcut menu. Pick on the **Section Scope** tab of the **Drawing View Properties** dialog box. A blue box appears on the left side of the dialog box. As you pick components in the view, their names will appear in the box and the components will be excluded from sectioning. Pick the shaft, nut, washer, and one of the bushings. You may have to zoom in when selecting parts; if you accidentally pick on a part more than once, the part will be removed from the list. When finished selecting components, pick **OK** to exit the dialog box. Now, SECTION A-A follows accepted drafting conventions. See **Figure 16-6**. Whether the bushing is sectioned or not may depend on a given corporate standard.

You can easily change the section view into an isometric view. Right-click on the view and select **Isometric Section View** from the shortcut menu. Now change the display style to Shaded. Return to the section view and study the results.

Figure 16-5.
The **Section Scope** tab of the **Drawing View Properties** dialog box is used to control the sectioning applied to the section view.

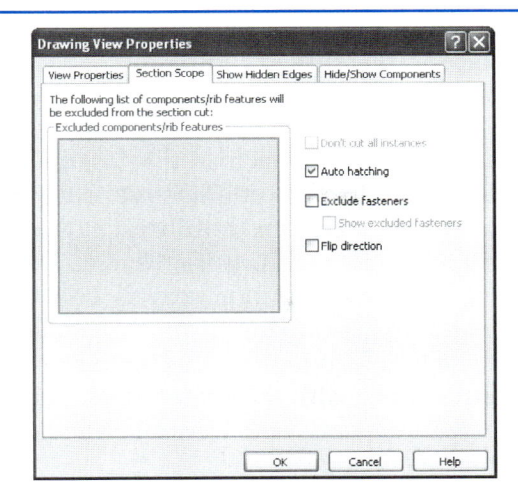

Figure 16-6.
The section view after removing section lining from standard components.

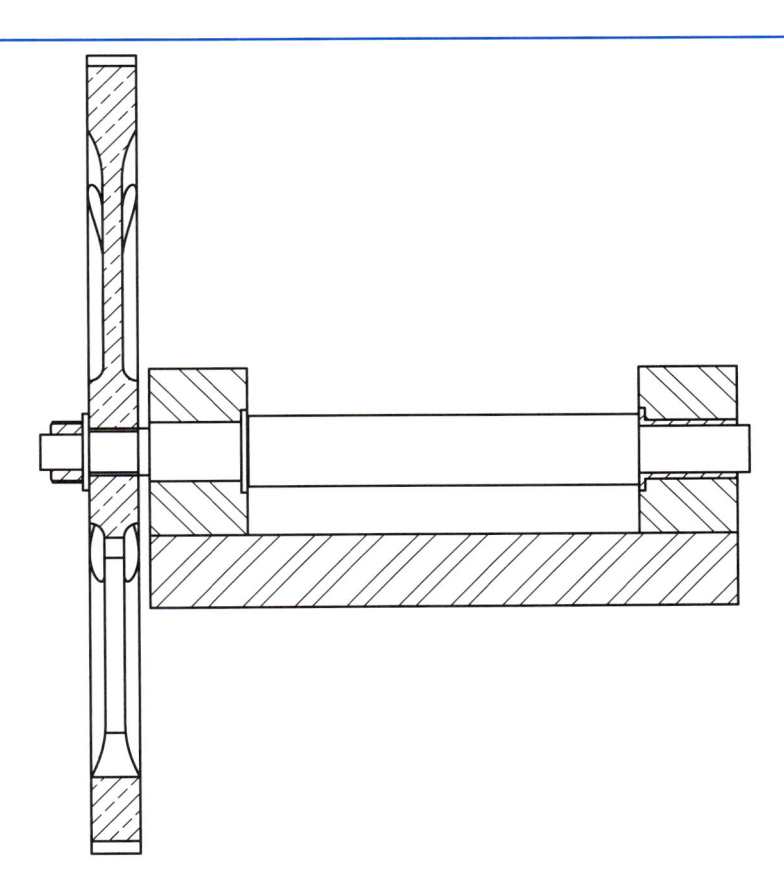

Creating Annotations

As you learned in Chapter 9, various types of annotations can be applied to 2D drawings. All of the annotations that can be applied to a part drawing are available for an assembly drawing. This section discusses some of these annotations.

Adding Dimensions

Dimensioning an assembly is similar to dimensioning a part. You can add model dimensions or reference dimensions to an assembly drawing. For this example, you will add reference dimensions to the top, front, and section views. Reference dimensions are

Chapter 16   Assembly Drawings

added to assembly drawings in the same way they are added to part drawings. After activating the appropriate dimensioning tool, select the part edges or centerlines. Once the proper geometry is selected, the dimension can be placed on the drawing.

Before applying dimensions to the views, change the display style of the front view to Hidden Lines Removed. Also, access the **Document Properties** tab of the options/properties dialog box and pick on Dimensions to change the primary precision setting to 2 places. This creates a custom drafting standard named ANSI-MODIFIED in the file. Rename the custom standard to Chapter_16. This is done by picking on Drafting Standard and then picking the **Rename** button next to the **Overall drafting standard** drop-down list. Next, change the size of dimension and annotation text in the drawing. Pick on Dimensions and select the **Font...** button in the **Text** area to change the text height for notes to .25". Also, check the **Scale with dimension height** check box in the **Arrows** area. Change the text height for annotations and view labels by selecting the appropriate items in the **Document Properties** tab.

You will now create centerlines and center marks in the top view using the **Centerline** and **Center Mark** tools. See **Figure 16-7**. When placing the vertical centerlines, you may need to drag them so that they extend past the upper and lower ends of the assembly. After adding the centerlines and center marks, use the **Smart Dimension** tool to place the dimensions as shown in **Figure 16-7** to complete the top view. In the front view, create center marks at the centers of the two gears using the **Center Mark** tool. Then place a horizontal dimension between the two gears. This documents the distance between the two gear shafts. Use the endpoints of the center marks to place the dimension. When selecting the center mark of the large gear, hover over the section line to highlight it, right-click, and select **Select Other** from the shortcut menu. Then, select Center Mark from the **Select Other** dialog box. This selects the center mark instead of the section line. In the section view, place the dimensions shown in **Figure 16-8**.

After placing a dimension, you may need to alter the value or the appearance of the dimension text. There are several techniques available, as described in the next sections. Choose the appropriate one for the situation at hand.

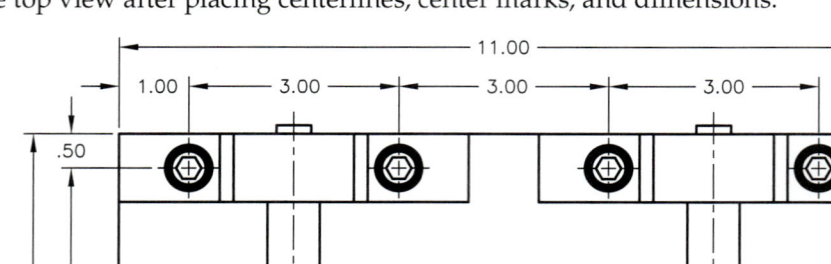

Figure 16-7.
The top view after placing centerlines, center marks, and dimensions.

Figure 16-8.
The section view with dimensions.

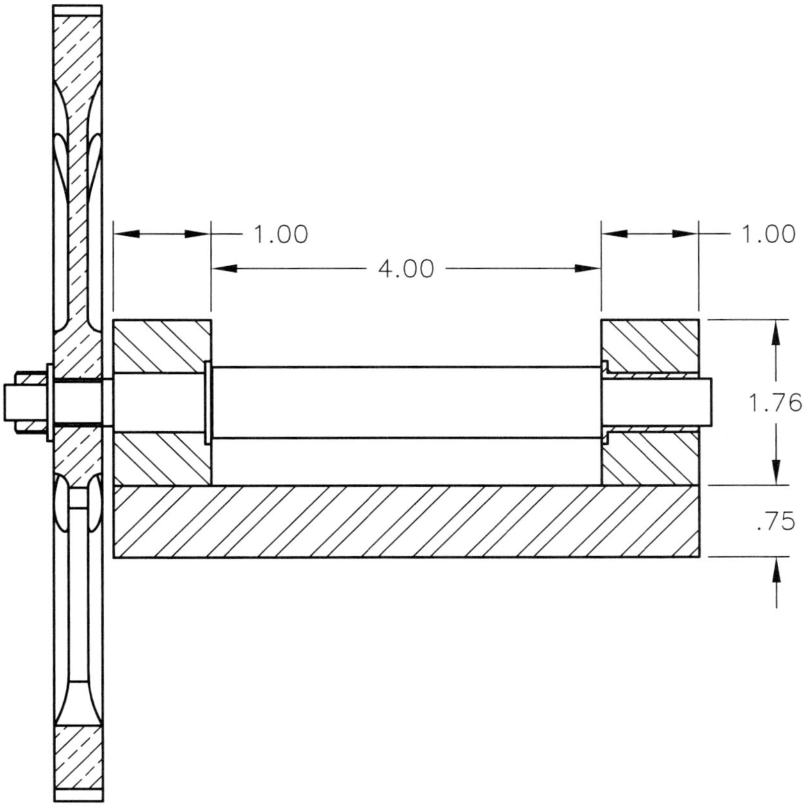

Adding text to the default dimension text

At times, text will need to be added to a reference dimension, such as TYP, REF, or 6X. To do so, pick on the dimension text; the **Dimension Property Manager** is displayed. In the **Dimension Text** rollout, the default value is enclosed in chevrons and appears as <DIM>. The default value can be deleted, but you'll get a message informing you that the tolerance display will be disabled if you delete the dimension value. You are asked whether you want to continue to do this; in most cases, you don't. Instead, you can add text to the dimension by placing the cursor at the end of the chevrons (or at the beginning) and then typing the necessary text.

Do this for the two dimensions in the top view shown in **Figure 16-9.** To add TYP to the 1.00 dimension, you will have to place the cursor at the end of the chevrons and press [Enter] to start a new line. For the .50 dimension, just start typing after the chevrons. The TYP designation signifies that those dimension values are typical for similar features in the assembly. In this case, the distance from the corner of the base plate to the location of the hole is typical for all similar holes.

Adding tolerancing information

To add a tolerance, pick on the dimension to display the **Dimension Property Manager**. In the **Tolerance/ Precision** rollout, use the **Tolerance Type** drop-down list to select the type of tolerance desired. As shown in **Figure 16-10,** change the 6.00 dimension between the gears in the front view to a maximum tolerance. In the **Tolerance/ Precision** rollout, you can use the **Unit Precision** drop-down list to set the number of decimal places used in the value.

Replacing the dimension text

Occasionally, you will need to replace the default dimension text. Add a thickness dimension to the large gear shown in the top view, **Figure 16-11.** Then, in the

Figure 16-9.
Adding text to dimensions.

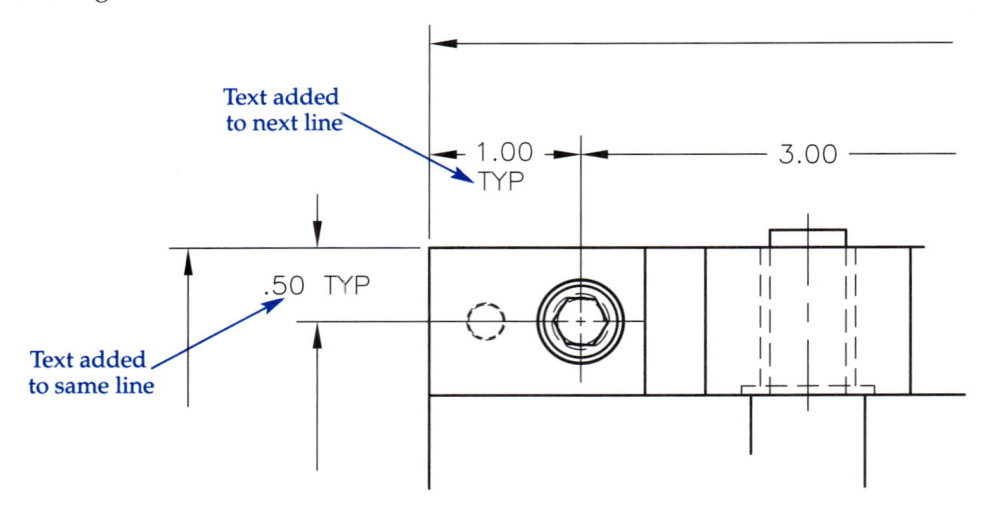

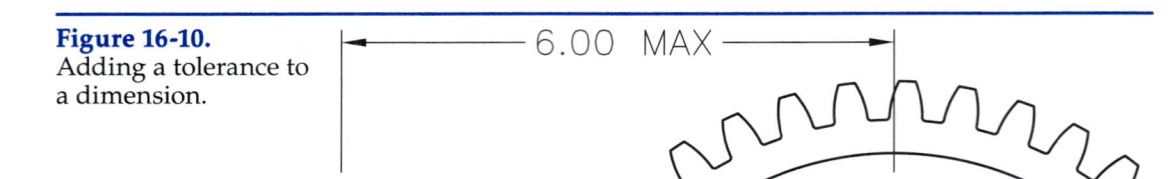

Figure 16-10.
Adding a tolerance to a dimension.

Dimension Text rollout of the **Dimension Property Manager**, highlight the default value <DIM> and type in the letter S. Pick the **Yes** button in the warning box and finish completing the text to read SEE VENDOR PRINT. Pick the green check mark button to finish. This dimension now displays the text you entered in place of the default value.

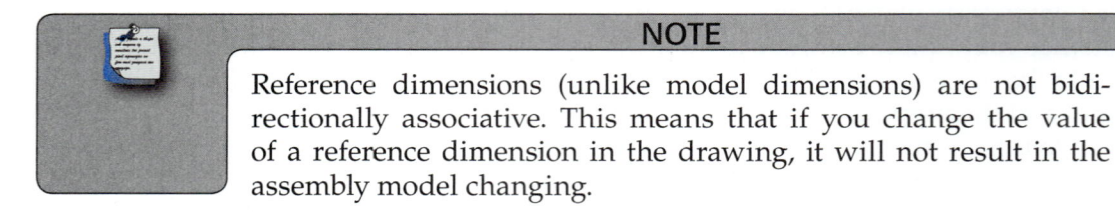

> **NOTE**
>
> Reference dimensions (unlike model dimensions) are not bidirectionally associative. This means that if you change the value of a reference dimension in the drawing, it will not result in the assembly model changing.

Adding Leader Text

Leader text is added to an assembly drawing in the same manner it is added to a part drawing. See **Figure 16-12**. To add leader text, pick the **Note** button in the **Annotation** tab of the **Command Manager**. In the **Leader** rollout of the **Note Property Manager**, pick the **Leader Left** button to place a left-handed dogleg leader. Then, pick a point on a tooth of the large gear and pick in the drawing to locate the text. A text box and the **Formatting** toolbar both appear. Type the text shown in the figure in the default format and then pick the green check mark button. Add a leader note on the smaller gear with the text 20T PINION GEAR.

Creating a Bill of Materials (BOM)

A *bill of materials (BOM)* is a table of information used to identify and describe the parts required for an assembly. There are two types of BOMs that can be created—a

Figure 16-11.
Replacing the dimension with a note.

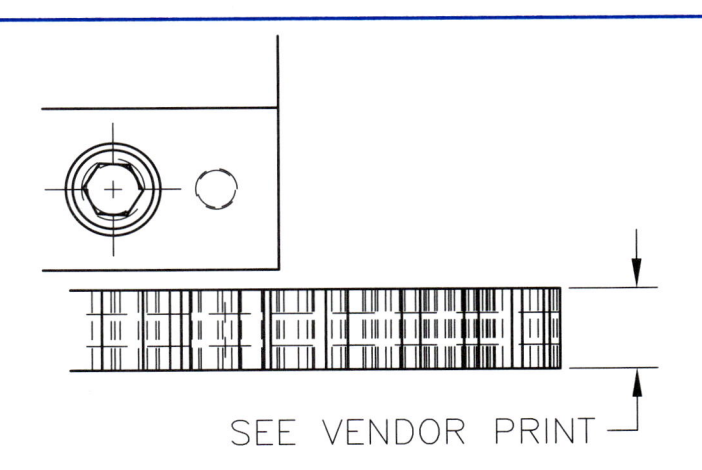

Figure 16-12.
Adding leader text.

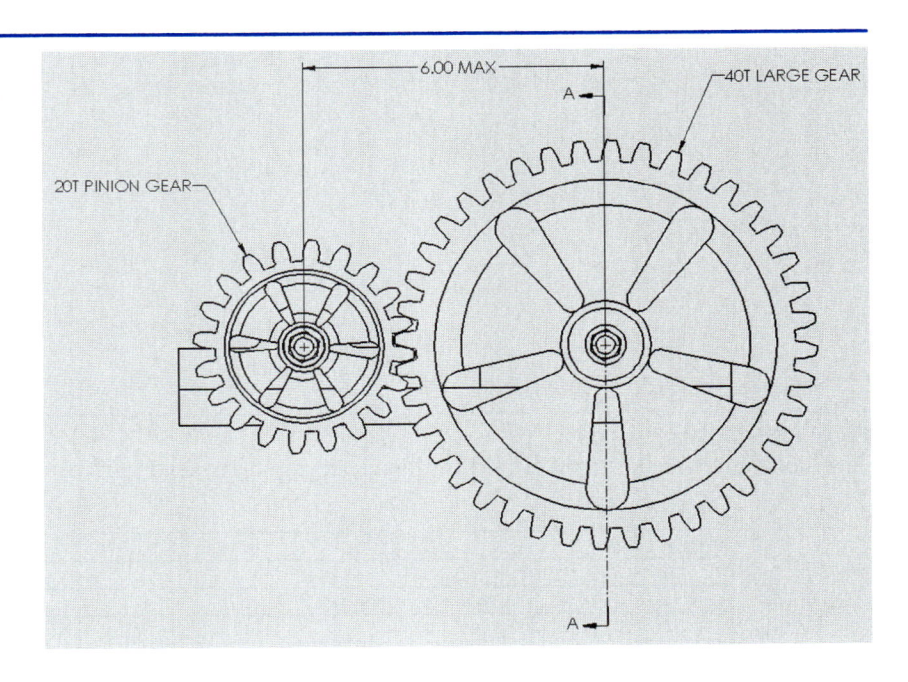

table-based BOM and an Excel-based BOM. A drawing can contain either one, but not both. This section will describe the use of a table-based BOM in an assembly drawing. The table format is flexible and can contain both information associated with the part and nonassociated details. We'll start by inputting the default BOM into the assembly drawing.

In the **Annotation** tab of the **Command Manager**, select **Bill of Materials** in the **Tables** drop-down list. Pick a view in the drawing to specify the model for the BOM. Since all views in this drawing are generated from the same model, you can pick any one of them.

In the **Bill of Materials Property Manager**, the **BOM Type** rollout has three options. See **Figure 16-13.** These options are important for assemblies that contain subassemblies where you might only want the top level of the subassemblies listed. The **Top-level only** option lists top-level parts and subassemblies, but not parts in the subassemblies. The **Parts only** option is used to list all the parts in the assembly and the subassemblies, but not the subassemblies themselves. The **Indented** option is used to list subassemblies and parts, and indents the subassembly parts below the subassemblies.

Since this assembly contains only parts, the default **Top-level only** option is appropriate. Pick the green check mark button and locate the BOM in the upper-right corner of the drawing. Zoom in on the BOM. See **Figure 16-14.**

Chapter 16 Assembly Drawings

Figure 16-13.
The **Bill of Materials** Property Manager.

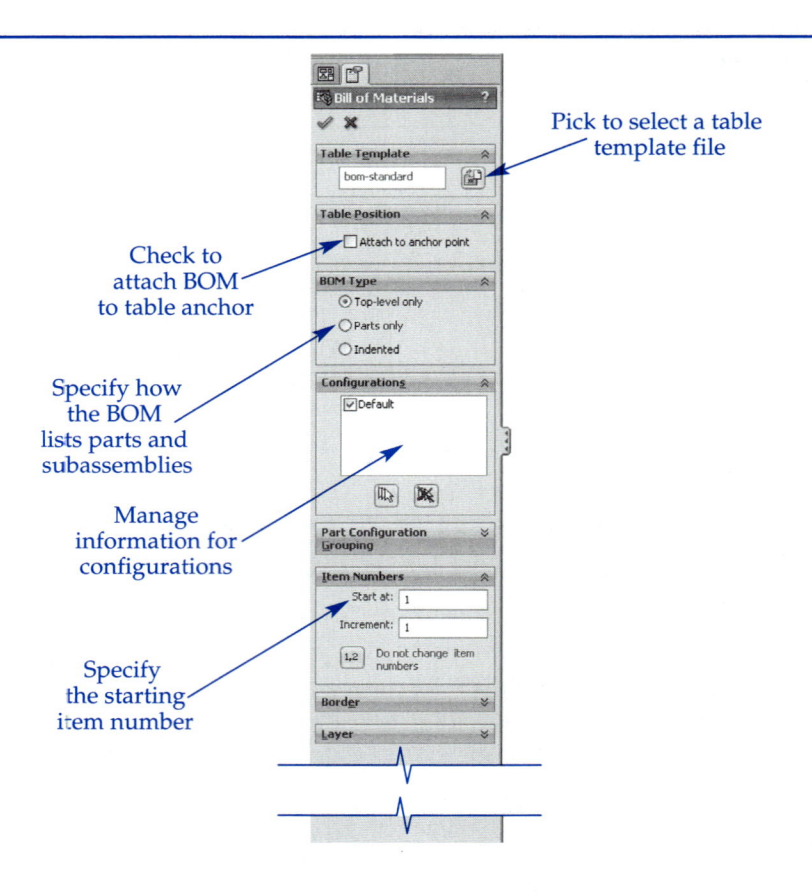

- Pick to select a table template file
- Check to attach BOM to table anchor
- Specify how the BOM lists parts and subassemblies
- Manage information for configurations
- Specify the starting item number

Figure 16-14.
A bill of materials has been added to the upper-right corner of the drawing.

ITEM NO.	PART NUMBER	DESCRIPTION	QTY.
1	Base		1
2	CR_Locating_Pin		8
3	Bearing_Block	MACHINED ON CNC #3	4
4	Bushing		4
5	Shaft		2
6	Pinion_Gear		1
7	Large_Gear		1
8	Washer_-375		2
9	Hex_Nut_-375_24		2
10	Cap_Screw		8

There are four columns in the BOM. The item number, part number, and quantity columns are required and cannot be deleted. The description column is displayed by default, but it can be deleted. Information that is displayed in the description column must be added to a part in order for it to display. As you can see, the bearing block is the only part with a description added, but we'll now add one for another part.

Open the file Bushing.sldprt. Select **File>Properties...** to display the **Summary Information** dialog box and pick the **Custom** tab. In row two, pick in the **Property Name** field to activate the pull-down menu. Select Description from the pull-down menu. In the **Value/Text Expression** field, input PURCHASED PART. In the **BOM quantity:** drop-down list, select Description. See **Figure 16-15**. Pick **OK** to close the dialog box. When you return

Figure 16-15.
Entering a value for the description property in the **Summary Information** dialog box.

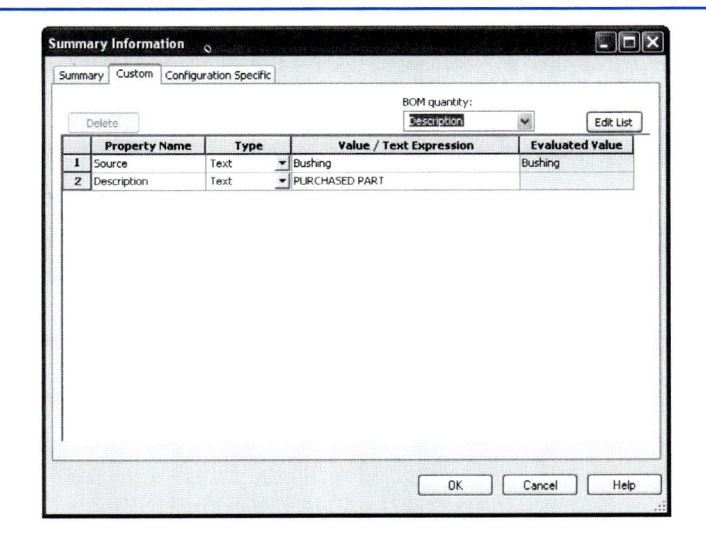

to the drawing file, the text appears in the BOM. See **Figure 16-16.** By default, the BOM is automatically updated when a change is made in the assembly. This is a system setting that can be accessed by picking Tables>Bill of Materials in the **Document Properties** tab of the options/properties dialog box. By default, the **Automatic update of BOM** check box is checked.

You can manually input text into any field in the BOM, but to do so, you must break with the data in the external model. For example, double-click in the description field for the shaft. A warning box appears and asks whether you want to break the link. Select **Break Link** and then type in CASE HARDEN in the field. To exit table editing, pick on the drawing outside the BOM. If you need to open the **Bill of Materials Property Manager**, pick on any field in the bill of materials and then pick on the move cursor in the upper-left corner.

Several other types of BOMs can be created when you first access the **Bill of Materials Property Manager**. Start by opening the file Bearing_Block.sldprt. Select **File>Properties…** to open the **Summary Information** dialog box. Notice that the Weight property has been defined and the value is the mass of the bearing block. Now return to the drawing file and create a new bill of materials using the **Bill of Materials** tool. In the **Bill of Materials Property Manager**, pick the **Open table template for Bill of Materials** button in the **Table Template**

Figure 16-16.
The updated bill of materials.

ITEM NO.	PART NUMBER	DESCRIPTION	QTY.
1	Base		1
2	CR_Locating_Pin		8
3	Bearing_Block	MACHINED ON CNC #3	4
4	Bushing	PURCHASED PART	4
5	Shaft		2
6	Pinion_Gear		1
7	Large_Gear		1
8	Washer_-375		2
9	Hex_Nut_-375_24		2
10	Cap_Screw		8

rollout. There are seven different table templates. Select the bom-weight template file. Place the BOM anywhere on the drawing and zoom into it. Note the weight column and the value for the bearing block. Delete this BOM by right-clicking on it and selecting **Delete>Table**.

Adding Balloons

Now that you have a BOM on the drawing, you can add *balloons*. These are numbered callouts that identify the components of an assembly. The numbers are used to correlate the items in a BOM to the drawing. They can be put on any view, but we'll use the isometric view. Zoom into the view. Balloons usually look better in line drawings than in shaded views, so change the display style to Hidden Lines Removed.

There are two tools in the **Annotation** tab of the **Command Manager** used to create balloons: **Balloon** and **Auto Balloon**. Start with the **Balloon** tool. Selecting this tool displays the **Balloon Property Manager**. See **Figure 16-17**. In the **Balloon Settings** rollout, the default balloon style is Circular, but there are nine other types. The default balloon size is 2 characters and that should be sufficient if the text is the item number and the total number of parts is less than 100. Pick on each part in the view and then locate the balloon. Note that there is a difference in the type of leader used depending on where you pick the part. If it's an edge, the leader has a filled arrowhead. If you pick on a face, the leader is a dot. Now put some balloons in the front view. The same part can have a balloon in several views, but that is not standard practice. A balloon can be deleted by picking on it and pressing the [Delete] key. Delete all the balloons except those on the two gears and one of the cap screws in the isometric view.

The **Auto Balloon** tool will place balloons in a view on all parts that do not have balloons in any other view. Select the top view, zoom in on the view, and select the **Auto Balloon** button in the **Annotation** tab of the **Command Manager**. The **Auto Balloon Property Manager** appears. In the **Balloon Layout** rollout, select the Circular pattern option and make sure the **Ignore multiple instances** check box is checked. Select the **Balloon Edges** radio button. With this option, the balloon leaders are attached to part edges. Note that every unique part has a balloon attached to it except for the gears and the cap screw, and that is due to the balloons in the isometric view. Pick the green check mark button. If a balloon is in an inappropriate location, you can pick it and drag it to anywhere you want. Now, delete these balloons and repeat the **Auto Balloon** tool. Place the remaining balloons in the isometric view. Create a circular pattern. Uncheck the **Ignore multiple instances** check box to see the results. Then, change the setting back and pick the green check mark button. See **Figure 16-18**. Save and close all files.

Figure 16-17.
The **Balloon Property Manager**.

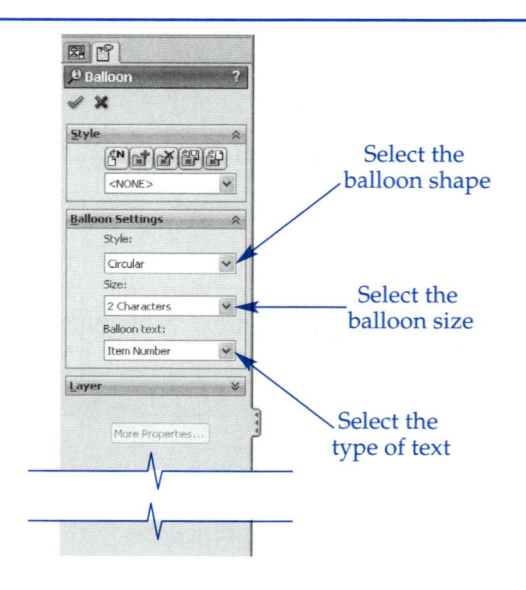

Figure 16-18.
The isometric view after using the **Auto Balloon** tool.

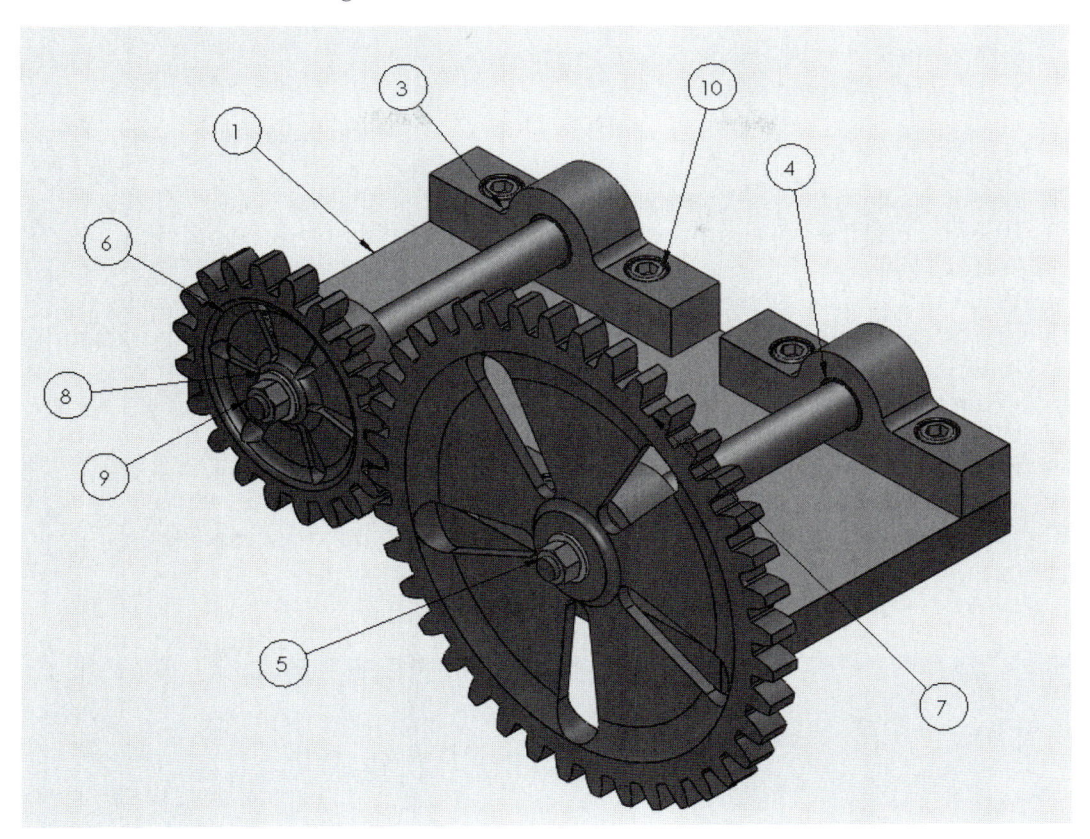

PROFESSIONAL TIP

When working with assembly drawings, it is common to have multiple sheets within the drawing file. This allows you to show part details when you cannot fit all of the necessary views on a single sheet. You can create additional sheets in a drawing file by right-clicking on Sheet1 in the design tree and selecting **Add Sheet...** from the shortcut menu. The new sheet will appear in the design tree and can be used to add views. You can change the sheet settings by accessing the **Sheet Properties** dialog box. Adding sheets to a drawing file allows you to have multiple sheets in the file without having separate drawing files. You can quickly switch between sheets in the file by picking on the named tabs that appear at the bottom of the graphics window.

Chapter 16 Assembly Drawings

Chapter Test

Answer the following questions on a separate sheet of paper or complete the electronic chapter test on the student website.
www.g-wlearning.com/CAD

1. What tool is used to project additional views from the base view in an assembly drawing?
2. Briefly explain how to change the display style of a view.
3. Briefly describe how to prevent certain components from being sectioned in a section view.
4. What tool is used to place reference dimensions in an assembly drawing?
5. Briefly explain how to edit a reference dimension to add the text characters TYP following the dimension.
6. What tool is used to place a leader note?
7. What is a *bill of materials?*
8. Describe how to add a bill of materials to an assembly drawing.
9. What is a *balloon?*
10. What tool is used to automatically add balloons to the drawing?

Chapter Exercises

Complete the chapter exercises on the student website.
www.g-wlearning.com/CAD

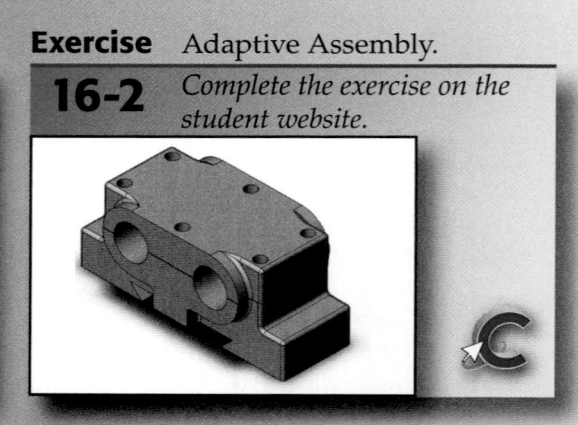

Exercise 16-1 Single Cylinder Engine. Complete the exercise on the student website.

Exercise 16-2 Adaptive Assembly. Complete the exercise on the student website.

Exercise 16-3 Sliding Clamp. Complete the exercise on the student website.

Chapter 17

Exploded Views and Animations

Objectives

After completing this chapter, you will be able to:

- Create exploded views.
- Modify steps in exploded views.
- Rearrange the order of steps in an exploded view.
- Use configurations to create multiple exploded views.
- Animate exploded views.
- Modify animations of exploded views to make the components move at the correct time and speed.
- Set different view angles in an animation to emphasize specific areas of an assembly.

Exploded Views

To show how an assembly is put together or taken apart, an exploded view of a design can be created. An *exploded view* consists of multiple steps that can be used to visualize the way parts fit together. Each step is known as an *explode step.* A single assembly file can contain multiple configurations with various exploded views of the assembly. However, each configuration of an assembly can contain only one exploded view.

Once exploded, the view can be animated to reassemble the components. Video files in AVI format can be created from the exploded view. The videos can then be viewed outside of SolidWorks. This allows you to share the animated exploded view with others who do not have SolidWorks.

A drawer for a wooden valet will be used as an example to study the features, principles, and steps in creating exploded views. The valet is designed to be built with simple hand tools, such as a saw, drill, and screwdriver. The final assembly of the components is shown in **Figure 17-1.**

In this chapter, you will be working on two of the subassemblies in the valet. The drawer for the valet consists of several parts and a drawer front subassembly. The first

Figure 17-1.
These two components from a valet assembly will be used in this chapter.

17E01_Drawer_Box_Top.sldasm

17E01_Drawer_Front.sldasm

subassembly you will work on is the drawer box top. Open the file **17E01_Drawer_Box_Top.sldasm** located in the Example_17_01 folder. See **Figure 17-2.**

Creating an Exploded View

Exploded views are created by adding explode steps to an assembly. Since the assembly is designed with components in their final locations, the explode steps must be created in an order opposite of that used to assemble the design. This can be thought of as taking apart the product.

Pick the **Exploded View** button on the **Assembly** tab of the **Command Manager**. Alternately, you can right-click on a configuration name in the **Configuration Manager**

Figure 17-2.
The box top assembly shown exploded.

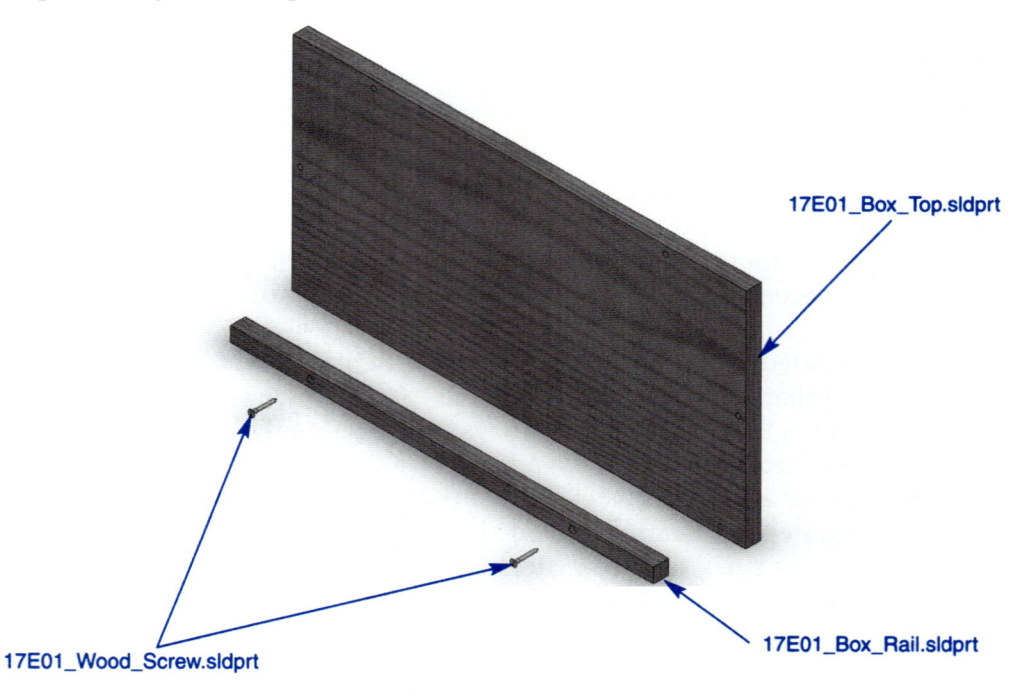

17E01_Box_Top.sldprt

17E01_Wood_Screw.sldprt

17E01_Box_Rail.sldprt

and select **New Exploded View** from the shortcut menu. In either case, the **Explode Property Manager** is displayed, **Figure 17-3**.

A *manipulator* is used to set the direction the selected components move in an explode step. The manipulator consists of three handles and appears similar to the coordinate system triad. For each explode step, the manipulator is aligned by default to the axes of the assembly, but it can be oriented to align with an edge or face of a component if needed. Simply pick the center ball of the manipulator and drag it to an edge of the part. The Z axis of the manipulator is aligned with the edge.

To add a translational (movement) explode step, select one or more components. Then, use the manipulator to pick a direction for the step. Components can be freely dragged to a distance from their assembled position or a value can be entered in the current units to precisely place the part. Continue as follows to create an exploded view of the 17E01_Drawer_Box_Top.sldasm assembly. Normally, the two wood screws would be selected for the first explode step. However, in order to demonstrate editing exploded views later in the chapter, the box rail will be moved first.

1. With the **Components of the explode step** selection box in the **Settings** rollout active, select the box rail, either in the graphics window or using the flyout design tree. The name of the component is displayed in the selection box. Also, the manipulator appears in the graphics window.
2. Pick the blue (Z) axis on the manipulator to set the direction of movement. The other axes on the manipulator are hidden. Make sure the blue axis is pointing away from the box top part. If it is pointing toward the box top, pick the **Reverse Direction** button in the **Settings** rollout.
3. In the **Options** rollout, uncheck the **Auto-space components after drag** check box if it is checked.

Figure 17-3.
Moving the rail as the first explode step in the exploded view.

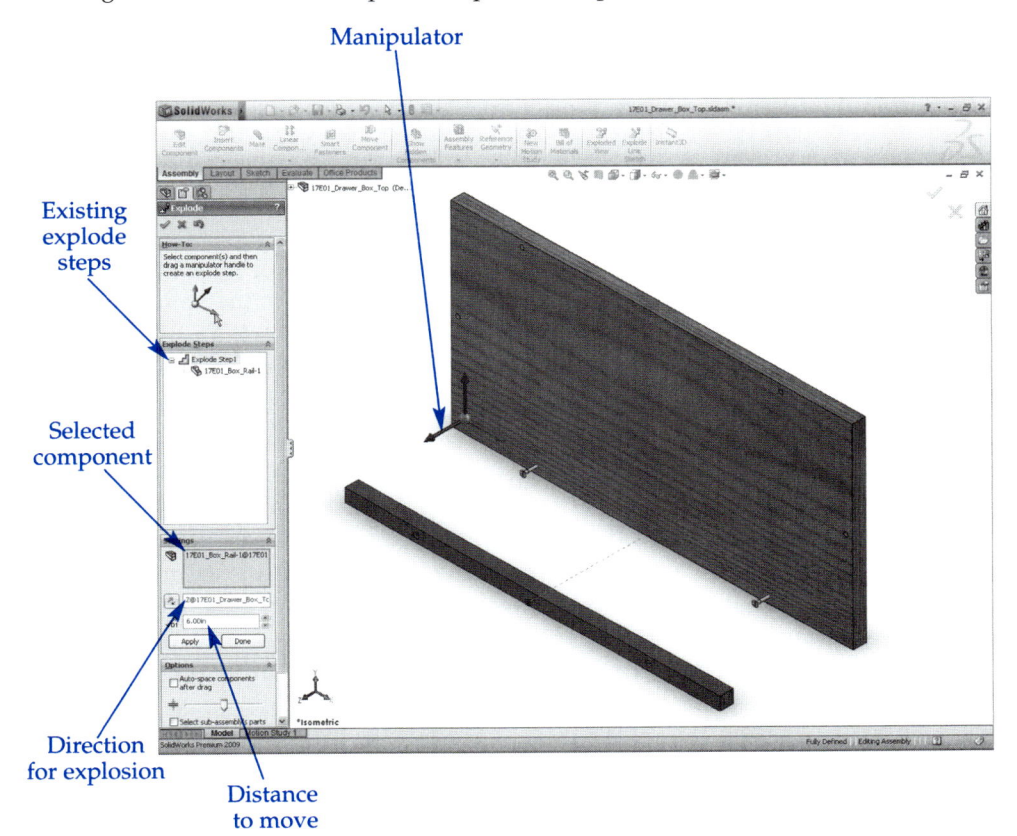

Chapter 17 Exploded Views and Animations 285

4. In the graphics window, drag the manipulator until the box rail is about 1" or 2" away from the box top. When the mouse button is released, the step is created and displayed as Explode Step1 in the **Explode Steps** rollout.
5. Press the [Ctrl] key and select the two wood screws.
6. Using the manipulator, set the direction of movement away from the box top (in the same direction the rail moved).
7. Enter 6 in the **Explode distance** text box in the **Settings** rollout and pick the **Apply** button. A second explode step is added.
8. Pick the green check mark button at the top of the **Explode Property Manager** to create the exploded view.

The assembly now appears in its exploded state. Display the **Configuration Manager**. Note that ExplView1 has been added to the branch for the Default configuration. This is the exploded view.

To collapse an exploded view, right-click anywhere in the graphics window or on ExplView1 in the **Configuration Manager** and select **Collapse** from the shortcut menu. The assembly returns to an assembled state and ExplView1 is grayed out in the **Configuration Manager** to show the exploded view has been suppressed. To view the assembly in its exploded state again, double-click ExplView1 in the **Configuration Manager**. You can also right-click on the name of the exploded view in the **Configuration Manager** and select **Explode** from the shortcut menu.

PROFESSIONAL TIP

As shown above, an exact value can be set for the explode distance by selecting a direction on the manipulator, entering the distance for the explode step in the **Explode distance** text box in the **Settings** rollout of the **Explode Property Manager**, and picking the **Apply** button in the rollout. This allows you to be more precise with the explode steps in the exploded views you create.

Animating Exploded Views

An exploded view can be presented as an animation to view the movement of components in the order in which they were exploded. In the **Configuration Manager**, right-click on the name of the exploded view and select either **Animate explode** or **Animate collapse** from the shortcut menu. If the view is currently exploded, **Animate collapse** appears in the menu. If the view is currently collapsed, **Animate explode** appears in the menu. After making the menu selection, the **Animation Controller** toolbar is displayed and the components are animated. See **Figure 17-4.**

The **Animation Controller** toolbar is used to control the speed of the animation as well as how the animation is presented. Picking the **Slow Play** or **Fast Play** button on the right-hand side of the toolbar decreases or increases the playback speed. If neither button is selected, playback speed is normal. To play the animation, pick the **Play** button.

Picking the **Playback Mode: Loop** button forces the animation to repeat from the beginning when played. Picking the **Playback Mode: Reciprocate** button forces the animation to play in a continuous loop from beginning to end and back to the beginning. This appears as though the assembly is being continuously assembled and disassembled. The **Playback Mode: Normal** button causes the animation to play once and then stop.

SolidWorks assigns an equal amount of time to each explode step in the exploded view. The speed of the components during the animation is controlled by the distance each has to travel and the number of steps to complete the movement. The screws

Figure 17-4.
Playing an animation of the exploded view.

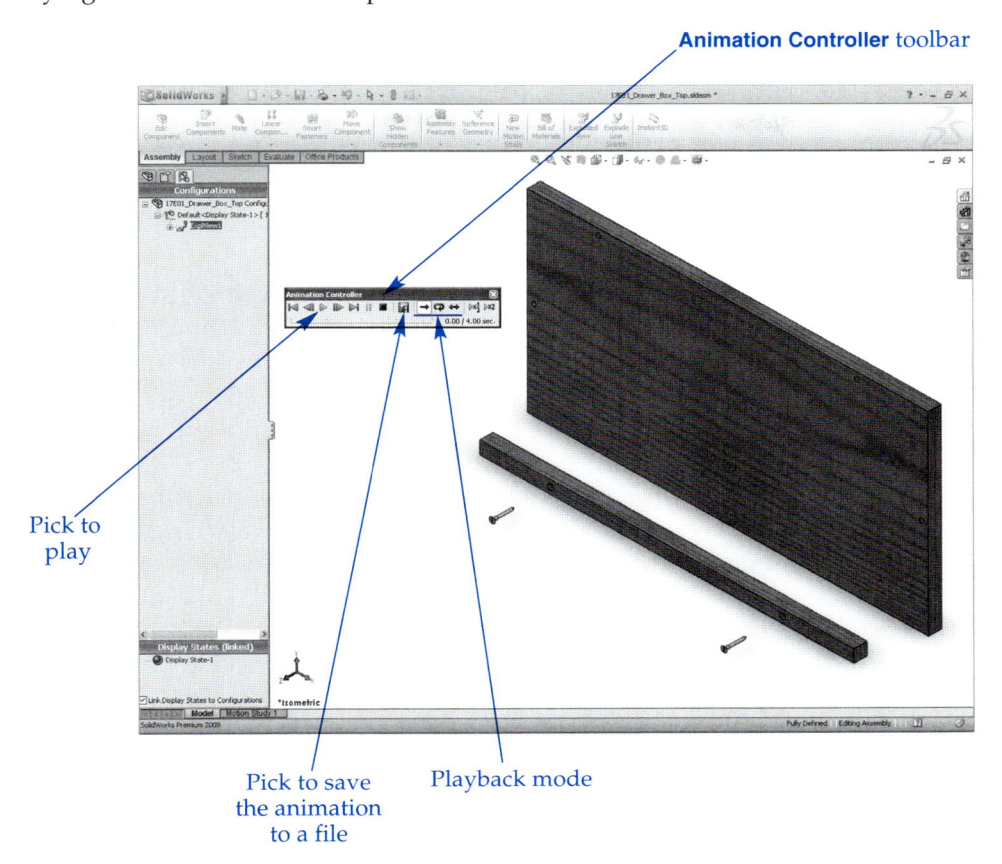

move quickly since they travel 6″. Compare this with the shorter distance the rail must travel during its step. Later in this chapter, the **Motion Manager** will be used to fine tune the speed of steps in an animated exploded view.

> **NOTE**
>
> The animation of an exploded view is a calculation-intensive operation and may require a high-end graphics card. If parts "drop out" of the animation or do not appear when they should, it is likely that your graphics card is not up to the task.

Editing Exploded Views

The screws should be assembled after the rail moves into place. However, notice how they move through the rail and then the rail moves over the screws. The explode steps must be reordered to accurately display the assembly operations. One wood screw will also be removed from the second explode step and a new step will be added. If the animation is playing, stop it by picking the **Stop** button and then close the **Animation Controller** toolbar.

In the **Configuration Manager**, right-click the name of the exploded view and select **Edit Feature** from the shortcut menu. The **Explode Property Manager** is displayed. This is the same **Property Manager** used to create the exploded view. The existing steps are listed in the **Explode Steps** rollout. Expand the tree for each step to see which components are moved, **Figure 17-5A**.

Figure 17-5.
A—The initial order of the first two steps. B—The order of the first two explode steps are reversed. C—A third explode step has been added and the order rearranged.

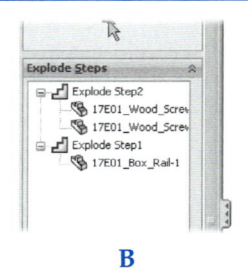

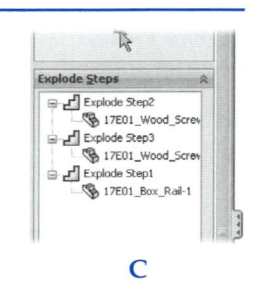

          A   B   C

The animated motion is applied in order of the steps in the **Explode Steps** rollout, from top to bottom. To correct the motion, the existing order of steps needs to be reversed. In the **Explode Steps** rollout, drag Explode Step1 and drop it onto Explode Step2. Now, Explode Step2 appears above Explode Step1, **Figure 17-5B.** Also, right-click on Wood_Screw-2 in Explode Step2 and select **Delete** from the shortcut menu. This removes the screw from the explode step.

Now, select Wood_Screw-2 in the graphics window or the flyout design tree. On the manipulator, pick the blue axis to set the direction of motion away from the drawer top. Next, enter 6 in the **Explode distance** text box in the **Settings** rollout. Finally, pick the **Apply** button in the rollout and then the **Done** button to add the explode step.

Notice that Explode Step3 has been added to the **Explode Steps** rollout. However, it is at the bottom of the list, which means the second screw will move after the rail. Drag Explode Step3 and drop it onto Explode Step2. This reorders the steps so the two wood screws are moved before the rail. See **Figure 17-5C.** The first screw moves before the second screw.

Pick the green check mark button at the top of the **Explode Property Manager** to apply the changes to the ExplView1. Now, when the exploded view is animated, the rail is assembled first and then the screws are assembled one at a time. After the animation plays, close the **Animation Controller** toolbar. Then, collapse the view if necessary to return the assembly to its assembled state.

To change the distance moved in an explode step, expand the tree for the exploded view in the **Configuration Manager**. Then, right-click on the step to change and select **Edit Feature** from the shortcut menu. The **Explode Property Manager** is displayed with the explode distance for the step shown in the **Explode distance** text box in the **Settings** rollout. See **Figure 17-6.** For this example, right-click on the explode step for the rail (Explode Step1), enter 3 in the **Explode distance** text box, and pick the **Apply** button in the rollout. Then, pick the **Done** button in the rollout to change the explode distance for the step. Finally, close the **Property Manager**.

Now, animate the exploded view. Notice how the rail moves farther away from the top than it did before. Save the assembly file.

PROFESSIONAL TIP
When editing an explode step, the manipulator can be dragged to set a new distance. However, this is not a precise method of specifying a distance. Entering a specific distance in the **Explode distance** text box, as described above, may be a better method.

Adding Exploded Views to a Drawing

Start a new drawing (.slddrw) file based on an A-size sheet. Insert an isometric view of 17E01_Drawer_Box_Top.sldasm to the drawing. To change to the exploded view, right-click on it and choose **Properties...** from the shortcut menu. In the **Drawing View Prop-**

Figure 17-6.
Editing an explode step.

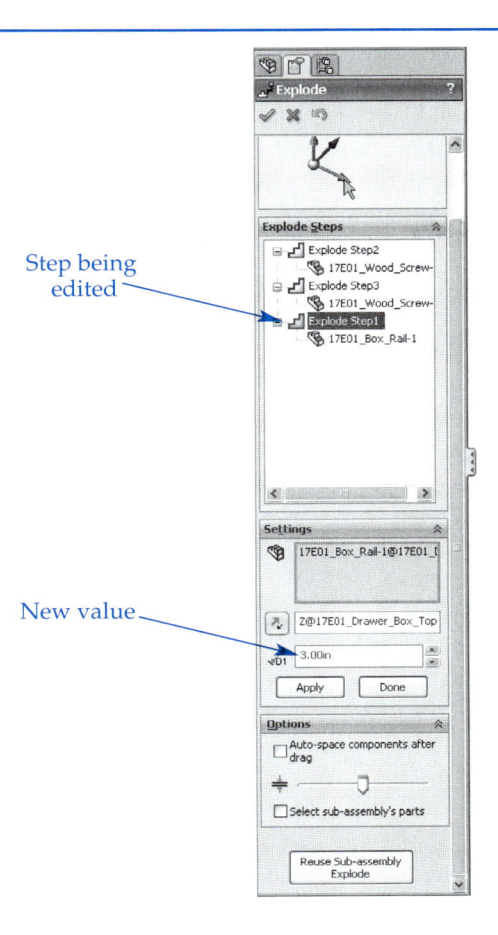

erties dialog box that is displayed, pick the **View Properties** tab. See **Figure 17-7**. In the **Configuration Information** area of the tab, check the **Show in exploded state** check box. Then, pick the **OK** button to close the dialog box and apply the changes to the drawing view.

> **PROFESSIONAL TIP**
>
> In the **Drawing View Properties** dialog box, different configurations may be designated for use in each view in the drawing file. This is useful for showing multiple exploded views or various states of assembly for the same assembly file in a drawing.

Figure 17-7.
Setting a drawing view to show the exploded view.

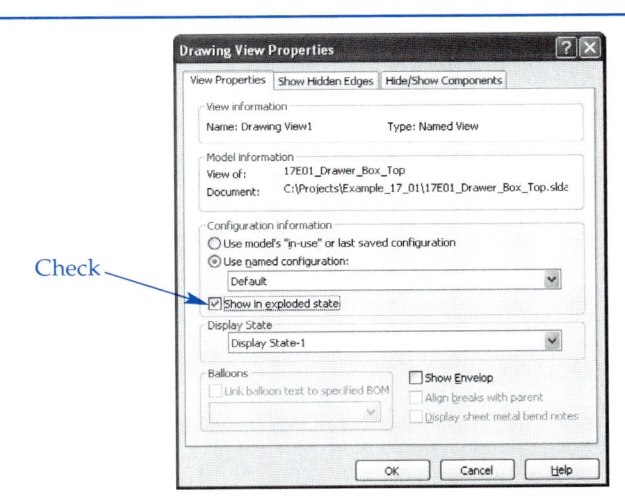

Chapter 17   Exploded Views and Animations

289

Creating Multiple Exploded Views

You can have many different exploded views of the same assembly in one assembly file. Each view is based on a configuration of the assembly. Note that each configuration can only contain one exploded view. Close all files and then open Example_17_02.sldasm. Open the **Configuration Manager** and look at the two configurations that appear in addition to the Default configuration:
- COMPLETE. All components are visible.
- FRONT WITH LOCK. Only the front subassembly and lock components are visible. The drawer sides, base, and back and the corresponding wood screws are hidden so you can better see the subassembly and lock. See **Figure 17-8.**

The configuration information is stored in the assembly file. This information includes:
- Visibility of components, sketches, and reference geometry.
- Colors and textures on components.
- The configuration names: COMPLETE, FRONT WITH LOCK, and Default in this example.

Now, create a new exploded view. Make the COMPLETE configuration active. Then, right-click on the COMPLETE configuration name and select **New Exploded View...** from the shortcut menu. Create the exploded view with:

Figure 17-8.
This configuration shows only the drawer front, including the lock components.

Figure 17-9.
The components in the drawer assembly are moved to create the exploded view.

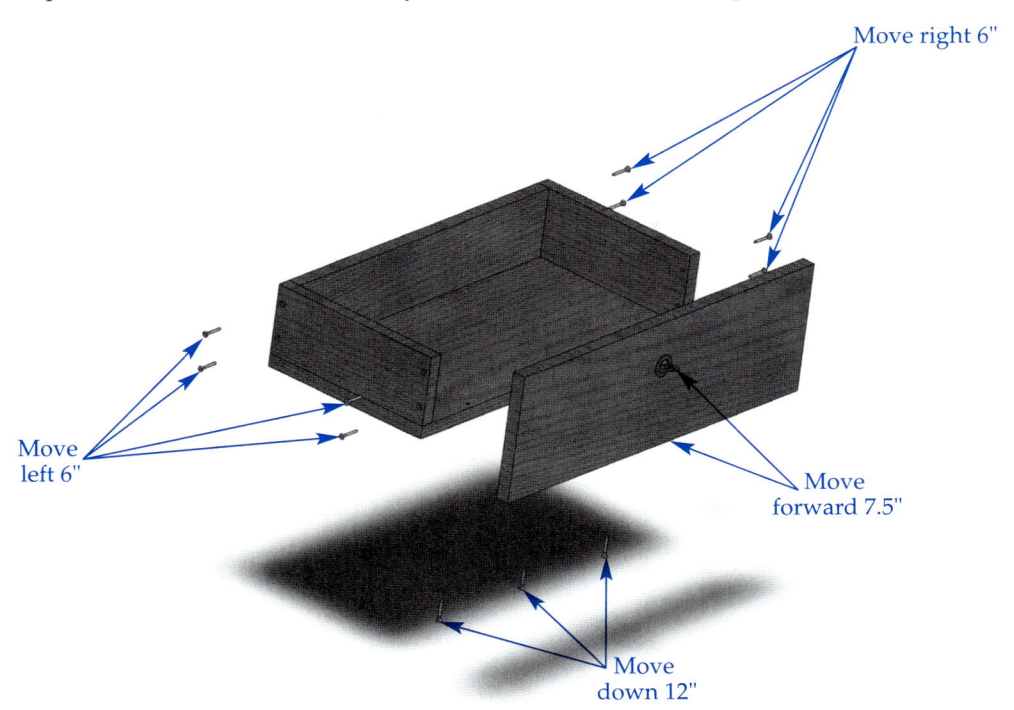

- The 17E02_Drawer_Front subassembly and the five lock components moved out 7.5″. See **Figure 17-9.**
- The four screws in each side of 17E02_Drawer_Front moved out 6″.
- The three screws in the bottom of 17E02_Drawer_Front moved down 12″.

Start a new drawing file based on a C-size drawing sheet. Insert a 1:5 scale view of the assembly. Select the saved view Iso Front. Next, right-click on the view and select **Properties…** from the shortcut menu. Display the **View Properties** tab in the **Drawing View Properties** dialog box. In the **Configuration information** area of the tab, pick the **Use named configuration:** radio button and select COMPLETE from the drop-down list. Also, check the **Show in exploded state** check box. Then, pick the **OK** button and save the file as Example_17_02.slddrw.

In the assembly file, activate the FRONT WITH LOCK configuration. Then, right-click on its name in the **Configuration Manager** and select **New Exploded View…** from the shortcut menu. Create an exploded view similar to that shown in **Figure 17-10.** Since the drawer front is a subassembly, you will need to select the components contained within it in the flyout design tree. Once the view is created, a new exploded view named ExplView2 is listed in the FRONT WITH LOCK branch in the **Configuration Manager**.

Insert a new view in to the Example_17_02.slddrw drawing. Set the scale to 1:2 scale and select the saved view Iso Back. If necessary, edit the view to show the exploded view. See **Figure 17-11.** Save and close all files.

> **PROFESSIONAL TIP**
> You can rename exploded views. This can be helpful in an assembly that contains multiple exploded views.

Chapter 17 Exploded Views and Animations

Figure 17-10.
The components of the drawer front are moved to create the exploded view.

Figure 17-11.
Two views have been added to a drawing and set to show the exploded view.

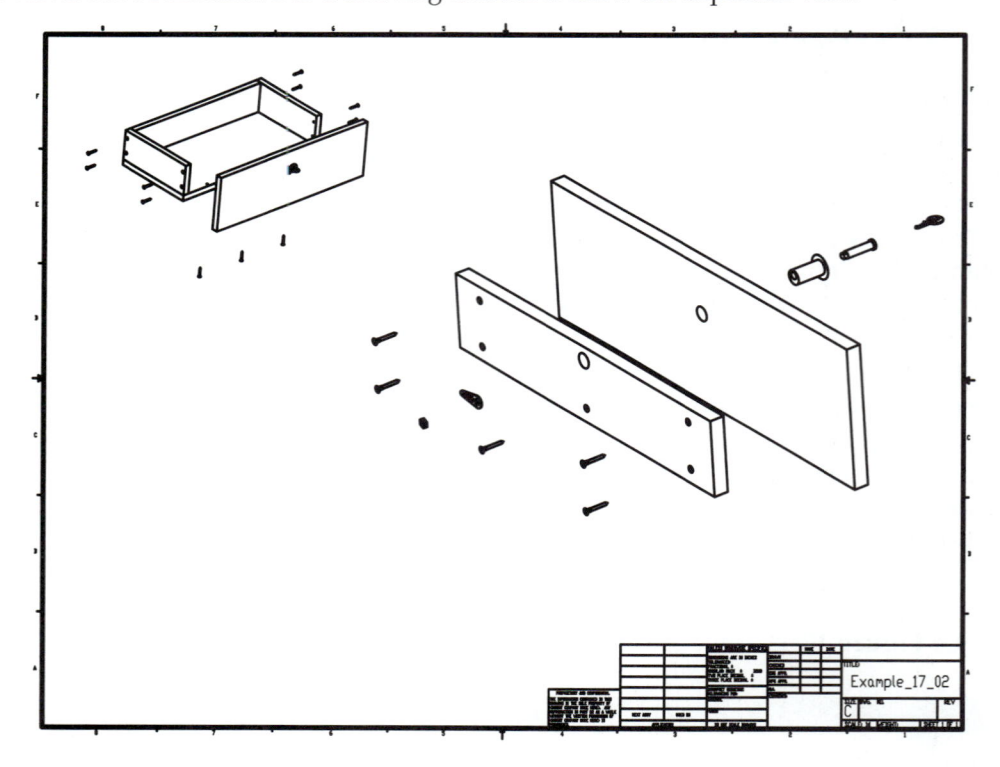

Using Exploded Views in Animations

Open **Example_17_03.sldasm**. At the bottom of the graphics area, pick the **Motion Study 1** tab. Play the animation that has been saved in the file. In a complex animation like this one, it is best to start out with a storyboard of the steps you want to see. A *storyboard* is a list of the steps in the animation and may contain some rough hand sketches, **Figure 17-12.** The storyboard for the drawer front is:

1. In the isometric view, put the drawer subfront on the drawer front from an original position about 3″ away. All lock parts are hidden.
2. Insert four of the screws all at once from an original position of about 7″ away.
3. Insert the fifth screw in from an original position about 7″ away. Zoom in on the screw.
4. Rotate the viewpoint, make the lock parts visible, and install the lock housing from an original position about 7″ away.
5. Install the lock tumbler from an original position about 8″ away.
6. Install the flag from an original position about 7.5″ away.
7. Bring the nut up to the end of the lock tumbler.
8. Rotate the nut 360°. At the same time, move the nut .1″ onto the lock tumbler.
9. Change the view to a front view. Bring the key in from an original position about 9″ away.

In the following sections this animation will be created using the **Motion Manager** to modify an animation of the exploded view. Most of the desired assembly animation will be added using an exploded view. All of the steps from the storyboard need to be considered in the reverse order during the construction of the exploded view. After the explode steps have been created, a motion study will be created from the exploded view and used to complete the animation. Using the **Motion Manager**, rotation can be added to the components to add realism to the exploded-assembly animation. Also, the view orientation during each step of the animation can be specified and component visibility can be controlled using the **Motion Manager**.

Figure 17-12.
Storyboards should be used to plan an animation. Storyboards help in planning the animation and also serve as a record of what needs to be done.

Chapter 17 Exploded Views and Animations

> **CAUTION**
>
> Save your work before starting a motion study. Also, after starting a motion study it may be best to return the time slider to the 0 second mark before saving the file. If a file containing a motion study is saved with the time slider at a time mark other than the 0 second mark, problems may be introduced into the file.

Creating the Exploded View

Close Example_17_03.sldasm without saving any changes. Then, open the file Example_17_03_Original.sldasm. This is the same file, but without the animation added. First, create a new exploded view based on the Default configuration. Complete the following steps to create the exploded view that will be used as the foundation for the final animation. Be sure to pick the **Done** button to complete each step before selecting the components for the next step.

1. Select the key as the component to explode and move it 9" away from the drawer front.
2. Select both the nut and the flag and move them .1" from their location away from the end of the lock tumbler.
3. Select the nut again and move it another 9" from the end of the lock tumbler.
4. Select the flag and move it another 7.5" from the end of the lock tumbler.
5. Move the tumbler 9" out from the drawer front.
6. Move the lock housing 7" out from the drawer front.
7. Move the center screw on the back of the drawer front 7" out from the back. Remember, you must select the components in the subassembly in the flyout design tree.
8. Hold the [Ctrl] key and select the four remaining screws. Move them 7" out from the back.
9. Move the door subfront 3" out from the back.
10. Select the green check mark button in the **Property Manager** to create the exploded view.

Right-click on the name of the new exploded view in the **Configuration Manager**. Pick **Animate Collapse** in the shortcut menu to preview the animation. Check to see that all steps are correct. Make any changes needed to correct the sequence and then save the assembly file.

Creating the Animation

Now, you are ready to create the motion study. Close the **Animation Controller** toolbar if it is displayed. Then, pick the **Motion Study 1** tab below the graphics window to open the **Motion Manager**. Pick the **Animation Wizard** button in the **Motion Manager** toolbar. The wizard is started, **Figure 17-13A**.

In the first page of the wizard, pick the **Collapse** radio button. This will create an animation of the parts being assembled, rather than disassembled. Then, pick the **Next** button. In the second page of the wizard, specify an animation duration of 9 seconds and a start time of 0 seconds, **Figure 17-13B**. These may be the default values. Finally, pick the **Finish** button to create an animation derived from the exploded view. Animation keys are automatically created based on the exploded view. Pick the **Play from Start** button to preview the animation.

Editing the Animation

Now, the **Motion Manager** can be used to modify the animation. First, rotation will be added to the nut. If a rotation is created during the final movement of the nut, it will appear as though the nut is being threaded onto the cylinder.

Figure 17-13.
A—The first page of the animation wizard. B—The second page of the animation wizard.

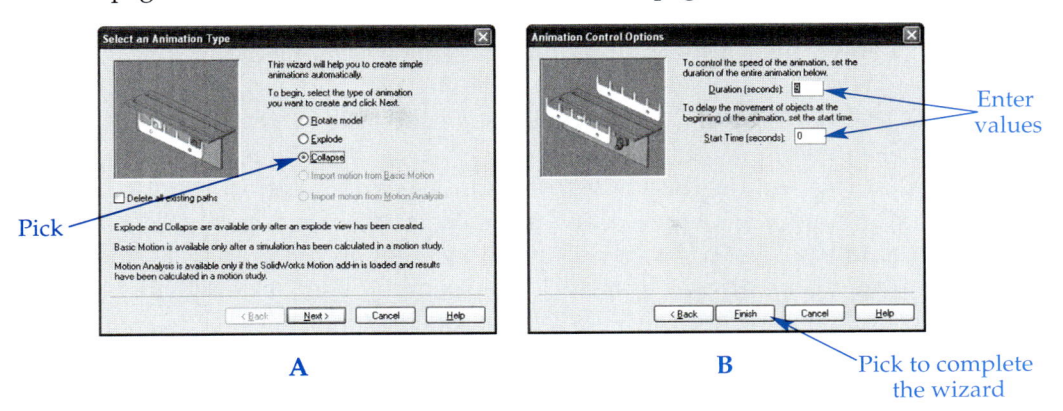

A

B

Pick

Enter values

Pick to complete the wizard

Adding rotation

In the **Motion Manager**, locate the animation keys for the .1" translation (movement) of the nut and flag. The first key should be at the 7 second mark. The second key should be at the 8 second mark. Expand the animation tree for the nut and the flag. Then, drag the time slider and watch the preview in the graphics window. When the nut and flag begin to move at the same time, the time slider is on the first keys for this movement, which should be at the 7 second mark.

Pick the **Motor** button on the **Motion Manager** toolbar. In the **Motor Property Manager**, pick the **Rotary Motor** button in the **Motor Type** rollout. With the selection box in the **Component/Direction** rollout active, pick the inner diameter of the nut. Since the threads are right hand, make sure the preview arrow points in a clockwise direction. If not, pick the **Reverse** button in the **Component/Direction** rollout.

In the **Motion** rollout, select Distance in the **Motor Type** drop-down list. Then, enter 1080 in the **Displacement motor** text box, 7 in the **Start Time** text box, and 1 in the **Duration Time** text box. This specifies that the nut will rotate 1080 degrees (or three full turns) starting at the 7 second mark and over a total time of one second.

Pick the green check mark button to apply the motor. Then, preview the animation by picking the **Play from Start** button in the **Motion Manager** toolbar. The nut should now move to the end of the lock tumbler and then turn at the same time it moves the final .1". The rotation may not be apparent at this point due to the zoom level. Later you will change the view for this part of the animation.

Changing views

The next step is to set required views for the sequences as noted in the storyboard. Place the time slider at the 2 second mark. This is the time mark where the center screw begins to move into the drawer front. Now, zoom and rotate the view until the exact view you want is displayed. Orient the assembly so the back of the drawer is visible. Zoom in to the middle of the drawer front, but keep the center screw visible in the graphics window.

Next, locate the Orientation and Camera View branch in the animation tree. Select the branch and then pick the **Add/Update Key** button on the **Motion Manager** toolbar. This adds a new key in the Orientation and Camera View branch at the 2 second mark that contains information about the current view. As the animation plays, the view will switch from the original isometric view to the view you established at this point.

Pick the **Play from Start** button to preview the animation. Notice how the view immediately begins to change. This is incorrect as it does not allow you to view the subfront and the other four screws being assembled. To correct this, you must add another key to the Orientation and Camera View branch of the animation tree. The easiest way to do this is copy the first key to a point before the key you just added, such as the 1.5 second mark. Hold down the [Ctrl] key, pick the first key in the Orientation and Camera View branch, and drag it to about the 1.5 second mark. Once you release the mouse button, a copy of the first key is added, **Figure 17-14.** Now when you pick the **Play from Start** button, the isometric view remains until the 1.5 second mark, then the view transitions into a close-up view of the screw.

Now, copy the key for the view from the 2 second mark to the 3 second mark. This will be the time mark where the animation transitions into the next view. Move the time slider to the 3.3 second mark. Adjust the view in the graphics window so you can see the front of the drawer and the lock assembly. Then, select the Orientation and Camera View branch and pick the **Add/Update Key** button.

Continue placing keys until the view changes resemble those specified in the storyboard. Preview each change by picking the **Play from Start** button. To change the view for a key, set the view as you want it at the proper time, then right-click on the view key and select **Replace Key** from the shortcut menu. Remember to copy view keys as needed to delay the transition in views.

Setting visibility

The visibility of the components needs to be set for each sequence. To change the visibility of a component using the **Motion Manager**, drag the time slider to a desired point in the timeline. Then, right-click on the part in the design tree or in the graphics window and pick the **Hide Components**, **Show Components**, or **Change Transparency** button from the shortcut toolbar.

Figure 17-14.
The first view change has been added and the keys adjusted as needed. The view shown in the graphics window is the beginning of the animation. As the animation progresses to the first key, the view will be changed.

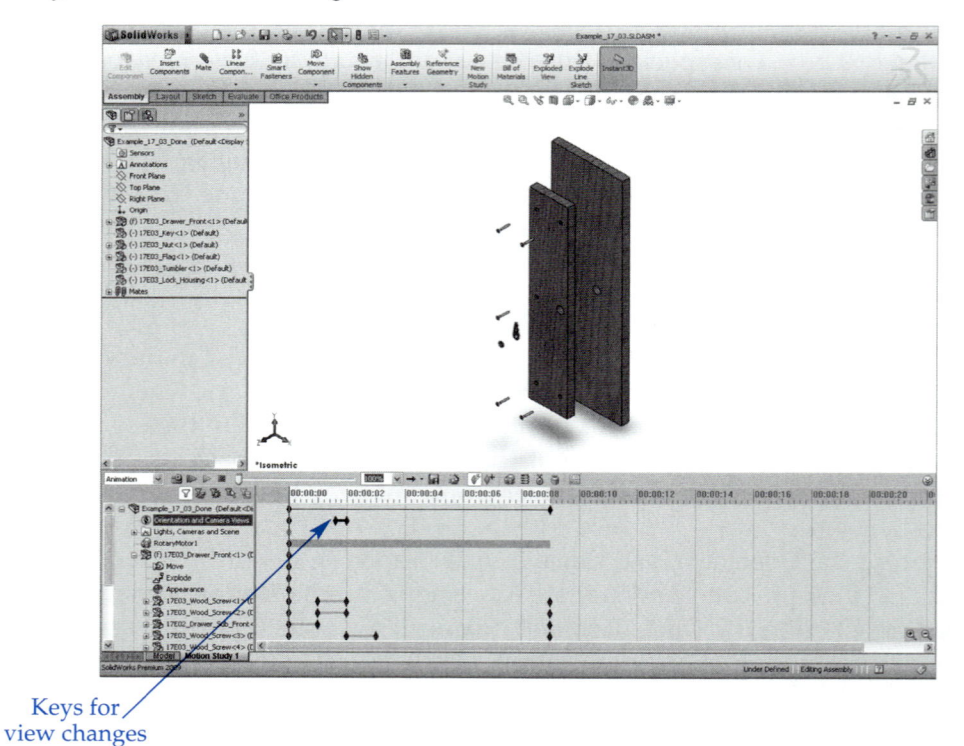

Currently, all parts are visible throughout the entire animation. The lock parts need to be hidden at the beginning of the animation. To accomplish this, position the time slider at the 0 second mark. Select the key, lock tumbler, and lock housing. Then, right-click and pick **Hide** from the shortcut menu. Next, copy this first key to the time where the parts should start to be visible (about the 3.5 second mark). The parts will be hidden from the 0 second mark to this point.

To make the components visible, move the time slider to the end. In the design tree, right-click each component and pick the **Show Components** button from the shortcut toolbar. The components will now be visible from the second key to the end.

Play the animation to check your work. If the animation is correct, save and close the file. If not, make corrections as needed. Animating complex assemblies in the **Motion Manager** can be a time-consuming process, though the results can be quite impressive.

Chapter Test

Answer the following questions on a separate sheet of paper or complete the electronic chapter test on the student website.
www.g-wlearning.com/CAD

1. What is an *exploded view*?
2. Each step in an exploded view is called a(n) _____.
3. List two ways to start creating an exploded view.
4. What is a *manipulator*?
5. How do you animate an exploded view without using the **Motion Manager**?
6. Briefly describe how to reorder the steps in an exploded view.
7. How can you have multiple exploded views in one assembly?
8. What is a *storyboard*?
9. Which tool in the **Motion Manager** is used to create an animation from an exploded view?
10. How can you add rotation to an exploded view?

Chapter Exercises

Complete the chapter exercises on the student website.
www.g-wlearning.com/CAD

Exercise 17-1 Slider Clamp.
Complete the exercise on the student website.

Exercise 17-2 Exploded View Drawing.
Complete the exercise on the student website.

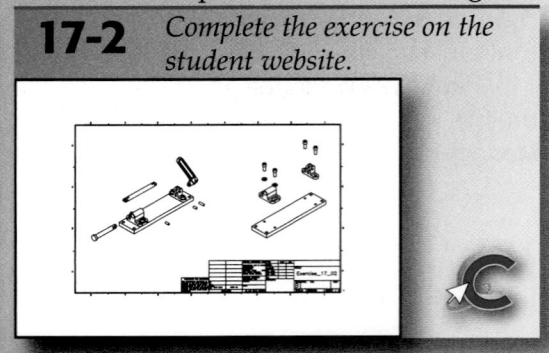

Exercise 17-3 Clamp Linkage.
Complete the exercise on the student website.

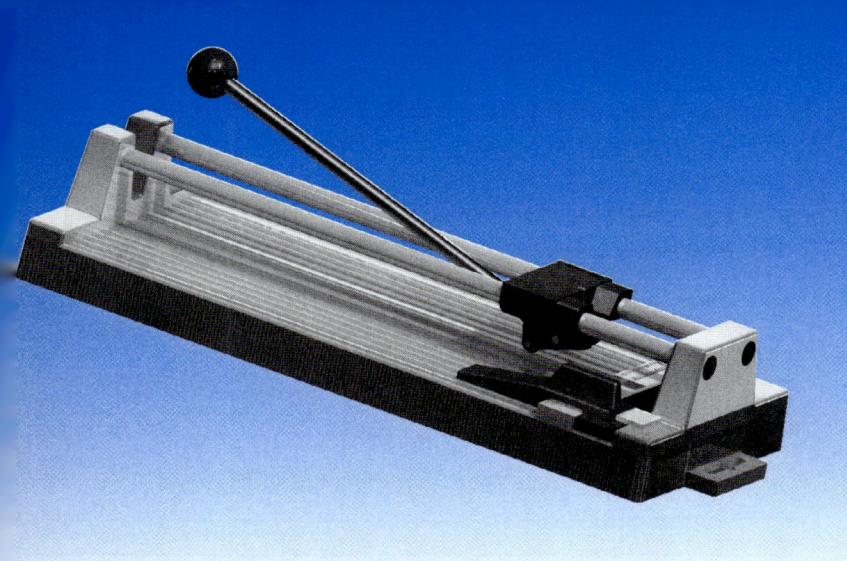

Index

2D drawings, 21
2D part drawing, 153–156
2D path, 192
3D sweeps, 197–199

A

adaptive location, 236–237
adaptive parts, 236–240
adaptive size, 238–240
Add Equation dialog box, 73–75
Add Relations Property Manager, 61
aligned section views, 162–163
ambiguous profiles, 62, 71–72
angle mate, 231
Animation Controller toolbar, 286–287
animation design tree, 232
animation key, 233
animations, 22
    animating exploded views, 286–287
    introduction to, 232–233
    using exploded views in, 292–297
animation wizard, 294–295
annotating drawings, 173–189
annotations, creating in assembly drawings, 273–281
arcs, 62–65
    drawing from within **Line** tool, 64–65
arrays. *See* patterns
assemblies
    applying smart mates, 214–215
    building, 207–222
    constraining edges of parts, 222–223
    copying inserted parts, 221–222
    creating, 207
    multiple-mate mode, 215–216
    placing fasteners from SolidWorks toolbox library, 220–221
    placing the first part, 208–209
    removing degrees of freedom, 210–214
    rotating the part, 209
    working with, 227–240
assembly, 20–21
assembly drawings, 269–281
    adding balloons, 280
    adding dimensions, 273–276
    adding leader text, 276
    creating annotations, 273–281
    creating bill of materials, 276–280
    creating views, 269–272
    section views, 271–272
assembly files, 27
assembly modeling, 20–21
assembly view
    creating parts in, 227–229
Auto Balloon Property Manager, 280
Auto Balloon tool, 280
automatic dimensions, 53
auxiliary views, 163–164

B

Balloon Property Manager, 280
balloons, 280
base features, 17–18
baseline dimensions, 183–184
base view, creating, 157–159

bearing block, 216
Begin Assembly Property Manager, 207–208
bidirectional associativity, 170
bill of materials (BOM), 276–280
Bill of Materials Property Manager, 277–280
bodies, combining, 139
body, 128
border, 155
Broken-out Section Property Manager, 164–165
broken-out section views, 164–165
Broken View Property Manager, 166
broken views, 165–166

C

cam mate, 247–248
centerlines, 175, 274
Centerline tool, 175, 274
center marks, 175, 274
Center Mark tool, 175, 274
chamfer dimensions, 184
Chamfer Dimension tool, 184
Chamfer Property Manager, 124–126
Chamfer tool, 124–126
Circle tool, 59–61
circular patterns, 126, 127–128
clearance holes, 114
closed-loop loft, 203
coincident mate, 211–212
collision detection, 230–231
Combine tool, 99–100
Command Manager, 25, 32
    Features tab, 48–50, 56, 64, 109
    Sketch tab, 48–50, 56
complex profiles. *See* ambiguous profiles
Configuration Manager, 251–254, 256–257, 286–288, 290–291
configurations, 251–257
    creating design tables from, 257
    creating in design table, 254–256
    creating new, 251–254
    working with, 251
connectors, 200
constraining
    new parts in assembly view, 228–229
    reference planes and axes, 233–235
construction geometry, 76–78
    surfaces as, 263, 265
context sensitive, 25
Copy with Mates tool, 221–222
Cosmetic Thread tool, 115–116
counterbored holes, 114–115

countersunk holes, 114–115
cropping views, 168
cross-sectional profile, 192
    creating, 195–196
curve-driven linear patterns, 126–127
curves, 46
    relations on, 51–52
custom standard, 174
cutouts, 71

D

datum, 183
default planes, 95
    and mid plane construction, 95–99
degrees of freedom, removing, 210–214
design intent, 19, 236
design table, 254–257
    creating configurations in, 254–256
    creating from configurations, 257
    editing, 256–257
Design Table Property Manager, 254, 257
design tree, 16, 32–38, 237–238
Detail View Property Manager, 164
detail views, 164
diametric dimensions, 80
dimensioning
    assembly drawings, 273–276
    in SolidWorks, 176–185
    isometric views, 185
Dimension Property Manager, 55, 75–76
    adding model and reference dimensions, 177–178
    adding text to default dimension text, 275
    adding tolerancing information, 275
    dimension styles, 178–179
    replacing dimension text, 276
dimensions, 52–55
    automatic, 53
    baseline, 183–184
    chamfer, 184
    changing, 34–35
    editing placed, 54–55
    manual, 54
    model and reference, 177–178
    ordinate, 183–184
Dimensions dialog box, 255
dimension styles, 178
dimension text, 275
    replacing, 275–276
display style, 31
distance mate, 212
draft angle, 145–146
drafting standards, 173–174

Draft Property Manager, 145–146, 148
drafts, 145–148
Draft tool, 145–146, 148
drawing files, 27
Drawing View Properties dialog box, 272–273, 288–289
Drawing View Property Manager, 158–159, 165, 169, 185, 271
drawing views
    aligned section views, 162–163
    auxiliary views, 163–164
    broken-out section views, 164–165
    broken views, 165–166
    creating, 157–167
    creating from assemblies, 269–272
    cropping, 168
    detail views, 164
    editing, 169
    full section views, 160–161
    half section views, 161
    partial sections, 161–162
    projecting, 159
    relative views, 167
    rotating, 169

E

editing in place, 218–219
Edit pull-down menu, 38
eDrawings files, 22–23
emboss, 143
empty view, 168
equations, 19
    using in sketch dimensions, 72–75
Equations dialog box, 19, 74–75
exploded views, 283–289
    adding to drawings, 288–289
    animating, 286–287
    creating, 284–286, 294
    editing, 287–288
    in animations, 292–297
    multiple, 290–291
Explode Property Manager, 285–288
explode step, 283, 288
externally referenced geometry, 47, 236
Extruded Boss/Base tool, 62, 65–66, 71, 87–88, 191
    embossing text, 143–144
    End Condition options, 88–90
Extruded Cut Property Manager, 90
Extruded Cut tool, 88, 90, 143–144
extruded surfaces, 260
Extrude Property Manager, 56, 65–66, 87, 260

extruding parts, 56–58
extrusion options, 88–92
    end condition, 88–90
    start condition, 91–92

F

faces, changing color setting, 86
fasteners, 220–221
feature-based modeling, 16–18
Feature Manager, 16, 32–38
    changing dimensions, 34–35
    renaming features, 35
    shortcut menu, 36
    working with features, 36–38
Feature Properties dialog box, 87–88
features, 16–17
    adding, 109–130, 135–151
    adding nonsketch features to parts, 109
    editing, 58–59
    renaming, 35
    working with, 36–38
    wrapping onto non-planar faces, 144–145
file management, 41–42
File pull-down menu, 38
file-renaming utility, 42
Fillet Property Manager, 117, 119–121
fillets, 117–123
    applying, 117, 119
    variable-radius, 121–123
Fillet tool, 117, 119–121
first-angle projection, 156
fixed, 209
flyout **Feature Manager** design tree, 33–34
Format Painter tool, 183
full section views, 160–161
fully defined sketch, 17

G

gear mate, 243–245
geometry, converting and projecting to sketch plane, 93–95
guide curve, 191, 200–201

H

half section views, 161
Help pull-down menu, 41
Hole Callout tool, 179
hole notes, 179–180
Hole Specification Property Manager, 218–219
Hole Wizard tool, 109–115, 179

Index   **301**

I

Insert Component tool, 229
Insert pull-down menu, 39
instance, 207
intelligent objects, 46
isometric views, dimensioning, 185

K

key, 233
Knit Property Manager, 265–266
knitted surfaces, 265

L

layers, 179
Layers dialog box, 179
leader text, 276
linear patterns, 126
line font, 271
Line tool, 59, 61–62, 77
    drawing arcs, 64–65
lofted surfaces, 262
lofting, 200
Loft Property Manager, 200–201
lofts, 191, 199–204
    basic loft, 200–201
    closed-loop, 203
    editing, 204
    open-loop, 203
    with guide curve, 201
loft synchronization, 200

M

manipulator, 285
manual dimensions, 54
Mate Property Manager, 211, 216–217, 243–246
mates, 21, 207
    coincident, 211–212
    distance, 212
    mechanical, 243–248
    removing degrees of freedom with, 210–214
    standard, 210–214
    tangent, 223–224
mechanical mates, 243–248
    cam mate, 247–248
    gear mate, 243–245
    rack and pinion mate, 245–246
Menu Bar, 26–29
    New button, 26–27
    Open button, 27
    pull-down menus, 38–41
    Rebuild button, 28–29
    Save button, 28
    Undo button, 28
Mirror Entities tool, 79–80
Mirror Property Manager, 79–80
Mirror tool, 79–80, 130
model dimensions, 176
    adding, 177–178
modeling motion, 21
Model Items Property Manager, 177
Model Items tool, 177
Model View Property Manager, 159
Motion Manager, 293–297
motion, modeling, 21
motion study, 232–233, 294
Motor Property Manager, 235
Move Component Property Manager, 231
multiple-mate mode, 215–216

N

neutral plane, 145–146
New SolidWorks Document dialog box, 26–27, 47, 154, 207
Note Property Manager, 179, 182–183
notes, 181–182
Note tool, 180–182

O

Offset Surface Property Manager, 263
Open dialog box, 27, 42
open-loop loft, 203
options/properties dialog box, 48, 174, 181, 274
ordinate dimensions, 183–184
origin, 49, 55–56
    visibility, 96

P

Pack and Go, 23
Pan tool, 31, 49
parametric dimensions, 176
parametric model, 18
parametric modeling, 18–20
part drawings, creating, 153–170
part files, 26
partial sections, 161–162
parts
    copying inserted, 221–222
    creating in assembly view, 227–229
    extruding, 56–58
    placing the first part, 208–209
    process for creating, 45–47
    rotating, 209

path, 192
    closed, 194
    profile not perpendicular to, 192
patterns, 126–129
    circular, 127–128
    curve-driven linear, 126–127
    linear, 126
    patterning the entire part, 128–129
pentagon, 77
pipe thread holes, 113
placed features, 18, 34
Plane Property Manager, 101–105
Plane tool, 101
Point Property Manager, 55–56
Polygon tool, 77
pre-selection method, 216–217, 267
Previous View button, 31
Projected View Property Manager, 159, 270
Projected View tool, 159, 270
Properties Property Manager, 55, 62–64
Property Manager, 51–52, 56, 59, 66
pull-down menus, 38–41

Q

quilt, 265

R

rack and pinion mate, 245–246
Rebuild tool, 28–29
reference axis, 101
reference dimensions, 176–177
    adding, 177–178
reference geometry, 18, 101
    creating and using, 101–105
reference planes
    angled from a face or existing plane, 103–104
    constraining, 233–235
    creating, 101–105
    normal to a curve, 105
    offset from an existing face or plane, 101–102
    on surface, 105
    parallel at a point, 105
    through lines/points, 104
reference point, 101
relations, 46, 51–52
    adding, 61
    review of, 66–67
Relative View Property Manager, 167
relative views, 167
revision symbol, 189
revision table, 188–189

Revision Table Property Manager, 188
Revolved Boss/Base tool, 80–82, 196
revolved surfaces, 260
Revolve Property Manager, 81–82
rib, 139
Rib Property Manager, 140
Rib tool, 139–142
rollback bar, 16, 37–38
Rotate View tool, 169
rounds, 117–123
    applying, 117, 119

S

Save As dialog box, 28
scribe, 143
Section View Property Manager, 160, 163, 272
section views, 271–272
setbacks, 122–123
sheet, 155
Sheet Format/Size dialog box, 153–154
Sheet Properties dialog box, 155–156, 187, 269, 281
Shell*n* Property Manager, 135–137
Shell tool, 135–139
    multiple shell thicknesses, 136–137
    shelling multiple features and combining bodies, 139
silhouette curve, 93–94
sketched features, 17–18, 34
sketches, 17, 45–47
    adding relations, 61
    circles, 60–61
    creating base features from, 47–51
    creating in drawing files, 168
    dimensions, 52–55
    editing, 58–59
    extruding parts, 56–58
    relations, 51–52
    relationship to origin, 55–56
    secondary, 85–87
    things that can go wrong, 65–66
sketching, 47–65
Sketch Text Property Manager, 143–144
Smart Dimension tool, 54, 73, 177, 179
Smart Fastener tool, 222
smart mates, 214–215
SolidWorks Explorer, 23
SolidWorks, introduction to, 15–23
SolidWorks toolbox library, 220–221
Split Line tool, 148–150
Split tool, 148–149, 263
standard mates, 210–214

Index   303

standard parts, 220
storyboard, 293
Summary Information dialog box, 278–279
Surface-Extrude Property Manager, 260
Surface Finish Property Manager, 180
Surface Finish tool, 180
surfaces, 259–267
    as construction geometry, 263, 265
    extruded, 260
    knitted, 265
    lofted, 262
    revolved, 260
    swept, 262
    thickening and offsetting, 262–263
surface texture symbols, 180
Sweep Command Manager, 262
sweep path, 192
Sweep Property Manager, 192–193, 199
sweeps, 191–199
    creating, 192
    practical example, 194–196
Swept Boss/Base tool, 192–194
swept features, creating, 191–192, 194
swept surfaces, 262

T

tangent mate, 223–224
tangent relation, 62
text
    adding, 180–183
    creating, 143–144
Text tool, 143
Thicken Property Manager, 263–264
Thicken tool, 262–263
third-angle projection, 156
threaded holes, 112–113
thread notes, 179–180
title block, 155
    editing, 185–187

Title Block Property Manager, 186–187
tolerance, adding, 275
Tools pull-down menu, 39–40
top-down modeling, 227
triad, 209
Trim Entities tool, 62
trimming circles, 61–62
Trim tool, 62

U

user interface, 25–42
    Feature Manager, 32–38
    file management, 41–42
    Menu Bar, 26–29
    overview, 25
    pull-down menus, 38–41
    view navigation tools, 29–31

V

variable-radius fillets, 121–123
view navigation tools, 29–31
View Palette, 155, 157–158
viewpoint, 31
View pull-down menu, 38–39
views. *See* drawing views
virtual component, 228

W

web, 139
Window pull-down menu, 40–41
work envelope, 21

Z

zero ordinate, 183
Zoom to Area button, 30
Zoom to Fit button, 30